LAND SO FAIR

Also by Firth Haring Fabend

The Best of Intentions
Three Women
A Perfect Stranger
The Woman Who Went Away
Greek Revival

A Dutch Family in the Middle Colonies, 1660-1800
Zion on the Hudson: Dutch New York and New Jersey in the Age of Revivals

A Catch of Grandmothers

Land So Fair

A Novel

Firth Haring Fabend

iUniverse, Inc.

New York Lincoln Shanghai

Land So Fair

Copyright © 2008 by Firth Haring Fabend

iUniverse books may be ordered through booksellers or by contacting:

iUniverse
2021 Pine Lake Road, Suite 100
Lincoln, NE 68512
www.iuniverse.com
1-800-Authors (1-800-288-4677)

Because of the dynamic nature of the Internet, any Web addresses or links contained in this book may have changed since publication and may no longer be valid.

The views expressed in this work are solely those of the author and do not necessarily reflect the views of the publisher, and the publisher hereby disclaims any responsibility for them.

ISBN: 978-0-595-47316-8 (pbk)
ISBN: 978-0-595-91594-1 (ebk)

Printed in the United States of America

For Caroline and Lydia,

and for Hugh, William, and Ione Elizabeth

and Theirs and Theirs

The Characters

Margrietje Cosyns, 1641-1724
m. Jan Pietersen Haring, 1633-1683

Marytie Blauvelt, 1670-1749
m. Cosyn Haring, 1669-1743

Aeltie Van Dalsen, 1696-1744
m. Jan Haring, 1693-1771

Margaret Blauvelt, 1725-1800
m. Johannes Haring, 1720-1798

Cathlyntie Mabie, 1757-1796
m. John J. Haring, 1755-1787

Geertje Bogert, 1789-1827
m. Johannes Haring, 1780-1868

Foreword

Land So Fair is an outgrowth of my historical poem *A Catch of Grandmothers* (2004), which in turn is based on my book *A Dutch Family in the Middle Colonies, 1660-1800* (1991), a history of the first five generations of the Haring Family in New York and New Jersey.

The novel is a hybrid of fiction and fact, but the basic biographical details about the main characters are accurate (with some exceptions necessary for the action), and the historical details come from the same sources and public records that inform both *A Dutch Family in the Middle Colonies* and *A Catch of Grandmothers*. Likewise, although the details have been rinsed in the river of imagination, the land disputes are based on published historical records, as are the church troubles, slavery, the material culture, particular historical persons, and the Revolution and its run-up and aftermath. A few minor characters are fictional.

I have taken certain liberties with the historical record. The French army did not march through Tappan on its way to Yorktown. I have, and without calling attention to it, occasionally put the recorded words of one public figure in another figure's mouth. (It was not Major Clough who made the remark about petticoats, but Governor William Livingston.) I have often appropriated statements of a public figure for a character to utter. Here and there, I altered the chronology of actual events to suit the narrative. I have telescoped events, and I have changed the birth dates of Margrietie Cosyns and Jan Pietersen Haring in order to allow four generations to interact with each other over the time span of the narrative, 1737-1800. Her actual birth date and his are given on the preceding page. They had three daughters together, in addition to their four sons. The cause of Haring's death and those of his three partners is a mystery.

I have indulged in pure invention. Caesar is fictional, but his experiences in 1741 at the time of the "great slave conspiracy" are those of the documented Caesar. The feelings of Margaret Blauvelt for George Washington are imagined. If she ever saw him, or he her, there is no record, but it is not credible that she would not have been in the crowds that came out to see him on those four highly charged occasions when he was in Tappan. I have entirely imagined that she was in his presence on another occasion (on Broadway, in New York City, as he was en route to Boston in June of 1775).

And, of course, I have imagined everything to do with the characters' daily lives and thoughts. The public record reveals only the bare bones of their existences: the dates of their baptisms, marriages, childbirths, deaths, the property they owned, the houses where they lived, the household goods and possessions inventoried at their deaths, and the times in which they lived. Secondary sources fill out and interpret the historical and cultural context of those times. All else is invention.

*   *   *   *

Those secondary sources were vital to the telling of the story. Particular works that I consulted are, for the land disputes, George H. Budke, "The History of the Tappan Patent," George H. Budke, "The Controversy Between the Proprietors of the Tappan Patent and McEvers and Symes," and Rev. David D. Cole, *History of Rockland County, New York.*

For slavery and the "Great Negro Plot" in colonial New York, the following works were essential reading: Thomas J. Davis, *A Rumor of Revolt*, Graham Russell Hodges, *Root and Branch: African Americans in New York and East Jersey, 1613-1863*, Graham Russell Hodges, *Slavery and Freedom in the Rural North*, Daniel Horsmanden, *The New-York Conspiracy, or A History of the Negro Plot with the Journal of the Proceedings Against the Conspirators at New-York in the Years 1741-2, in the Detection of the Conspiracy*, Edgar J. McManus, *A History of Negro Slavery in New York*, and for Pinkster, A. J. William-Myers, "Pinkster Carnival," in *Afro-Americans in New York Life and History*, and Shane White, "Pinkster in Albany, 1803: A Contemporary Description," in *New York History*. Jill Lapore's *New York Burning* was published in 2005 after I had finished the first draft of the manuscript, but I read it with great interest to confirm that I had "gotten it right." She certainly did.

For the church troubles, I consulted *The Ecclesiastical Records of the State of New York*, particularly volume IV, Rev. David D. Cole, *History of the Reformed Church of Tappan, 1694-1894*, and Adrian C. Leiby, *The Revolutionary War in the Hackensack Valley: The Jersey Dutch and the Neutral Ground, 1775-1783.*

For the Revolution, these works were central: George Athan Billias, ed., *George Washington's Generals*, George H. Budke, *Rockland Record, American Revolution*, James Thomas Flexner, *The Traitor and the Spy: Benedict Arnold and John André*, David Hackett Fischer, *Washington's Crossing*, Larry R. Gerlach, ed., *New Jersey in the American Revolution, 1763-1783: A Documentary History*, Adrian C. Leiby, *The Revolutionary War in the Hackensack Valley: The Jersey Dutch and the Neutral Ground, 1775-1783*, Craig Mitchell, "Bergen Summer 1779, The Enterprise Against Paulus Hook," Barbara J. Mitnick, ed., *New Jersey in the American Revolution*, Frank Moore, *A Diary of the American Revolution*, New-York Historical Society, *Narratives of the Revolution in New York*, Kevin Phillips, *The Cousins' War: Religion, Politics, and the Triumph of Anglo-America*, Barnet Schechter, *The Battle for New York: The City at the Heart of the American Revolution*, and John Evangelist Walsh, *The Execution of Major André*.

For George Washington, I consulted Joseph J. Ellis, *His Excellency George Washington*, James Thomas Flexner, *Washington: The Indispensable Man*, John P. Kaminski and Jill Adair McCaughan, *A Great and Good Man, George Washington in the Eyes of His Contemporaries*, Isabelle K. Savell, *Wine and Bitters*, and the works cited above for the Revolution.

For social background and material culture, I turned to Donna R. Barnes and Jane ten Brink Goldsmith, *Street Scenes: Leonard Bramer's Drawings of 17th-Century Dutch Daily Life*, Linda Baumgarden, *What Clothes Reveal*, Roderic H. Blackburn, *Dutch Colonial Homes in America*, Roderic H. Blackburn and Ruth Piwonka, *Remembrance of Patria: Dutch Arts and Culture in Colonial America, 1609-1776*, Edwin G. Burrows and Mike Wallace, *Gotham: A History of New York City to 1898*, Richard L. Bushman, *The Refinement of America: Persons, Houses, Cities*, David Steven Cohen, *The Dutch-American Farm*, John Duffy, *A History of Public Health in New York City, 1625-1866*, John A. Kouwenhoven, *The Columbia Historical Portrait of New York*, Peter G. Rose, trans. and ed., *The Sensible Cook: Dutch Foodways in the Old and the New World*, Kevin L. Stayton, *Dutch by Design: Tradition and Change in Two Historic Brooklyn Houses*, George Sturt, *The Wheelwright's Shop*, Wilfred B. Talman, *How Things Began ... in Rockland County and Places Nearby*, William E. Woodward, *The Way Our People Lived: An Intimate American History*, and various articles and essays in *de Halve Maen*, the quarterly of The Holland Society of New York, *South of the Mountains*, the quarterly of the Historical Society of Rockland County, and *Relics*, the quarterly of the Bergen County Historical Society.

For the works of all of these authors and editors, living or not, I am greatly appreciative. They were indispensable in developing the background of *Land So Fair*.

PART ONE

CHAPTER 1

▼

CROSSING

It was impossible to blot the ocean out of his vision, but the boy turned from the ship's rail to put it, at least, at his back. For weeks it had stretched endlessly everywhere in every direction as far as eyes could see, gray and purposeful, surging and hissing and tossing with a will of its own, almost a wicked will, it seemed. As if it had plans for him, he thought uneasily. He could swim a little, but he knew he would not have a chance of staying afloat in those briny deeps if he should fall overboard. He would be sucked under in a trice. He shuddered, recalling the sea monsters in a book he had seen in his grandfather's house, back in Hoorn, their gaping mouths, long sharp teeth, their rimless eyes mad with hunger.

"I am thinking again that Mother was right," he said to his older brother, beside him at the rail. "I am too young to go from home." He was eleven.

"It is much too late for second thoughts, Jan," Cornelius said cheerfully. He was twenty and raring for adventure. "We have made our choice, and we are almost there," he added. He gazed keenly westward over the sea. He couldn't get too much of it, cross the water fast enough, discern land soon enough. He was almost beside himself with impatience to be on that pleasant, promised shore they steered for, which the captain had assured him just this day could not be far ahead. "You will be in your promised land soon enough," the captain had said with a laugh that contained a note of mockery, Cornelius thought.

But what was there to mock, except perhaps his single-mindedness? He had been determined from the start to get to the New World without one hour's delay, as if he could control with his will the well-advertised vicissitudes of the journey. And so far, so far, there had not been one hour's delay, so that it seemed to him that in fact his sheer resolve was the cause of the swift and uneventful passage, not the calm weather or the captain's skill.

The seas had been so calm, in fact, and the rains so absent that the two, along with other male passengers, young and old, had been able to sleep on deck most nights, wrapped in duffle-cloth blankets against the ceaseless wind and the salt spray. "Below deck is hell," he had declared, after tossing in his narrow bunk for the first few nights. "The farting and snoring of the people are enough to make a man hate humanity. We will take our chances above board. And be that much closer to our beautiful destination."

"But what if it isn't the way they say it is?" said Jan. "What if it isn't naturally fruitful and there are not so many fine flats and maize lands as they say? What if we do not find brick work in Mana-hatta?"

"You are too much of a worrier, Jan. We will make our way. We have a good letter of introduction to those who can help us get a footing. And if we do not find our way immediately, our own townsman has testified to the abundance and variety of the food supplies. If worse comes to worst, we will pluck our sustenance from the forests and the air and the rivers and the streams."

The brothers were from Hoorn, the same little city on the Zuiderzee from where this townsman, Captain David de Vries, had sailed to New Netherland to seek his fortune—and live to write about it. "Don't you remember how he wrote of the pumpkins and melons, and the nuts of the trees, and the wild grapes?" Cornelius prodded. "Food for the taking is everywhere in New Netherland. One doesn't even have to grow it."

"The people do farm, though," said Jan. He had read all there was to read of New Amsterdam, the Captain's published account, some pamphlets, pored over some mysterious etchings for clues to his future, including one with palm trees and sugar-processing sheds, which indicated to him that the climate was mild, perhaps even hot. "They raise good grains and oats and peas, and good hops for beer."

"But if they did not, they could still live, for the forests are full of harts and hinds, and hares, and geese and turkeys, weighing, he has written, up to forty pounds," Cornelius insisted. "There are partridges, and meadow hens, and pigeons so numerous they blacken the sky."

"And fish," said the boy.

"Yes," said Cornelius. "Fish. We will eat fish, if nothing else, for there are so many fish one cannot name them all, or possibly count them. And you can catch them with your bare hands they are so plentiful. The Captain mentioned cod and haddock, and plaice, flounders, herring, sole, and *twaalf*, the favorite of our family."

At this mention of their family and their mother's succulent dish of stuffed *twaalf*, striped bass, the boy felt a lump rise to his throat. But he must be brave. He was only eleven, yes, but all agreed he was mature for his years, of good judgment, strong and healthy, and as reliable as the tides. "You must be a little man," his mother had whispered to him when they parted. He could not let his brother down, or her.

Published accounts of the New World, described so vividly by Captain de Vries—as well as by another traveler to that place when Jan was just a pup a year old, a man of law from New Netherland who had visited Hoorn on his way to the Hague in 1652 to lay Petrus Stuyvesant's shortcomings before the States-General—those two accounts had persuaded their father that the New World was the place to be. Cornelius agreed instantly—anything to get away from Hoorn—and their father assigned Jan, his youngest son, to go with him as his apprentice in the brick trade. Their older brother, Abraham, and their sister Brechtje, would stay behind to be their parents' strength and help in their old age.

Their father had chosen brickmaking for Cornelius when he reached the age of fourteen, because the process was easily learned (Cornelius being an impatient student) and required no special equipment. Moreover, there was a universal need for the product, and from brickmaking he could rise to mason in time if he learned his trade well enough and made the right friends and learned to control his slap-dash-boom-bang nature.

Jan had had nothing to say in the matter, whether of brickmaking or of going to the New World, and out in the garden, when it became clear that she had nothing to say about it either, his mother had gathered him under her black cloak with the red trim and held him in her arms and wept on his head. "I wanted you to continue with your schooling," she whispered tearily into his mop of dark curly hair. He was the only one of her four children to have dark hair and green eyes, the only one in the whole city of Hoorn, in fact. All else were blond or brown-haired and blue-eyed. Further, he was the brightest, the most capable, the most promising of her brood. She could not bear to lose him. It was unfair! "Maybe I can still do that in America," he whispered back. "I will try, Mother." She wiped her eyes with her handkerchief. "Try," she said.

On the sixth day of the fifth week of their passage, a hauntingly sweet, fresh smell assailed the nostrils. "There it is! Land ahead!" said Cornelius, rushing to the ship's rail. "Smell it, Jan! It is the smell of a beautiful and fruitful land, as the Bible says of Canaan. We have not been led astray. We have not been sold a bill of goods."

"I smell plums," Jan said wonderingly. "And strawberries! And what is that smell of orange in the air? Palm trees and oranges in Mana-hatta growing!"

"I smell pine, and cedar," Cornelius said. "And roses, by God! And I could swear hyacinths and marigolds!"

The scented air bathed them in a luxury of flower, fruit, and forest. And then as suddenly as the land fragrances had come, the wind changed, and all was as it had been, with only the customary salty and fishy smells of the sea, and the smell of tar and wet rigging and moldy bread and unwashed people as the vessel plodded forward in its creaking rigging. "It can't be long now," Cornelius said hopefully. "We will be there any day."

✳   ✳   ✳   ✳

And he was right. Two afternoons later, the sweet fragrance came again, and all rushed to the rails to look west. Far away, shimmering indistinctly on the horizon, lay, as if loosed from a fraying garment, a long, thin, gauzy ribbon of green, bobbling gently on the gray waves of the sea.

"We have arrived," said Cornelius. "Now life begins, brother! In the fine year 1662!"

It took hours for the ship to reach the harbor, and the closer they got to the land the more familiar the little city seemed to them. Back lighted by the western sun, the stepped façades of the houses, the four-sided fort at the tip of the island, the Dutch flag flying over it, the *stadthuis,* the signal pole with its smoking rag to indicate an approaching ship (their own), the sails everywhere, the masts bobbing at anchor: "It is just like Hoorn," the boy said wonderingly.

As the sun sank in the sky, the captain ordered the anchor to be dropped in the road, and the passengers settled down for their last night on the water. "I can hardly wait till morning," Cornelius said. "I can hardly wait, brother!" Like all the passengers on board, except for Jan, he was in a state of high excitement to consider what the next day would bring. "I can't wait!"

"I can wait," Jan said.

"It promises to be very much like Hoorn," Cornelius said. "You'll be fine."

"The stars are just like the stars over Hoorn," Jan said. "Maybe I will like it here."

"I promise you, you will."

In the morning, skiffs and rowboats appeared to off-load them and the cargo and take all across the choppy harbor to the wharf. The two stumbled and clambered onto the pier. "I can't walk!" Jan cried, staggering over the planks on his sea legs. "And my head is swimming!"

"It's like the herring fishermen in Hoorn when they return from their catch," Cornelius gasped, lurching and reeling, reaching out to steady himself on his brother's shoulder. "It will go away."

They pulled themselves along, holding onto a rickety railing until they reached the firm ground.

"First let us find a place to stay," Cornelius said, "and then we will go and present our letter."

They rented a room, a dark hole in the first house they came to with a vacancy. They had to share a bed in the dark hole, whose owner extracted two weeks' rent from them in advance. "I don't like this hovel," said Jan.

"It doesn't matter. By two weeks from now, we'll be out of here," Cornelius said. "This town is fair to bursting with opportunity. You can just see it, can't you?"

Jan looked dubious. He remembered the copper etching he had studied so closely in Hoorn, a copper etching called "Nieu Amsterdam," drawn by an artist who admitted he had never been there. Yes, there was the church in the fort, there was the *stadthuis*, there were the flagpole and the signal pole, there were the buildings of the Dutch West India Company, the Company gardens, the ships in the bustling harbor, the neat gabled houses.

But what about the pigs and hogs that ran about in the mud of the unpaved streets? And where were the etching's palm trees and the sheds for processing sugar cane? Where were the half-naked slaves? All the black people he saw were fully clothed, although shabbily, he noticed. And where were the elegant, high-hatted merchant and his wife, he standing proudly before his casks of tobacco and bales of fabric, she with her overflowing basket of produce? He saw only ordinary tradespeople at their work, coopers, blacksmiths, masons, carpenters, tailors, shoemakers, glaziers, turners, bakers, weavers.

And peddlers crying their wares. Peddlers everywhere, selling everything. "Oysters here!" "Hot Shrimp!" Women spread laundry on every bare spot they could find in their gardens, and all of them had something to sell, cabbages and carrots here, butter there, rabbits in cages, old clothes, a basket of turnips, hot warm waffles, cinnamon wafercakes. They each bought one of these and wolfed them down. "Do you want to buy a hearth brush?" a peddler demanded of them. "Here's onions," shouted another. "Pot lids here!"

The bustle of the streets was almost overwhelming. Jan felt faint. He swayed unsteadily, gripped onto a fence to keep his balance. He leaned against the fence until his head cleared, then sat on a log to finish his warm wafercake, feel the ground under his feet, firm and unmoving. It was good to be out of the sea wind, to feel the sun warm on his back.

With their letter of introduction safely stowed in Cornelius's wallet, which was tucked in an inside pocket of his shirt, sewn there by their mother, they asked directions to the *bouwerie* of Cosyn Gerritsen van Putten, a *rijtuig-wielen*, wheelwright. A woman pointed the way. "Beyond the wall built to keep the English out," she said. "And down his wagon way to the west."

"He has an odd name," Jan said, as they trudged into the fields beyond the wall.

Cornelius agreed. It was the Dutch word for a kind of window frame, pronounced *ko zine*. They had never known anyone named so, at home.

"Things are like home here, yet different," Jan said. "Pigs don't run in our streets. Peddlers are not everywhere you look. I think the settlers do as they please here."

"He brought his name with him," Cornelius said. "Putten is in Gelderland, far from Hoorn. That is why we have not heard it."

"It goes to show what we don't know about our own land, much less this place."

They found the wagon way and wandered down its bushy length across the fields planted with wheat and fragrant buckwheat and rye, past the orchard, past cows grazing in the pasture, past the barn and sheds, through the kitchen garden alive with ducks and chickens and pigs, and finally to the house and the wheelwright's shop.

It was a busy place. Two workmen, one young, one old, labored one at a chopping block, the other at a table set on sawhorses. Axes and adzes, saws, squares, and tools they knew not the names of lay all about. The two workers looked up to squint at the strangers suspiciously.

The man they sought was under a spreading tree outside his shop, turning a wooden winch in the hub of a huge wooden wagon wheel, one foot braced for leverage against a sturdy spoke. He was a short burly man, surrounded by wheels and wagons in various stages of construction, and dung carts and wheelbarrows, ploughs and harrows awaiting repairs.

He greeted them, suspiciously, too, for he had not been expecting them. But their appearance appealed to him, and after all they were from Hoorn, where his favorite aunt lived, the aunt who had promised to name him in her will, and they carried a letter from her. "Come into the house for a glass of fresh cider," he said.

They stepped across the work yard into a dark, low-ceilinged house, which was divided into two rooms, one on either side of a central hearth and chimney. It was the old-fashioned flat type of hearth, with no sides to it, just a hood above it to let the smoke rise up the chimney. Jan looked around him, noticing curtained beds in the corners, just like at home, chests for clothing, a small octagonal table, brass candlesticks, and on the table in the center of the room and on shelves beyond, in the pantry, pewter bowls and platters, trenchers, spoons, earthen jars, copper pots and pans, plainer than his own house furnishings in Hoorn, but enough like it so that he felt at home.

He told them to sit at the table in the south room, where a winding staircase in the corner led to the garret above. "Vroutje, come!" the wheelwright roared. "Bring the cider and the seed cakes!" She came down the stairs, his wife, a harried young mother with two at her feet and another rising under her apron.

While she prepared the refreshments, he read the letter. "She asks me to help you find work," he said. "And since my dear aunt Suzannah in Hoorn is a sister-in-law of an aunt of your own, that is enough of a recommendation for me, my boys. My *bouwerie* adjoins the *bouwerie* of the Director General of this place, Petrus Stuyvesant, and he is wanting help in building a chapel. So as you know bricks, you will be welcome."

"A chapel?" asked Cornelius.

"We, all of us in this neighborhood beyond the wall built to keep the English out, go to the Director's *bouwerie* every Sunday afternoon in the good weather to hear the *dominie* from Brooklyn preach and pray," Cosyn explained. "He is a newcomer here, but he has already more than hinted that the Director build him a proper chapel. He finds preaching in a barn to be undignified, and I agree. I will take you over there to meet the Director General when you come again on Sunday. You will wear your best clothes," he added. "And we will attend to the conditions of your employment after the preaching."

Jan felt comfortable in Cosyn's house and among his children, especially his merry, crowing three-year-old daughter, Grietje, who made everyone laugh with her high jinks. Encouraged by the attention, she rolled herself up in a ball and executed three little somersaults in a row. Jan laughed out loud at her. She was blond and plump and pretty, and green-eyed, like him, and she gobbled her seed cake in a comical way to make him laugh some more.

Before they left that day, Cosyn gave them a tour of his workshop, his timber yard, the smithy, the lathe house where a workman was turning a wheel hub. He was proud of his lathe. "We used to have to round the hubs with an axe," he said with satisfaction. "This is a big improvement."

They waded through a great litter of wood chips and shavings, a foot deep in some places. Jan loved the busy place. He asked all the questions he dared, and Cosyn, flattered, explained what the tools were for, and the process involved in mortising, and footing, and shaving, and boring, and wedging wheel rims, all new terms to Jan. "It seems to me a lad I know would like to work here, too," said Cornelius, winking.

Jan blushed. "I am going to be a bricklayer."

"A brick*maker*, first, then a bricklayer," Cosyn corrected him.

On Sunday, they returned, in their best clothes, and Cosyn with Vroutje and her two in tow led them, just as if they were part of the family, Jan thought, back down the wagon way to the Director's *bouwerie*. They gathered in the barn to hear the *dominie*, and Jan was amazed to find almost a hundred worshipers in all, including many from the negro families living in the neighborhood.

After the service, the children rushed outside to play in the fields around it, black and white together, without thought to color, and Cornelius discussed the conditions of employment with the Director, a proud-looking man with a wooden leg, and the foreman of his farm, who would be the brothers' *baas*.

Jan would have rather been with the children. He was only eleven, after all. Vroutje noticed where his eyes were wandering. "You can play with them, too," she said. "Go ahead."

And he did, that evening, and often in the long summer evenings when the brick making and chapel building were done. The second time he joined them, he touched arms with a cheerful black boy about his own age, comparing the hues of their skin, his so fair, the other boy's a warm brown, not black like some of the others. The boy laughed. "My father was white," he said.

They became good friends that summer. His name was Jan de Vries. Was the name de Vries a coincidence? Jan wondered. Or did the Captain from Hoorn father him? He lived alone with his mother and brothers and sisters in a tumble-down cottage in the lane alongside the north edge of Cosyn's *bouwerie* where the other negro families lived. They were freed slaves, he learned. And they owned their own land, scrubby and rocky as it was.

*   *   *   *

After two weeks sleeping together in the dark hole, the brothers moved to the Out Ward, near their work, and found room and board in a pleasant sunny little cottage on Petrus Stuyvesant's *bouwerie*. The garret was theirs. They had to share it only with their landlady's corn and herbs drying on the rafters, and the rats and mice.

Jan soon found that he did not like the brick trade. Not only was it hard work, and hard on the back, but it had to be conducted under a broiling sun that he wasn't used to. There was no such sun in cloudy Hoorn.

His job was to go to the clay deposits on the bank of a little stream that traversed the *bouwerie* and shovel the material out of the bank into a heap in the open air to cure and temper in the elements. The cured clay then had to be kneaded. His *baas* showed him how to knead it with his hands.

"I don't like this work" he said to his brother of the kneading. "I don't like this dirty work at all."

"The alternative is to walk an animal back and forth across the heap, so that their hooves do the kneading for you," Cosyn said. "Try goats."

He tried goats, two belonging to the Director. But the goats were too rambunctious for the work, butting each other frolicsomely and leaping about and trying to get loose from him to graze on the grassy bank of the stream. An old mare was more cooperative. He led her back and forth for hours on end. "Nothing will make me like this work," he said again and often to his brother.

With rake and shovel, together they mixed the clay with water and sand and in the drying shed tamped it into frames with brick-shaped sections. They then pressed these green bricks out of the form and left them to dry in the shed. They had to be completely free of any moisture before they could be used.

When the bricks were dry, they stacked them outside of the shed to produce a sort of kiln, made a hot wood fire in the middle of the kiln, and fed wood to it until the *baas* was satisfied the bricks were done. It was disconcerting to them how many bricks turned out to be useless, fit only to be thrown into the brick dump. These the *baas* called noggins, or pluggins, or clinkers, and he threatened to dock their pay for them.

"The worst part is carrrying the hod of mortar to the chapel site," the boy told Vroutje, who had taken quite a liking to him. "It is too heavy. It breaks my shoulder."

She sympathized and gave him food to strengthen him, build him up, every time she saw him.

While Jan made bricks, Cornelius and the *baas*, both wearing tall, wide-brimmed hats, laid the bricks to form the foundations and walls of the chapel. Now Cornelius, feeling the dignity of his hat and his profession, decided to adopt a proper surname, instead of using his father's name. His father was

Pieter Jansen: Pieter, son of Jan. Cornelius was Cornelius Pietersen: Cornelius, son of Pieter. "I have decided to make my last name Haring," he told Jan. "To honor the great catch that has made Hoorn famous."

Jan laughed. "Why name yourself for a fish?" he said.

Every Sunday evening, *Dominie* Selyns, a nice man, stopped by to admire their work.

Yes, a nice man, Jan thought, but when the chapel was finished, the *dominie* announced that he had decided not to baptize the black children any more. "Isn't it a sin not to baptize?" Jan asked Cosyn and Vroutje.

"He must have his reasons," said Vroutje doubtfully.

"He thinks they want their children to be baptized just so they can be free," said Cosyn. "A Christian can't be a slave."

"I thought they were free," said Jan.

"Not the children," Cosyn said.

Jan looked at Vroutje. "It is true," she said. She seemed sad about it, and it was sad. "I am godmother to many of them," she added. As if that made it better, the boy thought.

It took a whole year to complete the chapel, and when it was finished, Jan decided he would make bricks no more.

"What will you do?" Cornelius asked.

"I am going to ask Cosyn Gerritsen van Putten to take me as an apprentice wheelwright," Jan said, flushing.

"It is a long apprenticeship," said Cosyn, when the boy approached him. "You start by making a wheelbarrow, and it usually takes seven years to make one, for a beginner."

"Seven years to make a wheelbarrow! I'll be nineteen."

"That's the age I was when I opened this shop," said Cosyn. "It grows every year. It's a good business to be in. Everyone needs carts and wagons. And there's never an end to mending them. Even though the ones I make are meant to last a lifetime, they still need mending every year."

＊　　　＊　　　＊　　　＊

When it was finished, the chapel was much loved by the neighborhood. Even from south of the wall throngs came on Sunday afternoons to hear the *dominie*, a better preacher than their own, and to relax before and after under the locust trees shading the chapel, and to picnic at the tables the Director provided.

And then, exactly one year after the chapel was finished, an English fleet suddenly appeared in New York harbor and announced that the colony was theirs. Jan was thirteen.

The people were stunned. They had known that the Dutch and English were at war, and they knew that the English coveted New Netherland, wedged as it was between New England and Virginia. But they had not expected this.

"We have been farming this land for a generation," Cosyn shouted furiously, pounding the table with his fist. "Now what?"

The English agreed to let them keep their Dutch church and their inheritance customs, but the Dutch families knew in their hearts that further changes were in store for them.

"We are in limbo," Cosyn stormed. "Neither here nor there. What can we do?"

"Dutch and English understand we must get along together," said Vroutje hopefully. "And besides, our numbers are much greater than theirs. They have to treat with that fact."

"That fact will not last forever," Cosyn warned. "They will be coming in great hordes from now on. You'll see."

Cornelius and Jan saw the handwriting on the wall, too. "We must begin to learn English," Cornelius said. They went to school in the evenings to study the tongue with a schoolmaster straight from London. "See, Mother," Jan wrote. "I am keeping my promise to you, continuing my education."

✳   ✳   ✳   ✳

Jan much preferred wheelmaking to brickmaking. The timber Cosyn bought was up the Hudson, behind the towering cliffs along the river that soared up to the eagles' nests. He loved sailing up the mighty river on Cosyn's yawl to the sawpits deep in the forest, where they went on foot, along Indian paths. He loved to lie in a sea of fragrant ferns, watching the sawyers in a rain of sawdust cross-saw the oak and ash and elm and beech into the boards and planks and wagon shafts of Cosyn's specifications. And he loved sailing back, with the sawn lumber stashed on board midships, loading it on wagons to take it to the work yard, stacking it so that the air cured it without warping. "Not anywhere near the horses," Cosyn said. "The ammonia in their piss will kill the wood."

And he loved Cosyn and his kin. Their aunt's introduction had given the brothers as if a ready-made family, and all was calm and peaceful among them as the years passed. The English occupation was not as onerous as feared at first, especially in the Out Ward, which seemed to exist beyond the rulers' notice. In short, Jan was happy. He finished his apprenticeship along the way, and he developed a secret intention of marrying Grietje Cosyns when she was old enough. Eighteen, he estimated, would be about right. Or maybe seventeen, judging by the way she was shaped. She was only thirteen, but she had been wearing stays for two years already and was nearly as tall as he. Four more years, he told himself, and I will make her mine. This thought pervaded his being and put him into a pleasant and perpetual erotic fog.

But then, in 1672, to his and everyone's dismay, Grietje Cosyns, age thirteen, upset the happy apple cart by announcing she wanted to marry a stranger who had come into their midst, a stranger from Munsterlandt.

Cosyn and Vroutje were shocked and appalled and tried to dissuade the girl, but she would not be dissuaded. At last Vroutje seized a long carving knife and chased her around the kitchen garden with it, shouting at her to give up her wanton idea. "A German no less," Vroutje screamed. "A German busting out of his tight pants and his naked hairy legs in my face! How dare you? What can you be thinking of, you wretched girl?"

But Grietje was set on marrying, and she could run faster than her mother and vault over the fence of the kitchen garden to boot. "Twelve is the legal age in Dutch law," she shouted over her shoulder as she ran. "And Dutch law is the law in New Netherland, even though the English have come with their own law. So there!"

Vroutje, panting, knew when she had lost a battle. But she stood in the garden, carving knife raised to plunge it in her child's chest anyway.

Cosyn approached her and whispered something to her. And Vroutje lowered the knife.

"Come here," he said to Grietje.

She came.

"You can marry," he said. "But you cannot live with him. You must live at home, with us, until you have attained a more decent age."

"That's good," said Grietje saucily. "I didn't want to live with him anyway. I'd have to cook and clean all day."

"What she means is all she wants to do is …" Cosyn muttered.

"I could wring her little neck," said Vroutje. "And do worse to him, yes, I could gladly cut off his balls. A German no less."

Grietje's intended, Herman Theuniszen from Zell in Munsterlandt, a bold, handsome lad, was under the legal age for males, only nineteen, two years younger than Jan, who was so shocked at the turn in events that he was knocked speechless. "Yet," he said to Cornelius, when he recovered somewhat, "I recognize there is a certain animal quality to him that must appeal to a woman."

"She's not a woman," said Cornelius. "She's a little girl."

"She looks like a woman," said Jan.

"You must get the written approval of your father," *Dominie* Samuel Drisius told the lad severely. "It is the law."

Of course, everyone except the amorous couple hoped approval would be denied. But it was not. When it finally came from over the sea, six months later, *Dominie* Drisius married them, still with an air of disapproval, in the Dutch Church in the Fort.

"If I had known she wanted to get married, I would gladly have married her," said Jan.

"You marry Grietje? She's like our sister."

"She's more than a sister to me," Jan said dolefully.

"She's too young to marry. Thirteen years old."

"But she looks older," Jan said. "She looks at least eighteen." She was tall and strong with a well-developed bosom within her stays and a waist just begging to be clasped, and a sassy way of walking—and talking.

Jan mourned.

*   *   *   *

A year after Grietje married her Herman, the Dutch surprised themselves and the world by taking back the colony from England. The inhabitants of New Amsterdam were infused again with a great sense of hope and promise. That year, even though he was only twenty-two, Jan was appointed by the new administration to be a *schepen,* a magistrate of the court in the Out Ward. He was young for such a responsible position, but people could see that he was a special sort, mature, capable, intelligent, trustworthy, a leader they were lucky to have, no matter his years, and he could speak English better than most Dutchmen. Now he took the same name as his brother. "I will now be known as Jan Pietersen Haring," he declared. "But I am not named after the fish. I am named to honor Jan Haring the Hero of Hoorn, who hauled down the colors of Admiral de Bossu in the Zuiderzee one hundred years ago this very month." Now it was Cornelius's turn to laugh. "You have a big head in more ways than one," he said.

Jan had also begun to think seriously of his future. With his fellow *schepen,* Wolphert Webber, he gathered together a group of men, including his brother, of course, and Cosyn's son, and Jan de Vries and some of the other free blacks in the neighborhood, and they pooled their resources with the intention of buying a good-sized parcel of fertile land north of the Out Ward and south of the little village of Harlem at the top of the island.

But the authorities would not sell it to them. "We intend to hold on to that land until its value rises," they told him curtly. "You'll have to look elsewhere."

The men were deeply disappointed. "We have to get another dream," Jan said. He began to remember the land up the river, behind the Palisades.

*   *   *   *

The same year that Jan became a *schepen*, and Grietje was a new bride, she got herself talked about for a different sort of escapade. She had discovered Hendrick Pietersen's horse trampling her buckwheat. Without a thought, she jumped on him bareback and galloped him to the Fresh Water and left him there, from whence he strayed deep into the woods. An irate Hendrick Pietersen went to court and demanded of the magistrates that Grietje be condemned to search for the horse and deliver it to him at her own expense. Whereupon she went to court to defend herself.

"Without her father's help," people whispered. "Without even her stupid husband's help. She went before the magistrates to defend herself, at age fourteen. What nerve she has!"

She went, and she was acquitted. "You have every right," the court said, "to defend your buckwheat fields."

"So there," she said to the people.

"I regret it wasn't to my court that Hendrick Pietersen hauled her," Jan said to Cornelius. Hendrick lived south of the wall in the jurisdiction of the court that met in the city hall. "I would have acquitted her in a minute."

"She is a brave girl to go to city hall and stand up for her rights before those important officials," Cornelius said. "She is a feisty one."

"She is expecting a baby," Jan said sadly.

"How do you know?"

"Her mother told me."

"Her mother wishes you were the husband and father."

"I, too," said Jan. He would never find another to match Grietje. "Why did she marry that German?" he said. "He can't even be bothered to learn to make a wheelbarrow." Herman had turned up his nose at wheelwrighting, instead had hired himself out as a farmer to a rich man with a big plantation on the East River.

Suddenly, things began to happen fast again, all too fast. In 1674, the English returned, and this time, the Dutch knew, the jig was up. They had better look for greener pastures. This time it was for good. All were dashed into gloom. It was the last straw that the authorities had traded away their dear *colonie* for some god-forsaken swampland in South America. They began to speak of making their plans to leave Manhattan and start over again in the panther-, bobcat-, wolf-, and snake-infested wilderness. But a wilderness uninfested by *Engelsmen* at least.

That same year, Grietje had her baby, a girl, which did not live, and then her handsome, reckless husband died, thrown from his horse as he galloped much too fast down Broadway on a black gelding that he had borrowed for the day.

And then Cornelius said one day, "I cannot bear living with the English. I have decided to go back to Hoorn. What will you do, brother? Will you go with me?"

"I am going to stay here," said Jan. "After she recovers from her losses, I am going to pay court to Grietje."

He was shy with women. But when Vroutje judged that enough time had passed since her daughter's double bereavement, she encouraged him to approach her. She was seventeen now. He was twenty-five. "Do it before some other unsuitable foreigner appears on the horizon," Vroutje said.

Grietje laughed out loud when she learned that he had never slept with a woman. She laughed a lot, he thought. Everything amused her. "What were you waiting for?" she teased.

"For you," he said. "You're the only one for me."

"Why?" she asked.

"Because you have green eyes, like me. We are meant for each other." There was much more to it than her green eyes, though. She had smited his soul. He loved her spirit. And in the worst way he wanted her to be his wife and the mother of his children. She had just the guts and courage to be both well.

She laughed again. "I will teach you how to do it in no time," she said.

He learned the art of love fast, at her direction. He was good at it. They were good at it together! "I am the happiest man in the world," he murmured into her abundant blond hair.

They married, in the chapel he had helped to build. She bore him four sons in seven years.

*   *   *   *

They lived in the little house her father had built for her when she became pregnant at fifteen. "It is very crowded here, Grietje," Jan said, as the babies kept coming. "I want to move."

"Where shall we move?"

He described to her the fair land up the river, behind the awesome Palisades, where her father went to supervise the sawyers cutting his timber, the sparkling *kill* flowing into the river from a break in the cliffs. "We poled along the *kill* inland from the river for three miles to a clear place where the Indians grow their corn and squash. The hills to the east behind us were blue in a certain light," he told her. "It was a wondrous place. I want it."

She laughed. "I'm tired of this place, too," she said. "We need land for sons."

He gathered another group of men together, and with his English friend the hatmaker Samuel Edsall to translate, and his neighbors Smith and Blauvelt, he sailed up the river to that fair land in the fall of 1680 and negotiated with the Tappan Indians for 16,000 acres, the Tappan Patent it was called when the royal governor signed the papers. He acquired three shares in it, about 3,000 acres. "Not without my help," Grietje reminded him.

"Not without your help." According to the law, by his marriage to her he was the owner of the little house where they lived, and her good fields sowable and mowable as well, her dowry both from her first marriage and her second. He kept the house, because they would need a place to live until their new house could be built. But he sold some of the fields, not all, and he sold the100 beaver skins that had been part of her dowry to him, and he put the proceeds toward the funds needed to buy the goods the Indians wanted for the land.

*   *   *   *

The comet star appeared in the southwest on the ninth day of December 1680, at about two o'clock in the afternoon on a day of fair sunshiny weather, a little above the sun. What was it? A bright ball of fire hurtling across the sky. No one had ever seen such a thing before, in the daylight. The people were frightened and alarmed.

And then, to the great astonishment and apprehension of all, it returned the next day, a great bright ball, at about twilight, in the western sky, and when the sky darkened the bright ball had a long fiery tail or streamer. It appeared again the next night. And the next. It returned every night for weeks, shooting across the sky, and from the beginning all took it as a sign, a portent of evil. Undoubtedly it was God warning them of dreadful punishments to come if they did not change their sinful ways, repent.

The people begged the *dominies*—who did not have to be begged very hard, they were as terrified as everyone else—to proclaim a Day of Fasting and Humiliation, and everyone fasted and prayed and confessed their sins and begged for mercy all the day long, even the children. Finally, it stopped coming. But they could not forget it, or forget what it seemed to portend.

They planned to move to the land in the spring of 1684. And then tragedy struck. In December 1683, Jan Haring and three of his partners in the land venture were on a sloop in the Hudson River, sailing to Tappan with sawn lumber purchased of Cosyn to build a sawmill. The water was rough, the tide strong, the currents swift. Just past the *Spuyten Duyvil,* Hell's Gate, the boat began to take on water and sink. As it went down, a mighty timber that loosed itself from the stack midship struck Jan on the head with a great thump and knocked him overboard. He uttered one piercing scream and disappeared. Gerrit Blauvelt dived after him and pulled him to the surface, but he was already drowned.

With utmost difficulty, the three partners made it to shore, pulling their friend's body with them, but within a month of each other they had all died of various complications of the accident: Ide van Vorst of a broken neck, Gerrit Blauvelt of pneumonia, Cornelius Smith of bleeding in the stomach. As the people saw their leaders exterminated, one by one, over the space of a month, they could not help but remember how the comet star had hurtled through the night skies as the men negotiated with the Indians.

The survivors of the four were stupefied with grief, deprived of their husbands and fathers and sons, of four of their thirteen leaders almost simultaneously. "How will we ever clear and settle that wilderness land without those four strong men?" Grietje wailed. "How will we ever turn that forest to fields, build our houses, mills, and barns?" They had dreamed of it, a land of waving grains and grasses, of every garden vegetable they knew and every kind of fruit tree known. "How?"

And to make it all the worse a couple of other partners in the venture, remembering the celestial phenomenon, sensed trouble ahead, lost interest in the project, decided to "postpone settlement" for another generation, or so they said. "It is really that they have got cold feet," said Grietje scornfully. "They do not want to give the Destroying Angel they think hovers over the place a chance to lay them to waste. The cowards."

"You should sell the land," Cosyn said. "You will not have enough hands and backs for the work of clearing it and building your houses and barns and mills. Give it up."

"No," said Grietje. "I will not give up our fair land. Or our dream to be rid of the English. I want that land for my sons, and theirs, and theirs."

"It will be near impossible," Vroutje warned.

"We'll see," said Grietje. She never looked grimmer.

"You'll need a new husband," said Cosyn.

"You can be sure of that," Grietje said. "With the four sons of Jan Pietersen Haring to raise."

After an interlude of mourning, Grietje Haring, née Cosyns, ever resourceful, looked around for that new husband. She found him in Daniel de Clark, a neighbor, a lusty young man, seven years her junior.

Again, people were shocked. Daniel de Clark, seven years her junior! It created a scandal, like her first marriage at thirteen. People smirked. They whispered. She overheard someone refer to her as an "old vixen of thirty-five, robbing the cradle." She took that person to court for slander (she was twenty-six), and the court made that person apologize. The idea that anyone could think she was thirty-five!

And as they had when she was a headstrong young girl and insisted on marrying, everybody got over it.

Daniel de Clark, as young as he was, came into her widow's share in the land, a thousand acres, Dutch law again, and became the leader of the families, in place of Jan Pietersen Haring, drowned.

Without more ado, they gathered up her four children and his two and the necessities of life, and the tools to clear the land and the seeds to plant it, and they moved to Tappan to start their new life.

CHAPTER 2

▼

WOMEN

The day began hot. The Hudson Valley was a hot and steamy place in the dog days.

On a country lane, the house baked in the morning sun.

The high-breaking gambrel roof covered a huge garret where the heat would build up as the day wore on, acting like an oven to cook the rooms below.

Its sandstone walls, two feet thick, packed in the heat too. The house would be unbearable by noon, even with the windows and doors open to catch whatever air stirred. Not even the deep eave hanging over the long south-facing front of the house would be a defense against the blazing sun this day, or the fragrant locust trees planted for their shade on the east and west sides.

A woman appeared at one of the twin doors, or at least the top half of her appeared. It was a so-called Dutch door, the bottom half kept closed to keep the ducks and pigs out and the children in. No children of her own needed to be kept in. Hers were grown. Only an infant granddaughter, learning to crawl, must be confined.

She was fifty-nine, in this year of her Lord 1737. She shared the sandstone hotbox with her husband, Cosyn, who had built it in 1704, and their three daughters, Marretie, twenty-three, Margrietje, nineteen, and little Maria, fourteen. Their eldest, their son Jan, now thirty-seven, and his wife Aeltie and their brood lived nearby. Jan had married young to the schoolmaster's daughter. A good match in beauty and brains at least, even though her apron had risen a month sooner than it should have, and even though her dowry was nothing to crow about. And even though they were but nineteen and eighteen.

As soon as the harvest was in, Cosyn was planning to build a new house for themselves on his land a mile or two to the southeast and let Jan and Aeltie have this house. The house where they were living now had grown too small for them, or them too many for it and their eight children. A new one came along every two years, and they were bursting out of the walls and windows.

It was a good house, hers, though not the very best in the area. The house of her mother-in-law, Grietje Cosyns, was the best. But hers was one of the best, wider and deeper than most, with two large rooms on the first floor, each with its own front door, and two smaller rooms behind. And, up the stairs tucked into the corner of the *groote kamer,* that huge garret. Their slaves had cut and hauled the sandstone from an outcrop on the Palisades, helped him and his brothers and their slaves raise the tulipwood beams, roofed the place with cedar shakes from the pungent white cedar trees that grow along the Hackensack River. They built it in 1704 as if it had to last for 500 years.

The windows in the rear rooms gave out on her kitchen garden and chicken coop, the duck pond and the icehouse, the great barn off to the left about 200 feet, the *speelhuis,* where they took their meals in the summer, the summer kitchen, where the slaves slept, the smokehouse, hay barrack, the manure pile, the malodorous necessaries, one for the family, one for the slaves, and, beyond all that, their sustenance—the orchards, the fields of grain and corn, ripening for the harvest. One could say in fact that the windows gave out on their hope, she often thought, for it was only by selling the surplus of the harvest, the grain, the flour they made of it, bacon, bread, butter, apples, garden seeds, nuts, honey, corn-meal, onions and shallots, smoked beef and pork, that they could hope to rise, continue to improve their holdings, purchase seed and tools, livestock and slaves, hire day labor, acquire the niceties of life, leave something for the next genera-tion.

Her name was Marytie. Her one and only English friend, Hannah—forever hungering for things English in this peculiar Dutch enclave on the west side of the Hudson where she had found herself—calls her Maria, with the accent on the first syllable, English style. But that is Marytie's youngest daughter's name, and they put the accent on the second syllable, Dutch style. For herself she prefers Marytie, although she lets Hannah have her way. She is especially kind to Han-nah these days, now that her peculiar husband, a harsh and suspicious German, is threatening to move with her and their daughter Eliza up into the mountains. He doesn't care for the Dutch. Doesn't go to their church, although there is no other. Doesn't drink in their taverns, although there are no others. In fact, he is so peculiar that he doesn't drink! Hannah believes he wants to keep Eliza away from the young men who have lately begun to notice her and her suddenly big bouncing breasts that she does not enough to conceal.

She saw him, across the lane, skulking out of the woods, sticking in the shade of the trees at the woods' edge, slyly skirting her domain: the wolf. He lapped at the water in the duck pond. *In the duck pond like a sitting duck,* she thought. He had been after her chickens for a week. "That wolf is as good as dead," she muttered to her slave woman, Dina, who had also seen the creature.

She turned from the door, lifted her husband's musket down from its place on the chimney wall, and stepped swiftly back to the door and out onto the front *stoep.* The musket was always loaded, its powder in a paper cartridge, its lead ball ready to be fired. He did not notice her. He wanted a chicken too badly.

She was a tall, strong woman, and she knew very well how to shoot. She raised the musket and aimed. Behind her, Dina clapped her hands over her ears. Marytie brought him down with one shot and with, from him, one unearthly screech.

The Board of Supervisors paid a bounty on wolves. She replaced the musket on the wall and took up the rapier that had come down to her husband from his grandfather, whose name he bears: Cosyn. She remembered him, that old Cosyn, remembered him from her childhood, strutting cockily around New York City with the sharp little sword displayed at his waist. In the heyday of the old Dutch *colonie*, when the little city was called New Amsterdam, he had been a minor player there. The wheelwright. Everyone needed the wheelwright.

Besides the rapier, she took a spade with her too and walked across the yard toward the body of the wolf. The wolf was not a he, as it turned out; it was a she.

Too bad. With two swift strokes of the sharp little sword, she sliced off its ears, an acceptable substitute for the head the law required of the official wolf catchers, wrapped them, bloody, in a handkerchief, and tucked them into the deep dimity pocket tied around her waist, over her skirt and petticoat. Four shillings and sixpence nothing to sneeze at.

The red clay soil was not easy digging. And the act of digging a grave, even for a wolf, was for her not an easy association. Of their eight blond *kinder*, they had buried four, in this same red clay, two bonny sons and two daughters. Suddenly drenched in sweat, bowed with memory, grief and, yes, fury, even now, years later, she leaned on the spade and raged, silently: *It was not fair! Those four innocent little bodies.*

She had raged to God after each one: *It is not fair!*

And after each one she had stayed home from church, angry at the Lord for taking what he had given. But they had drawn her back each time, the *dominie*, her mother, her husband, his mother and stepfather, her son Jan, her only surviving child by the time the fourth had died, her sisters and brothers, her aunts and uncles, her friends and neighbors, quoting scripture, warning of the consequences, the dreadful consequences of disobeying his Commandments. Thou shalt remember the Sabbath Day to keep it holy, they insisted.

She stepped down on the spade again with her heavy leather clog, urging it into the hard-packed clay with all the energy her rage could muster. This mother wolf would have a shallow grave.

In the end, she could not tolerate the prospect of eternity in hell. She went back to church each time. It was how, they promised her, she would meet *them* again. The sinless ones she had buried. But, then, she wondered about that. And maybe they wondered too. It wasn't something they talked about: Was there really an after life? Was heaven an actual place? Or was it a state of mind? Or was it just a trick to scare you into believing?

She often wondered this. Was hell a geographical place, or just a thing invented by holy men to make you fearful? Was anything up there, down there?

As if these theological thoughts had forced her to her knees, she knelt and shoved the wolf into the shallow cavity she had made and covered it with a few spadesful of the red clay and spread on the top of it some brush. Crows and rats would soon come to feast on it, and it would stink in a day. But it would have to do unless someone else, Cuff, wanted to dig the hole deeper.

From a wooden bucket hanging on the coop, she scattered corn for the chickens and went back to the house. In the distance Cuff was plowing, getting a fallow field ready for the winter wheat. In the house, Dina, no relation to Cuff that they knew of, was on her hands and knees, scrubbing the kitchen floorboards, already white with daily scrubbing.

She was restless suddenly, wanted company. Had something on her mind today she needed to talk about. Her three daughters and her young grand-niece Margaret Blauvelt, who was visiting for the summer, had gone off to cool in the Hackensack River, float on its clear cedar-shaded waters in their shifts, right off the hard-packed bank. At least she hoped they would keep their shifts on. You never knew who might be lurking in the bushes. A day laborer had murdered a slave woman from one of the other farms there not so long ago, cut her throat. He claimed she had stolen from him. So of course there was no penalty to pay, it being a capital crime for a slave to steal from a white. She shivered. It was a lonely place, a place where the slaves went at night after their work was done. Their drums and their doleful chanting drifted through the woods when the wind was right.

Summer was the time for long visits, and her daughter-in-law Aeltie and her children had gone to spend the week with Aeltie's widowed mother, a Holland-born woman who spoke almost no English. Cosyn and Jan have been gone all week as well, gone by *sloep* down the Hudson to New York City to meet with the factor on Pearl Street, to discuss the price of wheat, the prospects for the coming harvest. And to consult with Cosyn's elder brother Peter, their county's delegate to the New York Assembly, about the wicked plot that had come to light, the sinister plot two Englishmen have hatched to rob them of their land.

Not that her Cosyn was much of a conversationalist! Of the four brothers who inherited the land their father had acquired from the Indians so long ago, he was the different one. A quiet, retiring man, he was always busy in the fields or the barn, or doing his accounts, supervising the slaves and the hired hands, serving in the militia, where he was a captain, going off to his church meetings, never calling attention to himself. He has been a deacon on and off for years in the Tappan church. And an elder, too. He was to serve again as elder in the fall. His name in Dutch meant window frame, *kozijn*, and he was as strong and quiet and dependable as a window frame should be.

They have been married for going on forty years. Unlike some she could mention, they had married for love, not because their families urged them to, with a shrewd eye to the mutual long green fields they would one day come into. That they had come into those bountiful fields was the cream on the milk. The milk for them was ever the best part.

They had known each other since childhood, but she could still remember the day she had looked at him with new eyes, the day she had decided that he was the one for her, that no one else would do. She was thirteen; he was fourteen. *You are mine*, she would whisper to herself at night. *Know that you are mine. I have made you mine.*

He was tall—and dark, unlike the blond folk who peopled the community. His hair fell like a soft dark wing across his wide, serene brow. His eyes, green colored, saw everything. His lean and muscular body caused her pulse to speed up when she was anywhere near him.

But he was not one to commit himself to anything until he was sure it was the right thing for him. She watched him watch her from afar, making up his mind about her, and then one day, when she was eighteen and he nineteen (the same as Jan and Aeltie), he came acourting. And then after that exciting time of getting to know each other in the courting, kissing, touching way, he asked her if she would seal their troth, and she agreed.

She remembered how they had set a date for this encounter (a time when she would be clean of blood). And then, without further ado, one fragrant summer eve they walked together into the woods to a place he had prepared for them, a chamber safe from prying eyes formed by the branches of a spreading beech tree. And there on a surprising bed of sweet hay, he spread a linen sheet and gently laid her down and kissed her, and kissed her until she was panting, until they were both panting and sweating, and then, resolutely, he raised her best apron and her skirt and her petticoat and her shift, the one with the lace on it, while she focused hard on the dense-leaved branches of the beechnut tree waiting for what was to happen to her. A fleeting image crossed her mind: Of him, that day, driving past her house with a load of fresh hay in his wagon. How should she have known it was to be her betrothal bed? She watched with fascination as he let down the fall flap on his leather breeches and held gently in his hand for a moment the sturdy member she would come to love, as if he were instructing it, or encouraging it, and then he bent to seal their pledge with it. Later, and many times thereafter that summer, they would take off all their clothes and lie naked together under the beech tree, exploring each other's ardent, willing bodies, taking their pleasure with all carnal abandon.

But enough of memories. She wanted to talk! There was work to do, of course; there was always work to do, but not today. She put the wolf's ears on a shelf in the *keuken,* changed her plain work apron to a silk one embroidered with vines and flowers, put on her bonnet against the sun, and set off in the heat to visit her mother-in-law, Grietje Cosyns, a mile or so to the east. She was sure that Grietje, her best friend, would have some good advice about this thing that was on her mind this day.

Grietje's house, as she neared it on the bridge over the spar *kill,* appeared through the orchard. It was a very fine house. It was smaller than Marytie's, but it was made of brick, imported from over the sea, and the two fireplaces, one in the *keuken* and the other in the *groote kamer,* were surrounded by handsome lavender-colored tiles depicting Bible stories, from over there too. Delft.

A large and useful hallway separated the two front rooms, a place where extra trestle tables loaded with food could be set up when they celebrated together, family and the friends, and where children played games in the bad weather. The hallway did not have stairs to the second floor, just a ladder, though it was not a mere garret up there, but a second floor divided into proper chambers where long ago when they first built it her still-unmarried youngest son and her stepson, de Clark's boy, slept.

Grietje had not only the best house but the best flower garden in the area, and on the south side of the house the best herb garden, full of herbs both to make her cooking tasty and herself and her family strong and healthy.

She had been working on the flower garden for thirty years, had modeled it on the formal garden of Peter Stuyvesant's mansion house in the fort at New Amsterdam on the island of Manhattan.

As he had, she had laid out long and narrow rectangular beds, bordered with low hedges of boxwood and rosemary, that stretched themselves out in the sun perpendicular to a center path leading out of the west façade of the house. Their flowers were bunched densely together in the Dutch manner, by type, sunflowers here, carnations there, tulips, lilies, anemones, violets, roses, marigolds, each having its own little plot of earth within the borders.

She kept the seeds of the annuals carefully labeled with each type in its own little white paper, so that she would not mix them in with each other at sowing time.

Her mother and father had brought them originally from over the sea when they came, in the last century, seeds, seedlings, bare roots, and rooted slips of hawthorne and holly and linden trees, too, the roots tucked in a tub of rich earth ready for planting on their land when they got it. They had brought nuts, too, and peach and plum stones, cherry and apricot pits and apple seeds from the fatherland, and trees from all of these grew handsomely in Grietje's orchard ninety years later.

She sat at the table in the *keuken*, deep in thought, as if in a faraway place, as she often seemed to be these days, her head resting on her left hand.

Marytie said her name softly. "Grietje?"

Grietje started up, stared at her as if she didn't recognize her, so far away in her thoughts she had been. She looked distressed, Marytie thought.

"You startled me," she said. "Marytie. I almost didn't recognize you at first. What's wrong with me?"

Was it the land problem that was troubling her? Marytie wondered. Or was it something else? She was still hale and hearty at seventy-eight, although Marytie had noticed lately a certain slippage, that distant look in her eyes at times, the green eyes she had given to Cosyn. As if, Marytie thought, with a shiver, as if she was pondering fields where sheep may safely graze.

"I am sorry I startled you," Marytie said. "I came to talk."

"I am writing a letter," Grietje said, "to my son in the Assembly. To give him my advice about the problem. I am just finishing it."

Yes, it was the land problem, of course. Marytie frowned at the mention of it.

It was so hot that Grietje had shed her skirt and the petticoats she normally wore, even in the hot weather, sat in her stays and a sleeveless summer shift edged in lace around the neck and armholes. Marytie admired the way she had kept her figure. Of course, the stays helped. *"In Engels,"* she added proudly.

Her dog-eared wordbook, the list she kept of Dutch words and their English equivalents, was at hand. "I have one last sentence to write," she said, turning to the letter. "Sit by me while I finish." Dutifully, Marytie sat at the table with her, although she was itching to tell her news.

The old lady bent to her work. Her hair was grayer than she knew, Marytie noticed.

She insisted on writing *in Engels* when she wrote to her son in the Assembly, even though it was difficult for her, and even though she hated the English themselves. Arrogant praters, calling the Dutch men *boors* and the women "butter-boxes," of all things. ("And by the way," she had said indignantly to one and all when she first heard that outrageous term applied to one of them, "I am anything but a butterbox. A butterbox doesn't catch three good husbands." She was tall and stately and as proud as any Englishwoman, even going on eighty.)

Yes, she hated them, rude Englishmen. But she was still determined to know their language. "You can't know your enemy if you don't know their language," she often muttered. And she would know her enemy. She had underlined in her wordbook the word for *vijand*: enemy. She hated them most of all for having so brusquely removed them from power, for upsetting the applecart, coming and taking over the *Duits colonie* they loved and deeming it English.

Arduously, she had spent the whole hot afternoon composing this letter to her first-born son, Pieter (which he spells Peter, for he had understood how to climb the English ladder). He had named his first daughter after her, as tradition expected, but he spelled it the English way, too: Margaret. She was more than proud of him as Orange County's representative to the New York Assembly. And so, as often as she wrote to him she wrote in English, the language he spoke in the Assembly, the language of politics and business, the language for getting on in life, just to prove to him that she could do it.

One must have English to rise. They have all finally understood this by now in the year 1737. Her son would not be in the Assembly without it. She missed him, her first-born and most promising of her four sons, so capable, like the father he had hardly known. He had been gone eighty days this year on the Assembly's business. "He will be home soon," she muttered, "to help with the harvest, and not too soon either, for his farm, as I have not been shy of pointing out to him all summer, is going to pot."

Her loathing of the English had been stirred afresh by the news that they had come again—to this their new land and were trying another takeover here that her sons and the other farmers of Tappan would most likely have to spend their substance fighting in the courts.

This is what had happened so far: Two years before, in 1735, Lancaster Symes, a notorious land grabber with connections in high places, purchased property adjoining the Tappan Patent on the west from a *schurck*, a rogue, named John McEvers, and with deed in hand had laid claim to a strip of land east of the Hackensack River that the patentees had always and ever assumed was theirs. It *was* theirs, those flat, fertile fields and propitious sites on the river! How dare anyone claim that land? But they had dared. And now they had a fight on their hands.

She finished the letter and showed her effort to Marytie. *"I see in the papers that the Assembly does not do much but discord,"* she started out. But she quickly cut to the chase. It was not the bickering Assembly that bothered her. It was the land problem: *"I hope that God will not impose more upon us than we can bear regarding the patent. If what the King's Governor has once given away can be broken by another Governor then there would never be an end, and in that case one would never be safe in this world!"*

And then she wrote of how she hates Lancaster Symes. *"If I ever see him face to face, I will spit in his eye."*

And finally, imperious as usual, she wrote her concluding sentence, the one Marytie had patiently sat waiting for her to compose: *"Here is what I want you to bring me when you come: eleven yards of that morning crepe otherwise I can't put any lining in my nightfrock for winter, a small piece of blue check, a piece of white Flemish, 2 small pieces of multi-colored cotton, some salt, and a cask of rum."*

She ended her epistle by commending her son herewith into the protection of the Most Highest and signed it Your loving Mother.

Marytie praised it.

Grietje looked grimly gratified. "It is not easy work, writing in that terrible language," she said.

She put the letter aside. She was still steamed up over Lancaster Symes. She repeated her threat to Marytie: "I mean what I wrote," she said. "I will not hesitate to spit in his eye if I ever meet up with him. I am not afraid of a mere man."

And then she lapsed into that reverie state again, slipped away into her past, Martyie guessed.

Yes, Grietje was remembering the past, the year 1673 when she was a young married woman (of fourteen) and discovered Hendrick Pietersen's horse trampling her buckwheat. She remembered jumping on that horse and riding him bareback to the Fresh Water and leaving him there, with a smart slap on his rump. He galloped away, whinneying, into the woods. And when Hendrick Pietersen demanded of the court that she be condemned to search for the horse and deliver it to him at her own expense, she went to court to defend herself. She didn't ask for her father's help, or her husband's, as other women would. She went herself before the magistrates at age fourteen. And they acquitted her. She had every right, the court said, quite kindly, to defend her buckwheat fields.

Marytie cleared her throat and drummed her fingers on the table to draw her back. Grietje came to and looked at her. "So, tell me, what less would I do now at age seventy-eight to defend my share of the Patent lands?" she demanded.

"Nothing less. We must defend the land," Marytie assured her. "Don't worry, we will defend it. It is ours, forever."

Grietje sighed a great sigh. "It calms me to hear you say we will not let ourselves be cheated out of our own property. Say it again."

"I promise you. We will not let ourselves lose our land."

"*Dank u,*" she said.

So at last Marytie could change the subject and get on with her news, the unwelcome news that Jacobus Demarest, a widower, had come courting her middle daughter, Margrietje, Grietje's namesake. (Or one of them. There were three or four others, her children and grandchildren all prolific bearers and all more than glad to honor her in this Dutch way.) "He came again last evening to announce that it was his last offer," she said glumly. They, she and Cosyn, had not treated it seriously up to now; hoped if they ignored him and his offer he would go away and forget about it. But now there was a new twist. Now it seemed that Margrietje had actually become interested in the notion of being the man's wife.

"I do not at all like the idea of Jacobus Demarest marrying my daughter," Marytie fumed. "He is closer to my age than to Margrietje's!" (This was an exaggeration, but Grietje didn't point it out.) "And if he was going to look in our direction, at least he might have looked at Marretie." She took it as an insult that he had passed over Marretie, her eldest daughter. "I don't like the man. I never liked him."

Grietje remembered him. "His mother was a great friend of mine," she said. "Yes, I remember him from way back, though he is Hackensack, not Tappan."

"And that is another part of what I don't like about him," Marytie exploded. "He will take her from here to that place."

"It is not so great a distance away," Grietje said.

"True, but it is an irksome trek by horse and wagon through the forest." They both well knew the bumpy, rutted lanes, sometimes so bad the wagons had to turn back for the mud. "And far enough that that church, his church, will become her church." Small comfort that the same *dominie* served them both.

"And besides, why does he have to want Margrietje? What is wrong with Marretie if he needs a wife, a mother, to bring up his three children with Lea De Groot, deceased?"

Grietje shook her head, bit her lip, bit her tongue. She knew, of course; they both knew it. It was because Margrietje was so pretty and Marretie was so plain. Grietje sighed. Looks were important. It satisfied her that she had kept hers, even into her old age, kept her teeth, kept her figure, kept her dark blond hair, though she had to admit it was a little faded these days ("laced with silver," as she liked to put it). She was as vain as could be about her looks, whose condition she kept track of in the glass into which she gazed numerous times a day when she stopped before it to pile her hair ("laced with silver") on top of her head, skewering it there with the help of an imperious tortoise-shell comb. Her second son Cosyn resembled her very greatly in his looks, though not in his temperament. He was a stolid, quiet man, took after his father—not like her, volatile and opinionated.

But even so, Grietje had a different take on the matter. "He is a Demarest, after all," she pointed out, "and they are one of the best families among us." Even though there had been a scandal when the Indians accused the settler, an uncle of this Jacobus, of selling rum to them so that they knew not what they were doing in parting with their hunting grounds.

"Among *us?*" Marytie said scornfully. "They're French."

"They've become Dutch," said Grietje. "Almost." She and Jacobus Demarest's mother, Rachel Cresson, the daughter of Huguenots from Picardy, had been fast friends for a long time, although Rachel was fifteen years younger and had been dead already these ten years. "And he has a good farm."

Those long green fields again.

Marytie further disturbed herself by thinking of the sex they will have, he so experienced, her girl so not.

Grietje was thinking of the same thing. "The Demarest men are said to be lusty," she said. At least, that is what Rachel Cresson, with her three husbands, just like Grietje, had reported of her first husband. The Demarest husband she had lost to a falling tree.

"I suspected it," said Marytie grimly.

Sex was a subject that even at seventy-eight had not faded from Grietje's recollection. She had stored for keeping her memories of those pleasure moments when flesh shuddered and caved in like quicksand, when her flesh and his were one. She retrieved them whenever she pleased. She was always well disposed to men and they to her. Perhaps it was less justice, she sometimes thought, a little guiltily, that the magistrates had meted out to her that time of the horse in her buckwheat fields (and other times, too, when she had gone before them) than admiration for her comely and fearless and, yes, somewhat *koket* coquettish self.

There was one more thing bothering Marytie: Margrietje's probable long widowhood marrying a man nineteen years her senior.

At last, she wore her doughty mother-in-law down. "Yes, there are drawbacks to the match," Grietje finally admitted. His age. The slight to Marretie. His three children. The distance. The probable long widowhood. "Therefore, you must make him a hard bargain," she determined.

"Then let us think of what it shall be," said Marytie quickly.

And so it happened that Jacobus Demarest, that summer of 1737 when he next came calling to get an answer to his final offer for Margrietje's hand, so it happened that Cosyn persuaded him to buy a 261-acre farm of Jacobus's uncle for 280 pounds. "I already have a farm," Jacobus whined. "But that farm is for your three children by Lea De Groot," Cosyn pointed out. "You should buy a farm for Margrietje and the children you will have together." And so, reluctantly, Jacobus Demarest did as he was told.

Then the banns were published, and Margrietje Haring set a date to become the bride of Jacobus Demarest in the Tappan Reformed Church, when the *dominie* came on his next quarterly visit to do the baptizing and marrying, and the communion. And nine months and three weeks after the wedding, she bore Jacobus a son. To Cosyn and Marytie's chagrin, they did not name the child Cosyn, as was expected. Cosyn and Marytie couldn't have known it at the time, but ten children would be born to Jacobus and Margrietje between 1738 and 1760, and not one of them would be called after their grandparents. "He is an independent *bastaard*," Cosyn said of him curtly. Frenchman thumbing his nose at their cherished Dutch naming customs. "He didn't want to have to buy his uncle's farm. He wanted our pretty Margrietje Haring for nothing."

*   *   *   *

On her way home that day, Marytie caught up with her daughters and her niece, walking back from the river and its now-contested east bank. Their aprons were wet from the wet petticoats and shifts underneath, from floating in them in the river, *zwemmen* in the funny way they had developed of navigating their bodies underwater, like fish, then lying on their backs so still in the river's shallow waters, on its hard-packed clay bottom, that schools of curious minnows swam up to them to investigate, tickling them, making them shriek and splash the little creatures away.

At the house, they doffed the aprons and petticoats and laid them on a hedge in the sun to dry, and, shapely as they were, walked about in their thin summer shifts, which soon dried too.

That night, stifling in her airless bed, Marytie heard the wolf, howling for his mate, lying in her shallow grave.

Lying in her close bedbox, Marytie felt like howling for her mate, wanted him home. He has been gone for nearly a week. She wanted to lie with him and pledge their love again.

My dearest One, she whispered, as if she were praying to him, rather than to God. *I hope that God will give us what is blissful for us.*

For them, blissful meant each other forever and the family forever on the land.

*   *   *   *

After Marytie left, Grietje wandered into her garden, where her thoughts returned to Rachel Cresson, married first at nineteen, widowed not long after, when that tree fell in the wrong direction and crushed her lusty young husband to death.

Rachel's father, she remembered, a lively, friendly Frenchman, was always called *Pierre le gardinièr,* because over the sea he had been a gardener to the Princes of Orange. In fact, this employment by such eminent noblemen lent a certain air of distinction to him, so much so that his friends and acquaintances had taken to referring to him respectfully in this way: *Pierre le gardinièr.* He even took to referring to himself in a double first-person as *Moi Pierre,* I Pierre. Funny little man, she remembered.

When the Labadists, those two radical French-speaking Dutch pietists, came in the 1670s, they visited him on his plantation on Staten Island, and he jumped for joy, they reported, to be speaking French with them. But then he wasn't so happy when they converted his son Jacques to their curious sect. That Jacques, who five years later in 1684 was found hanging by the neck in a cockloft in his house, and no one was sure if it was an accident or not.

The thought of Rachel Cresson's lusty husband brought on a reverie of her own three husbands, lusty, too, though it must be said that the third one, lately always napping in the rocking chair, had sadly lost his vinegar. Daniel was seventy-one now, and they have all agreed that he had not aged well, though they imagine he will outlive her, he being seven years younger. By rights, he should have gone to New York with Cosyn and his son Jan this week to meet with Peter Haring about the Englishmen's threat to their land, plan their strategy, talk to a man of the law. But he has been content to sit in his rocking chair and let others do the work of defending the Patent. She is disappointed in him, she has confided to Marytie more than once.

The first husband she had married at thirteen, though her parents and all their friends and relations were shocked and appalled and tried to dissuade her, to no avail. At fifteen, she had a baby girl with that husband. It died. Then he died of a broken neck from galloping too fast down Broadway on a horse that suddenly decided to jump a fence. He was a reckless, dashing fellow, full of charm.

She pined for a while, more than a year. Then she married Jan Pietersen Haring. He had come fresh from Holland at age eleven, but when she married him he spoke English better than she did. She had with him four sons in seven years, and every one of them lived. Good blood, her people had said approvingly. Of her three husbands, he was the best. She remembers how proud she was to be marrying a man who had been chosen a magistrate in that brief period in '73 and '74 when the Dutch took New Netherland back from the despised English and then lost it again after fifteen heady months. That was when they had decided to thumb their noses at the English in New York and move to this place, where they could be themselves by themselves.

The sheepskin land grant from the English governor confirming the transaction hung on her whitewashed wall to this day. "It is the only English thing in my house," she often said. "Not counting our clothing." The colonies, to their discontent, were not allowed to manufacture textiles on a large enough scale to make them free of English manufactures.

And then, just before they were about to make the move, without warning, that second husband upped and drowned in the Hudson River, intestate to boot. A widow again. "And here we are, fifty years later, four generations on the land,

and still having to defend it. It is *schandelijk* shameful!" She spoke aloud, although she was alone.

The land was one thing. She could brood about it, and out loud, without apologizing. But those other things, all that was so long ago, Grietje thought, annoyed with herself for wasting her good time dwelling on the past, raking over all those old memories. But she had noticed that her mind was turning more and more these days to the past. Was she reviewing things for her Maker? she wondered. She touched her silver-bound Psalm book in the deep linen pocket tied around her waist, her favorite pocket of many and one she herself had embroidered with flowers and vines in silk thread.

She turned and looked back at her precious brick house with its high-pitched roof and its long eaves, so Dutch-like, the year it was built worked in bricks all across its front: 1 7 0 0. She recalled often, and always with a shudder, how they had nestled in that nasty pit house for two summers, back in the first days. Dark and dank, humid, soggy, the bark-roofed pit in the ground was essentially a cellar for the house-to-be, six to seven feet deep, and as long and as broad as they needed. They covered the floor and walls with timbers to keep the earth in place, put over it beams to form a ceiling and a roof of spruce branches on the beams, and covered the spruce with bark and sod, so that they could live dry and warm in it, until the sawmill was up and running. They partitioned it to make chambers, one for living and eating, others for sleeping. A small fireplace with a stick and mud chimney provided warmth on the cool nights. They cooked above ground, under the trees.

Then came a frame house of sawn timbers, a rough house. And then the brewery. And finally in 1700, with the profits from the brewery, they had the means to build this fine place. She would have been surprised to learn that the most famous man in the country would stay in it on four occasions, make it his headquarters, fifty years after she lay in her narrow place. But that is sixty years in the future, and the house will no longer be theirs then, but another family's.

At the edge of the pasture, she sat on a bench on the mossy bank of the spar *kill* in the shade of a great willow tree and opened her Psalm book with the silver binding and latches. She read only a few lines, though, before her eyelids began to droop.

He hath led me beside the still waters, she thought, not irreverently. *And now he maketh me to lie down in this green pasture.* With her Psalm book as her pillow, she lay herself down on the mossy bank and curled her long legs up under her shift. Before very long, lulled by the slapping of the creek against the bank, she slept.

CHAPTER 3

▼

WORK

Marytie's grandniece, Margaret Blauvelt, turned twelve in the year 1737. Two months later, the blood came.

She didn't notice it. Even though her mother had told her to be expecting it. The slave woman Suki noticed it, when she picked up the girl's shift for washing. Suki showed it to the girl's mother, the small brownish-red stain the size of an egg on the back of the shift, and her mother showed it to her, almost like an accusation. Margaret was taken aback that this had happened to her without her realizing it. In fact, she felt chagrined to think that her body had acted in such an important matter without her knowledge, or assent. Even at twelve, she liked to be in charge of things.

Her mother gave her the linen cloths she had prepared in advance and told her, overly severe in her tone, Margaret thought, to expect this to happen every month. She went on. "You are no longer a little girl. You have become a woman. You must protect your body now," she added sternly. "No more horseback riding. And wear your bonnet in the sun, and be modest. No swimming in the river in your small clothes unless we are with you. And keep yourself strong. In a few years, when you marry, your body will need to be strong to bear new bodies."

Of course, it was no surprise to hear *that*. All married women bore a baby every two years. But in "a few years?" Oh, no, Margaret thought. It was much too soon to think about marrying. And why could she no longer ride her horse? What was the connection? Something told her not to ask.

She washed herself, tied the linen cloths around her body, and took to her bed.

* * * *

When it was over and she had washed the cloths and dried them on the line and folded them away for the next time, she sought out her friend Eliza.

Eliza lived with her mother Hannah, an Englishwoman, and her dour and forbidding father, Gerhart Hafnagel, in a small house on the south bank of the Slote, the creek or *kill* that ran from the mountains through Tappantown to the Hudson. To distinguish it from the many other creeks and *kills* in the area, this creek was sometimes called the spar *kill* after the spars of sailboats tied up at the wharf.

Gerhart, a German, was a woodcutter and an ironworker in the mines in the mountains, where he had a cabin. He came and went, and the little household was happier when he went, but never truly happy, even when he was away. They were a family whose members seemed not to be meant for each other, was how Margaret put it to herself.

It was planting time. School had ended for a while. "School has ended for me for good," Eliza said sulkily "I am too old to continue. There is nothing more to learn from that dull schoolmaster." She was fifteen. She lolled in the shade of a fragrant locust tree, her heavy-lidded eyes half closed, fanning herself. Grasshoppers sprinted through the grass, bees sucked the clovers' liquid, orange butterflies flitted crazily as if drunk on nectar over the flowers her mother had planted in an effort to brighten up the place. Her bosom lavished itself upon her low bodice. She was a pretty girl, with a fair complexion and curly dark blond hair, brown eyes. Her lips were cherry red and full and pouty.

"I thought you liked Mr. van Blarcom," Margaret said, surprised.

Eliza laughed. "*He* likes me," she said. "And my mother likes *him*. She considers him a good catch for me. Even my father agrees, for once." She laughed again.

"Aren't you a bit young for that sort of thing?" Margaret asked.

"No, Little One. I am not a bit young for that sort of thing," Eliza mocked. "The fact of the matter is, I have my eye on someone else." She called Margaret Little One, even though Margaret was taller. A humming bird hovered over a choice marigold, sucking.

"Who?" Margaret was all agog.

"Maybe I'll tell you, and maybe I won't," Eliza teased. "*You* are a bit young for that sort of thing." And then suddenly her mood changed. "I hate my father," she said in a low, fierce voice. "I am going to run away from here."

Margaret was shocked. "You hate your father? You would run away from your home? What could be so bad?"

"He's a misogynist," Eliza said.

"A what?"

"A man who hates women."

Margaret was taken aback. All the men she knew seemed to like women.

"And I hate him for it," said Eliza in that low fierce voice. "He won't let me be free to do what I want to do."

"And what is that?"

"I want to walk in the woods with someone."

Margaret was shocked again. "Who?"

"Not Mr. Prissy van Blarcom, Little One!"

"I am not so little any more," Margaret said loftily.

"And what is that supposed to mean?" said Eliza, narrowing her eyes.

Margaret told Eliza her news and told her too that her mother had laid down some new rules for her new estate. No more horseback riding, for one.

"Hmmm," Eliza said.

"How do you decide who to marry?" Margaret blurted out. This question had been sorely bothering her ever since her mother's comment that she would marry "in a few years." She tucked it here into the conversation casually, where she thought it would fit, and not draw attention to herself, rather make it seem as if it were Eliza she was concerned with, not herself.

It worked. "Who said anything about marrying?" Eliza snapped, glaring at Margaret.

"I was just wondering," said Margaret meekly.

After a long pause, Eliza spoke, answering Margaret's first question. "I have my eye on … a handsome ferryman," she said dreamily. "I don't know his name yet, but I soon will. And maybe I will marry him. And maybe I won't."

Somehow, Margaret did not doubt that she would soon know his name, and more. Her friend was way beyond her in the growing-up things.

"Who do *you* like?" Eliza inquired.

Margaret blushed. "Do you know that Johannes Haring?"

"I think so," said Eliza. "Is he the one with the somewhat large head and the dark hair?"

"Yes." Margaret liked the shape of his head. It was like her own. "We are second cousins," she said. She liked his grave, green eyes. She liked his hands. They were square-shaped, like animal paws. She liked his dark coloring, so different from all the fair-haired fellows in the neighborhood. She liked the way his dark hair fell across his forehead and had a wave to it. "His grandmother, Marytie Blauvelt, is my great-aunt, because he and I share a great-grandfather in common. They called him the *blau boer,* the blue farmer," she added primly, although she suspected Eliza would not care about this detail.

"Who?"

"Our great-grandfather."

"Why blue?"

"No one remembers."

"Silly," said Eliza. "How can a farmer be blue? I don't care about family," she added carelessly. "I'll start my own family when it pleases me. Or maybe I won't. Maybe I will just live for myself. Anyway, isn't this Johannes a little old for you?"

"Yes," Margaret admitted. He was seventeen, much too old to notice her. For the last two years he had been studying surveying, or law, she wasn't sure which, maybe both, at a school in Hackensack. He boarded there. "I seldom catch a glimpse of him anymore," she said, "but when I do my heart beats like a trapped bird."

"What a confession," said Eliza dryly. "What an original *simile.*"

"And I have an urge to run up to him and sink my fingers into his mop!" she said.

"It sounds like the real thing," said Eliza in her lazy voice. "Running your hands through his mop. Ugh. But if that's what you want, Little One, set your cap for him."

Margaret loved to learn these English phrases from Eliza. *Set my cap for him!* she said to herself. *I will do just that.*

* * * *

Soon after this conversation, Margaret began having strange feelings, feelings of being overcome by smoke, or fumes, or water, a sensation of water rising over her head. Several times these sensations woke her in a panic in the middle of the night, and she screamed out for help. Her mother and father jumped from their *bedstede* and came running, and she rose from her own bed in a kind of stupor and fainted away in her mother's arms while her father ran off to get a cup of water to dash in her face and her groggy brother peered at her from around the bed curtain.

After this happened three times, her mother, looking as if she could smack her good and hard, told her never to do it again. As if she had been doing it on purpose.

"I have nothing to do with it! It just happens!"

"Don't let it happen again."

Of her mother's five children, only Margaret and her brother Teunis had survived. So perhaps she was riven with fear, Margaret decided. With fear that Margaret was announcing some peril of her own with her fainting fits that would take her away too.

Eliza's mother, Hannah, diagnosed the fits as the vapors, something natural to women, but Margaret's mother took no stock in such an English idea. "Get over it," she commanded.

And so she did. After her mother outlawed the fits, they did not come again. But she remembered them, and she wondered what had caused them. She decided they had to do with her not wanting to be a woman so soon. She wanted to keep on going to school and learning as much as she could from Mr. van Blarcom. She would even like to go to that school in Hackensack and study something useful, but that school was only for boys. Yet her brain needed food, just as theirs did, food for knowing what the world was all about! No, she did not want to be a woman yet, especially a married woman. She had things to do before she settled for marrying.

"I do not want to even think about marrying," she said to Eliza the next time she saw her. "Not at all. After marrying, life seems to be over for a woman. Nothing but babies after that."

"There is more to it than babies," said Eliza in a sing-song voice. "If you think how the babies are made."

"What do you mean?"

"Why aren't you allowed to ride horseback any more?"

"I don't know."

"There is much pleasure and delight in making babies," Eliza said knowingly.

"What do you mean?"

"You've heard your parents, no doubt," said Eliza. "Or haven't you?"

Margaret flushed, felt weak in the head. She couldn't help but be reminded of the not completely stifled cries and moans and deep breathing she heard emitting from her parents' curtained bedbox on occasion. "I know men and women couple to have children, just as animals do, of course," she stammered. But she hadn't connected the cries and moans with the idea that there was pleasure and delight in the process.

"Animals!" Eliza laughed and went on to tell her tales of the "bliss," as she put it, enjoyed by human animals.

What it had to do with horseback riding was beginning to be clear.

*   *   *   *

That summer, around the middle of June, Margaret's mother sent her to stay with her husband's aunt, Marytie Blauvelt, ostensibly with the idea that Marytie would teach her how to cook. But Margaret suspected that the real reason had to do with her mother's opinion that she was spending too much time with Eliza, who indeed did fill up her mind with many lurid facts. "That one is not a good influence," she had overheard her mother say to her father. "She is running her mother a merry chase this summer." And another time, one dark night just before she fell asleep she heard her murmur to her father that Eliza had too much an eye for the men. "Early ripe, early rot," he muttered. Until then, Margaret had thought that expression applied only to fruit.

If a ripe *girl* meant that her mouth was cherry red and as if containing ripe fruit her bodice burst with her breasts, Eliza was ripe. Margaret hoped she would not rot.

*   *   *   *

Her great-aunt, Marytie Blauvelt, was the sister of Margaret's grandfather Abraham Blauvelt and the wife of Cosyn Haring, one of the original settlers of Tappan. Many of the houses in the area were poor, homemade things, crooked and shabby. But not theirs. Marytie and Cosyn had a handsome, well-built stone house whose fields and woods ran to the Hackensack River. It was plainly furnished, though. Plainer than Margaret liked. When she had her own house some day, she had already planned how she would fill it with fashionable furniture and bright colors and pictures in frames and mirrors and all sorts of fine things found in the shops in New York City.

Marytie and Cosyn had a yawl, too, which they owned in common with Cosyn's three brothers. This they kept moored at the Tappan Slote, where the *kill* met the Hudson River, and where Margaret's other grandfather, Teunis van Houten, had started a store many years ago, the only store in the area. When he died, just this year, her mother, Elizabeth van Houten, inherited a share in this profitable enterprise. They had sold their own farm and moved to a house next door to the store in order to help with the management of it. Margaret was their only daughter, and she knew that, with her outset in mind, they were already setting aside choice linens and house furnishings from the store as they arrived on consignment from New York City. Margaret liked this alteration in their circumstances. She liked not having to live on the farm anymore. It was more interesting to live next to the store, and just down the embankment from Eliza. But it was interesting to be at Marytie's house, too, for Marytie was a great storyteller and knew all the family history.

At Marytie's house, Margaret was amazed at how much work there was. "There is never an end to the work," Marytie sighed. "There is never an end to it, and everyone works, on a big farm like this."

"At our house," Margaret said chummily, "the work is not so complicated any more because we have only a garden and a cow and some chickens now. One man and a woman can easily handle it all."

"Not here," Marytie said. "Definitely not here."

"Your slaves have a long day of it," Margaret observed. "Ours did, too, when we lived on the farm."

"Yes, they do have a hard day of it, and a hard night of it too, if you want to know," Marytie agreed. "It can be no fun sleeping on pallets out in the smokehouse."

It had not taken Marytie long to notice that her little niece had a sharp eye and a quick mind. She was a good companion for Maria, who was not as *matig* mature as she should be at fourteen. That was because Marytie had babied her. After all, she *was* her baby, born when she was forty-five, a surprise to all.

"Do they complain?" Margaret asked.

"Not in so many words," Marytie said.

"I used to notice that ours had their certain ways of complaining, but not in words so much as in actions," said Margaret.

"That's their way," said Marytie. "At least the younger ones."

*   *   *   *

The slaves did the worst of the work, of course. Cuff and his son Caesar toiled on the manure pile, moving the pungent dung from barn to pile and in dung carts from steaming pile to furrows in the fields. Cuff and Caesar moved the necessaries when their stinking contents rose too close to the seat for comfort, dug new pits, being careful to take into consideration the prevailing winds. Cuff and Caesar, along with slaves borrowed or rented from the surrounding farm and a few day laborers hired for the job, were already digging the cellar hole for the new house that Cosyn and a carpenter would start building in the fall.

Marytie knew the process by heart, for this would be the third house Cosyn had built, and he had helped with a dozen others: They would line the pit with rocks to ground level, without mortar, to prevent frost heave, raise the foundation, load into wagons the H-bents and anchor beams, posts, corner braces, and rafters, joists, and studs all sawed at the mill by the mill hands and drive them to the site of the house. They would put the pieces all together like a puzzle, starting by laying strong wooden sills above the damp line, strengthening with mortar of mud and hogs' hair the sandstone blocks of the walls, finally raising the roof. "Of work there is no end," she said again.

*   *   *   *

Margaret Blauvelt was interested in slaves; she asked Marytie endless questions about them. Marytie told her what she knew. "Cuff, now about thirty-eight, is the grandson of a slave named Nate that Cosyn's people bought in Manhattan, straight off a boat from Jamaica, in the 1670s," she said. Nate had spent a few years out of Africa getting seasoned under brutal conditions on an Englishman's sugar plantation there. "His spirit was broken, even before they bought him."

Marytie had never known Nate, but she had heard tales of him from her husband and from his mother, Grietje Cosyns. Heard that, haunted by his memories of Jamaica, and by the treachery of the trusted African chieftain who had sold him to the English, he had toiled in their fields in silence, mute for thirty years.

"He's dead now?"

"Oh, yes. Poor Nate is long dead and gone, laid to rest with the others behind the church," Marytie said, "on the edge of that little ravine, or down in it. Who knows?"

"Can we go there to see the graves?"

"There's nothing to see," said Marytie. "The shells and pottery they decorate the graves with have a way of disappearing."

"So none of the survivors can ever be sure who lay where?"

"Yes," said Marytie.

"Sad," said Margaret.

"Yes, it is."

"What about Cuff's father?"

"That was Ben," Marytie said. "He is long gone too."

"I guess slaves don't have the opportunity of growing old," Margaret Blauvelt said.

"You are right about that. Most of them don't," Marytie said. "Their lives are hard."

Cuff and Caesar did the dirty work out of doors. Dina did it indoors. The granddaughter of a slave, also long gone, bought off the same boat as Cuff's grandfather, Dina was not Cuff's wife. Cuff's wife, Caesar's mother Nell, lived and labored in a household in New York City. Tom, the father of Dina's children, was on the farm of Cosyn's brother Cornelius; their several children were scattered on other farms about the Patent.

"And so it goes," said Marytie.

"Where did Dina come from?" Margaret asked.

"Oh," said Marytie vaguely, "Dina's mother Nelltie was given to me when we were both three years old. We grew up together. When I married, Nelltie became part of my dowry. I could sell her if I wished, or I could keep her and bequeath her to my children. I kept her, because I was fond of her."

"And so Nelltie's children belonged to you, too."

"Yes," said Marytie. "Of them I kept Dina. She's now about thirty."

"And the others?"

"I sold them to my nieces and nephews," Marytie said. "I am ashamed to say so, but I did. I'm glad Nelltie never lived to know it. She and I were good friends."

"You were playmates," said Margaret.

"Yes," Marytie said. "And more. All those years, first playing together, then working side by side. We prepared food together, nursed each other when sickness struck, were there in childbirth for each other. We buried some of those same children we had delivered to each other."

"It was almost as if you were sisters," Margaret said.

"There was a bond such as that, yes. I taught Nelltie to read a little along the way, too, an effort not approved of by some, I might add."

"What about Dina?"

"I taught her to read, too," Marytie said.

"Does she have children?"

"Yes."

"Where are they?"

"I kept one," Marytie said. "The one we call Jemmy."

"You can't keep them all," Margaret said.

"No, you can't. They get under foot and require as much attention as white children, believe it or not. And they are an expense. We have to feed and clothe them. And then there are their injuries and sicknesses to tend to. And the expense of their funerals. They are more trouble than they're worth, to speak the truth."

"The children don't know they were born to slaves and bound to be slaves," said Margaret. "But they learn soon enough, don't they?"

"Yes," said Marytie. "Soon enough. Now there is work to be done, my dear," she said briskly, ending the discussion. It had gone on long enough.

*   *   *   *

Marytie had plenty of work to do, but Dina did the work Marytie did not have to do, as it was in every household with a slave woman or two. She scrubbed the floors on her hands and knees, and she scoured the kettles and crocks and pitchers and pans and jugs and jars with her bare hands and the lye soap it was her job to make twice a year out of meat grease and saved ashes from the fireplaces. She milked the cows morning and eve, hefted the milk to the house in buckets, made butter and cream and cheese of it. She carried the garbage out to the pigs and hogs running about in the yard and carried wood in from the woodpile, armload after armload. She kept the cooking fires lit all day long all year round for the three meals a day they made together. She kept water ever boiling in kettles hanging in the fireplace, carried it in steaming pails to the copper tub where she stirred the dirt out of the laundry with a big stick and a handful of that nasty lye and meat-grease soap. She carried water to another tub in a corner of the kitchen for the family's baths. She slept in a lean-to built off the smokehouse. Cuff and Caesar slept in the smokehouse itself on pallets on the brick floor underneath the hams and sides of beef hanging from the ceiling.

Dina's labors did not mean that Marytie and her three daughters spent their days idly. Hardly. The family's survival depended on their work as much as it did on their men's work, free and slave, in the fields and orchards. Their work, the never-ending labor of preparing the household's food, meant, first, preserving it: salting beef and pork and venison, and shad and mackerel from the Hudson, pickling, smoking, preserving everything they could for the winter months, parching corn, hanging the apples and herbs and peppers to dry in the garret, stocking the root cellar with potatoes and carrots and turnips and beets and pumpkins and apples. Everything that could be preserved was preserved.

Only when the food stores were arranged in sufficient quantity for their needs did they turn to their spinning wheels. In the winter months, from the flax of their fields, which Dina had helped Cosyn and Jan and the male slaves and the hired laborers pull in the month of July, they spun thread and made linen. From it they wove some cloth and sent some out to be woven. The fabric produced then went to the mill where the weave and texture were refined, and then it went elsewhere in the neighborhood to be dyed and made up into clothing by the tailor.

From the flat fabric they themselves fashioned the household towels, sheets, bed hangings, and curtains, and some of the ordinary clothes they wore on their backs, like women's shifts and work gowns and bed gowns and men's simple work shirts. They spun the short and broken fibers on a coarse wheel to make summer garments of tow for the slaves. For their best outfits, they bought imported cloth from England, wools and worsteds for men's coats and breeches, silk for their waistcoats, linens and fine brocaded silks and velvets for the ladies, and printed polished cotton from India, and soft, light silks from China, and had them made up in London's fashions. Garments too complicated to fashion themselves or beyond the capabilities of the local tailor they bought ready made in the city, as did the slaves, who found their natty jackets and waistcoats and hats in the second-hand shops in the city's narrow cobbled streets.

Whether homemade or city-bought, silk gowns went to the silk scourer to be dry cleaned with mysterious substances found in nature, and Dina washed the ordinary clothes and the household linens in her boiling cauldron. And then, when they were old and worn out, Marytie and her daughters tore all these garments and household linens into strips to make rag carpets and into squares to make colorful quilts, the flax of the fields fulfilling its final destiny.

That morning, before it got too hot and before the girls disappeared again to the river, Marytie required them to finish whitewashing the stone walls of the cellar with buttermilk paint, an annual chore, to keep it clean down there. They made short work of it and were off, twittering down the lane by noon, as carefree as birds. Margaret Blauvelt stayed behind. She had her blood again, now for the third time, and every time it came she took to her bed until it was over, as if it were a sickness, or as if she wanted to sleep it off, ignore it, resist the meaning of it.

*   *   *   *

Grietje Cosyns had mentioned that she wanted to get to meet this Margaret Blauvelt she had been hearing about. "She is said to have her eye on my best great-grandson," Grietje said to Daniel. "I want to look her over." He only grunted.

"I think today is a good day to pay a visit to my mother-in-law," Marytie announced, when the girls were gone. "She wants to meet you. There's no need for you to stay in bed. You are not sick."

Margaret rose. She was eager to get to know Grietje Cosyns, too, the great-grandmother of the one she had set her cap for. "I know her by sight from church," she said primly, "but we have never had a proper conversation together."

✱   ✱   ✱   ✱

Marytie was worried about Grietje. On leaving her the day before, she had got to the end of the path where it met the dirt lane to her own farm, when she remembered her bonnet. She could not walk home the two miles into the west sun without her bonnet, or she would have sunstroke. She retraced her steps, went back, to find Grietje gone, not in the house, and Daniel asleep again in his rocking chair. On some instinct, she looked toward the *kill*, and there on the ground under a huge willow tree lay a form, Grietje's form, alive or dead she could not tell.

She ran to her down the garden path and across the field where the cows pastured. She was alive, her chest rising and softly falling, but dead asleep on the cool mossy ground, her head on her little silver-bound Psalm book, her legs curled up under the skirt of her shift.

It was disturbing to say the least. What was she doing lying on the ground like that? Practicing for death? Bargaining with God for some future *welwillendheid*, some benevolence perhaps undeserved?

Now, the thought made her shiver. Then, she had stolen away, so as not to waken her and be caught a witness to some private drama between the woman and her Lord. But it troubled her. Life without Grietje? It was hard to imagine.

And then, just as she was deciding to hitch up the wagon and trot over to see her dear mother-in-law, down the lane came Grietje herself, in her riding chair pulled smartly along by a spirited mare. "I have come to meet your niece," she called out. "I have come to meet Margaret Blauvelt."

Marytie was rejoiced to see her! "You are well!" she cried.

"Of course I am," said Grietje. "When was I not well?"

✳   ✳   ✳   ✳

The three sat at the table in the *speelhuis*, and drank sweet tea and talked of the old days, before the English took over, when Dutch customs prevailed. "Were there slaves back then?" Margaret asked.

"Of course," said Grietje. "How could we get along without slaves? But back then, the slaves were treated almost like family. They even lived under the same roof with us, though in garrets and cellars and lean-to's attached to the kitchen end of the house. Not like today, quartered in the smokehouse with the hams and the beef."

"The Dutch dreamed up the idea of half freedom," Marytie said, stirring her tea. "They were pragmatic people. They reasoned, why shouldn't a slave be free to go about his own business, as long as he understood that he had to work for his master when required?"

"Hmmm," said Margaret. "It saved them his upkeep."

"It did that."

"Things are different, now," Grietje said. "Some used to consider it a sin to own another. But now many maintain there is no sin in it at all. They are not quite human, they say. So they don't mind it as we would. And the Bible condones it, they say, if you read it right."

"They quote II Corinthians 3:17," said Marytie: "Now the Lord is the Spirit; and where the spirit of the Lord is, there is liberty."

"You mean that what matters is spiritual freedom from sin, not physical freedom from slavery?" inquired Margaret Blauvelt.

"Yes," said Grietje. The girl had a quick mind for sure.

"But you notice they don't go on to quote verse 18," said Marytie: "'And we all, beholding the glory of the Lord, are being changed into his likeness from one degree of glory to another; for this comes from the Lord who is the Spirit.' The verse says 'we all,' not 'you whites.'"

"Nowadays, certain *dominies* refuse to baptize the negroes' children, even though it was the practice in the old days," said Grietje. "I am godmother to half a dozen of them and my mother before me." She still remembered the first one who had announced he was no longer going to baptize them, back in the Out Ward. What was his name? *Dominie* Selyns, she remembered. Nowadays it was quite the custom.

"Why do they refuse?"

"They say they seek nothing by it but the freeing of their children from slavery, without pursuing piety and Christian virtues."

"Why do they say that?" Margaret was mystified.

"Because it used to be believed that a baptized person could not be a slave," Marytie said. "Now, that is no longer believed, and law was written to make it so."

"And besides, the *dominies* today don't want to interfere with a man's property," said Grietje. "That could make a man stay home from church. Or not pay his tithe."

"Well," Margaret said, "you have to admit that slavery makes sense: owning someone who will do your work for you for nothing, or almost nothing."

"In theory it makes sense," said Marytie. "But it has a price."

"And not only in pounds and shillings," said Grietje. "The price is, they take exception to the institution."

"Yes, and they have risen up. And been put down. And they may again rise up. That's the price, the worry of it."

"It wasn't difficult to stamp out their insurrection that time, in 1712," said Grietje. "But we knew then and we still know now in our hearts that we can never rest easy as long as unfree people are in our midst. Yet we persist in it."

"How many slaves do you own?" asked Margaret.

"Eight," said Grietje.

"There's no alternative," said Marytie.

Eight, thought Margaret. She was silent for a moment.

And then Grietje said, "There is an alternative. It is to pay wages to free people."

"But we don't go there," said Marytie wearily.

"Because the profit columns in the owners' account books would suffer in that case?"

"You are the child of a long line of merchants," said Marytie dryly.

"The French say *cherchez la femme,*" said Grietje. "I say *cherchez* the pounds and the shillings."

✳   ✳   ✳   ✳

Their views on slavery were something Marytie and Grietje had long had in common. But since that slave uprising, even though it was twenty-five years ago now, they no longer spoke so openly of the injustice of the system as they used to. They still spoke of it, but quietly, between themselves, as they were doing now.

"To have no *vrijdom*, it is hard to imagine it," said Griejte. "Hard to imagine where the deprivation of it will lead someday."

"Yes," said Margaret. She shivered. "How does Aeltie feel about it? And my cousins?"

"My girls are not given to thinking much about it, unfortunately," Marytie said. It was a sorrow to her that her own children did not see the wrong in it. "But Aeltie has strong feelings against it," she added almost apologetically.

They had learned this when the story circulated of a certain slave woman, who, upbraided by her mistress for having another baby ("another mouth to feed! another interruption in the work pattern! more confusion in the house!"), went out of her mistress's house with her newborn babe in her arms that winter day and gently placed it face down in the snow to die.

"What?" Margaret cried. "She killed her own baby?"

"Calm yourself," said Grietje.

"But *did* she?"

"Yes," she said. "And Aeltie stood up in church that Sunday and announced that the Lord ought to come to wipe our evil from the face of the earth for driving one of his creatures to such wickedness."

"Aeltie is not the *voorleser's* daughter for nothing," said Marytie. "It caused quite a stir."

"It caused a stir, because the congregation knew she was right."

*   *   *   *

Marytie's views had been shaped by the Bible, too, and also by *Dominie* Bertholf, who came from Hackensack to preach and perform the sacraments four times a year, and whose preaching stirred her spirit so at age sixteen that she rose up in the congregation and praised the Lord for her salvation. When Aeltie stood up that day and invited the Lord to punish them for their sins, Marytie couldn't help but recall that moment in her life when she had publicly declared she was the Lord's and he was hers. "I am in God's heart, and he is in mine," was how she put it.

She had been struck by the *dominie's* conviction that God loved all his children and so too must they. Thus she was as kind to the slaves as local custom permitted, although of course they had to do their work and do it readily and do it right. Cuff and Dina did it readily and did it right. But Caesar, sixteen now, lately did not. Caesar was a different kind of slave from his father and the others of Cuff's generation. She had had to have a talk with Caesar on more than one occasion in the last year.

Grietje had come by her views in another way. She had spent her childhood on her father's eighty-acre *bouwerie* in the Out Ward, adjacent to the *bouwerie* of Petrus Stuyvesant. "That was the neighborhood beyond the wall built to keep the ever-bold English out," she said in a dreamy voice, remembering. "Our neighbors, on nine or ten small farms stretched out alongside my father's wagon way, were various negro families. They had once been slaves belonging to the Dutch West India Company. The Company freed them after they had finally accomplished what was considered to be enough hard labor for any lifetime, even for those not quite human. And the Director gave them land. Not the best kind of land, of course, but the swampy land or rocky land that no one else wanted. He granted those farms to some of them in the 1640s, before I was born," she went on, "and I grew up playing with the children of the former slaves. Bowling on the green, ice golf in the winter, spinning tops, one old cat, jack straws. It was the most natural thing."

Marytie noticed again how Grietje dwelt these days on that pleasant, innocent time, so long ago.

"My second husband," Grietje went on, "the father of my four sons, also came naturally of a liberal turn of mind. This was because he was born and raised in the most tolerant country in Europe."

Margaret Blauvelt knew about Holland, of course. She had learned at home that freedom of the conscience was permitted there, where they had come from, although not publicly in any but the Reformed Church. (Even so, the authorities winked at the Jews and Catholics who worshiped in their secret synagogues and house churches. The idea was, her father said, better to let them do it than to risk the disorder that might result from trying to stop them.)

"That's why no one was in the least surprised when he invited two of the free blacks from the Out Ward to unite with himself and his other friends in the Tappan venture," Marytie said.

"So, it was regarded as normal that blacks might be interested in the same advantages that the white families were anticipating getting out of the move?"

"Oh, yes, dear niece," said Marytie. "It was so."

"Years ago," Grietje recalled, "way back then, I used to agree with him, my husband, my best husband, that there is no difference between bond and free, as the Bible says, but that all are one in the Lord. But nowadays, it's clear there are differences between us." She sighed. It was as if their now four generations in bondage had caused alterations in their nature and character, as if the new laws in the new century had dashed any hope they could ever be free and made them sullen and lazy and angry beyond words.

"When did it change?" asked Margaret.

"It began to change long before you were born, with the uprising in 1712." Grietje warmed to her tale. It was flattering the way the girl hung on her every word. "It began when a group of slaves conspired to upend New York City and perhaps the system of slavery in the process. They hid their muskets in an orchard on the outskirts of town, and then set fire to a barn. When the whites came running to put the fire out, the slaves burst from their hiding places and killed five of them, wounded six."

"How did they happen to have muskets?"

"They were given them, of course, and taught to shoot them."

"Such dangerous men were given muskets and taught to shoot them?"

"The same is true today," Marytie said.

"Of course it is," said Grietje. "Because we have to trust them. We need them to know how everything on our farms works. They hunt for us. They protect us."

"Cuff has a musket," said Marytie. "He hunts for us and for himself too."

"Our slave has no musket," said Margaret.

"You live in town. Your slaves had muskets when you lived on the farm."

Some town, thought Margaret. *One store and a wharf.*

"Do you want to hear the rest of the story?" said Grietje.

"Yes!"

"Other whites came to the rescue," Marytie said. "All able-bodied men were armed to hunt them down, the militias were brought in from Long Island, Manhattan was cordoned off at its northern end, to prevent their escape. They drove the slaves into the woods. Hopeless and starving for food, the leaders committed suicide after a week of being hunted down. Seventy of their followers were arrested, twenty-seven brought to trial, twenty-one convicted and put to death by many imaginative means: they were burned alive, racked on the wheel, gibbeted on the gallows, left to hang alive in chains as a warning while the crows came and pecked at their eyes and their flesh."

"I feel like throwing up," said Margaret faintly.

"Well, don't," said Grietje. "It's just our history."

"And then, new laws were passed," she went on. "And freeing slaves began to be illegal. No more the easy half-freedom devised by the practical Dutch, either, when a slave could be at liberty to go about his private business, so long as he would work for his master when his master required it. No more the custom of their living together under the same roof. White people were afraid of them now, afraid of being murdered in their beds at night. Off to the smokehouse with them. No more the quaint notion that they were human beings with feelings and ambitions of their own. No more the days when a freed black could actually own an indentured white servant, even marry a white woman or a freed slave woman a white man. Now in this English world of ours, under this English law, things are very different. Trust is gone. Laws are posted for all to understand."

"But they still have muskets," Margaret said.

"Slavery is now recognized as legal," said Marytie, ignoring her. "There is no social stigma attached to the trade. All the best people buy and sell, and all the worst. Buccaneers, magistrates, freebooters, merchants, pirates, lawyers, Captain Kidd, clergymen of all persuasions."

Auctions were held weekly in New York City, sometimes daily. "It is a disgrace," said Grietje, "and in my opinion it will come to no good in the end. But there it is."

"And one does not have to go back twenty-five years either," Marytie reminded them. "Just a few months ago, in May, two slave women were punished for stealing a kettle worth tenpence. They were stripped to the waist, tied to a cart, and lashed forty times: five lashes at the City Hall, five lashes at the corner of Wall Street, five here, five there, five at the corner of Broadway, by the English Church, and five on their return to City Hall, forty lashes in all."

"It must make them all the more angry," said Margaret, wonderingly. "And it must make the whites all the more fearful."

"Oh, yes, everyone sees the trouble lurking in the system, but no one has the courage to do away with it."

Other changes had come about too. "Now those who can be made to work harder and longer are made to work harder and longer," said Grietje. "And they die sicker and sooner because of it."

"And what of those who can't be made to work harder and longer?"

"They are the younger ones," said Grietje. "They are impudent and careless, focused on how to escape their lot—but in most cases not daring to, though the papers are full enough of runaways."

"And these days," Marytie said, "few marry. And even fewer are interested in the church."

"And something else is different, too," said Grietje. "It's curious, but they used to have real names, like Andries d'Angola, Lucas Pietersen, Anthony Portuguese, Jan de Vries, Catharina Negrinne. Now we call them Cato and Caesar and Scipio, Pompey and Horatio and Cicero."

"A little touch of comedy to mock them with their distance from the ancients," said Margaret.

"Yes," said Grietje. "To diminish them by the absurd comparison." (This niece of Marytie's was a quick study.) "The women today are called Bessie, a cow's name, Dina, Nell, Cate, Suki. No surnames any more, no way to trace themselves in family lines." She had served as godmother to them in the old days, in the Dutch time, when it was common that they were allowed to have their offspring baptized. She was godmother to both daughters of Maria Anthony and Salomon Pieterszen, Mary and Jannetie; godmother to Lowys, son of Claes Manuel and Lucretia Lowys; godmother to Salomon, son of Willem Willemsz and Maria Solomon. Maybe others, too, that she had forgotten.

"Our Suki has a child named Bett who will be my slave when I get older, and one called Tom, who will be my brother's some day," Margaret said.

Grietje didn't seem to hear her. She had slipped back again into memories of her dark-skinned childhood companions and the games they had played. "We played hoops together," she murmured, "and marbles, mumblety-peg, hop scotch, tug of war, leapfrog, tag, blind man's bluff. I played dolls with the little girls, and my brothers and their brothers marched together, brown and white, in mock militia company parades, Dutch style, down *de heere straet*, Broadway."

As she thought about those days now, in her old age, the childish games, the play, seem to have been but emblems of the real life that was to unfold, if only one could have interpreted them correctly. "I've asked myself lately," she said musingly, "is hoop rolling a symbol of the futility of life? Or is it an emblem of continuity, of eternity? Or is it one thing for slaves: futility, and another for free: a reassuring continuity? Is flying a kite a worthy symbol of one's aspirations to heaven? Or is it, when the winds dash the thing to the ground, a reminder of life's uselessness, disaster? What do you think?"

"'The world and its whole constitution/Is but a children's game,'" Marytie said, quoting a famous Dutch poet.

"Metaphors," said Margaret. She had learned of metaphors and allegories, analogies and similes, from Mr. van Blarcum. "*Love language and make it do your bidding*," he would say.

They talked of these existential things that day, under the canopied *speelhuis*, Grietje and her daughter-in-law, and her daughter-in-law's grandniece. (One fine specimen of young womanhood, in Grietje's opinion.) And Margaret loved the talk. She couldn't get enough of it.

But at last it was over. Grietje stood. "I must be on my way," she said. "You may call on me at any time, Margaret Blauvelt. I am just down the lane and over the *kill*. A matter of a mile south and a mile east."

When she was gone, they talked between themselves of the slavery matter, Marytie and Margaret. "It is part and parcel of our lives' most curious dilemma," Marytie said.

*   *   *   *

Cuff came across the barnyard. "The tide is coming in," he said. "I'll go to meet the yawl."

"We'll go with you," Marytie said. "I can shop. And Margaret, you can visit with your family while they bring the boat in."

"I need shoes, Missus," Cuff said.

"So you do," she said. His toes stuck out of the ones he was wearing.

Cuff was parsimonious. He made no bones about the fact that he saved every penny he got his hands on to buy Caesar's freedom. And Caesar made no bones about the fact that he wanted his freedom bought. He did not like being a slave, and he had lately showed a disinclination to, well, to slave. By law, the slaves received their maintenance, their clothing, their medical care when needed, and the men twelve or fifteen pounds a year in wages, the women half that. As they all did, Cuff earned a little extra by selling the produce of his garden plot, his eggs, firewood gathered in the forest, the skins of animals he hunted. While they were at the river, shopping at the store, waiting for the yawl, he would busy himself collecting cattails. Slaves and other poor folk used the fluff from the plenteous cattails along the river's edge to fill their mattresses. The excess they sold in the city on their day off, Sunday. But when he needed new shoes, as he did now, she must give him money to buy them. It was the law. They always put off replacing their shoes for the longest while, though, because the kind of shoes made for slaves rubbed their skin raw and raised blisters the size of toads until they were broken in.

"Caesar needs shoes, too," he said, over his shoulder, as they rode down the lane toward the Hudson.

"Caesar will have to ask me about his shoes himself," she said sharply. "You know, Cuff," she added, "I have had to speak to him about his sulkiness again. He is getting quite out of hand."

"Yes, Missus," he said.

All the talk of slavery with Grietje in the *speelhuis* had made Marytie a little uneasy. On her bench in the wagon behind Cuff driving down the bumpy, dusty excuse for a road, she wondered at her wisdom in putting herself and the girl alone in this lonely spot in the company of a man from whom and from whose grandfather, father and mother, wife and son all liberty had been taken for going on a century. Why wouldn't they have risen up back in 1712? They had ample cause. Why wouldn't he now? Why wouldn't he stop the wagon in this lonely spot, strangle them, dump their bodies in the swamp, run away to freedom? He wouldn't, she knew, because he knew what would happen to all of them if he did. As a few years ago, when two slaves on Long Island decided to murder a white family. For their crime, they were hung alive in chains and impaled on rapiers, but only partially impaled, so that death was prolonged for hours. By such methods their masters hoped to make themselves safe.

He tethered the horse to the hitching post, and helped them down from the back of the wagon. The yawl was in sight out in the river. With no wind and the tide on the ebb, it would be an hour before it could get into the *kill*, six in the evening. She had been expecting him earlier in the day, on the morning tide. She supposed that they had left the city at three in the morning at high water, as planned, but that the wind had been against them, so that the tide spent itself and they had had to put ashore at Yonkers until it flowed again.

Cuff held the door open for her, and they went into the store together. Almost as if a parody of man and wife going about their household shopping, she thought uncomfortably.

Cuff bought his shoes and put them in the wagon, rolled up his trousers, and in his old shoes headed for the cattails. His legs would be covered in leeches when she saw him next. But he would have earned a few more pennies to put toward the 200 pounds necessary to buy Caesar's freedom.

She greeted her nephew and his wife. "And how is our daughter doing with you?" her nephew inquired, as if Margaret Blauvelt were not standing right in front of him.

"Margaret Blauvelt is a treasure," said Marytie. "We enjoy having her. She makes me think. We are becoming good chums."

"Is she learning to cook?"

Marytie laughed. "Oh, yes. The fun things. We'll get to the serious food later."

After a few polite words with her mother, Margaret skipped off to find Eliza, up the Slote.

"We will collect you on our way past the house," Marytie called after her.

Marytie moved among the wares: barrels of tobacco and lard, casks of rum and Madeira, barrels of sugar, sacks of flour, casks of gun powder, Bohea tea, pepper, ginger, molasses, rice, ladies' blue gloves, ladies' stockings, men's stockings, nightcaps, needles and pins, awls and flints, bright bolts of striped fabric, flowered petticoats and skirts and jackets, kerchiefs to cover one's bosom, thread, sand for scouring tin and pewter, sickles and scythes. She bought whitewash brushes, scrub brushes, black lead to clean the plate, linseed oil. They cannot clean the house without these things. And a small paper of mints, for Caesar, to get on his good side again after having taken him to task for his lazy ways.

She studied a pair of copper candelabra. She had had her eye on them for some time, wanted them for the new house they were planning to build after the wheat and rye fields were sowed and the meadows cut and cut again for winter fodder for the animals, after the slaughtering and butchering time, after the apples were picked and pressed for cider.

She resolved to put a deposit on them. Instead of keeping them for her new house, though, they would be for Margrietje, she decided, rather grimly, if she went through with her intention of marrying Jacobus Demarest. They would be for her new house only if that unwelcome prospect did not come to pass.

She put her purchases in the wagon and walked down the lane to the salt marsh where Cuff was cattailing, his grizzled head just visible above the waving fronds. The yawl was slowly moving up the *kill*. Her son Jan was poling it toward the dock. Cosyn was taking down the jib. Even from a distance, she saw something in their faces that made her shiver. Things had not gone well in the city then.

CHAPTER 4

▼

LAW

Grietje knew they had planned to sail on the morning's high tide. But evidently they had missed it. She had been listening for them all day, dashing to the door very time a horse and wagon clip-clopped down the plank road past the north end of her farm. Now it was almost evening. Where were they?

Then she heard another wagon coming on its way. She ran to the front *stoep* to make it out: the sorrel mare and the bay drawing the curvaceous wagon she had been looking for all day (one her father had made in his shop fifty years ago). They were back from the city! And there was enough daylight left to follow them.

She hitched her mare to her riding chair and hurried after them to hear the news. She had a feeling it would be good news. She flicked her whip on the mare's flank to speed her along.

She also wanted to take another gander at Margaret Blauvelt. She liked what she had seen so far. She was a pretty thing, and bright as a bee.

But, first, the news. "What did you learn?" she asked her son eagerly, when she caught up with him at the barn.

"We learned there is trouble," he said shortly. He unsaddled the horses, while Cuff and Jan started unloading the wagon. She looked around for Caesar. Where was he? she wondered.

"What trouble?"

He could tell she was raring for a fight. He shook his head, as if to shake the words loose, but they didn't come. "Later," he said.

"No. Now. Tell me now," she said. "I have been waiting for two years." She followed him into the barn where he hung up the saddles. "Please!"

"Soon," he said.

She followed him to the *speelhuis*.

"Now," she said.

"The trouble is …" he began. But he couldn't go on. He sat heavily at the table under the canopy of grape vines.

"Go on," she said. "It has been two years!"

He spit it out in a growling, stifled voice, the words sticking in his throat: "The trouble is, the crooked Englishmen who are trying to do us out of our land are succeeding."

It had all begun back in the 1680s, when the royal governor, Thomas Dongan, applied his signature to the Patent, for wittingly or unwittingly (this was unclear; he was a man well known for doing favors to those who did favors for him), he signed an inexact description of the land that now exposed it to attack.

"And what did our man of law that we pay so handsomely have to say about this?" Grietje demanded.

"Our man of law," Cosyn said slowly, trying to get it straight, "our man of law has told us that it was more likely not the governor who is to blame for the faulty description."

"Well, then, who was it?" asked Marytie.

"It was most likely the anonymous scribe who penned the document," he said.

"It does not matter one fig who is to blame," Grietje snapped.

"No, it does not matter," he said wearily. "What matters is, our deed from fifty years ago describes the western boundary line of the Patent as running south to north to a place called the Greenbush, but it leaves out what they say now is a crucial phrase: '*as the river runs.*'"

"What nonsense!" cried Marytie. "For fifty years we've owned that land. And just think of how we have improved it in those fifty years."

Margaret Blauvelt sat at the table with them. Grietje, even in her distress, noticed that the girl was sizing it all up, understanding. She listens well, she thought. And as well she might. It was her land, too, that was in trouble.

This fact was not at all lost on Margaret Blauvelt. She had heard of it from her father and mother. The trouble was, the Hackensack River made a wide bend to the west along the way from the two points on it that marked the south and north ends of the Patent, and if a straight line were drawn between those two points, a swath of land seven miles long and as straight as an Indian's arrow, and from a third of a mile to a mile wide, bulging westward like an Indian's bow, fell into that bend.

And two years ago, two cunning Englishmen had seized on the oversight of the hapless scribe, or whoever it was, who had left out that phrase "*as the river runs*" and laid claim to that fertile, flat, and lovely land, where her own grandfather and father, and Grietje's sons and their families and Marytie's family and their brothers and brothers-in-law and the other families, and the friends and their families had for these many years lived and made very great improvements. Every one of them had received land on the east bank of the Hackensack out of the original 16,000 acres, and there they had built their houses and barns and outbuildings and mills. And roads, too, such as they were, muddy, rutted things, but requiring much painstaking labor to carve out of the earth, even so.

"And we have our plans for even more improvements to come," Grietje Cosyns said sharply. "What does our fine lawyer have to say about that?" The five surviving patentees had agreed to meet in a year or two to divide up the balance of the land, held in common ever since 1704. It was time. Their grandchildren were coming of an age to marry and were needing land of their own.

But the facts of the matter were so bewildering, so difficult to take in that over and over again they had to repeat to themselves and each other what exactly the trouble was.

"As the river runs!" Marytie fumed. "It is ever the case that rivers and streams are natural boundaries in land transactions! It is never the case that they are not!"

"According to the man of law," Cosyn said wearily, for he was very tired of it, "it must be spelled out. It must say in so many words '*as the river runs.*' These days, it is not enough to assume it. English law is the law of the land, and English law demands it."

"My father says our people bought it during English times," said Margaret.

"But Dutch law was still in effect at the time they bought it," Cosyn said dully. "According to our man of law."

Bitter controversies, accusations, debates, and demands had occupied those two years. Cosyn and his elder brother Peter and their sons and Marytie's brothers and their sons had been to the city more than once to see this man of the law. He was an old family friend, the son of the translator who had gone in 1681 with their father and Margaret Blauvelt's great-grandfather, the blue farmer, to negotiate with the sachem, Memsche, and his lieutenants, Jan Klase, Micheramick, Anason, Aliaque, and Mendwose. "It does not look good for us," Cosyn said, shaking his head. "It does not look good."

Grietje steamed. She recited from memory exactly what they had paid the Indians for their beloved land of milk and honey, this Dutch Canaan in what had so inexplicably become English America: "The fathoms of white and black wampum we paid, the guns, pistols, blankets, kettles, bolts of fabric, coats, hoes, gun powder, tools, shirts and stockings, rum, beer, everything they demanded—a small fortune in goods! How can it be that the land we got in return is now being taken from us? What good is the law in that case?"

His voice was harsh and angry. "If we have to go to court to settle it, we will go to court. We have agreed on that."

They drank sweet tea in the waning light and pressed their spoons into a big bowl of *sappaan*, made puddles of milk in the warm mush, felt comforted by the familiar food and by the decision, finally, to go to court. "The court will take our side," Marytie said. "And that is that."

She walked Grietje back to her riding chair. "That niece of yours is a bright little thing," Grietje said as she climbed into the seat. "Though her head's on the big side, isn't it?"

"Yes," said Marytie. "And there's a lot in it, too."

"We are agreed on that," Grietje said.

✳   ✳   ✳   ✳

But the comfort was short lived. They lay, he naked, she in her shift, sweating in their airless *betse* that night. "I am weary of it," he said again. "And despite my brave talk, uncertain of the outcome, if you want to know the truth."

"Two years," she said. Beside him in the sweltering darkness, she turned on her side and reached out to lay her hand on his hard naked chest. It was not an invitation, as it would have been in the old days, when they were so ardent for each other. It was a gesture of condolence. He laid his hand over hers.

"I'm unmanned by it," he said. "I can't think of anything else."

They were too troubled to sleep. After a time he sat up in the bed with a groan, baffled. "Let's go out," he said, half desperate, pulling his shirt on.

They left the stifling bed and wandered outside onto the *stoep* and sat in the dark on the bench. Cicadas raged in the trees, a deafening roar of mate seeking mate. She thought of the wolf decaying in her grave. Her mate had found her at the end of the day that day, had pawed at the brush and clay covering her form, briefly. "I killed a wolf while you were away," she said. "A female. Her mate came. I saw him, once. I think he has left, place of death for him."

"Maybe for all of us," he said grimly.

"Don't say that," she said. "A contract is a contract. A deed is a deed."

"We'll see."

The sky was full of shooting stars, as it was every August. Although, thank God, never again with that dreadful comet star that had scared the wits out of everyone way back in 1680. Although she was only a tot at the time, she could still remember it, or at least remember how people had never stopped describing it for years afterward, so that perhaps it only seemed to her that she had seen it. It appeared the year the families had decided to buy the land from the Indians.

Thunder began to rumble in the distance as they sat together in the dark on the stoop, looking at the stars and she thinking of the ominous comet with the long tail that had terrorized them that time and that none of them had ever forgotten. "Do you remember the comet star?" she asked.

"Of course," he said. He was only three or four at the time, but they had pointed it out to him in the western sky night after night, and of course people talked of it for years afterward. "And I remember how everyone said it meant trouble," he said. "And they were right. We have had more than our share of trouble here, from the beginning."

"Land so fair, peace so rare," she said. It was what everyone always said about the Patent.

She remembered all too well the trouble. The thirteenth child of Gerrit Blauvelt, the blue farmer, and his wife Marretie Moll, she was born in New Amsterdam in 1678, when the Dutch still called it that. They refused to call it New York. As it was in Grietje's life, the number thirteen had been significant in her life, too. (Between themselves, they had often remarked at the coincidence.) She was the thirteenth child of her parents, and she was thirteen when she and her widowed mother and her sister left the city for Tappan in 1691. Thirteen families, two of them her brothers' families, had joined the venture to move here. And she was thirteen when her heart first leaped for Cosyn, her beloved.

Her family had intended to make the move much earlier, in 1683. But just then, at the very worst moment, her father died. He died the same month, December 1683, as Cosyn's father, drowned in a terrible boating accident. Pneumonia took her father, a third partner in the venture died of his injuries, and soon after a fourth, until the survivors were reeling with it, convinced all their leaders were singled out for extermination, one by one. And they all recalled the comet star that had hurtled through the night skies as the men negotiated with the Indians.

"It's been bad before this," she said. "And yet we have succeeded." Now fifty years later, their fields yielded their plenty, their cattle were fat and sleek, their woods and fields were full of blueberries and artichokes and grapes, strawberries, wild apples, nuts, God's free gifts to them. Their kitchen gardens flourished full of vegetables and healthful herbs, their orchards of fruits. These gifts they had planted and cared for, and they had thrived.

"Yes," he said, "but even so, at the back of our minds isn't there always the thought that the venture was cursed from the start?"

For yet another catastrophe had overtaken them at the beginning: The royal governor, the very same one who had signed the confirmation of the Patent in 1686 lacking that crucial phrase "as the river runs," announced, six months after signing it, that their land was in the Province of New York—not, as they had of course believed, in the Province of East Jersey.

What an unforeseen debacle. Its East Jersey location had been the whole object of buying it from the Indians in the first place! At the Patent's most southern point, the Hackensack River ran up against a low-lying swampy area where profit-seeking Dutchmen, used to managing water ways, naturally envisioned digging a canal to the head of navigation on the Hackensack. In this way, they could trade their surplus crops and their timber down that river, legally avoiding the Hudson River and New York's port duties for the tax-free havens of Perth Amboy and Burlington.

But the men on the Governor's council had other ideas. They coveted the trade of the farmers of Tappan for the imposts they could levy on it, and they moved to frustrate the patentees' ambitions by putting a bee in the Governor's bonnet that he snatch their lovely land into New York. And the Governor was only too willing to snatch. As he complained, those "Dutch farmers of Tappan have only a *pretended* right to the Hackensack River ... only a *pretended* right to pay no custom or excise inwards or outward. And besides," he added censoriously, "they also have the advantage of having very *fine* land."

"As if Dutch farmers do not merit land as fine as the mighty English deserve," the Tappan people said among themselves, in disgust, when they heard this.

So, with the Governor's fateful decision, their land was usurped into New York. Instead of pleasant dreams of tax-free commerce, if they dared to proceed with their canal building they would legally be smugglers. Trouble indeed.

"English law determined our future in that case," she said. "Is it to do so again?"

"No," he said. "We will not let strangers come and read the law their way and take away our land. We have a deed. It must be honored. We have to believe that."

She looked away into the night. Brave talk again, she thought. "I will believe it," she said. It was too disturbing not to.

Before long, the wind bent the branches of the locust trees to the ground and great wet drops of rain began to fall. Lightning now brightened the sky so lately full of shooting stars. The cicadas quieted down, as if in fear of what was to come hurtling at them through the branches where they had crawled to mate.

They went back into the house, freighted with sleeping humanity—daughters, grandniece.

But what if he was wrong? What *if* the English and English law were to determine their future? They crept into their *bedstede* and waited for the cool to come through the room's open windows, the question haunting his mind, so that, when he finally dropped off, he groaned in his sleep and flung himself from side to side. But she put it out of her mind and dreamed that night of the place he had prepared for them, when she was eighteen and he nineteen, the sweet bed of hay under the spreading beech tree, that private place, on the now-threatened land, where he had laid her down and made her his own.

✴   ✴   ✴   ✴

The next morning, after breakfast, they sat together in the shade of the *speelhuis* for an hour. He told her more of what he had learned in the city and of the expense and trouble they would have to go to, to clear the title to their land. She loved his handsome face, tinged with worry now, beloved face whose stress she longed with her kisses to smooth away, hold to her bosom, soothe with comforting words. But she felt helpless to relieve his cares. Unmanned, she thought. It is doing him in. There is no balm in Gilead.

And then he told her something else that bothered her, too. On Sunday week, he and Jan had spotted Caesar in the city skulking around a grog shop, off limits to slaves, with a bunch of his fellow slaves and some boisterous whites known to be careless of the laws and customs. "The sort of whites who sell the slaves liquor, and let them gamble and make merry, despite the law."

"Caesar is going to be a problem," she said. This summer, he had taken to vanishing as soon as darkness fell on Saturday nights, reappearing only on Monday mornings. They suspected he went to the city, of course, and with others from the farms around, and now they had proof. They all knew how to catch a ferry, maneuver the rafts they hid in the reeds, how to "borrow" a skiff or a rowboat at mooring in the *kill* and slip away with the tide. No matter how many laws the whites made, they could not seem to prevent them from traveling across land

and water to congregate with each other, frolic at the taverns in the Out Ward, drink liquor together, sing, dance, gamble, lie together.

And conspire, no doubt, to throw off their hated yokes, she thought. Sunday was their day off, by law, and on Sunday mornings in the city, while the whites were at church, the streets filled with rowdy, randy blacks of both sexes and all ages dancing and diverting themselves. And small wonder. As Grietje often pointed out, such randivouzing was life's only pleasure for those kept in the same manner as the beasts of the field.

They gathered on weeknights, too, in the good weather, right here in their own neighborhood. Marytie often heard them, randivouzing off in the woods, singing and chanting their songs of complaint, dancing in the moonlight, shaking their rattles, drumming, chanting their doleful African rhythms, chanting their anger at their lot, the chants binding them in a fellowship that whites well knew to fear.

They were said to have no souls. But what did that mean? That when they died, they perished like the beasts? Some said so. But when Marytie heard their plaintive wailings from the woods, their rattles and drums, their cries to gods she believed they knew (*Hi-a-bomba bomba bomba, Hi-a-bomba bomba bomba*), she was convinced they had souls—of their sort.

They had many ways of resisting their bondage, these younger slaves, like Caesar. They stole easily, they fenced their purloined treasures in the taverns of the city, they incited others to riot, they ran away, they even on occasion killed their masters. The less adventurous ones simply worked as slowly as they could get away with to show their disrespect for those who would own them.

The smartest, strongest ones saved their money and bought their freedom. But that was harder than ever these days, since the law was made that required the master to post a 200-pound bond and guarantee the freedman twenty pounds annually for his maintenance, measures to ensure he would not be a burden on the authorities. Cuff saved every penny he could to buy his boy's freedom, for of course he would have to compensate Cosyn, but the taller and sturdier Caesar became on the farm's wholesome produce, the more he was worth. A year ago, before he had begun to sprout up, he was worth forty-five pounds. This year sixty pounds. It would be a long time before Cuff had that total saved up. He had close to a hundred, he had told her, but there was a long way to go.

What kind of slave was Caesar turning out to be, she wondered that day, after Cosyn had left for the flax field. The saving-money kind? The lazy kind? The thieving kind? The running-away kind? The kind who murdered his master and wife and children and was burned at the stake for his crimes?

She shivered. She had known him since his birth, at which she had been present. Would she be present at his death? No, she said firmly to herself, thrusting the idea out of her head. He had been the playmate of her own children. He was not the murdering kind. He was the running-away kind, she decided. He was practicing for it by slipping away into town on Saturday night, and some Monday morning he would not be there when they wanted him.

CHAPTER 5

▼

RIVERS

That summer Cosyn took his women folk sailing out on the wide Tappan Zee, and even all the way down the river to New York a few times. It seemed odd to Margaret to be walking with her cousins down the wharf past her family's store and her own house, and boarding a sailboat moored right outside of it, odd not to be living with her family any more, just waving to them as she passed by, calling out a hello and goodbye. But it was an old custom among the Dutch to send their children at a certain age to another family for a time. They say this was because their parents loved them too much to discipline them, as they should be, when the time of rebelling at rules came upon them. There was another reason, too. It was considered a part of a child's education to live in another family for a time, see how others did things, and Marytie's household was ideal for Margaret in more ways than one, Marytie being full of stories about the old days and Margaret being hungry for history. In Margaret's case, there was a third reason, she knew: to separate her from seditious Eliza.

Margaret hardly missed her own family. She liked staying at Marytie's house. She liked everything about it, especially her second cousin Maria, fourteen. They quickly became best friends, and Margaret confided in her that she had set her cap for Johannes Haring, Marytie's grandson. "Tell my mother," said Maria. "She will make it happen."

"I will make it happen," Margaret said airily. "When I'm ready."

There were few rules in Marytie's house. The girls could do almost anything they liked, it seemed. But she did have that rule about horseback riding. None of her girls rode. "Why not?" Margaret asked her one day when they were alone. (She asked to test Eliza's stories.)

Marytie blushed. She gazed at Margaret for a long moment, and then cleared her throat and took the plunge. "It is to avoid calling a girl's attention to the area of her body meant only for her future husband to know," she said primly.

Now Margaret blushed. Yes, she recalled, yes, bouncing on a horse's back did draw her attention down there in a certain way, as Eliza had said.

*   *   *   *

Her mother had explained to her that she was going to Marytie's to learn to cook in the old Dutch way, for Marytie had a book of recipes and liked to make the fancier ones, the ones the slaves didn't have time to master.

Margaret had told Eliza this, when she went to say goodbye to her. Eliza merely sniffed. "It is how they are preparing you to marry," she said. "The way to a man's heart is through his stomach. Everyone knows that."

"Well, if I have to go through a man's stomach to get to his heart, he isn't worth the trouble," Margaret said, chagrined that she had been tricked into marriage preparation without knowing it.

"If you like to eat, you shouldn't mind learning to cook," Eliza said. "My mother does all the cooking in our house, but I'm going to have a slave to cook for me some day, so I'm not going to bother learning," she added,

In the summers, all the cooking was done out of doors in the summer kitchen, and the family took its meals out of doors, too, under an arbor, its canopy a grape vine heavy with fruit, in the shade of the big fragrant locust trees that Dutch people always planted around their houses.

The first dish Marytie taught Margaret and her cousin Maria to make was not such a very useful one, in Margaret's opinion, but Margaret supposed her aunt thought it would amuse them to make cold currant soup.

First they had to go out in the yard and strip the little red currants from their stems, enough for a great bowlful, for Marytie's sisters and brothers and their children were coming the next day to celebrate the feast of John the Baptist, and cold currant soup was a tradition in the families on that day. (Margaret Blauvelt's excitement grew as the red fruit deepened in the bowl, for she was expecting Johannes Haring, the son of Marytie's son Jan and his wife Aeltie, to be among these relatives on the feast day.)

Picking so many currants was the hard part; the sharp rough stems cut the girls' fingers. After they had filled the huge bowl with the berries, Marytie instructed them to pour rainwater from the barrel on the fruit, to clean it, and then pour over it some Rhenish wine and a little clean water, sweeten the brew with sugar to their taste, and then pour the brew over white bread in a dish for themselves, and let it set until the bread was soggy. They sprinkled it with more sugar and cinnamon. And good it was.

They set a vat of it, covered from the flies, in the *kas met plancken*, the closet with shelves, in the summer kitchen, to await the relatives.

The wagons full of family arrived the next day, but Johannes was not among them. Margaret was crushed. "He must have more important things to do," she said.

"What could be more important than a feast day with the family?" said Maria.

Marytie's nephew Gerrit was almost exactly Margaret's age, and Marytie put him and Maria and Margaret in charge of taking all the children ten and younger into the woods to gather green walnuts, the traditional day to do this being St. John's Day, before the shells of the walnuts got hard. The older ones stayed at the house to help with the food preparation. The little ones were Elisabeth, ten, Frederick, eight, and Sara, five. And another Gerrit, from one of Marytie's sisters, and Pieter, and Jacobus, and from another of her brothers a third Gerrit, and Samuel, and another Jacobus, seven, and the twins Maria and Lydia, four. And from yet another brother a fourth Gerrit, and Cornelis, and Willemptie, seven. They were seventeen in all, traipsing noisily off into the woods. The four Gerrits were named in memory of Marytie's father Gerrit, the *blau boer*. The hills to the east did appear blue in a certain light, so perhaps that is how he got his name, Margaret supposed.

The walnut-picking custom was not new to Margaret. She had done it many times before. The ground was littered with these nuts, and they gathered baskets of them. Then, back at the house, those who had patience for it sat at the table under the grape vine and with small pins pricked holes in the shells and set them to soak.

Later, in the afternoon, the three "chaperones" took their fourteen charges to the Hackensack River. They walked for a good half-hour into the bright summer afternoon, until at the end of a long sandy lane they found themselves at the white sand dunes that mysteriously cropped out of the red clay soil in the woods on the east bank of the river. Like the soft bright promise of a beach in paradise, the shining white sand dunes sloped down to the water and its firm-as-wood red-clay cedar-shaded bottom.

They took off their shoes and stockings and ran to it. Margaret and Maria lifted their skirts and waded in to cool their legs. Margaret felt almost delirious with freedom. She cupped the cool water with her hands onto her hot flushed face and throat. They drew straws to determine who would stay with the little ones, and who would go to the lovely deep water around the bend. Margaret drew the short straw, and Maria and Gerrit thrashed upstream with the older of the fourteen cousins, where they could swing out over the river on a rope tied to the branch of a big oak tree, while Margaret stayed behind with Sara, Jacobus, the twins, and Willemptie. "We will take turns!" Maria shouted over her shoulder.

When the older ones were around the bend in the river, and the little ones were splashing naked in the shallow water, she took off her apron and pinafore and pocket and waded into the river waist deep in her linen shift. She sat on the bottom and let the water cool her from the long walk in the hot sun. She looked down at herself and admired the way her budding breasts floated so nicely within her shift, and she stood and tightened the wet fabric to her body, to accentuate her bosom and her waist. *A young woman,* she thought, caressing her pretty figure. She was beginning to get used to the idea. She smoothed the wet cloth over her stomach.

Then, from the corner of her eye, she saw him. She had seen him before: a hired man on one of the farms about the area. He had a large ruddy face, and he was steadfastly watching her from under a willow tree up the embankment. It took her a moment or two to notice, to her astonishment, that he had let the fall flap of his breeches down and was methodically rubbing his exposed member, which even from the distance that she was from him had clearly taken on a size and shape she had never seen, although Eliza had described it, laughing.

He did not, and then somehow she knew he could not, take his eyes off her. She understood that she had something to do with what he was doing, and that he could not stop doing it. Suddenly, she remembered a dog that had latched onto her leg one day and taken some awful and intentional pleasure from her limb, excitedly thrusting itself upon it, and her throat contracted in a powerful spasm.

She heard herself utter a little scream, and then she sank to her knees in the water to cover herself and began to paddle frantically upriver to the others, keeping her body under the water, away from his leering eyes, abandoning her little charges without so much as a thought to their welfare. She was very sorry that she had disobeyed her mother and disrobed down to her small clothes. "Help!" she shouted to the cousins. "Maria! Come! Help!"

They came to her from every direction, running through the grasses, jumping out of trees, splashing wildly down the stream. "What's the matter? Where are the little ones? What have you done?"

"Back there!" she gasped.

When they got back to the place, he was gone, and the little ones were perfectly fine.

"Why did you make us come back?" they demanded. "What's wrong with you?"

She was out of breath and panting. She couldn't tell them the truth, of course. "I saw a huge snake," she said lamely. What she had seen was far more alarming than a snake; that soft little thing she had witnessed on her brother many times, what had made it so hard and big and stiff? It had to do with her, somehow, and from the look on his face it had to do with pleasure and delight. It made her feel quite sick, as when the dog had pleasured himself on her leg.

*   *   *   *

After that, she stayed close to her aunt's house—and to her aunt. She tried to put the memory of him out of her mind and fill it instead with Marytie's tales of their large family and how it had got to this place and intermarried with the other families, so that they were almost all related to one another in some way or other. But the image of the hired man strenuously abusing his awful thing was etched in her brain, and she lay awake at night seeing it. That is where the babies come from, she thought dully. That is what I must submit to when I marry, and I am very sure I will not get any pleasure or delight from it.

She did not tell Maria about it. First, it was too horrid, and then also too much her own fault for caressing her nearly naked body in public. She should have kept her clothes on, as her mother had told her to.

Attend to the walnuts, she told herself grimly. Forget about it.

Every day that week and more, Margaret and Maria were responsible for changing the walnut water and boiling the walnuts with sugar until their shells dissolved, and then they stuck cloves in some of the meat, and cinnamon in others, and then boiled them some more, adding sugar as they went, for ten days, until they were done. They left them in the syrup and ate them all summer.

Tasty, but again not real food, in Margaret's opinion. Not the kind that might be the way to a man's heart.

Still, Marytie seemed to want them to learn the arts of candying and pickling before they got on to the real food. As the orchard ripened, the girls learned to candy pears, and quinces, and apples. They learned to pickle small cucumbers. They learned to make quince marmalade, both the red kind and the white kind. They learned to preserve apricots and peaches and plums and cherries and currants. And finally when Marytie thought they had had enough of these dainties, she started to teach them how to cook what might appeal to a real man, a hungry man, one coming in, say, from surveying the metes and bounds of the Patent and those around it. *One like Johannes Haring, studying that very subject in Hackensack,* Margaret thought dreamily.

"We are going to make veal meatballs," Marytie announced. This was possible because the itinerant knife sharpener had finally come to the door and sharpened all the knives in the kitchen. Marytie had been expecting him for weeks.

It took the girls working together with very sharp knives more than an hour to chop, nay, to mince, all the veal and the veal fat as fine as Marytie said they had to be. To the minced meat, they added mace and grated nutmeg and salt and pepper, and kneaded it together with very finely minced orange peels. "Shall you make one big meatball, or many little ones?" Marytie asked.

"Many little ones," the girls said. And when they were formed, they stirred and rolled them around in frying pans, until they were cooked through and gave off a delicious smell.

Marytie taught them how to stew a hen with orange peels. First, they roasted the hen on the spit until almost done. Then they peeled oranges and cut the peels into quarters and boiled them and then put them and the hen into a clean pot, with Rhenish wine and sugar, and let it stew some more, and they dished it up sprinkled with cinnamon powder. And it was delicious.

"How about a lemon heart?" suggested Marytie. "It's very appealing to the menfolk," she added slyly, with Johannes Haring in mind. She had learned of Margaret's secret from Maria.

Margaret blushed.

Again, they minced veal and veal fat with sharp knives, and added to it the spices and the peels of a fresh lemon cut into little pieces, and egg yolks, one per pound of meat, and crushed rusk, and mixed it all together in the form of a heart. "This will make a man your sweetheart for sure," Marytie said. "He'll be eating out of your hand before you know it."

Margaret blushed again. They stewed the heart in water, and then added to it the juice of unripe grapes, and butter, and the peel of a salted, boiled lemon, and boiled it some more. They served it with a sauce of unripe grape juice beaten with egg yolks. It was perfect. *Johannes Haring is a lucky man, and he doesn't even know it yet,* Margaret gloated.

*   *   *   *

One morning, with the heat wave past, and the air cool and sprightly, and with the question (*are we not in charge of our own destiny?*) still in her mind, Marytie collected Grietje, and they went in the wagon, Grietje, Marytie, Aeltie, Aeltie's *kinder*, Maria, and Margaret Blauvelt, to ride the disputed land, the lovely Edenic, now disputed land, as if they were of a mind to encounter what remained of its virgin self, take stock of the improvements forced upon it by their aspirations, their brute power, and challenge it to be faithful to them.

Marytie drove, and Grietje bounced Aeltie's baby, little Maria, one year old, on her knee. Maria was Grietje's great-grandchild, and she doted on the little blond thing, as she did on all the babies and infants, and on all the children and adults, too, who shared her blood. She sang the familiar old nursery song to her as they jogged down the bumpy lane:

> *Trip a trop a troontjes,*
> *De varkens in de boontjes.*
> *De koetjes in de klavaer,*
> *De paarden in de haver.*
> *De eenjes in de water-plas,*
> *De kalf in de lange grass.*
> *So grott mijn kleine Maria was!*

They drove west down the lane toward the Hackensack River, then south through forest not yet cleared, under towering oaks and maples and pines, sandy soil now, not clay, and then clay again, past long flat green fields newly planted with wheat and rye, past sandstone farmhouses like the ones they live in, past farmers plowing, farmhands sowing, slaves toiling on the manure heaps, children playing, carefree blond *kinder*, ignorant of the threat to their future. "What if we have to give it up?" Marytie asked. "We and ours have built these houses, raised these barns, erected these mills for sawing wood, grinding corn, milling wheat, fulling cloth, cut these very wagon lanes out of the very forest!"

Before coming, they had been promised this: that the land they were buying from the Indians was plentifully supplied with lovely springs, inland rivers, and rivulets, wherein were very good fish and waterfowl. And they had found it so. The forests were thick, and insufferably hard to clear, but there was also natural open ground, as promised, meadows fit for plowing, previously cleared by the Indians, and pasturage for their animals. Deer and turkeys were free for the taking, pigeons so abundant they darkened the sky in flight, salmon, shad, sturgeon, lobster, oysters, crabs thick in the Hudson, trout and perch in the Hackensack and pike and eel. Strawberries grew so plentifully in June on the meadows that the ground appeared to be laid with a red cloth. The rivers were their natural roads for transporting the wheat and flour they would sell, the pelts, tobacco, iron if the rumors turned out to be true, fish, pork, beef, salt, corn, timber for ship masts.

"It is like paradise," Aeltie said, wonderingly, as they rolled down a sandy shady lane to their favorite place. (Margaret Blauvelt realized that it was *that* place they were heading for, that place of the hired man who had violated her privacy and her innocence, too, she suspected.) "How did the serpent enter it?"

Aeltie was the daughter of the schoolmaster and *voorleser*, their reader of prayers and Psalms and a printed sermon not of his own making on all those Sundays but four when the beloved *dominie* came from Hackensack to marry them and baptize them and offer them communion. She was given to Biblical language and theological thoughts, but Marytie knew her Bible, too. "The serpent was here first," she reminded Aeltie. "It was Eve's disobedience that ruined Eden."

"So, we are to blame for the *onrust*, the kettle of fish we are in? What exactly did we do to deserve this *verdreit*, this trouble? What rule did we disobey?" She had been born in the Old World, spoke English well, but remembered her Dutch too. And it was good Dutch, not the dialect they had begun to slip into, they born on this side of the water.

"It's a good question," Margaret Blauvelt piped up. "What *have* we done to deserve this trouble? How is it that suddenly we are not in control of our own futures and fortunes? What have we done to deserve such a problem?"

(*We*, Grietje noticed. She was right into it, one of them, as she should be.)

"We have done nothing at all to deserve it!" Grietje said. "The land is ours. It is no one else's. We will fight for it, and we will win the fight."

And then Margaret Blauvelt surprised them all by jumping to her feet in the back of the wagon and shouting to the heavens, "This Land Is Our Land! Do You Hear Us Up There?"

Her girlish silliness restored their humor, and Marytie remembered the crabs in the Hudson River when they had first come to this place, when she was a girl of thirteen. "Their claws were the color of the flag of the Prince of Orange, orange, white, and blue," she said, "and we took that as a sign that the Dutch were to people the country, and the country it was to belong to them."

"And we were right," said Grietje.

Suddenly, the sandy lane gave way to the shining white dunes rolling down to the river. Margaret Blauvelt shuddered, remembering the hired man leering at her.

"What's wrong?" Grietje said.

"Nothing."

"A goose walked over your grave," Grietje said.

It was a well-known saying, but it didn't make her feel any easier.

It was a mystery to everyone how this abundance of soft white sand had come to be on the river bank at the end of the clayey red fields, billowing there like a divine apparition. "God threw it down here for our pleasure," Grietje said firmly, and they believed it was the only explanation.

The Hackensack was as always: clear and clean and red bottomed from where the clay started again. White cedar trees grew along its east bank, and around the bend, out of sight, was the ancient oak tree with a rope for swinging out over the oxbow and dropping into the cool stream. The west bank was reeds and cattails as far as the eye could see. They laid the baby down to sleep in the wagon in the shade of the pungent cedar trees, and Aeltie's little ones stripped off their clothes and jumped into the water, while Margaret Blauvelt and Maria took off their shoes and stockings and launched the canoe hidden in the reeds and paddled away up the creek, where it curved to the north. The canoe was a white cedar tree trunk, hollowed out with fire by Cuff years ago. White cedar was the best, the girls knew. It floated so lightly on the water. Such a canoe would last for twenty years. Theirs was large enough to hold six persons.

As the girls disappeared around the bend, Marytie remembered the days when *they* would take a canoe to their secret spot, undress in a private place in a bend on the shore and float together in the cool waters, kiss in the dappled sunlight, stand naked on the hard clay bottom in water chest high, pressed together like two spoons, make their love on a linen sheet spread on the mossy bank under the shade of a pin-oak tree. She smiled to herself at the memories. Aeltie would probably not believe it. It would probably never cross her pure mind that such things had gone on between her husband's seemingly so-proper parents.

When they were out of earshot of the older women, Margaret, in the stern of the canoe said softly, "Maria, do you remember that day when we were all here, and I screamed and made you all come back? I said I had seen a snake?"

Maria stopped paddling and turned around to Margaret. "Yes?"

Margaret rested her paddle, too, and told her what she had really seen.

"What!" said Maria.

"It was disgusting," said Margaret, shuddering. "Never come here alone."

"You can be sure of that," said Maria. "Repulsive Englishman."

"How do you know he was English?"

"Dutchmen don't hire themselves out," said Maria. "Besides, only an Englishman would do such a thing."

*   *   *   *

After she told Maria about it, the memory of the hired man subsided and finally she put the scene out of her mind and thought no more of him.

And then, she saw him again. Maria and her sisters had gone to visit one of their aunts for a week, and Margaret was alone, leaving a meadow, where she had gone to pick blueberries.

This time, he was with another man. The second one, Billy, was English, she knew, so they probably both were. Billy came on and off through the growing season to work on the farm of one of her mother's sisters. The two stepped out of a thicket into the lane she was walking along on her way back to Marytie's house with a bucket of blueberries. "So, little Dutchie," the first one called out to her, in an insinuating voice, the one she had seen at the river. "Eliza's friend, ain't you?"

She flushed and her heart began to pound. She tried to get past them, but they barred her way.

"Not riding horses anymore, are you?" Billy said. "Why not, girl?" He leered.

"Let me pass," she said tersely. They laughed and took a step toward her. The first one reached out as if to take her physically. "I saw you looking at me that day by the river," he said. "Did you like what you saw, Dutchie? You stared good and hard."

She threw down the bucket of blueberries and ran as if for her life away from them down the dusty lane, slipping to safety under the bottom rails of the fence enclosing Marytie's buckwheat field. Behind her, she heard them laughing. She landed in a patch of nettles. Her heart was fluttering madly, like the wings of a bird trapped in a net.

But they wouldn't dare come on her uncle's property, she knew, so she picked herself up out of the nettle patch and walked with as much dignity as she could muster across the field, not looking back.

"We have a right to be here, too, you know," Billy shouted, heaving the bucket over the fence after her. Margaret thought he meant by this that they, the Dutch, acted as if the whole place was theirs. She had been taught that it was. She hurried toward the house shimmering ahead in the late morning sun, "*We have a right to be here, too, you know,*" echoing in her head.

Marytie appeared at one of the twin front doors.

"Who were those men?" she asked.

"I don't know," she said half-truthfully. She knew who Billy was.

"You mustn't talk to strange men," Marytie said.

"I didn't. Honestly, Auntie. They spoke to me. They frightened me. I dropped my blueberry bucket and ran. I'm covered in nettles."

She stayed close by her aunt all that day, picking the tiny nettles out of her arms.

It was a day so hot that her whole body dripped with sweat in the sweltering house. She longed to go to the river to cool off, but it was out of the question to go alone. She was safe only in the house, with Marytie. She tried to put the two unsavory men out of her mind, but then she began to wonder how Billy, the one who worked for her aunt and uncle in the planting and harvest times, knew Eliza. And how did they know she didn't ride horseback any longer? Had they been watching her from the woods? Something made her blurt out to her aunt that one of the men she had heard shouting in the lane knew her friend Eliza.

"Ah?" said Marytie, as if she were waiting for Margaret to expand on this confession. Margaret did not. She had said too much already. Marytie was no doubt well aware of her parents' opinion of Eliza.

"How do you know he knew Eliza?" Marytie asked after a while.

"He asked me if I was her friend," Margaret said, reluctantly.

"I heard of a woman who took up with a hired man, and it ended in tragedy," Marytie said in a thoughtful voice. She shook her head, as if it was something she still couldn't believe. "She was a married woman, but this hired man took a fancy to her and she to him. And then her husband caught on to it. He took her into the woods to a cabin he had and strangled her and hanged himself," she said. "They didn't find the bodies for weeks, until someone stumbled upon the cabin in the mountains. They had two little children, too, poor things. At least he had seen to it that they were in his mother's care before he did it."

Margaret was horrified. "What could cause a man to do such a terrible thing?"

"A man can be possessed by the demons of jealousy," Marytie said. "She was his lawful wedded wife, and he couldn't trust her."

Margaret was shaken by the story, not only by the unsettling idea that not every wife was to be trusted, but that not every husband could forgive. She thought of Eliza's father and his cabin in the mountains, and his bad temper and possessive nature. Eliza had better be careful, she thought.

"It has to do with property," Marytie explained. "Suppose she conceived a child with her lover. How would the husband know that it wasn't his? In such a case, his property could be diverted from what he thought was his true child and heir to a false one. They say it's a wise man who knows his own father."

For Margaret, it was too much adult knowledge all at once. She shook her head as if to shake the words away.

"One day," Marytie said, changing the subject (or maybe not changing it but going from one violent memory to another one, somehow for her benefit? Margaret wondered later). "One day, not too long ago, I killed a she-wolf."

Margaret felt as if a fainting fit was just around the corner.

CHAPTER 6

▼

CHURCH

On the second day of August in the year 1737, they rose at the first crowing of the roosters chorusing each other from the treetops where they slept. It was four in the morning. In the dark, they sleepily dressed in their Sunday best, stowed baskets of food under the wagons' benches, fragrant *taerts* and smoked meats, a bucket of *kool slaw, olykoeken*, cider to wash it all down, and the peach brandy, of course. By the time they were ready to leave, the roosters had gone back to sleep and would not crow again until the day dawned in another half-hour.

They piled into the wagons for the bumpy trip to Hackensack, where the newest little Margrietje, two weeks old, was to be baptized. There were Jan and Aeltie and their eight in one wagon, and Grietje and Marytie and Cosyn and their three daughters, and Margaret Blauvelt in the other. Margaret loved living with them and had developed a close bond with Marytie, even confiding to her that she had "set her cap" for Marytie's grandson, Johannes Haring, unaware that Maria had already told her mother this secret. "Aren't you rather young to be thinking of that?" Marytie had said. "Oh, no," said Margaret. "I am older than my years."

And so she was.

"Maybe *he'll* be there today," Marytie whispered, as they jogged along the rutted road.

"Maybe," said Margaret in a dreamy voice. After all, he was still in Hackensack, boarding now with his law tutor, having decided that the law was more interesting to him than surveying, she had heard. She liked to imagine getting him alone in a quiet place where she could *learn him*, learn what he thought about things, learn what future he saw for himself, learn whether she was the one for him and he for her.

They rattled southward into the dawning sky, snacking on cherries and peaches and cold bread, quaffing cider. The air smelled of wet grass and turned soil, of humus and the ammonia of the fresh manure dropping on the road in front of them, a pungent and familiar mixture that pleased all of them.

After they were out of sight, Cuff hitched up an old wagon. Rather than stay on the farm and fret and mope all the day long about Caesar frolicking in the city with his unruly friends, it was better that he drive Dina to the Tappan church, where they could climb up the steep ladder into the gallery and join Tom and the other slaves to listen to the prayers and Psalms and sermon of the *dominie*. As always, they would listen as carefully as possible to his every word, hoping to catch a clue to the mysterious relationship that white people talked of between the rite of baptism and freedom. They had been baptized long before this *dominie* came to town. But they were not free.

✳   ✳   ✳   ✳

The infant Margrietje to be baptized was the daughter of Brechtie Haring and the granddaughter of Cosyn's brother Peter, now home from the Assembly for the harvest. The godmother was yet another Margrietje, another of Peter's daughters (though he calls her Margaret) and the sister of the mother. The families were so close and shared so many names in common that it was a mighty puzzle to the English how they ever kept each other straight.

The baptism was taking place at Hackensack instead of at Tappan not because the *dominie* had already made his summer visit to Tappan in June, before the birth of this infant, and will not be back again until October. No, that *dominie*, Guiliam Bertholf, had become too old and fragile for the rigors of the circuit and confined himself these days to his Hackensack flock. Tappan now had its own fulltime *dominie*, Frederick Muzelius, a most unpopular man among the families. This family was going to Hackensack, to Bertholf, because, lately, there was talk in the air, a great awakening of religious talk, some of which had to do with the idea that infants dying unbaptized were consigned directly to hell. For, though they might be sinless, the awakening preachers told them, the original sin of their first parents had to be washed away by the living water of baptism, or their eternal welfare was imperiled.

But *Dominie* Muzelius did not take stock in religious "awakenings" or "living water" any more than he considered slaves qualified for baptism, and so there was a general dismay with him among some of the congregation, him and his set ideas, his refusal to consider new things. Some of the families wanted a preacher like Bertholf who would talk to them of the new birth and the warming of their hearts for Christ—not at all Muzelius's cup of tea. So, only an awakening preacher would do to consecrate their tiny one. Some of them remembered all too well another Brechtie Haring, their sister and aunt, who had given birth to triplets one bitter cold December's night and died two weeks later, the same day as her three infants were baptized. One of them died, too, soon after, a female. But at least she had been baptized—and by a man of their own convictions.

Baptism was a fraught matter in more ways than one. Way back when, before the matter was clarified in the law, which it finally had been in 1704, Grietjc and Marytie often worried between themselves that children of slaves did not have the same advantage as the children of free: the gift of Christianity, which, of course, entailed baptism. It was clear to them from their ardent Bible-reading that a Christian should never prevent the uninitiated from access to Christianity, with its incomparable offers of grace and redemption. But, over the years, the persistent and troubling notion kept cropping up that a baptized person could not be kept in slavery. Thus, fewer and fewer had the courage to baptize their black possessions as they had in the old days when it was quite common, for fear that the slaves would then demand their freedom. And nowadays even more perplexing questions seemed to come up: Are they really quite human? If not, do they really require baptism?

The baptizing of slaves, which before the English took over some of the Dutch *dominies* had practiced as a matter of course, fell into disfavor after the English came, because of this argument it gave rise to concerning their status. But in 1704, when Cuff was four years old, the Assembly had settled the question by proclaiming that the baptizing of slaves in no way could be taken as a reason for having to give them their liberty.

Slave owners drew a deep breath. It was a great relief. They could have it both ways. When the *dominie* next came to Tappan, Marytie and Cosyn took Cuff to the church, where—along with a flock of wailing black babies brought thither by their owners, and a swarm of black toddlers his age—they presented him to the *dominie* for the sacrament. A pack of raggedy black youth of the neighborhood, of an age when, if they were white, would long ago have been baptized, were also brought to the pulpit that day. Of course, their owners watched them carefully to determine if the sacrament would suddenly invest them with some intrinsic potency, as their Catholic forebears long ago in the old country had believed: Baptism's power set one free, no matter what the law said.

The *dominie* did not record these baptisms in the same *kerk-boek* where he recorded the baptisms of white infants, but rather in the scanty pages of his *swart-boek,* "black book," for such was the custom of the society. But at least he recorded them as having received the sacrament commanded by the Lord; at least he made a human record of their having been ingrafted into the body of Christ where they would be maintained unto the resurrection of their bodies to eternal life. But what happened to that *swart-boek*? After he no longer came to them, did his successor, that disruptive, argumentative, often drunken and profane man Muzelius throw it away? No one would ever know for sure. All they knew was that it had disappeared, never to be seen again.

"Down the well, probably," Grietje guessed. "Or into the necessary."

And at least that good and faithful one who had baptized them had attempted to catechize the poor things on his quarterly visits to the community. This was a nearly hopeless endeavor, though, for few of them had enough learning to construe even the simplified catechism he had compiled for them, and they had little time or opportunity or encouragement to review their lessons in the three months before his next appearance. They had to work. They were expected to work as soon as they were capable of moving wood into the house, milking cows, throwing garbage to the pigs.

Marytie thought about all this, their practice of slavery, their treatment of the slaves, as the wagon bumped along the rutted road to Hackensack. Although the morning was turning out to be a warm one, she shivered a little. She never stopped disquieting herself with the idea that they or theirs would have to pay for it some day. And now Margaret Blauvelt, too, was gripped with the notion that slavery would be their undoing in the end. Marytie had never been able to spread the idea to her own daughters, so she felt somewhat uneasy at having passed it on to her brother's granddaughter. "But there we are," she had said helplessly to Grietje and Aeltie. "One either sees it, or one doesn't."

As they arrived at their destination, wagons from all directions were converging on the Green in front of the church. Children threw their hoops on the ground and jumped out of carts and wagons, spilled off to run about with their siblings and friends and cousins until the service started. The men gravitated to men under the sycamore trees, to mull over the land problem. Of course, somebody had to say it: "land so fair, peace so rare." The women drew together, eager for news and gossip. Courting couples or those with a thought to courting removed themselves from their elders and flirted together in the graveyard, out of sight and earshot. Slaves led the horses to the trough to drink. And when they had all had a good little visit, the *voorleser*, preceding the *dominie*, both on foot in their formal black suits, approached along the lane and all went into the sanctuary to hear the Word of God. Margaret looked everywhere, on the Green, in the graveyard, in the church, but the elusive Johannes Haring was nowhere to be seen. She was crushed again.

✴   ✴   ✴   ✴

"Of course, the Word of God is important, and we must hear it," Grietje always said. "But Sunday is also fun day, family. The *world* of God is important, too." The intensity of her feeling for their world, for the physical beauties of the round blue hills they farmed at the feet of, the long green fields, the sparkling rivers and *kills*, the ever-changing sky, the seasons bringing each its delectable sights and sounds and smells, equaled her devotion to her family, and almost equaled her love for Him, or even surpassed it, if she were honest. Although, if she were honest, and she was, she knew that was a sin. Still, they had been taught he would forgive.

Dominie Bertholf sighed as he gazed down upon them from his high pulpit. They were a restless lot, his flock. Indeed, the fidgeting, the foot tapping and adjusting of hats and collars and skirts, the undercurrent of whispers and clearings of throats, the occasional loud sigh, the rustling of Sunday silk, the shuffling of feet, the coughing, the passing in and out to the necessary in a corner of the churchyard, formed a kind of unmusical but inevitable antiphone to the sung Psalms, the prayers, the baptism, the sermon. He knew they were impatient to be out in that beauteous natural world with their families and the friends. He knew it was hard for them to sit still for two hours for thinking of what lay just beyond, after this first necessary part of the day was over. But finally, finally, he got through all the liturgical bits and came to his sermon, and on one of his favorite texts: "Come unto me, all ye who labor and are heavy laden, and I will give you rest." And then they could go!

Once his long closing prayer was over, that is.

He understood his flock. He understood they were heavy laden, with work, with cares, with debt, with their knotty land problem, with the daily concern for survival. He understood that many among them were feeble in spiritual knowledge and that one must be gentle with them, not frighten them away with tales of hell and damnation, as some overly zealous men of God were apt to do, not arouse their anxiety over the state of their salvation. No, rather nurture them with the story of God's love for them and teach them to trust in a merciful deity's promise that he will not snuff out a smoking wick or break a bruised reed.

Someone had called him an "itinerating apostle," for in his prime his flocks had been scattered from the Raritan to the Passaic to the Hackensack and over the river to Tarrytown on the east shore of the Hudson, and wherever he went to serve them he had never forgotten what the authorities back in the Old World had told him at his ordination: "We encourage you to harmony and mutual peace, which is the great lesson, warning and commandment of Our Lord Jesus: to love each other, avoid all the opportunities of displeasure, yield in pursuing the peace, show always the gentle spirit of Jesus Christ." Because he remembered these things and loved the people, and did not overly agitate them with prospects of reprobation and damnation, he in turn was well loved himself by them.

When he was done with his final long prayer that morning, they poured out of doors onto the Green, and at the picnic tables set up under the sycamore trees, they feasted on ham and goose and spinach *taerts* and pickled quinces, cherry *taerts* and melons, and candied walnuts, all washed down with cider and peach brandy, until their bellies were full and their heads tiddly. And then the old man catechized the children for an hour, even the black ones, while their elders sipped their peach brandy some more, and then the children went whooping out of the church doors to roll hoops on the Green again, and all was good.

It was time to join his old friend Grietje Cosyns under a shade tree. "It is always good on Sunday, fun day," Grietje said to him, giving him her hand in greeting. He put his other hand over hers, enclosing her slender fingers in his big mitts. Her heart gave a little leap at his touch. He was a virile thing, even in his old age. She had always had a secret sweet tooth for him. And she suspected that he had always had a secret yen for her, too, which no amount of candor would ever pry out of his most honorable self. Still, she liked to flirt with him a bit. No harm in it. She arranged her kerchief modestly over her bosom, not really intending to call attention to that still shapely flesh. Or did she?

She held the new baby, her newest namesake, the now safely baptized one, in her arms and softly sang to her:

> *Slaap, kindje, slaap,*
> *Daar buiten loopt een schapt.*
> *Een schapt met witte voetjes*
> *Dat drink zijn melk zoo zoetjes.*
> *Slaap, kindje, slaap.*

He smiled at the image she sang of. But, of course, he thought, the little one, dressed in her tiny shirt of fine white linen and the long-sleeved linen Christening sacque that had been worn by so many of her sisters and brothers and cousins when he baptized them, was well asleep, and the world would never know if she was dreaming of a sheep with four white feet drinking milk so sweet. In her sleep, the baby raised a tiny mitt of Flanders lace, with its cut-out thumb hole, to her little rosebud mouth and sucked, and Grietje's heart leaped again, with love and thanksgiving. And so did his. Their eyes met as if to say, *Life is rich. Life has been good to us.* Which was true, even though they each privately suspected that life was coming to a close. They were old. How much more time could be left to them?

After the feasting, the family had no intention of calling it a day, but got back in the wagons and went on to the household of the just baptized one for gift giving and *kandeel* drinking. A silk cushion decked with white ribbon hung on the door to signify the occasion, and another feast was spread. The gifts were silver porringers and silver spoons and *kandeel* cups. The *kandeel* was made from a family recipe, a mix of three gallons of water, seven pounds of sugar, oatmeal, spices, raisins, lemons, and two gallons of Madeira wine, all steeped for a day and a night.

The *dominie* traveled with them. There was plenty of room, as the children knew the way to the house and ran off to it ahead of the wagons. He sat beside Grietje, beside her like man and wife, she thought, and holding hands no less, which was something new. Does he know something that I don't know? Grietje wondered to herself, for he had never been so affectionate with her before. Holding hands like a courting couple! "Are you ill, friend?"

"I'm in good health," he said. "As much as anyone can know that. But lately I do wonder how much longer I will have to visit with you, one of my oldest and dearest friends. And lately I do wonder," he said, gazing down the road over the caravan of wagons proceeding from the Hackensack Green to the next celebration, "I do wonder what comes after. I can't help but wonder."

She looked away into the sky. *What do you mean, after?* she wanted to ask him. There were two things *after* could mean: Did he mean after death, *to one's soul?* Or did he mean after *his* death, *to those of his left living?* And what will happen to her soul? And what will happen to those of hers left living? She wanted answers to such questions.

"I wonder the same," she said, gazing down the road, too. She would literally be surrounded this day, as she always was on Sundays, by her descendants, her children, grandchildren, great-grandchildren, the fifth generation in America already. "What follows this?"

"And how will they get along?" he said, seeming to take her second meaning. "And how many of them are there of yours to get along, well or not?" he said. "Or can't you count them? I have not nearly so many as you. I can count mine on my ten fingers."

"I have scores," she said, "and more to come." Of great-grandchildren there were already, she counted on her fingers, thirteen (that number again) with one on the way in October. "And with many more ahead, for some of my sons may have more children, and most of my grandchildren have not yet even married, nor have any of the great-grandchildren, of course."

"When that generation starts birthing, there will be a great flood of your descendants to baptize."

"Like Sara," she said, "'the Lord blessed me fruitful and multiplied me exceedingly.'"

"Now, friend, you know, of course," he chided her affectionately, "the blessing was upon Abraham, not Sara."

"I do not think the Lord minds my taking a little liberty with his word," she said in her coquettish way. "I am confident that he is fond enough of me to overlook even worse things I have done. And besides, friend, whatever his book says, in my book women are as good as men. You know that."

He chuckled. He knew she was referring to the time she had gone before the magistrates at age fourteen to represent herself in what she always called Hendrick Pietersen's *beklagenswaardig* pitiful little suit against her.

"Yes," she said proudly. "I am thinking of that, as I often do. I am proud of it. Most women in my day sent their husbands, or their fathers, to defend them in court when they got into trouble. But that was not my way. I am as brave as any man."

He would not dispute it.

At the house, they sat together in a corner, and she eyed the younger women about her. Who among them, she wondered, would have her *geest*, her spirit of independency? Who would rise, when she and Marytie were gone, to steer the family toward the future? Aeltie, of course, the wife of Cosyn's only surviving son. She showed promise, had a good head on her shoulders. Grietje had her eye on Aeltie. And maybe Margaret Blauvelt after Aeltie, if Margaret Blauvelt married Grietje's best great-grandson, as it was said she had in mind to do. But that would be another age, she knew, and she would be long gone. *After.* It was a problem and a mystery, whichever way it was meant.

*   *   *   *

Finally, in September it was settled, and on a brilliant afternoon Marytie walked to Grietje Cosyns's house to tell her the news: "Jacobus Demarest has bought a farm," she said glumly.

Grietje saw that it was too difficult for her to spit out the rest. Grietje had to supply it: "And our Margrietje has agreed to have the banns published?"

"Yes." Marytie buried her face in her hands and shook her head. *No, not yes!* Her head rang with *No. No, no, no, no!* But it was too late.

"The fat is in the fire, then," Grietje said crisply. "We must make the best of it. It is not the end of the world."

The Sunday after their intention to marry had been registered with the authorities and the two Sundays after that, the banns were read at the Tappan church to announce the betrothal of the widower Jacobus Demarest and the fine-looking Margrietje Haring. And in October, on a day when the maples and birches burned red and yellow against a cobalt sky, and the sycamores and the locust trees rendered themselves russet and gold, their being no objections to their union—"at least none that anybody can hear," Marytie muttered to Cosyn—they were married in the *groote kamer*. It took less than a minute.

Marytie did not at all care for the way they looked together, that burly *groot zwaarlijvig* Jacobus Demarest in his rusty black suit and her dainty slender daughter in her new yellow quilted damask dress and her gray silk slippers embroidered with pale flowers, the latest style. Nevertheless, the deed was done, and Marytie knew she would have to fork over the copper candelabra.

Although the wedding ceremony was over in the twinkling of an eye, the wedding frolic lasted all night, with rum and wine and food aplenty, roasted turkeys, ducks, geese, and chickens, roasts of beef, suckling pig, hare, and rabbit, with their sauces, stewed turnips, cabbage salads, desserts galore, custards, *taerts,* fried sweets. All night the slave fiddlers played in the great barn, and the guests danced and caroused, and in the morning when the roosters were done with their first and second chorusings and the sun appeared in the eastern sky the men had a horse race, with a gallon of Madeira wine the prize, and when that gallon was consumed, the guests roused their children, sleeping on every possible flat surface they could find in the house, and finally took their leave.

Well before midnight, the bridal couple had left the barn, with much fanfare and foolery behind them, for their marital bed—Marytie's dear *betse*—the cupboard bed in the *groote kamer*. And Marytie, who knew that the betrothal had not been sealed aforehand in the way that hers had been, under the beech tree, could not help but imagine the weight of the impatient husband thrusting itself upon and into the supine, surrendered body of her daughter in the very bed where she had been conceived and born. There will be fresh blood on my clean sheets by now, she thought grimly, in the little hours of the morning when she lay awake thinking dark thoughts. She and Cosyn huddled together that night in the feather bed in one of the back rooms while a determined lusty man slept soundly nearby, having deflowered their elfin child.

The next day, in the afternoon, when everyone had slept it off, the whole party would ordinarily have climbed into their wagons and bumped and rattled along the road to Hackensack to the home of the bridegroom's parents for another feast. But since his parents were long gone to their reward, Marytie did not have to put herself out for that particular tradition. She said her goodbyes at the wagon's side, and when they were down the lane and safely out of sight she went into her house and lay face down on her *betse*, lay on the blood of her daughter and wept for all her daughters living and dead, and all her sons, living and dead.

"What is this life that has been given to us?" she sobbed when Cosyn came to her. "What are we supposed to think of it, to do with it? What is it besides eating and sleeping and working and worrying, and giving birth and marrying and burying our dead and losing our living ones to others' appetites?" In the privacy of her cupboarded and curtained bed, she relived her grief when those babes of hers had been taken, four in a row, remembered her grieving prostration at her bitter losses. And relived her anger now at those who had said it was unreasonable of her to prefer her pleasure in her enjoyment of them to the eternal joy they had come into when they left her. "Who cares about eternal joy?" she had stormed then. "I want them in my sight. I want them in my arms."

"I want *her* in my sight," she sobbed now. He tried to comfort her, but she was inconsolable, mourning her beloved *dochter* Margrietje, gone from her for all practical purposes. "Gone!" she moaned. "She's gone!"

"No, no, no," he soothed her. "She is still ours. She will be with us many times."

And two months after that, on Christmas Day, 1737, she had occasion to weep again, when Marretje, the plain one, not to be left on the shelf, married Johannes Bogart in another ceremony taking half a minute, if that. He was four years her junior, only nineteen, of slight build, compared to his wife, and slightly cross-eyed. But he was another one with long green fields in his future, and it was considered a very suitable match on all sides in that respect, and as it turned out it had been Marretje's own idea. She, as one who might not have so many chances to find a husband, had sized him up as one who might not have so many chances to find a wife, one who would appreciate her good dowry, one who was canny enough not to turn her down because of her long horsy face and big teeth and dun-colored hair. She had a good heart, after all, and wide hips. He could see she would make him a good and true wife and be a good mother to his offspring.

As she had for Margrietje in October, Marytie produced yet another set of copper candelabra for this occasion—in addition, of course, to the usual *outzuit,* the full set of furniture for setting out on married life, expected by every bride from her parents—as well as a slave woman purchased of a neighbor and a couple of cows.

The prospect of married life made Marretje's long plain face glow that day with excitement and anticipation, and love, too. She actually seemed not only to like but to love the little squinty-eyed fellow when she threw her arms around him and danced him up and down the hall of her grandmother's house. And she could actually look quite *aantrekkelijk* pretty when love came upon her, Marytie marveled.

*   *   *   *

She was married on Christmas Day, but Christmas was nothing special among them. Indeed, some hardly knew when the day rolled around, for the church authorities in *patria* had frowned on it as a Popish festival with pagan roots, and Reformed people had never got used to marking it in any special way. The children got their treats in their wooden shoes from St. Nicholas and his helper Swart Pete on the saint's day, December 6. So, when church was over that Christmas Day, it was not Christmas that was on their minds, but another wedding feast.

Some got back in their wagons after the brief little wedding and clopped to Grietje's house, down the road and over the *kill,* for the festivities, and some, including the aged *dominie,* who had come from Hackensack for the occasion, and the *voorleser,* walked to the house to stretch their legs. Afterward, the people would remember it as the last time, or perhaps the next-to-last time that their dear former pastor would walk that walk, for he declined and died soon after. The new *dominie* did not attend the festivities. He did not like the company, as they well knew. Nor did they like him, as he well knew.

In packs, according to age and fleetness, the children ran as fast as they could to get to the party, much faster than the walkers and the heavy old horse-pulled wagons, and they were there before anyone else, so that they had to wait outside, and peek through the windows, to see the treats and special foods being laid out on the tables in the hallway by the slaves.

"And so it goes," Grietje said, with satisfaction, to Guiliam Bertholf.

"Yes, so it goes," he said. He knew just what she meant.

Year in and year out they poured into her house on occasion after occasion. And so it went, he thought and she thought, the never-ending cycle of births and marriages, work and play, sickness and death. "I've been meaning to ask you something," she said.

He knew what was coming. He had been asked that question many times, and many times he had not answered it truthfully, out of compassion for a worried soul.

"Yes?"

"What follows? Is there a heaven?"

He looked into her questing eyes. She could take it, he decided. She would know if he was not truthful. "I have asked myself that question many times," he said slowly. "And the truth is, I don't know. Is there an after life, or does the after life exist only in the memories that others have of us when we are gone?"

"The Bible says there is."

"Yes," he said. "'In my father's house are many mansions. If it were not so I would have told you.'"

"And so?"

"It could be a figure of speech," he said. "Though it is heresy to say so."

"What is the Kingdom of God, then? Another figure of speech?"

"I think the kingdom is, perhaps, not up there," he said slowly, "but will appear here, on earth, when we love our neighbors as ourselves, forgive our enemies, make our world as good as it is possible to be."

She sighed. "I knew you would say that," she said. "My world is almost as good as it is possible to be, if it were not for Lancaster Symes. And he is one neighbor I will never love. So there you are. There is no heaven for me, for I will not forgive him."

"Let us hope that that problem will be resolved in a peaceful way," he said. "Then you will forgive and forget."

"If I should live so long," she said. "But I agree with you, in fact, dear *Dominie*. *We* are supposed to bring the Kingdom of God about. That's how I read it."

"I, too," he said. "But it's a tall order for creatures so frail and flawed."

CHAPTER 7

▼

RUFFLES

The grains and hay were reaped. The men drove the wagons laden with the harvest and jumping with grasshoppers, butterflies, and locusts into the great barn. They forked the hay up into the loft, stored the corn in bins, shoveled the wheat and the rye into barrels to take to the miller for grinding. Summer was over.

"School is starting," Marytie said. "It is time for Margaret Blauvelt to leave my house and go back to her own home."

"But I don't want to leave," Margaret cried. "I want to stay here. I love your house!" And she loved Marytie, who was not only full of interesting information, but playful as well. Her own mother (she loved her, of course) was never playful.

"You can come again next summer," Marytie promised. "And we will see each other in church on Sundays." She said this although she knew it was not true. She would be at her married daughters' churches on many a Sunday. "And at other times, too," she said. "It is time for school to start."

"I can go to school from here," Margaret pleaded.

"No, it's time," said Marytie firmly.

So, blotting tears, Margaret gathered her clothing into her valise, and Cuff drove her down the dirt lane and then down the plank road to the Slote and her family's house. She focused on his old straw hat bobbing in front of her and on a fat bumblebee that sat on it, along for the ride. "I don't want to go home," she said to the bee.

He thought she was talking to him. "You will come back," he said.

He helped her down from the wagon and carried her valise to the front door. "Goodbye, Cuff."

"Goodbye, Missy," he said. He was sad to see her go. She was a lively thing around the farm.

The tears came to her eyes again. She wanted to throw her arms about him, but that was not done.

Inside, she found no one at home. She set down her valise and walked through the house, calling for her mother. There was no response. "Mother? Where are you? I am home."

She went next door to the store and found Eliza there, weeping on Margaret's mother's neck. "What is it?" she asked in wonder, to see her mother with her arms around the girl she didn't approve of. "What has happened?"

Elizabeth van Houten looked up, annoyed to see her daughter. "Weren't you expecting me?" Margaret said.

With a sharp thrust of her chin, her mother shushed her out of the store.

"Hardly the homecoming I had in mind," Margaret said, hurt. Her mother glared at her over Eliza's head.

She went out and sat on the wharf in front of the store and watched a colony of ants busying themselves with the hill they were making where the sand met the reeds. The tide was coming in. Sloops plied up and down the river far out in the channel. One sailed into the *kill* to unload its cargo on the wharf, bolts of fabric, casks of rum and Madeira, crockery, everything that was needed by the people of the area was sold in the store. Her father went in and out signing drafts and bills of lading.

At last, Eliza emerged. Her face was flushed, and her bosom heaved in her bodice. The flesh around her left eye was bruised and swollen, and the eye itself was red.

"What happened?"

"My father hit me," she said.

"Why?" Margaret was shocked.

"I walked in the woods with Cornelis," she said sullenly.

"Who is Cornelis?"

"The man I love."

"The ferryman?"

"Yes."

"What do you do when you walk in the woods?"

"You hug and kiss, silly, what do you think?"

"Did your father see you?"

"Yes. He followed me. He came at us with his musket. He frightened Cornelis away. He ran off. And then my father struck me across my face. Now I will run off. And for good. I have not told your mother so. So kindly don't you tattle on me. It's my own business," she added fiercely.

"Where will you go?"

"To the city. Where else?"

"Will Cornelis be there?"

"I will know tonight, when I jump on his ferry," she said grimly.

"And if he's not?"

Elizabeth van Houten appeared in the doorway to the store. "Come in, Margaret," she said in a voice not to be disregarded.

"I will go anyway," Eliza said in a low, determined voice. "I'm leaving here with or without him."

"Write to me," Margaret whispered. "I want to know that you'll be safe."

"Goodbye, Little One."

"Goodbye, Eliza. I thought we would be friends forever."

Eliza laughed. "Forever is a long time."

"You laugh at every thing and any thing," said Margaret sadly.

"Friends forever, then," said Eliza. "It's a promise."

That night, a moonless, windless night still as death, except for the breathing of her parents in sleep, Eliza rose from her bed and, wrapped in a lightweight woolen cloak, slipped out the door. It was pitch black outside, and she stumbled and stubbed her shoe on a rock here and slipped on a mossy patch there and walked into a branch that stung her cheek where it was bruised. This is not going to be easy, she thought grimly. Especially if he is not there.

But he was there. The ferry came in on the tide, and a boatman jumped off. Cornelis tossed a line to him to secure the vessel so the few passengers could board, including two slaves she knew, Caesar and his friend Pompey. It was Saturday night. They were going to the city for their frolicking.

She jumped aboard.

"Eliza!" Cornelis said. "What are you doing here?" He was astonished to see her. And he did not seem all that glad to see her either. He would warm up in the city, she decided.

He was staring at her black eye, which was apparent even in the dim light of the ship's lanterns. "Did your father do that?"

"Yes."

"It wasn't necessary," he said gruffly. "But I suppose you might have expected it."

"I didn't expect it. That's why I'm off to find a new life," she said.

"In the city?"

"Yes."

"Where will you stay?" he asked.

"With you," she said.

He gaped at her. "I sleep in a room with four men!"

"That can change," she said, sashaying past him to a corner of the deck she had spied out for herself.

It was dawn and low tide when they arrived at the steps at Comfort's dock at Crown Street, and she was tired and hungry. She had sat up awake all night, wrapped in her cloak, afraid to drop off lest one of the leering boatmen molest her while Cornelis was busy with the sail. She had hoped at first that she could trust Caesar and Pompey to watch out for her, but after an hour they went below deck to play at dice.

He booked a room at a tavern a few doors north of Comfort's Inn and paid in advance for the next night as well. But he himself had to make another run with the ferry over to Perth Amboy, he said. He would be back by noon. She went into the room and fell asleep on the bed in her clothes.

He never came back. She waited for him for days that September, standing on the wharf, examining every boat that docked.

"He has fled to safer ports," said Mary Burton. "A man doesn't take very well to a musket pointed at him by an angry father." Mary was the indentured servant of John Hughson in whose tavern near Trinity Church Cornelis had booked the room. Eliza was grateful for the room, but as he had paid for the chamber for only two nights, on the third day, she had to begin working in the kitchen in return for her lodging and board. "Little better than a slave," she thought bitterly, washing greasy pewter trenchers and cups in cold water. And she had to share a bed in the garret with her kitchen mate, a slave named Sarah.

That first night in Sarah's bed, she lay awake in fear and dread while Sarah slept. What is to become of me? she asked herself. What have I done? She could not go home. Her father would beat her for running away. She wouldn't give him the satisfaction. She tossed and turned, at her wits' end. *I need something,* she thought. *I need I need I need I need … somebody. I'm all alone.* She hadn't ever needed anyone before, as far as she could recall, unless she counted her mother, when she was a helpless tot.

In the dead of night, Sarah stirred, groaned, woke. Eliza lay still as a poker. Soon Sarah's body began to shake violently, as if, Eliza thought, she was imagining she was strangling someone. In her waking moments, Sarah, who was nearly as white as Eliza, because she had been fathered by a white man, was half-consumed by rage that a white man's appetites had doomed her to slavery. So it was natural for Eliza to suppose, lying there next to her in the dark, that it was her father Sarah was strangling in her nocturnal imaginings. Then she began panting heavily, emitting a series of little cries and yelps, and then at last she heaved a great sigh of contentment and quieted down.

After this strange exhibition occurred a second night, it began to dawn on Eliza that it nothing to do with a violent rage. It was something else. After the third time, she was sure of it. She rolled close to Sarah's body on the bed when it was over and put her hand in the small of Sarah's back. "Did you pleasure yourself?" she whispered.

Sarah froze. "That's for me to know," she said.

"You did."

"It's none of your business, white girl."

"Pleasure me," Eliza whispered, in the dark, pressing her body against Sarah's.

"What!"

"I mean it. I need someone to comfort me."

"Do you think I'm your slave?"

"My lover," Eliza said.

Sarah sucked in her breath sharply. "You're mad," she said. "I can't do that."

"Yes, you can."

"I can't."

"We can. Do it now."

They put their arms around each other and kissed with their warm mouths closed at first, and then open. And then, their hands went naturally where desire guided them, to breasts first, and bellies, and warm, smooth thighs, and then, oh, yes, "oh, yes!" Eliza cried. There is pleasure and delight in it, indeed, the coupling of humans, she thought contentedly, when it was over.

They pleasured each other often, and they whispered to each other that it was their reward at the end of a long day of domestic drudgery. "No one has to know. It is between us," Sarah whispered.

"Yes," Eliza whispered, kissing her. "Between us."

And then one night when Eliza went to the room, a black man was in the bed. "You can't sleep here any more," said Sarah, rolling over, turning away from Eliza at the door. "My man is back."

Disgusted, Eliza thrust her few things into her valise and went to look for Mary Burton, who lived in another room in the garret.

"Now what?" she said. "Where do I go now?"

"You need money," said Mary.

"And how do I get money?"

"There are four ways," said Mary. "You can work for wages, as you do, you can steal, you can sell your pretty body for it, or you can find a man to marry you."

"That's nice."

"There are no others, that I know of," said Mary.

"What would you do?"

"I would do the fourth. But this time find one in ruffles," Mary said. "With your good looks and handsome figure it shouldn't be hard. A ferryman isn't fine enough for you."

"It's not likely I'll find anyone in ruffles in this scurvy place," Eliza said. "There are mostly blacks, and all breaking the law in more ways than one."

The law said they couldn't gather, couldn't be out at night, couldn't drink and gamble, couldn't get merry together and dance, but they did all of those things, and more. "There are too many of them, and not enough constables to control them," said Mary. "They do just as they please."

Eliza laughed. She admired them, their defiance of the authorities, taking what freedom they could, right under the noses of the sheriff and his men. A carefree lot, they were determined to have their pleasures, despite their bondage, and make merry in their taverns and grog shops, despite the law. That's the spirit, she thought, so unlike her own cold, distant father and her scared-mouse of a mother, going to bed with the birds. She was well out of that dull household. She didn't miss it in the least, or her mother, and certainly not him.

She preferred being among them, as they drank their rum punch together, played on their violins, softly talked their business together.

"What is their business?" she asked Mary.

"Stealing," said Mary. "They break into the cellars of taverns to steal a cask of gin, or break into a warehouse to relieve the owner of a bolt of cloth or two."

"And then what?"

"They have no large places to hide and store their booty, so they can't steal in volume, and they can't sell it themselves in a public place. They would be caught and hanged."

"What do they do with it?"

"They sell it to Hughson, who pays them a sum and then transports the goods out of town to his mother for resale. Hughson is called a fence," Mary Burton said.

So there was working for wages, which she didn't care for, or stealing, or selling her body. Not counting Sarah, and she didn't really count Sarah, because it wasn't the real thing with her, a woman, Eliza's body was still her own. She had not given it to Cornelis, although she had intended to, when he so cravenly disappeared. But she could not imagine selling it. "It makes me shudder to think of it," she said to Mary. "Hundreds of strangers poking me. Though I would like to be poked."

"Find yourself a husband," said Mary. "He'll poke you enough."

"Why don't you find yourself one?"

"I'm only sixteen," said Mary. "And besides, I had a poke. I don't care for what it gets you."

"What does it get you?"

"A baby."

"Do you have a baby?"

"I had one. It died."

"I'm only sixteen myself," said Eliza thoughtfully. "I'm ready for the husband. But not the baby."

"They go together," said Mary.

As she pondered how to raise herself out of Hughson's kitchen, Eliza saw her best opportunity to be in fencing, and one night she recommended herself to one of the slaves, smooth-talking Toby whose cocky manner she admired. "You steal. I'll fence," she whispered.

Toby pinched her on the cheek and said, "How about if you steal with me. *And* you fence."

"I'll make more than you."

"That's all right. You need more than me. You don't have an owner."

"Very well."

"Swear your everlasting secrecy," he said.

"I do. And you too," she said, holding out her hand to him.

He pressed it to his chest. "I do," he said. "And make sure you know, girl, that the gallows await thieves, even white and female ones. So we must not get found out."

"We must not, that's for sure."

Together, she shivering, they broke into a nice little shop that very night and stole silver coins out of the cash box and a pair of silver candlesticks. It was child's play. She sold the coins and the silver candlesticks to a gaudy woman who owned a tavern on Williams Street, gave Toby his share of the proceeds, bid adieu to Mary Burton and Sarah and the scullery, and got herself a room of her own. It was in the house of a free negro named Francis, all she could afford, but at least she had her own space and a pallet stuffed with straw.

The next night, they robbed another store, and then another. She soon had enough money to buy herself a new bonnet and a red satin kerchief that Mary said looked lovely against her fair English skin and her dark eyes and curly dark blond hair, and the glass told her that Mary was right. Bedecked in these new items, she set about finding herself a man.

She returned to the shop she had robbed on her first night stealing. It was a high-class shop, with expensive and stylish merchandise, and she had noticed in passing it in daylight that a handsome young man managed it, and he wore ruffles. A little bell tinkled as she opened the door, and he looked up at her from behind the counter. He flushed at her comely face and full figure. She wore a becoming blue bonnet, and the folds of her red satin shawl did not disguise the burden of her bodice.

"Good day, Madam," he said, bowing slightly, drinking in her features.

"Good day," she said in her gravest voice. "I was passing by here yesterday, and I believe I dropped my lace handkerchief in the street. Did anyone turn it in?"

"Oh, no," he said. "Anyone who found a lace handkerchief in this street would be sure to keep it for themselves."

"How dishonest," she said. "I would return it if I found it."

"There are some that would," he said. "But they're few and far between these days."

"Shocking," she murmured.

"Do you live near here?" he asked.

"Yes, I lodge in the neighborhood."

"Alone? No family with you?"

"No, no family. I'm quite alone." She cast her eyes down, as if her aloneness were a condition not so agreeable to her.

"My name is Thomas Pyke," he said. He spelled it for her: P y k e.

"How do you do?" she said, holding out her little gloved hand. "I am Eliza Shaw." Shaw was her mother's name. She did not want to tell him her own too-German-sounding name: Hafnagel. She hated the name.

He took her hand in his and pressed it warmly.

"Is this your shop?" She asked this to flatter him into thinking that she thought him grand enough to own such a fine shop himself. In fact, she assumed he was a clerk hired to work behind the counter.

"Yes, it is," he said.

Now it was she who flushed. Ruffles indeed. And on the first try.

"I was just about to close it to take my midday meal," he said. "Would you do me the pleasure of accompanying me to the coffeehouse?"

Her eyelashes fluttered with a will of their own. She had never been to a coffeehouse, the fashionable alternative to the taverns and grog shops frequented by slaves and the lower sort of whites. "Why, yes," she said grandly, as if it were an everyday thing for her. "I don't mind if I do."

He laughed and gathered his hat and his gloves and locked the door to the little shop she had unbeknownst to him so recently robbed, and together they walked sedately up Broadway to the King's Arms, just north of Trinity Church. She prayed to God that no one from Hughson's would see her passing by on the arm of such a propitious specimen, and her prayer was answered.

Thomas Pyke was a bit of a piker, a speculator, in a small way. It was how he had got his shop started, playing at cards at first to build up a little nest egg, then parlaying that nest egg into small silver and china objects acquired by his wife in London, don't ask how, then each small sale into the acquisition of more profitable items, always with the help of his enterprising wife. He looked on Eliza, with her fine breasts gleaming like porcelain in the candlelight of the little curtained booth in the coffeehouse, as a gamble of another sort. He mulled in his mind how many such meals he would have to supply her before he could get her up to his rooms above the shop and undress her, kiss each rosy breast, bury his face in her warmest places, make her his own. His temperature rose at these thoughts, and he fanned himself with his napkin.

She was not unmindful of the effect she had on him.

CHAPTER 8

▼

CAESAR

It's time, Grietje said to herself one day. She had made up her mind: It was time to wrap her books in brown paper and present them to her dear Marytie.

Lovingly, she smoothed the worn cover of *De Medicyn-Winckel, The Medical Shop,* and wrapped it and laid it in a basket. For her children's health—not one of her four sons had died, or even been seriously ill—she believed she had in particular to thank that little book of practical information and also *de Verhandelinge van de opvoedinge en ziekten der kindren, The Little Book on Child Sickness).* "Little treasures," she murmured to herself, carefully folding the paper around the books. "What would we have done without you on so many occasions?"

In her opinion, sickness was the only one of life's certainties that one could hope to avoid. The rest were inevitable. "One is born, one plays, one works, one marries, one gives birth, one dies. But one does not have to be sick," she said to Daniel, somnolent in his rocking chair by the window. He merely grunted. She sighed. She couldn't imagine what was ailing him; he had no energy, no zest for life any more.

That she had been remarkably healthy all her many years she attributed to her avoidance of the city with its crowds of the likely diseased, to her garden with its medicinal herbs, and to her medical books. To educate herself to recognize the diseases that abounded in their world and to try to avoid them, and if that failed, to cure them, she had made it her business to study these useful books, which had informed her of all the diseases known to medical science, from childbirth fever, which often took mother and child together, to throat distemper to the bloody flux that visited in the summer to scarlet fever to the *struma Africana*, the galloping consumption that killed off the slaves, to measles. A measles epidemic way back in the '80s had left 500 dead in Canada and caused her to attend to her herb garden with renewed concentration.

And then there was the bilious plague, also called yellow fever, with its flushed face, scarlet lips and tongue, fever and chills, yellow skin, and the black vomit that indicated bleeding in the stomach. It had appeared mysteriously in New York in the year 1702, and the English governor, Lord Cornbury, had fled the city with his household and taken refuge in, of all places, Tappan, much to her displeasure. He was heartily disliked by the Tappan people for his unconcealed contempt for their Dutch ways, and she stayed home from church for weeks that time, so as not to have contact with him or his.

The disease she dreaded the most was not yellow fever, though, but smallpox, perhaps because she was so vain and the disease so disfiguring. It was her lifelong fear that it would attack her and she would become covered in oozing *kinderpocken* pustules and scars forever. It had broken out in New York in the late 1680s, just after they moved to Tappan, to which it fortunately did not travel, though it might well have, as they were just a morning's sail from the city on a flow tide and a brisk wind. She had held her breath till it was over.

When it appeared in Boston in 1721 she wrote to her son in the Assembly to urge him to introduce a bill to begin variolation in New York, as they were doing in Boston and as she had heard they did even in remote Turkey. Even in primitive Africa variolation was known. Her husband's slave Congo, said to be the son of a prince or a chief of his tribe in that place whose name he bore, claimed to have undergone the procedure as a child. Six thousand were afflicted in Boston in 1721, in a population of just under 11,000, and 844 died, the papers said, and there would have been many more had not the English divine Cotton Mather undertaken to see that children were inoculated in the arm with pus obtained from a patient acutely ill with the disease. "Why can't New York do the same?" she wrote to her son. She nagged and nagged him about it. "Take the juice of the pox, and cut the skin and put in a drop. It's easy." But, to her annoyance, there was great resistance in New York to Cotton Mather's cure.

This day, without much thinking about it, because she had been meaning to do it for some time now, Grietje methodically finished wrapping her dear books and then tied a blue ribbon around her medical volumes and another around her precious household bible *Het Vermakelijck Landtleven*, a compilation of everything from information on diseases and the medicinal herbs to cure them to

designs of gardens and flower beds, arbors and sundials to a calendar of the culti-
vation of fruit trees and vegetables. Within its covers was also her indispensable
cookbook, *De Verstandige Kock*, along with instructions for beekeeping, butchering, and baking, all the information one needed for the management of a proper
household in the country, which hers surely was.

She put them all in the basket and added to it *Den Ervaren Huyshouder*, full of
practical advice to the "experienced housekeeper" (i.e., herself), a much-loved
religious book, a book on the rearing of Christian children, and that book with
the frank and interesting details of the delights of the married life, *Venus Minsieke
Gasthuis* (this little volume was as well worn as the cookbook for they had both
traveled much about the neighborhood). And then she put the basket in her
riding chair and drove over to Marytie's house and presented the basket to her.

Marytie was shocked, for she understood at once what this act meant. Grietje
was getting ready to leave them. It dealt her almost a physical blow, that unwelcome idea, as if someone had thumped her on the back with an ax handle. Her
stomach lurched, and tears blurted into her eyes from some deep well of sadness
within her, whose source was her already too many losses, too many deprivations.
But to be deprived of Grietje? Oh, no, she thought. Not yet. Not yet. I'm not
ready.

All those times they had enjoyed each other's company, and each other's
advice and counsel, each other's fears and tears, and joys, too, passed in a dizzying
procession through her mind. They had had more occasions than they could
count to celebrate, and to weep and bewail, the fates of their loved ones.

She put her arms around her and kissed her gently on each cheek. "*Dank u,
lief schoonmoeder*," she said.

What would she do without Grietje? What would she have done on the most
recent of these events, she wondered now, that most ambiguous of occasions,
when they had been unsure whether to rage or sigh in relief, when their *lieveling*
darling granddaughter and daughter, Maria, Marytie's youngest, six months
pregnant, finally got her man, her unworthy, swelled-head, lazy boy-man, to
marry her. She was a mere sixteen, he a callow nineteen. Of course, she had been
eighteen and Cosyn nineteen when they married, but eighteen was not sixteen,
and she had not been with child, and Cosyn had a future. Nobody could say that
for Maria's chosen one.

Marytie was beside herself with disappointment when she learned of the pregnancy. "I hope and pray she'll lose it," she said through her teeth to Aeltie, to
Cosyn, to Grietje, to her married daughters, to her son. "I pray for it, though it

be a sin. But I pray for it. Then it might blow over." But she didn't lose it, and it didn't blow over.

"There is only one thing to do," said Grietje grimly. "We must bite the bullet."

She convinced Marytie to make the best of it and gamely order the bride's *outzuit*, though how it would fit into the hovel that was all he could provide for their darling was hard to imagine. "At least," Grietje ventured, "we will not have to bear the shame of an *onecht kind* bastard child in the family."

"I will have to provide them a better house," said Cosyn. "I won't have her in his hovel."

For Grietje, for Marytie and Cosyn and their other daughters, and Jan and Aeltie, it was almost more than they could bear, to witness such a favorite granddaughter and daughter and sister have to wheedle and beg a man to marry her, and such a man, connected to the patentee families only by law, not blood. The common wisdom regarding the choice of a marriage partner was summed up by a Dutch poet: Choose a spouse "not rich or mighty grand, but like to you in goods and land," but this advice the besotted Maria had blithely ignored. Her chosen mate was a well-favored, ruddy, joking fellow, but he had hardly a *stuyver* to his name, let alone goods and land. "Unless you count his horse and that one-room thing he calls a house," Grietje snorted.

"At least he's Dutch," said Marytie bleakly.

Grietje was not one to let disappointment overtake her, but this test was a hard one. Still, she managed to put it behind her. "It's a great life if you don't weaken," she muttered to Daniel.

"Ya," he muttered back.

"I shall carry on," she said.

She carried on, tended her herb garden, fed her chickens and her ducks, studied her wordbook in her spare time, wrote her letters to her four sons, went to church, and took satisfaction that at seventy-nine nine great-grandchildren, including Maria's near-bastard, would be born to her in the year 1738 alone, nine *onnozele schaapjes*, little lambkins. But, nevertheless, it was with a heavy heart that she went about her routine these days, a heart that seemed finally to admit that there were more troubles in the world than one could shake a stick at.

And then, in this cheerless state of mind, she died. She had known it was coming. Hadn't she predicted it, told the *dominie* she felt it coming? She didn't want to die, not yet. Certainly not as the disputes over their land on the east bank of the Hackensack were coming to a head. She wanted to live to see the outcome of that long battle of the nations! For she always thought of it as that: the Dutch defending their precious land against the English again, a battle they must win, they must win.

But one afternoon, lost in her faded memories of the past, brooding over the green land's wound that had to be healed, must be healed—land so fair, peace so rare, she muttered to herself—trying to imagine the unimaginable future of her huge family with herself not among them, she felt her brain come under attack. One side of her face froze up, the right side, and her arm on that side lost its power. A vision of all the heft she had lifted down the long years with that arm came before her eyes, and she uttered a cry that no one heard.

She was alone, on the bank of the *kill* near a great weeping willow tree whose last brown leaves had been whipped away by the winds of autumn nights, alone. She stumbled half blindly toward the bench under the tree, her left arm reaching out for it. Behind her was her precious house. She made a move to try to see it, but a further dimness came upon her eyes, and a sudden severe headache caused her stomach to heave. She lowered herself to the bench, felt herself vomiting, felt the warm vomit fall into her lap. And then she felt herself tipping off the bench onto the ground.

She lingered for several hours, at first in a sort of coma, when she could half sense the things that were being done to revive her, and the attentions of her old slave woman Dell, and Marytie and Aeltie, murkily perceived. She lingered, still alive, though unconscious for some time, when she sensed no more, perceived no more, and finally breathed her last.

It was one of the largest funerals the place had ever seen. The house teemed with family and men friends, women not being allowed at funerals, other than the closest relatives. The kitchen and summer kitchen were full of slaves, male and female, from all the farms around, preparing the feast. Latecomers stood on the *stoep*, peeked in the windows at the body, laid out in its Sunday best in the *groote kamer*, craned their necks to hear the frail and ancient *dominie* for, as they feared and later knew for certain, it was the last time he would ever come to them. He spoke of time, the livings' time and the deads' time, God's time and mortal's time, the world's time and eternal time. Grietje's time on earth was over. "She is in a better place," he said, "where sheep may safely graze."

Marytie mused on this image, not entirely convinced.

The body in its pine box was taken to the graveyard on the shoulders of the pallbearers, representing the four generations connected to her: her third husband, her four sons, two of her grandsons, and that best great-grandson, Johannes Haring, back from studying law, or perhaps it was theology, in Hackensack. The people weren't sure what he studied. He was always studying something. A bookish fellow.

They wore black gloves and long black scarves, and into the narrow place dug for her behind the church by their slaves, they lowered the box on ropes, and the *dominie* said a prayer. Then, they returned to the house and the women, and the party began.

The women and their slaves had made all ready, with tables in the hall and in both rooms laden with bottles and glasses, pipes and tobacco, platters and bowls of food, baskets of bread, cakes, and special treats. Out near the barn, the male slaves had been roasting an ox and a hog since the night before, and the men set long planks on sawhorses to carve the beasts upon and brought the meat all juicy and delicious with fat into the house.

The eating and drinking and frolicking went on for hours, all day and into the night, and the guests consumed a cask of rum, two casks of Madeira wine, two of beer, and mountains of food. They smoked pipes, men and women together, and admired the pallbearers' gifts, mourning rings and silver mourning spoons, that Grietje had had the foresight to have made and engraved in the city, long before her demise. There was no sign of sadness, or any prayers, or pious and solemn references. She had had a long and blessed life. Why should they be sad? Rather, gossip, news, horses, crops, children, accidents, births, marriages, sickness, deaths to be expected when the weather changed, and a possible lawsuit over the land occupied their attention. In the midst of death they were in life and glad of it, even though they had their troubles.

✻   ✻   ✻   ✻

And so it was that in 1738, Marytie Blauvelt, age sixty, wife of Cosyn, took Grietje's place as the matriarch of the Haring family.

"Why not Peter's wife, Grietje Bogert, as the wife of the eldest brother?" some wondered. But the thing was, *that* Grietje was too tied up with her van Houten and Blauvelt and de Baan and Myer daughters, all giving birth in either Hackensack or New York City that very year. Besides, that Grietje was focused on improving her family's fortunes in the city, where her husband was a member of the Assembly, and where she made it her business to mingle with the right people, the people who would advance his career and the careers of her promising sons, Abraham and Elbert, and her son-in-law, Adolph Myer. *That* Grietje couldn't be bothered with country matters, even if they were issues that would ultimately affect her interests and her family's future, like the land problem, the intractable Lancaster Symes problem. Let Marytie do it.

And besides, everyone in the family knew that Marytie was the logical one to step into the shoes of her mother-in-law. After all, wasn't it Marytie to whom Grietje had given her beloved books? Wasn't it Marytie to whom she had left her tortoise-shell comb and her silver rings, her cambric caps and her lace-edged linen handkerchiefs, her damask jacket lined with fur, her beaver cap, her silver spoons, her silver goblets and brandy cups? According to her will, her share in the house and land, her money, those Jacobuses and Holland stivers and English shillings, her gold and silver coins, her ells of wampum, her household goods, her slaves, her cattle and sheep, were to be divided among her sons, but she left to Marytie the things she really loved, the things that made her Grietje.

Grietje had as good as decreed it: Once she was gone, she, Marytie, was to be the thinker in the family, the main pray-er and petitioner to God for its welfare. And the one to see to the bitter end the fight for the defense of the land they rightfully owned. Never give up that fight! That was one of Grietje's legacies to them all, their entitlement to the land she had helped buy with her own two dowries, and helped clear and civilize with her own two hands.

*   *   *   *

Marytie took her office seriously. Its dignity came upon her. She stood straighter, arranged her long, graying blond hair on top of her head and skewered it there with the imperious tortoise-shell comb, just as Grietje had done. She felt capable, calm, and courageous. Leadership ennobled her. She felt benevolent and benign. She prayed for wisdom and kindliness.

She prayed for the temporal welfare and the eternal welfare of all the family and the friends. And of the slaves, too. And as always, she even prayed that slavery would end, somehow, although in this petition she did not pray with her usual confidence in the verse *Ask and ye shall receive*. Still, she continued to ask. She considered it her duty.

Bereft of her now three married daughters, all gone away, for the first time in her married life Marytie might have had time on her hands, but that was not to be. Dina was failing, and Marytie had to take up some of the slack. The poor faithful slave, who had been her property from the day Nelltie gave birth to her, and her friend, too, over the years, was no longer of much use at age thirty-nine. She was worn out. They would keep her, of course. But they would have to find another to do her work, and sooner rather than later, because Marytie's time was better spent in attending to the land problem, and to her children and her grand-children, than doing chores and cleaning house and cooking. Aeltie with her eight, Marretje and Margrietje with one a piece and one each on the way, and Maria and her new-born infant were scattered all over the Patent and as far away as Hackensack, so that she was often traveling from place to place to lend a hand in their birthing and rearing.

Still, the land came first. In the family's yawl the *Bontekoe*, and often in bigger vessels, sloops in service as ferries up and down the Hudson, she sailed, and more than a few times, that summer of 1738, down to New York with her husband and her son and two of her brothers-in-law and their sons and her brother Johannes Blauvelt and his sons and Lambert Smith and his sons to call upon Peter Haring in the New York Assembly for his advice.

And Margaret Blauvelt, too. Margaret was back. She had begged to come for another long summer's visit, "to continue the cooking lessons," she said. Marytie had laughed. "I have taught you all I know about cooking," she said. But Marytie remembered that she had promised to have her back a second summer, and she was glad to have her. She was good company, especially with Grietje gone, and her three daughters married and out of the house.

It was their habit, when they went to the city on the matter of the land prob-lem, to moor the boat at Comfort's dock on Crown Street and walk down Broad-way and east on Wall Street to City Hall. Marytie loved the crowded, bustling city. "There are said to be two thousand and a half buildings in it now, including almost a thousand houses," she told Margaret breathlessly, clearly in awe of the place. They admired the handsome dwellings of red and yellow brick, their stepped gables, their pleasant *stoeps*. And the newer houses, too, with their roof-tops decked with balconies. Fancy brick mansions were cropping up on the filled-in land on the East River, three stories high, with handsome windows giv-ing out on the river views, and balconies, and many chimneys and ornamental urns and pots adorning their tops, and, without, orchards, stone kitchens in the gardens, and fine flower beds extending to the river. In some estates, hanging gar-dens adorned the banks of the river, and all had pleasant summerhouses at the water's edge.

"Things are much improved in the city since former times," Marytie said with satisfaction. "I remember the days of having to step over piles of garbage and dodge grunting pigs and hogs and smell the stench of stinking weeds and the loathsome sewers running down the middle of the streets." Now at least in the better neighborhoods the streets were mostly paved with cobblestones and lined with fine locust trees and beech and lime trees and elms, and laws required the inhabitants to rake up all the dirt and filth into heaps, to be carried off each week by the cartmen and thrown into the rivers, "the way it should be," she said.

"But it floats in the water," Margaret protested, wrinkling her nose. "Why don't they just burn it?"

"Burning is good, too," said Marytie.

The City Hall was at the intersection of Wall Street and Broad Street. In this bustling building met the Assembly of the Province of New York, the Common Council, the Mayor's Court, and the Supreme Court. In the basement was the city jail. The Dutch still remembered, and it still rankled, that the stones in the foundation of the City Hall had come from the foundation of the wall that had given Wall Street its name. As Marytie put it, "the stones from the famous wall built by us to keep the bold English out now support the English government that so boldly put us out."

"I hate them, the English," said Margaret fiercely.

"They are quite repellant," Marytie agreed. "And quite unnecessary, too. We did fine here on our own."

They collected Peter this day, and with him leading, the whole group trooped from the City Hall through the crowded streets to the lawyer in his office near the Bowling Green, to reassert the Hackensack River as the western boundary of their land, and to claim and reclaim all the land east of that river within the north and south bounds of the Patent. "Divers of the inhabitants of Tappan for many years have lived and made very great improvements secure in the knowledge that the river was their western boundary, just as it was named as the western boundary of the two patents lying north of theirs," Peter Haring told him.

"I know, I know," said the man of law impatiently. "You have made that clear before. But it is the language. The correct language is lacking."

"Those other patents do not say 'as the river runs,'" Peter pointed out. "Why should ours have to?" They were determined to lodge these facts firmly in the lawyer's head.

"You must supply proof that you own that land," the lawyer said.

"'As the river runs' is understood!" Marytie exploded. "That *is* the proof. Just because two English swindlers became joint owners of the land on the west side of the Hackensack River does not mean they own our land on the east side of it."

"But they have claimed they own it, and they do continue to claim it," the lawyer calmly repeated. He was just as determined as they were to get the facts lodged in his head as he was to get that particular fact lodged in their stubborn Dutch heads. "You will have to make an accommodation with them. Either get them to back down, or pay them for the land they claim."

Schurkachtig schelmen! They cursed the men to hell on their way back through the cobbled streets to the river and home. Marytie conjured a vision of them bound to stakes with bridles in their mouths, rods under their arms, and notes pinned to their chests: *Dief,* Thief! *Leugenaer,* Liar! *Oplichterij,* Swindlers!

Margaret was wondering to herself if this pickle they were in had something to do with their being Dutch in an English world.

"It's because we're Dutch," Marytie fumed, as if she had read Margaret's thoughts. "They think they can take our land and we won't fight back. Whenever did the Dutch not fight back against the English?" She knew her history.

"I am beginning to think that the land has made many troubles for us in this new world," Margaret said slowly. "Owning land is not a wholly good thing, is it?"

Cosyn looked at her sharply. She was a quick study all right. Land was at the bottom of everything, good and bad. Land sought, bought, cleared, planted, harvested, bequeathed, disputed, confiscated by governors. And now they were trying to steal it in a swindle, by God!

"Land so fair, peace so rare," Marytie muttered. They could count on trouble when it came to the land.

✳   ✳   ✳   ✳

With such fierce thoughts still in their minds, one sultry day in late September of the year 1738, after Margaret Blauvelt had gone back to her own home again and her schooling, Marytie hitched up the wagon, collected Aeltie and her two youngest daughters, not yet in school, and drove to the Hackensack to take a dip in the cool water. It was one of those sticky, humid autumn days more like summer than summer.

As they approached the river down the sandy lane and the white sand dunes billowing as soft and clean as one of their feather beds, they discerned, in the reeds across the water, the head and shoulders of a negro. A negro holding a plumb line. "I do believe surveying is going on," said Marytie. Some distance down the bank of the river, on their side of it, a white man peered through a telescope mounted on a tripod. The horse and wagon that had conveyed them and their equipment hither were secured to a tree.

"*Intrigant,*" said Aeltie. "And look over there." Over there, what they recognized as Lancaster Symes's sorrel mare was tethered to another tree, while what must be Lancaster Symes's clothing adorned a gooseberry bush. In the distance, around the bend in the creek where the water was deep and cool, they heard the sound of splashing and singing.

"Lancaster Symes is taking a dip in the river this hot and humid day," Marytie observed, "while his men measure the land he is trying his best to steal from us."

"That slave's black legs will be gray with leeches sucking his blood by the time he stumbles out of the reeds," Aeltie said.

"Like Lancaster Symes sucking our blood," Marytie said, suddenly angry enough to spit. She couldn't help but think of Grietje, who never did get the chance to spit in Lancaster Symes's eye as she swore she would do if she ever saw him face to face.

Marytie was far too circumspect to spit in a man's eye, especially a naked man's eye. But she was not above teaching this man a lesson. She looked at Aeltie. "Shall we?" she said.

Aeltie looked at the shirt and the breeches on the gooseberry bush, *onbedui-dend* insignificant garments fitting the *geringschatting* runty physique of a man with an *ongezond* unsavory character! "The moment is made for us," said Aeltie primly. "If would be a shame not to take advantage of the opportunity."

They climbed down from the wagon. Aeltie's two little girls ran to the stream, flinging off their aprons and wading into the water in their shifts. Aeltie picked up the aprons (in case they should have to make a quick getaway) and put them in the wagon. Then she approached the gooseberry bush and tied knots in the arms of Lancaster Symes's linen shirt and flung it over her head to fill it with air. Gently, she let the ballooned garment down upon the river, where it floated slowly south on the current, away from its unwary owner. Her little girls clapped their hands and laughed out loud. Their shrieks of pleasure made Aeltie and Marytie chuckle.

Marytie did the same with the trousers. And again the little girls shrieked and clapped their hands. "Shhhh," Aeltie said. The slave across the river in the cattails smiled broadly, and the man down river trained his telescope on the slowly sinking clothing but did nothing to retrieve it or to alert his employer.

To entertain the spectators further, Marytie lifted Lancaster Symes's small-clothes on the end of a long stick and flung them up into the air, high enough so that he might even catch a glimpse of them, from around the bend in the river, as they descended lightly upon the cattails on the far side of the water. Aeltie laughed out loud, and the girls crowed with delight at this surprising scene.

"Shhhh! That's enough," said Marytie, suddenly uneasy. "We must go now. Hurry!"

Aeltie put the children, who began to wail loudly at having to leave so soon, back in the wagon, while Marytie untethered the sorrel mare and stung her smartly on her flank with a handy willow switch. The mare reared up, neighing in pain, and galloped off up the sandy lane.

Hastily, before an irate and naked man should run after them, they got in their wagon and hurried after the sorrel mare until she was out of sight and they were home.

"We have done a good job. Grietje would have been pleased," said Marytie, satisfied.

It was learned later that an infuriated Lancaster Symes wanted to sue for damages in court, but he failed to identify the perpetrators. His slave claimed he hadn't noticed a thing, for which prevarication he was severely beaten.

*   *   *   *

It was not until the next summer, the summer of 1739, that their counsel, Richard Edsall, seeing no other route to solution of the boundary problem than a court fight, drew up a bond whereby the freeholders of Tappan agreed, under penalty of a forfeit of fifty pounds each, to pay each his respective proportion of the legal expenses that would accrue for the preservation of the Patent of Tappan. "So to court we will go," said Cosyn harshly.

"But first you must go to the Governor," the lawyer said.

William Burnet had a reputation for liking the Dutch, as not many royal governors before him had. English and Dutch were like oil and water. But then he was a Scotsman, so perhaps that explained it. He received them affably on the front porch of his mansion in the old fort near the foot of Whitehall Street. The site was another that the Dutch well remembered. As Marytie gazed out over the bustling harbor flecked with white caps and tacking boats of every description, she recalled that it was in this very the mansion that the Dutch Directors General had lived.

The Governor asked all the familiar questions and looked carefully at all the relevant documents. "To my regret," he announced at last, "further measurements are required."

"But that is another and an unnecessary expense," protested the men.

"I am sorry, but it is necessary," the Governor sighed. "I shall sign a warrant to the surveyor general for a survey."

"We already have a survey, or as good as one in our Indian deed," Marytie cried.

"I regret," he said. "I am sorry for you, but the law requires it."

They went home in a funk, in deep despair.

"If they can be so unashamed as to claim our land, we can be so unashamed as to claim theirs," muttered Abraham Haring, Marytie's third and youngest brother-in-law of three.

"What do you mean?" Cosyn asked.

"I mean to carry the war to the enemy's camp. You will see what I mean. One lie is as good as another these days."

His scheme was to claim the western boundary of the Tappan Patent to be seven miles west (not east) of the Hackensack River, and he managed to convince the inexperienced deputy surveyor who came to measure the land that this trumped-up lie was fact. In time, the surveyor neatly showed it as so on the map of the Patent he produced for the court. Abraham laughed his head off at the ease with which he had gulled the man. But his brothers were not happy, especially Peter. "As the county's representative to the Assembly," he said, "I cannot afford to be connected to the wrong side of a land hoax. Besides, it is a desperate hoax bound to backfire."

Which it soon did, for by this time, Symes and McEvers were busily selling off lots of the Tappan land to their English friends, and they persuaded one of the buyers, one George Marley, to retaliate by bringing a suit in ejectment in the Supreme Court of New York against one of the Tappan in-laws, Jacob Flierboom, a landowner in the disputed territory. George Marley claimed title to Jacob's land, for which he could show the court a deed that looked perfectly correct signed by Symes and McEvers.

"The Court has given judgment for the plaintiff," Cosyn reported when he heard the news.

"What!" cried Marytie. "That George Marley? That one who had the impudence to buy land from those who did not own it and then to sue the rightful owner!" She was beside herself.

"You have said it," said Cosyn.

"What now?"

Various affidavits of writs of possession followed, and various petitions relative to the judgment against Flierboom, and then, as they were all quite exhausted, the Supreme Court issued a final writ, ordering all to "honor" the claims of Symes and McEver.

"Honor? Honor?" Marytie said. "What is honor in this case?" The decision stuck like a toad in her throat, in all their throats.

"Murder and mayhem are just around the corner," Abraham predicted.

And he was half right. They didn't murder anybody, but one dark night, shouting imprecations and wielding knives, Abraham and his sons and sons-in-law and nephews set upon the Englishmen, Symes, McEver, Marley, and three others, in a tavern on the road to Hackensack. They beat them bloody and slashed them up, but not enough so that it was fatal. The sheriff and his men apprehended them and threw them into the Tappan jail, to await trial.

But, considering their imprisonment unjust under the ambiguous circumstances, another group of the Tappan landowners, young hothead cousins and in-laws, stormed the jail and freed Abraham and company, leaving the sheriff and his constable behind bars in their place.

As soon as the sheriff and his constable managed to free themselves and find their horses, they galloped to Cosyn's house, Cosyn being the captain of the local militia, and ordered him to call out the troops. Cosyn saddled up his horse and did his duty, promptly rode around the neighborhood rounding up the militia to search for the escapers and the escaped, which was not so easy, since the perpetrators knew the good places to hide and the militia knew them, too, and so did not look in those places for them.

Then, finally, in the fall of 1739, all the parties suddenly gave up the fight and settled. But it was a severe setback, that settlement, to the five surviving Tappan patentees. In truth it was a humiliation, for in addition to the legal fees of fifty pounds each, they now had to bind themselves to pay 100 pounds each to Symes and McEvers in return for title to their own land in order that it be legally conveyed (*reconveyed,* they continued to insist), to them, the five survivors. This amount was more than the value of the goods they had given to the Indians in exchange for title at the beginning, nearly fifty years before.

*   *   *   *

This humiliating transaction occurred in October of 1739, the worst year in Marytie's life.

Afterward, in her heart she felt that they, or at least she and Cosyn, had given up the fight over the land in grief over the death of their darling Maria that month, just six months after her second child was baptized. One day she was alive and well, and the next day she was six feet under.

What was mere land worth now in comparison to that lost treasure?

It had started with a sharp pain in her stomach that caused her to collapse in a faint on the floor right in the midst of a family gathering to celebrate the harvest. When she came to, she remembered the sharp pain, "as if something in me burst," she said wonderingly, but the pain was gone, and so she and they gave it little more thought. A few hours later, though, she began to feel bloated, and her stomach indeed did swell, and she was very uncomfortable. By the next morning, she could hardly stand. Her chest was tight with pain.

The doctor came and examined her. "She's bleeding inside," he said glumly.

"Bleeding inside? From what?"

"A rupture," he said. "Of a blood vessel, or an artery."

"What can be done?"

He shook his head. "When this happens," he said, leaving his sentence dangling.

She was gone by the evening, and the doctor came again and opened her up, and sure enough her insides were filled with her own blood, pints of it, which Dina sopped up with linen cloths. "That's what caused the chest pain," the doctor said. "The blood was pressing on her lungs."

The slaves dug her grave in the morning, and they buried her in the afternoon.

Marytie felt she was dying, too, was already dead and buried. She wished to die. She thought of filling the pocket around her waist with rocks and walking into the Hudson River. She thought of throwing herself down the well or off a cliff of the Palisades. She looked in the barn for the rat poison. They had taken it away, for they suspected she would look for it. She relived again her grief at all the others she had lost. But this one, this death, this last loss was the bitterest of all bitter pills to swallow.

"It is his fault," she said tonelessly. "It is his fault."

"Why is it his fault?" Cosyn asked her, though he knew the answer.

"Why did she have to marry him? Why did she have to love the wrong man, that cocky penniless Ralph Eckersen? Why? Why?"she raged. "Now she is dead. It must have had something to do with her second pregnancy, so soon after the first."

And to add insult to injury, before the mourning period was over he remarried. "That *begeerte* lustful *jongen*," she railed when she heard it. "Within months he has remarried! And so my grandchildren by my darling Maria now have a stepmother, and who is it but their own aunt and my own niece, Rachel Blauvelt!"

"What have we lost? What have we lost?" Cosyn grieved too for his little lost pet, their last love child, the one they had babied and spoiled, married at sixteen, dead at eighteen. They clung to each other in their *bedstede*. They wept. "That clever rogue knows how to pick his brides," he said. "Rachel Blauvelt is not like to him in goods and land, by a long shot, any more than Maria was."

In addition to the farm that Cosyn had felt obliged to provide for his pet daughter Maria in order that she not have to live in the hovel her husband provided, now his cousin, the new wife's father, had to produce a handsomer dowry for *his* daughter than would otherwise be warranted, because the careless husband had shown so little talent in managing the farm he didn't deserve to have from Cosyn in the first place.

Marytie stopped eating. She had no appetite. She lay in her *bedstede* bereaved. She left off washing herself or brushing her hair. When winter was over and spring came, she got up from her bed and walked out into the woods, indifferent to the green haze of new leaf, the fragrant witch hazel, the jack in the pulpits, the skunk cabbage, favorite food of bears, not caring if she met up with a bear, a rattlesnake or a wolf or a panther or a rabid dog. It was immaterial to her, let them meet her, attack her, kill her. "I do not want to live," she said in that dull and toneless voice.

"Not even for me?" Cosyn said, frightened. "Not even for our other daughters and our son, and our grandchildren?"

"No," she said. "Whoever does these things to me has done one too many. I'm through."

Aeltie followed her, at a distance, to the edge of the sheer cliffs above the Hudson, through the forest of red oak, white oak, and black oak, black birch, maple, tulip, and ash trees. She followed through the shrubby undergrowth, thick with viburnam, poison ivy, wild grape, bittersweet, moonseed, stood near enough to her to snatch her back if she made a move to throw herself down the cliff, but not so near that she trespassed on her grief. She followed her back to the house and lay on the *bedstede* with her, fed her *sappaan*, cornmeal mush, on a spoon at the cherry table in the center of the room, washed her face and neck and arms, brushed her hair.

After Grietje's death, Aeltie had become Marytie's best friend and confidant and, of course, matriarch designate. When the time came for her, Marytie, to go, Aeltie knew that Marytie wanted to be sure she was coached in the role. Death being always just around the corner, it was never too early to plan ahead. And so, in the dreadful mourning period for Maria, it was Aeltie who played the role of head of family, Aeltie who prayed for its well being, made decisions, tried to calm and stabilize her half-crazed mother-in-law. And when the time for grieving finally began to come to an end, it was Aeltie who helped the woman to shape her feelings into manageable presences in her life, dispel the gross monsters of sorrow and distress that had suffocated her night and day with their insinuating power.

And as the pain and grief began to fade, Marytie, strange to say, began to feel closer to Aeltie even than to her own two only surviving daughters.

"Why should this be?" she asked Cosyn.

"Is it because you have calculated deep in a private part of your mind and soul that it is better not to love your flesh and blood too well, or at least not to seem to?" he said.

"Yes," she said. "That is what I have done." Of the eight children she had borne, only three remained now, and only two daughters, and they might be taken too, if that sinister horned and tailed black monster of death who had stolen her others noticed that she especially doted on those who were left.

*   *   *   *

It was a year before she got over the worst pain of losing Maria. By then it had become clear that the time for finding a replacement for the now visibly ailing Dina, who had a painful tumor the size of a muskmelon in her stomach, could no longer be put off. So, in the spring of 1740, when the ice in the Hudson had broken up, with Cosyn at the boat's long tiller and mainsail and Cuff on the jib and topsail, and two fattened cows tethered to the mainstays lowing piteously all the way, Marytie, still mourning, lowing piteously herself in her heart, and Aeltie sailed to New York on the *Bontekoe* to visit the slave market at the foot of Wall Street on the East River. Aeltie, though indignant at the presence of slavery in their midst, knew she needed to learn how to buy and sell these indispensable commodities when the necessity arose, as it now had in the case of Dina.

The tide as they set out was favorable on the wide Tappan Zee, where the ebb ran at two miles an hour, and a spanking breeze behind them filled the sails, so that they made good time, with Cosyn changing his mainsail from one side to the other depending on the direction of the river's many reaches. He pointed his helm hard up and kept it there until the boat was at an acute angle to her course, then the big mainsail would fill with wind on its other side and begin to swing around, and the boom passed over the stern's rail with a great roar, and they were on a new reach.

As they passed the Palisades, the river narrowed and the currents quickened. The tide was turning. Within five hours of sailing, the tallest chimneys and the spires of the city's churches came into view. They moored at Crown Street, Comfort's dock, and climbed up the steps, aslosh with briny water now at high tide. They hired a slave for two shillings and sixpence to help Cuff off-load their produce for the factor to sell, and while Cosyn led his two bleating cows to market

Marytie and Aeltie walked down Wall Street to the Meal Market to buy a new slave.

A slaver from the Caribbean was in port, and its frightened half-naked cargo was paraded on the deck for inspection and auction, all manacled and linked together with chains. A broadside advertised a "Parcel of likely Negro Men and Women also Negro boys and girls from the coast of Guinea, but seasoned in Curaçao," which meant they understood a little Dutch, a plus for those families who still spoke it. "The going rate for a woman aged sixteen to forty is forty-five pounds," Marytie told Aeltie. "Girls of twelve to sixteen years are less. Girls under twelve less than that."

"What about women over forty?" Aeltie asked.

"For them there is no market," Marytie said. "You will see them for sale, poor things. But no one wants them."

"We will look for a young woman of about twenty years," she went on. "And one who is hale and hearty. She should know how to do all sorts of housework, she should know how to brew, bake, cook, roast, and boil, make soap, wash, starch, and iron. She should be a good dairywoman and know how to card and spin cotton, linen, and wool. She should neither use tobacco nor drink alcohol. She should have a pleasingly deferential nature. She should have had the small pox. She should speak some Dutch and some English too, if possible."

"Should be married?"

"No! And she should not have any children."

"For slaves to have family distracts them from their work?"

"Exactly. How about this one?" she inquired, stopping before a young woman with a strong, healthy-looking body. She inquired of the auctioneer as to the woman's abilities and was assured that she was well acquainted with all the domestic duties that would be required of her, and to boot she was a decorous, well-mannered woman of good family. "Her father was a chieftain," the seller volunteered.

Aeltie looked at the comely woman and thought of Caesar. "This one will catch Caesar's fancy," she said. Even though he already had a woman in the city who had borne him a set of twins, he could take another in the country. Nothing to stop him.

"We will have to put up with it if she catches his fancy," said Marytie. "This is the one I want."

"If so, babies and years of children underfoot," Aeltie warned. "And years of the mother's labor interrupted tending to them. For even black children need to be tended to."

"Yes, they do. Slaves are more of a nuisance than anything," Marytie said crossly. "That's what we have to live with."

For forty-five pounds they settled on the comely one. "We will call her Hagar," Marytie said.

"But isn't that name *lastig* troublesome"? Aeltie wondered. "Wasn't it Hagar whom Sarai gave to Abram's embrace and who, when she conceived, looked with contempt on her barren mistress? Sarai dealt harshly with Hagar for that, and Hagar fled from her."

"The angel of the Lord made Hagar return to Sarai and submit to her," said Marytie calmly. "Sarai was the mother of nations. Hagar was a mere slave and a concubine."

Cosyn joined them just as the bill of sale was presented and read. "Know all men by these presents, that I, Robert Sandford, Captain, for and in consideration of the sum of forty-five pounds Current Money of the Province of New York to me in Hand paid by Cosyn Haring of Tappan the Receipt whereof I do hereby acknowledge do hereby acquit and discharge, and said Cosyn Haring his executors, Administrators and Assigns, have Granted, Bargained, Sold, and by these Presents do fully, clearly and absolutely grant, bargain, sell, and Release unto the said Cosyn Haring a negro woman name of Hagar purchased by Robert Sandford on the Coast of Guinea to Have and to hold forever."

When the document was duly signed and sealed and delivered in the presence of three witnesses, they walked back to the Hudson River. There was no need to put Hagar on a leash. She was clearly too frightened to try to run away. She trotted along beside them, whimpering.

It was near dusk, the tide was on the ebb again, and there was little wind. "Not a time to set sail," Cosyn said. They wrapped themselves in their cloaks and slept the night on pallets on the deck of the yawl, white in the stern, black in the bow.

Cuff thought longingly of the girl, who whimpered and moaned softly near him. She would be just right for Caesar. Although he knew that Caesar, now eighteen, had found a woman in the city and already fathered twins by her, it would be better for him to have a woman on the farm where he worked, at least until he, Cuff, saved enough money to realize his dream of buying him his freedom. Besides, if he took a shine to Hagar, there would be less reason for him to try to run away, which Cuff was afraid he wanted to do. Pinkster was just around the corner, when the slaves had all sorts of revolutionary ideas.

*   *   *   *

The slaves had Sundays off and the usual Christian holidays. But the best of these was Pinkster, the holiday on Pentecost and Pentecost Monday and Tuesday beloved for the freedom it gave them of a three-day break from their labor, the freedom to head for the city to meet up with their friends and family in fields just outside of the settled part of the city, and drink, dance, and make merry to their hearts' content for three whole days and nights.

Around the city markets they danced for eels, which they liked to eat boiled with a sharp lemon sauce, tooted on fish horns, banged their drums, played practical jokes on one another. For a penny a fable, the storytellers among them told tales of men who could transform themselves into flying lions and magic hares, of tricksters, of a tiger who slights a tortoise, and trappers who are trapped, of ant-eating dogs and talking drums, of a clever chameleon who wins a race for the chief's beautiful daughter by turning himself into a needle and sticking himself to the tail of the hartebeest, his competitor. Silly tales, the whites thought. Nonsense from Africa.

Their owners liked to think that the freedom they allowed the slaves on this annual occasion would, or at least should, make them content with their lot for the rest of the year. But actually, in their hearts they knew that something else was happening. As anyone could see, Pinkster gave the slaves the opportunity to bind themselves together into a league of their own, an opportunity that might again one day, as it had in 1712, lead young dissatisfied slaves like Caesar to play the last card in the hand that fate had dealt them, the card only they held: the card of insurrection.

They spent weeks in preparation for the holiday, practicing their story telling and drumming, on drums made from eel pots, planning a grand parade and the election of a Pinkster king, a king who in real life was but a slave. Yet for the one brief satisfying moment of his rule, the real society was mocked and turned upside down, rich fantasies enacted of power overturned.

And of course new clothes were in order. As the day approached, Caesar's excitement was palpable. He asked Marytie for money to buy a new pair of shoes, and he treated himself too to a new yellow waistcoat and a shiny brown hat from his own savings, and down the river he went along with all the other slaves and the whites of a certain class, too, on the first ferry after dark that stopped by the wharf at the Slote on Saturday night.

The Dutch loved the holiday, too, with its ecstatic overtones of the Resurrection and the coming of the Holy Spirit fifty days later to the Disciples. They were imbued with feelings of good will toward all at that blooming time, when the pink *blummachee* the English called azalea flowered on the wooded hillsides and birds nested and it was remembered that Christ risen from the dead had walked the earth for fifty days. It was a time when all was well with the world, the only time in the year when blacks and whites came together in a social way, and remembered remnants of African beliefs and African music and dance coincided with the mystical spirituality of the Christian holiday.

The Dutch celebrated it in church, but afterward they went to watch the high jinks, the children, black and white together, playing ninepins and walking on stilts about the market booths set up in the fields. In the booths, special baked goods of the holiday were sold and dyed eggs and other treats, and hucksters and peddlers hawked their wares and their cakes and ale. The Tappan slaves held a dancing competition with the Long Island slaves, dancing on boards held down at their ends by strong friends. Both created special hair styles for the occasion: the Tappan slaves braided their forelocks and tied them with tea-lead; the Long Island slaves made queues down their backs and tied them with dried eelskin.

Cuff joined the excursion to the city not for holiday fun but to try to keep an eye on Caesar and his motley friends. Marytie and Cosyn stayed at home and did not let Hagar go. Marytie did not want her to be introduced to the Pinkster festivities so soon upon her arrival in this new world, did not want her to see her fellow slaves drinking wine and ale and gambling and playing on their instruments, dancing and shouting so loud they might be heard a league off. Did not want her meeting a man she might want to take up with. (She and Caesar had not hit it off at all, to Cuff's disappointment and to Marytie's relief.) Besides, she was so homesick for her vanished land and family that she still whimpered to herself throughout the day and night. She would not enjoy herself at Pinkster.

Cuff arrived home on Tuesday, minus Caesar, in good time to do a round of chores before dark. "Caesar is coming on the night ferry," he said. "And Missus," he added, "I saw the girl Eliza there."

"Hannah's Eliza?"

"Yes."

"Was she alone?"

He shook his head. "She was with a man," he said.

"That ferryman Cornelis?"

"No," Cuff said."

"Who, then?"

"An Englishman," said Cuff. "A jack-a-dandy."

Marytie pursed her lips and frowned.

*   *   *   *

That afternoon, Marytie sat in one of the back bedrooms with Dina, where they had moved her, now that she was dying, fretting over how to tell Hannah about her daughter, when suddenly, she heard from outside in the barnyard an anguished shout. Cuff, normally a sluggish mover, ran from barn to house across the yard, scattering the ducks and chickens and pigs. She rushed to the door. "What is the matter?"

"My savings," he shouted. "My savings." His savings, stashed in a leather bag under the bricks in a corner of the smokehouse, were gone.

Caesar was the only flesh and blood Cuff had ever known, except for his own father, Ben. And now Caesar had betrayed him, just as his grandfather's chieftain in Elmina had betrayed *him*, poor mute Nate. He had stolen Cuff's hard-earned money, and run away perhaps never to be seen again. Marytie had been half expecting it.

It was a crime to run away, of course, and it was also a crime to harbor a runaway. "He might be found," she said, to give him hope, for many runaways were found. Whites had a duty to arrest any slaves found away from home and return them to their masters, who were permitted to whip them for their crime even unto death, there being no law against masters murdering their slaves. But of course Cosyn would never do that, and Caesar knew it. So he took his chance. Slaves who were determined to be free ran away the first chance they got. But Caesar had had lots of chances.

"What made him decide to do it now?"

"Pinkster," said Cosyn.

Together they composed the advertisement describing their vanished property: "Slave answering to name of Caesar, very black color, tall and strong, wearing yellow waistcoat, tow pants, and used beaver hat. Can fiddle very skillful. Can read and write some. May be traveling on a fake pass forged by his own hand. Can row and handle a sail. Reward. Twenty pounds."

Cuff had found that a woolen shirt, a homespun jacket, and a brown overcoat were missing, all saleable items, so they added that to the advertisement. "May have run to the city and mingling with an ill sort," Cuff wanted to add. He may have run to the city, but she had no confidence that he would be lingering in the city. But she added it anyway.

The next day Cuff went missing. Marytie searched for him in all the usual places. In the barn she smelled liquor. Brandy, to be precise. And there she found him, dead drunk in the grain loft. When he came to, hours later, sick as a dog, she gave him a potion to make him vomit and sweat. He wept, rocking himself back and forth on the *stoep*, moaning and keening, as if he were losing his mind. "We will go to look for him," she promised. "We will go tomorrow."

They went together, Marytie and Cuff, to give the advertisement to a printer and to look for Caesar in his usual haunts. They went first to his mother, Nell. "I heard he shipped out," she said saucily. "On a privateer bound no one would say where."

"Who did you hear it from?"

"From him himself, who else?" Nell said in a defiant way. "And I don't blame him. Should he be a slave for white people his whole life?"

"The money was to buy his freedom," Cuff said. "Now he's nothing but a runaway slave thinking he's free."

"More power to him," said Nell.

Now Marytie had to buy another slave, to replace Caesar. There was planting to be done, and all the other chores that Cuff needed help with. But this time she couldn't be bothered going to New York. Time was short. She went to Hackensack and bought Bill from a man they knew, a man who was sick and dying and had to give up his farm.

Bill didn't care for being bought and sold again. And he didn't care to sleep in the smokehouse with Cuff. In his old place, he had been accustomed to sleeping in a lean-to attached to the main house. He was sulky and uncooperative. Cosyn regretted buying him. He would like to have threatened to beat him if he didn't start shaping up, but he knew that wouldn't get him anywhere. So he built him a lean-to on the side of the house, and Bill shaped up, somewhat.

"What nuisances they are. They are like children, always needing sorting out. Always making trouble. Always requiring attention. We would be better off without them," she said to Cosyn, as she often did.

"If only we could afford to hire white men," he said.

"Maybe we can't afford not to," she said.

CHAPTER 9

▼

INSURRECTION

Cuff took his loss hard. He became distracted and morose. And careless. Chopping wood with a sharp ax, he split his big toe straight down the middle.

They got him screaming into the wagon and hustled him on the rough road through the forest to a barber-surgeon in Hackensack to have the toe sewn up with deer hide. A few days later it was infected. He sat soaking it in a bucket of salt water. From Grietje's now neglected herb garden, Marytie made an ointment of crushed calendula blossoms mixed with lemon juice to take the fever out of the nasty dark streaks of poison that rose up his swollen and shiny black leg.

His grief was worse than the pain in his foot. Bereft of the only living thing he loved, he mourned to have been so deceived. Marytie grieved for them both. She had known Caesar from his birth. Watched him grow up along with her own children.

Separated from his mother, Nell, at six, when Cosyn, though with regret, sold her to a man in the city, he had attached himself as if he possessed her to Marytie, made her his new mother, wouldn't let her out of his sight. The little shiny black boy with the ferocious will and the tall blond woman with the resigned demeanor made a strange couple, going everywhere together. Cuff would take him to the city on Sundays to see Nell, but it wasn't the same as having her near. He was inconsolable.

Yes, they had feelings, just like us, she thought, remembering his blasted childhood.

She missed his fiddling in the evenings, missed the doleful African chanting and drumming out in the woods at night (*Hi-a-bomba bomba bomba, Hi-a-bomba bomba bomba*), which he seemed to have been the leader of, for now that he was gone the music, such as it was, had stopped. The woods were silent, reproachful.

"Where was that privateer bound?" she wondered. "To capture Spanish treasure? To Africa to purchase slaves?"

"How would we know? It could be bound anywhere in the world."

"If Africa, will he try to escape again, this time back to his grandfather's village?"

He had no opinion.

"Aren't slaves more trouble than they're worth?" she said.

"They are," he said. "They are nothing but trouble, living and dying." Dina was still dying. She was forty. It was taking her a long time.

Shortly after Caesar ran away, she did die. In expectation, and well before his split big toe had incapacitated him, well before Caesar's disappearance, Cuff had made her coffin, shaped to fit the human form, wide at the shoulders, tapered at the feet.

Tom, her man, and Bill and Pompey dug her grave, in the wooded area down in the ravine behind the church allotted to the slaves. Dressed in their best, the blacks on all the farms about, led by Tom, paraded together to the burial ground, the men carrying the coffin. There they performed what their owners considered to be their heathenish African rites, accompanied by music and chanting and the curious body movements of their dances.

The men lowered the coffin on ropes into the grave, shoveled the dirt back into it, and they all, men, women, and children alike, some of them Dina's children, knelt on the ground to decorate the raw earth with pottery and clamshells and clay pipes. The children wept as they placed the objects on their mother's grave. This was to link the part of her spirit buried in the ground to them above it. Her spirit's other part, they believed, had already gone back to the village on the slave coast whose chieftain had sold her father to a slaver, and where his spirit and those of his ancestors had now reunited with hers.

No white person, not even Marytie, whose faithful servant and friend Dina had been since her childhood, attended the rites. But Marytie paid a sum to Grietje's old Dell for tending the body and decorating it with beads and amulets, after remembered custom, and for the gifts of food and rum that Dell would place on the grave in the morning. And Marytie let them have the gathering after the burial in her house. Of course, she paid the expenses of it, too, which came to a pound, for five quarts of rum, five papers of tobacco and four dozen pipes, and a pound of sugar. They all got very drunk very quickly, however, so that the party ended sooner than they would have liked.

With Dina and Caesar gone, and Cuff laid up, Hagar and Bill now did all the work, neither in a good spirit. Bill was sulky and hostile, Hagar careless. Hagar had discovered New York City and from the Slote caught a sloop there early on Sunday mornings, where in the taverns and grog shops she soon learned to drink and dance, make merry with blacks and poor whites alike. In the city, she found plenty of poor whites who owned no slaves and who thought no one should own them to fill her head with ideas of liberty and fairness, so that she came back to the farm even more indifferent to her duties than when she'd left. Marytie could have sworn she kicked over a pail of soapy water on purpose, one Monday morning.

One of these whites, John Hughson, the tavern keeper, laid on a great feast every Sunday, with mutton and goose on the table and plenty of rum and beer and cider, and this welcoming place became Hagar's favorite destination. Marytie tried to prevent her from going, tried to persuade her to go to church on Sundays, but she did not have the influence on Hagar that she had had on docile, faithful Nelltie and Dina. "Hagar is a different bird," she said to Aeltie.

"Do you blame her?"

"No," said Marytie, "wouldn't I do the same? If I were captured on the banks of the Hudson by an African chieftain and transported to his nation to slave in the hot sun? Wouldn't I run to fellow whites, if I could find them, to hear of liberty and fairness?"

"I would," said Aeltie.

*   *   *   *

Suddenly the year was 1740, and Marytie was sixty-two, Cosyn a year older. She felt strong, still, but it seemed to her that he was growing frail. Not everyone lived to be eighty, after all. His eyes were failing; his hearing too.

"Our lives are dwindling down," she said, walking with him one summer evening along the lane leading to the Hackensack River. "Look how we shuffle along, how we keep our eyes fixed on the lane. We never used to do that."

"I am afraid of falling," he said. "I lose my balance now, feel dizzy."

"How much time do you think is left to us?"

"Less than is behind us," he said. "That we can be sure of."

They tried to imagine their departure from each other. "Who will be left behind?"

"I will go first," he said sturdily.

"And I left behind? No! How would I get on without you?"

"I don't want to be left behind either. So I will go first."

With a moan in common, they turned and clung to each other for a long moment in the dusty lane. His body felt thinner in her arms than it had in the old days, his bones delicate and vulnerable.

"Mijn liefde, mijn lieveling," she whispered, with a catch in her throat.

He wiped his eyes on his shirtsleeve. "I am thinking it is time to make my will," he said.

"Because of the recognition that life is growing short? Or are you ailing?"

"I am fearful that the smallpox will come here," he said. An epidemic was ravaging the provinces. "In some places they say the living are scarcely able to bury the dead, whole families being down at once, and many die unknown to their nearest neighbors."

"Is it that, or is it the slaves?" More and more frequent occurrences of slave unrest were being reported that threatened them all with sudden death.

"I worry about that, too," he admitted. Up and down the coast, not only in New York and New Jersey, but also in Virginia and South Carolina and down through the sugar islands, the slaves were rebelling. "On St. John's, they killed sixty whites; on St. Kitts, they burned six houses before they were stopped."

"Yes, and in Jamaica, it took thousands of English troops to put down an uprising just a few years ago."

"It is very troubling," he said.

"It seems to me," she said, "that if you counted all the years of sullen looks and provocation, of carelessness, deliberate laziness, broken crockery, tools left to rust, all the ways they have of making known their resentment, it seems to me that unrest has underlain everything since at least the failed uprising of 1712."

"You exaggerate," he said.

"I don't. In the old world, they had a Thirty Years' War. Here, looking back, a thirty-years' war has been going on around us and we haven't credited it."

"I don't know about that," he said.

"Didn't the plot four years ago in Antigua in 1736 convince you?" Twelve hundred slaves planned to cache a large amount of gunpowder in the basement of the house where a celebration ball in honor of the King of England's Coronation was to be held. In the midst of it, they planned to blow up the house, slaughter the whites, dignitaries and all, take over the government, and inspire slaves all over the island to rise up as well. "It was discovered in the nick of time."

"It was quickly forgotten," he said.

"Human beings have a convenient capacity for forgetting calamity once it's over," she said. "Just as women forget the pain of childbirth, until the next time."

"Perhaps," he said.

"And what about that uprising on the slaver bound from Africa just a few years ago? That should have made believers of us. The slaves subdued the crew, murdered them in cold blood, and threw the bodies overboard, then sailed the ship back to the port where they had been captured to take their revenge on the chieftains who had sold them to the white men. At the time people said: *if they did that they'll do anything.* Before long, though, they put it out of their minds, forgot about it."

"If you want to know, I have remembered it," he said. "And that is why it is time for me to make my will."

"So it is the slaves, not the smallpox."

"Yes."

The violent uprisings of the past were in the air again. People began to discuss the uprising of 1712 again, out of earshot of the slaves, of course. The failed plot in Antigua in 1736 emerged from more recent memory to haunt daily life. Fear flickered in white hearts.

"Bill is lazy and insolent," he said, "and Hagar's indifference to her work grows every day."

"And that's all part of it," she said. "It's how they tell us that they want to be free. And they mean to be free. They will be free one day."

"Free to rise up and murder us? I never gave them any cause."

"Nevertheless," she insisted, "they are not free and they will not be content until they are."

"Haven't I been a kind master?"

"Yes, you have been a kind master, but they are slaves."

"I let them grow their own food, buy and sell as they can."

"Yes," she said.

"I let the men own guns, hunt and sell the skins, sell their cattail fluff, trade in second-hand clothes, visit their women on Sundays."

"That's true," she said.

"I let Cuff keep Caesar," he said, "even though I could have sold him when he got of useful age. But I kept him on for Cuff's sake. And what good did it do?"

She saw that he was beginning to doubt himself.

He sank into his thoughts, remembering how he gave them Sundays off, and half Saturday too, so they could tend their garden plots. He let them go freely about the farms to see their acquaintances when their work was done, even though it was against the law for them to mingle in groups of more than three, let them go to the city on their days off, and again at Christmas, *Paas*, and especially Pinkster. He had taught Cuff to sail, let him take the yawl across the river when they needed something from Mr. Philipse's mills, take the horse and wagon to Hackensack market to sell the farm's surpluses, buy their necessities, trusted him to come back with the right goods and the right cash. "They have always been deferential to me, hard working, never impudent or thieving. Even Nate, though he chose not to speak, was a hard worker and no threat to life or limb. And old Ben was a paragon. And Nelltie and Dina never gave us any trouble."

"Yes, but Caesar and Hagar and Bill are different," she said.

"Yes," he finally admitted, wearily, "it has perhaps been a thirty-years' war, right under our noses."

And yes, it was perhaps time to get his affairs in order. The most conservative and cautious of the four brothers, he was the first of them to make his will. They had all put it off out of superstition, unwilling to draw the attention of the watchful Reaper to their persons. But it was time now.

"Please," she said. "Don't leave it all to me. That's the old Dutch way."

"I mean to do it no other way," he said stiffly. He went to a man of law and in old-fashioned Dutch style, he declared her, his dearly beloved wife, his executrix and sole heir. This meant that, before their three surviving children got title to his property, even his only son to the farm where he lived, she, Marytie Blauvelt, was to have legal title to it all: the farm where Jan and Aeltie lived, the salt meadows on the Hudson, the woodlots on the mountain, the land on the Hackensack designated for Margrietje and Marretje and for poor dead Maria's two children, and of course the farm where she and he lived and all its appurtenances. She was also to have all his moveable estate and all the profits arising from the same. In order of their value, his slaves, livestock, paper currency, notes, bonds, cash, house, house furnishings, and farm equipment were to be hers and hers alone until her death, provided she did not remarry, which of course was unthinkable, and not only because of her age.

"I wish he hadn't," she fretted to her children. "You should own your farms now, not have to wait till I'm dead and gone. That is the modern way."

"He did it to ensure that we will continue after his death to revere you," Jan said.

"You would anyway," she said.

"It's best to have it in writing," he said.

"The old ways die hard," she said to Aeltie. "I will be a rich old widow if he goes first. But without the slaves to make it all possible, he wouldn't have it to bestow on me in the first place, and we all know it."

"They know it too," Aeltie said.

*   *   *   *

Just around the time that Cosyn wrote his last will and testament, a rumor floated through the city and countryside that King George had ordered the slaves in his American colonies freed. Yet the Royal Governor in New York, George Clarke, refused to issue the proclamation, for fear, it was said, of a mad rabble of embittered whites, their property turned free, rising up to overthrow his government, burn down his mansion, cut his throat.

The slaves had heard the rumor, too, and since the Governor would not fulfill the King's law, the slaves decided to take matters into their own hands. In the taverns and grog shops where they met, even though it was against the law, they concocted a plot. Their plot was that every male slave rise at midnight and cut the throats of his master and his master's sons, set all the houses and barns on fire, and the next day, in daylight, so they could plainly see what they were doing and who they were doing it to—and relish the terror it aroused—ravish the women and girls, and then ride the best saddle horses in the barns toward the Indians in French country—and freedom.

As in Antigua, the plot was discovered by the merest of chances, and about thirty conspirators were arrested. The authorities cut the ears off some of them, and some escaped with a whipping. Such light punishments were not enough to fit such a dreadful crime, they knew. But slaves were valuable property. As the owners reasoned, who would do the work if they were dead?

Only if the deed was heinous enough was their monetary value overlooked, as when, a few years after that aborted uprising in 1712, two slaves on Long Island were executed for attempting to poison their masters with arsenic. And then, one day, not long after he made his will, Cosyn came home from Hackensack with a dreadful new tale. "Do you remember Scipio?"

"Caesar's friend?"

"Yes." She knew him by sight. What had he done? She could tell by his voice and his tone that it was something dreadful. "What?" she said, trembling with fear. "Tell me!"

"He sank an ax to the full extent of its bit into the back of his master's six-year-old son," he said in a dull voice.

She grabbed onto a chair back for support.

"He cleaved his torso in two."

She began to shake, felt she was going to faint.

"Then he set fire to the barn and over a thousand bushels of grain stored in it."

"No," she moaned, feeling sick. "No. That little child. That innocent child."

No light punishment for that evil one. He was burned at the stake without further ado.

*   *   *   *

It came to a head in 1741, the year of the so-called great slave conspiracy that submersed all New York in panic and hysteria. It came at the end of a bitter cold winter, the coldest anyone could remember. "Roaring winds from the north are bringing such a frigid cold that the ink in my well freezes solid, even though I sit before a blazing fire," Marytie wrote in her diary. "Ten feet of snow has fallen and buried small houses and their occupants almost entirely. We cannot get to our necessaries; our houses have become disgusting stink pits of overflowing chamber pots."

It was so cold, and the people burned so much wood to keep warm that one and all were afraid they would run out of it. The rivers froze solid. Even New York harbor froze. Before the snow got too deep, men drove teams of horses from Staten Island up the Hudson as far as they cared to go. Animals froze to death where they stood, their carcasses not discovered until spring.

"Fires are a danger, as we huddle inside our houses, trying to warm ourselves around our hearths," she wrote. "The hearths roar and snap with hazards: burning coals flying up the chimney and landing on the roof, or hurtling through the room at night to light on bedding or a window curtain." The cold sucked the moisture out of frame buildings in the city, rendering them so much tinder.

What led to the conspiracy that fateful year? Was it the hardships of that winter? Was it one more generation of those born into slavery finally rising up to say *no more*? Or was it the visit of the evangelist George Whitefield to New York the summer before that spurred the conspiracy of the slaves and their poor-white sympathizers? This is what Marytie thought was the cause of it.

George Whitefield called not for the end of slavery; the time was not yet ripe for that. But he did call for the humane treatment of slaves. In an open letter to New Yorkers, he declared that in the south dogs were treated better than slaves. It was odd, he went on in his provocative way, that down there they don't rise up more often against their owners. Inflammatory talk. New Yorkers protested angrily that they treated their slaves as well and better than dogs. And they probably did. But it moved the discussion along.

From his open-air pulpit on scaffolding set up on the Common, the preacher bellowed that slaves should be instructed in the Christian religion and baptized.

"That is tantamount to saying they should be freed," people shouted back at him. For it was still a question that had never really been settled in Christian hearts. Despite the law to the contrary, there was serious doubt that a Christian could be a slave.

What really killed her beloved husband, Marytie often thought afterward, was the dreadful plot of the slaves in 1741. He was never the same after it. He declined steadily, and he died a broken man about two years after it was declared to be over. It was at first impossible for him to take it in that his slaves hated him so much that they would do what it was said that they would have done had they not been discovered in time.

"Our slaves were not involved in it," she said. "As far as we know."

"I was good to them," he kept saying. He took it as personal treachery, what they did, or planned to do, even if they weren't his own.

But in the end he finally came to understand that their precious dream, *their Eden*, their paradise had been poisoned from the start. "Our paradise is their hell," he said slowly, one day. He finally saw what she had been trying to make him see, that the uprising of 1712 had been only the first event in a generation of rebellion by enslaved people who refused in the end to be enslaved. It saddened him, tarnished his opinion of himself and all he had accomplished in his life. He felt humbled and humiliated by his own obtuseness.

No one ever knew for sure if there really was a plot, for in fact they did not carry it off, their terrible plan. In fact, the whole insurrection may have been just their *pijp droom*, their pipe dream, as the English called it, their fantasy of getting back that freedom they or their parents or grandparents once had known.

If he had learned of it, plot or not, it certainly would have killed Cuff, had he not died long before it of his infected leg, for who should be one of the prominent leaders of the insurrection but Caesar.

      *   *   *   *

Yes, Caesar had come back, but not to them. He had returned to New York after a few years at sea and, with forged papers, hired himself out as a freedman to a baker in the Out Ward. But this man, Vaarck, discovered his identity, and, as the law required, Vaarck informed his rightful owner. Cosyn would have none of the *verrader* traitor and troublemaker. He never wanted to see him again. He sold him to Vaarck for the going rate, sixty pounds, minus the unusually handsome twenty-pound reward he had offered when the scoundrel ran away.

His woman having died while he was on the high seas, although their bastard twins had survived, Caesar soon took up with a comely red-haired Irish prostitute named Peggy Kerry. Peggy was the worst sort of prostitute, it was said, a prostitute to negroes, but she gave up her trade when she met Caesar. She soon had a child by Caesar. Which meant that Caesar had three children that they knew of, two legally theirs of his first woman and living on their farm, cared for by the lackadaisical Hagar, and one in the city legally Vaarck's. Vaarck reported to Cosyn that Caesar paid Peggy's room and board in John Hughson's increasingly infamous tavern and visited her and their pretty little mulatto daughter after dark, when he had finished Vaarck's work.

"Why is his tavern so infamous?" Aeltie asked.

"Because he lets blacks cavort in it," Marytie said, "Slave and free together, and black and white together, too."

"It is where Hagar goes," Cosyn said.

"And where Eliza, big with child, has been seen, going in and out," Marytie said sadly.

*   *   *   *

The negro plot to burn the city, kill all the slave owners, and ravish their women-folk began to be found out on March 18, 1741, when Lt. Governor Clarke's fine house in the Fort went up in flames. By the end of the day all the buildings in Fort George were in ashes, and arson was suspected.

A series of fires over the next few weeks heightened suspicions into assumptions. The residents now believed for a certainty that it was arson, and that the slaves had done it. The city shivered in a turmoil of fear. The whites remembered that Charleston had gone up in flames just months before. Three hundred houses had burned to the ground in that unfortunate city, along with goods worth 250,000 pounds. This disaster was never attributed to negroes rising. But no one could be completely sure of the cause, either. "Charleston is on its guard, and now New York is, too," Cosyn said gloomily. "And so should we be on ours, even here in the countryside."

No sooner had he said this than news flashed over the region that seven barns in nearby Hackensack had gone on fire. Jack and Ben, friends of Caesar's, and well known to all of Bergen County as the surly property of Albert van Voorhezen and Derrick van Horn, were promptly burned at the stake before a great crowd. Slaveowners in Orange and Bergen counties shivered in their boots—and kept their muskets loaded and to hand and their doors locked tight.

Then a fire broke out in Pearl Street, near the mansion of Adolph Philipse, and Philipse's slave Cuffee was observed running from the scene. "The negroes are rising!" someone screamed. "The negroes are rising!"

Cuffee was seized and thrown into jail, along with a dozen or so other blacks apprehended by raging mobs of vigilantes.

A frightened City Council examined them, but found no evidence. The Lt. Governor appointed Daniel Horsmanden, a justice of the Supreme Court of the Province of New York, to look into the rumors of insurrection.

John Hughson was a prime suspect, because it was known that he sold liquor to blacks in his tavern, a crime, and it was said that he even fenced their stolen goods, a worse crime. All remembered that in the bitter cold winter just passed, Hughson and his wife, along with Caesar and his friend Prince, were accused of robbing one Robert Hogg. Hughson's servant, Mary Burton, white, had made the accusation against the four and had implicated as well Peggy Kerry. Mary Burton had it in for Peggy Kerry, because she had consorted with negroes for pay. Or so she told Eliza Shaw, who lived in a miserable little room under the eaves of the tavern and worked in the kitchen for Hughson's wife.

Daniel Horsmanden soon discovered that Hughson had a grudge against the rich people who made their negroes work too hard. He was said to have been overheard inciting his black friends to burn down the houses of the rich and kill them all, as had been the plan in the failed uprising of 1712, an uprising now much on everyone's minds.

The Lt. Governor announced rewards: 100 pounds to whites for evidence; forty-five pounds to free blacks or Indians for evidence; and twenty pounds, plus manumission, to slaves for evidence.

With these handsome incentives, evidence (or as some put it later, "evidence") began to pour in, of course. Trials started at the end of April. On May 1, Marytie heard that, on the basis of Mary Burton's evidence, no doubt sweetened by the promise of release from her indenture to Hughson, Caesar and Prince were found guilty of robbery and thrown into jail, a place familiar to Caesar who had been arrested before for burglary, and even condemned to death for it, burglary by slaves being a capital crime. He had been lucky that time. They had let him go. They would not make that mistake again.

Mary Burton was ordered to testify before Daniel Horsmanden's grand jury about the March and April fires, and about other matters. Brimming with self-importance, she testified in great detail. And of course her testimony was reinforced by the testimonies of slaves eager for that twenty-pound reward and their manumission. They were only too willing to report to the authorities how Hughson and his black conspirators kissed the Catholic Bible, brandished knives, and stepped inside a chalk circle on the floor of Hughson's alehouse, swearing allegiance to each other and to their cause until death, if need be. A friend of Hughson's, they testified, was said to be a Roman Catholic priest, who baptized blacks within that circle of chalk, assuring them that a baptized person could not be a slave. On these testimonies, perhaps perjured, people later thought, the Hughsons and Peggy were found guilty of receiving stolen goods and condemned to die by hanging.

But they were not the first to die. On May 10 Caesar and Prince were condemned to hang for burglary. Witnesses—fellow slaves and one-time friends—had testified that Caesar and Prince planned to burn the city to the ground and all the white slave owners with it. They testified that Hughson was to become King and Caesar Governor of New York, after the plot had driven the English out of the colony. But as the court could find no proof of these heinous claims, although it tried its best, burglary was fixed upon as the logical charge to be rid of the troublemakers.

When the news reached Tappan, as it did on the first tide, Marytie and Aeltie hurried to the city to see Caesar for the last time. Proud and mute on the scaffold, he refused to confess, ignored his interlocutor, ignored the hangman, his vengeful eyes darting about the crowd. His eyes lit on Marytie and stayed fixed on her face while the hangman tied the noose around his neck and pulled it tight against his ear.

He was accusing her of something. She felt it. He was saying she had failed him.

She remembered his whole life. She was present at his birth, rocked him in her arms when he screamed with colic, took him to be baptized, cleaned his cuts and salved his bruises, comforted him for the mother sold away from him, became his mother, taught him to read and write, berated him for his laziness and impudence, bought him peppermints to get back on his good side, tried to make a good and useful slave of him. She had failed in that, and she had failed him too, and that was worse.

The platform gave way with a loud bang, and he swung, his eyes popping out of his head. Beside him, Prince followed immediately. Their dead bodies were left on the scaffold on a little island in the Fresh Water Pond, within sight of Grietje Cosyns' former buckwheat fields. Marytie went home, sorely troubled.

After Caesar hanged, Cuffee, Adolph Philipse's slave, and Quack, property of John Roosevelt, were next. It was reported at their trial that Cuffee had said that "a great many people had too much, and others too little," and that his master "had a great deal of money, but in a short time should have less." They had no legal counsel, only the lukewarm testimony of their owners, and their friends, who were no friends, as it turned out. The jury in a trice pronounced them guilty, and Horsmanden as quickly pronounced their sentence: Death by fire. Chained to the stake with the bonfire flickering around their feet, Cuffee and Quack confessed to the crime they had been charged with: the burning of the Fort. They begged for mercy, but the crowd wanted to see them up in flames, and the Court thought it the better part of valor not to disappoint the crowd.

The deaths of Caesar and Prince and the Hughsons and Peggy and Cuffee and Quack were not enough. More, many more, were required before the city was appeased. In all thirty-five persons were either hanged or burned at the stake. Seventy-two blacks were banished to the West Indies and farther places.

The trials continued. Proof positive of the plot that had begun to unravel in March was pronounced in mid-June, while Caesar's body and Prince's still swung from the scaffold, and black gangs were everywhere, committing robbery and mayhem. Crime and revolution, it seemed, went hand in hand. By this time, every slave in New York, and there were more than 2,000 of them, was suspected of being involved in the conspiracy, and half of the city's male slaves over the age of sixteen languished in jail.

"Now," people said, with the benefit of hindsight, "how imprudent was the policy of seasoning the Africans in the Sugar Islands while they learned to obey their masters and to speak some Dutch or English. They learned there dangerous things as well."

Yes, rebellion was in the air in New York now as it had been down there and was again. Anthony Ward's slave Will, it was reported in the papers, had been involved in two conspiracies, the uprisings on St. John's and in Antigua. He was burned at the stake, confessing at the last minute that Moore's Cato had advised him to bring in many negroes to the plot. He must say, Cato told him, that he had set his master's house on fire, which would make the judges believe him. And so he said it. But was it the truth? Not even the justices were sure. "So rare it is to get the truth from these wretches," they complained.

The authorities passed laws to regulate the taverns and grog shops where the plotters met, duplicating laws already on the books, the serving of liquor to slaves was strictly forbidden (hardly for the first time), and the illegal receipt of goods stolen by slaves from their masters for the fencing of them was again made punishable by death. Other redundant laws were passed forbidding slaves to congregate on the Sabbath, to move about at night, to gather in groups of more than three, to gather for the purposes of gambling. But they were also ignored. And no law could regulate the whispered meetings that took place on street corners or in the fields where they continued to gather clandestinely out of sight of the authorities. Or meetings in the homes of free negroes. It was reported that Otello and Braveboy had been overheard plotting together by the Dutch Church after a frolic at some free negro's house in Bowery-land.

"All is changed," Marytie mourned. "Our lovely world is ruined. Beyond repair."

CHAPTER 10

▼

ELIZA

It took Thomas Pyke three midday meals, two evening meals, and a matter of claret to induce Eliza to visit his rooms over the shop. Climbing the narrow stairs behind him, she knew, even though she was a little tiddly from the wine, exactly what she was doing, and exactly what to expect once she entered the small dark room. Here he at once divested her of her cloak and the red satin kerchief that covered her voluptuous bosom.

He put his arms around her and began to kiss her mouth hungrily. She responded, but not too eagerly at first. She did not want him to think she was a loose woman, for she was not. She was a woman who wanted a husband in ruffles, a man who would provide her with a roof over her head and three meals a day. In return for which she was willing to do what he wanted, even to work for him, with or without pay.

Because he owned a shop, she had hoped that he would ask her to work in it, once she had given herself to him, and she in fact had already put this idea in his head over one of their intimate dinners. "I have experience behind the counter," she had said with great dignity. She was dissembling, of course. She was thinking of Margaret Blauvelt's parents' store at the Slote, where her experience consisted of looking longingly at the goods she would have liked to have been able to purchase.

He fumbled with the stays that pressed her sumptuous breasts high, and, breathing hard, released these warm pink globes from her bodice and slipped her out of her dress and her shift, until she stood quite naked before him. He was panting. He stripped off his own clothing, flinging it here and there about the room, and naked led her into the other room, his bed chamber, and laid her on the bed. He lavished his kisses on her face and throat and breasts, his member hard against her stomach, and she began to breathe hard, too, and pant, and then he entered her. She uttered a little scream, for it was her first time, with a man, and much different from Sarah's sweet petting.

They were inseparable after that. She moved into the rooms with him, and she worked during the day in the shop below, opening packages from his partner in London, charming English china, silver objects, bolts of fine linen and silk. Just the sorts of lovely things she used to steal, when she started out in the city. When business was slow, he would lock the door, draw the curtain over the window and make love to her standing up in a corner of the shop, or draw her upstairs where they would play games with each other to their hearts' delight, naked in the bed.

She was in love, for the first time. Cornelis was only a faded memory. Thomas was the real thing.

There was one matter she did not like. He wanted to pay her for her hours working in the shop, but he had an odd way of doing so. Instead of wages at the end of the week, he laid a shilling or two, or a crown, or a pound, depending on the sex of the night before, or for that matter, that morning, on the little table on her side of the bed, larger amounts for those times when she did what he especially wanted, taking his member in her mouth, allowing him to enter her from the rear.

She didn't care for these acts, or for this system of payment; it smacked of prostitution. But he just laughed when she protested. It reinforced for him that she was not a greedy girl, which he knew from having to coax her to perform the higher, or should he say the lower, offices, or the higher paid ones in any case. After a while she got used to it. She did not want to be a trouble to him. She was happy. Yes, for the first time in her life she felt happy! She tucked the coins in the silk pocket she wore around her waist over her petticoat and kept her own counsel. She wanted him to marry her, which he had promised he would do.

In the meantime, she wanted to dally with him on his bed, wantonly touch him where he wanted it most, kiss him all over, being kissed in return all over, talking together in the dead of night. Oh, it was sweet to sport on the bed with her darling, toying and playing without a care in the world. She lay with him thirty times, she estimated, before she became pregnant.

"I am with child, Thomas," she said shyly, one morning.

He looked decidedly unhappy at this news. "Do you want to get rid of it?" he asked glumly.

"Of course not! What an idea. I think we should marry. It's time."

He groaned. He sat up on the edge of the bed, doubled over in misery, his head in his hands. "I can't bear it," he said.

"Can't bear what?"

"My responsibilities."

"What do you mean?"

"My partner, in London. It's my wife. I'm already married, well and good."

"What!"

"I should have told you," he said, looking shamefaced.

She felt faint and clutched her head to steady it. "What!" she cried. "What did you say?"

"I'm sorry," he said. "I can't bear any more responsibility in this life of mine. You'll have to go."

"Go? Go where?"

"Go back to where you came from. Go back to your home."

"You're mad!" she screamed. "I can never go home!"

"It's customary that a young woman in your predicament can count on her family for support, especially if the father of the child is unable, as I am," he said coldly.

"You have no idea what my father is like," she cried in anguish. "He would kill me."

"Many young women have children out of wedlock," he said. "It happens all the time."

At this she swooned, the morning sickness coming upon her at the same time and making her feel so nauseated that she was sure she would faint away.

She rolled to the edge of the bed and sat up beside him and buried her head in her hands until the nausea passed.

"You'll have to go, Eliza," he said gently. "My wife is coming here next month. I was going to tell you. It was just a matter of time."

She began to weep. "I am going to tell her," she said. "I am going to tell her what kind of man you are."

"I think she already knows that," he said, with a laugh. "She's as bad as I am."

*   *   *   *

In a panic, Eliza packed her few things and caught a ferry to Tappan. What else could she do?

Her father strode across the room to her and struck her across her face. "You abominable fornicator," he said, white with rage. "You detestable, odious sinner."

Her mother wailed and wrung her hands.

"Filthy dalliance," her father said, as cold as ice. "You are to blame. You let him have carnal knowledge of you. You enflamed his lust with your lascivious carriage."

Her mother, weeping, said, "Your intimacy necessitates your being married, which I hope you have decided upon."

"He is already married," Eliza said dully.

"You loose vain wretch. You common harlot," her father said, with venom so deadly it seemed to hang in the air like a poisonous cloud.

She moved back to Hughson's tavern and took up her work in the kitchen again. She could think of nothing else she could do.

"Nothing else! Nothing else!" she sobbed, as she washed the greasy pewter plates and tankards in the dark scullery.

At Hughson's she had friends, at least. The sundry assortment of servants and slaves, and of course Hughson himself, and his wife and daughters, and Caesar and Peggy Kerry, and Mary Burton, and her old love mate Sarah; they were her friends and became her family of sorts.

Caesar was kind. He remembered her from the Slote, where he had often seen her on the wharf staring moodily out across the wide Tappan Zee like a lost soul. "You have legal rights," he told her. "You can accuse him before the court, and the court will make him pay you for seducing you with his falsehoods and flatteries."

"But before you go to court, go to him," Hughson advised. "Threaten to name him. He will pay you on the side rather than have his name known."

"What is his punishment?" she asked.

"There is none," Hughson said. "In the old days, they would have forced him to marry you, or charged him a fine, or whipped him. But things are looser now. It's no longer a crime."

"What if he doesn't pay me?"

"The law says he must pay half of the costs of the lying in and half of the annual support for four years."

She moaned, felt faint. "What if he doesn't pay?"

"Then you will be sent to the workhouse, for the child will be a public charge. You will work until it is old enough to earn its keep."

"What if he flees?"

Hughson shrugged. "It's common that they do," he said.

She went to see Thomas Pyke. "My good name and estate should not depend upon the mere word of a lewd woman," he said coldly, all their ardent lovemaking and wanton sporting forgotten. It broke her heart. She wept in front of him, but he was implacable.

When Marytie learned of the girl's predicament, she decided to intervene. In better families, when this happened, fathers paid their daughters' fines and supported them at home until they married. She went to see Eliza's mother. "If she fell on her knees and humbled herself to her father, would he take her in?"

"No," Hannah said. "He is a hard-hearted man. He is a hater with a long memory for what he hates."

"Will he not even confront Thomas Pyke to persuade him to pay?"

Hannah shook her head. "No."

"Will you?"

She hesitated. "If he doesn't come to know," she said.

"He won't know from me," Marytie said.

Together they went to New York and found Eliza, convinced her to let her mother help her to get a signed statement from Thomas Pyke ensuring the child's upkeep.

Marytie laid it out for them. "There are three possibilities," she said. "You can try to get a private agreement between him and Eliza arranging payments. Or Eliza can go before a jury and confess to fornication, which can lead to a ruling that he pay her costs and upkeep. Or failing that, you can bring a civil lawsuit to win maintenance. The private agreement is the best."

"Yes. A private agreement."

They went to his shop and confronted him. "If she goes to court, Thomas Pyke," Marytie said, looking him straight in the eye, "as a married man convicted of fornication with a single woman, you will be forbidden by the court to sell your property until your wife is granted a divorce and a settlement is secured."

He laughed. "Suppose she don't want a divorce," he said.

"Unless a private agreement can be arranged," said Marytie coldly, "it will be necessary to force you to acknowledge your paternity before witnesses."

"Why should I be persecuted for the mere act of begetting my own likeness?" he snarled. "She suffered me to have carnal knowledge of her body and she should be fined for her transgression."

"Be a man," said Marytie harshly.

Furiously, he took his wallet out of his pocket. He handed Eliza a wad of money. "Now be gone with you," he said, trying to usher them out of his store.

"Not so fast," said Marytie. She counted the money. "Twenty pounds," she said. "It is not sufficient. I have a paper for you to sign." She took it out of her pocket and handed it to him. "Sign this," she said.

He read the paper. "Twenty pounds a year for twelve years! You must be mad," he said.

"Sign it, or we will go before a jury. You will not be treated with sympathy, I can assure you."

"Take it back," he said, handing the paper to her. "And catch me if you can." This time he did manage to push them out of the store. He locked the door behind him and closed the curtains.

Months before the child was born, he closed the shop and disappeared from the city.

CHAPTER 11

▼

CHANGE

Margaret Blauvelt was sixteen in the spring of 1741, when Caesar swung from the gibbet. She was living in the city in the household of Johannes Blauvelt, her uncle, his harried wife having been delivered of her sixth child that spring. She was not a good manager, that aunt, Rachel Demarest. She was a nervous, anxious woman, given to bursts of tears and, ever since the electrifying evangelist George Whitefield had put them into her mind, overly concerned with disturbing thoughts of her eternal welfare. Further, she missed the country. Her husband had rashly sold his blacksmith shop in Tappan and moved the family to the city where he found work with a relative as a cooper. Having to learn a whole new trade at his age was neither wise nor easy.

With a new baby to care for, and only one lazy and indifferent slave in the house, and no mother or sisters or friends near by, she needed help.

"It is a perfect fit for me," Margaret announced to her family. "I will watch aunt's little boys in return for my room and board."

Her mother protested. "You are but sixteen."

"I am finished with my schooling, and I am in no hurry to marry," Margaret said. "I want to see the world a bit first." She wanted to leave the dull country for the city where she could perhaps listen to that exciting preacher, if he should come again, listen to him harangue the crowds on the Commons with their sinful ways and certain path to hell. Her mother and father and brother and she had all been to hear him the year before, when he first came, and he had impressed her so much with his eloquent rhetoric and his electrifying twin messages of doom and hope that she had been thinking of him for a year, wanted to hear him again. And again.

She begged and wheedled until she got her way. "For the summer, then," her father said. "Just for the summer."

She meant well. She really did intend to watch the little boys and play with them and teach them useful things. But then the conspiracy trials in the negro plot started, and they were even more fascinating than George Whitefield. She ended by spending more time watching the trials than she did the children. In fact, before long, she turned the boys over to their sisters, Grietje and Brechtie, who were old enough to mind them anyway, in her opinion, at thirteen and fifteen.

In the crowd that day in May of 1741, when Caesar swung, his eyes bugging out of his head, Margaret spied her great-aunt Marytie Blauvelt, and Marytie's daughter-in-law Aeltie, their eyes riveted on the figure on the gibbet. She recalled fondly her two summers with Marytie, when she was twelve and thirteen, and how she had "set her cap" for Marytie's grandson, that handsome Johannes with the green eyes and the thick, dark mop falling over his forehead. She had to laugh now to remember that childish infatuation. But, then, remembering it made her remember again what it was she had liked about him, and how the sight of him had once made her heart thump. She dashed across the street to catch up with them as they made their way through the crowd back toward the ferry.

"Marytie!" she called.

"My dear!" said Marytie, turning, almost forgetting the girl's name, she was so grown up, and Marytie so addled from the sight of Caesar hanged.

"Margaret Blauvelt!" said Aeltie.

"Margaret!" Marytie said. She was rejoiced to see her niece again, but she was in such a fearful state of agitation about Caesar that she could talk of nothing else. "I knew him from birth," she said, over and over again, as if she couldn't really believe it. "I knew him from birth. I tried to teach him. I tried to help him." She was beyond distraught.

Margaret saw it was not the ideal time for her to inquire into the whereabouts of her aunt's grandson (the last she had heard he was reading law in Hackensack, or was it theology?). But it did enter her mind that day, at sixteen, that she might one day marry him, after all.

That evening, she confided this to her aunt and uncle. "Stranger things have happened," said her uncle. "And there is, keep in mind," he said, "that matter of the fine farm he will one day come into, and its appurtenances, and the slaves, and of course your generous dowry to complement what he brings to you."

"Yes," she said thoughtfully. "There are those practical things to keep in mind." When the trials were over, she promised herself, she would go home and look for him to see if he still made her heart race.

The trials were held in the City Hall, an imposing building at the corner of Wall and Broad streets. Outside of it, in front of the triple arches and long-windowed façade, stood a cage for holding prisoners, a whipping post, a pillory, and stocks. The magnificent building was topped by a handsome cupola, which held a bell and a four-sided clock, and was guarded by a rooster weather vane. Living birds made it their own.

The Supreme Court was in the east wing on the second floor. Judges in gray wigs and black robes presided. The Grand Jury of seventeen men occupied the jury box, and the spectators arrayed themselves on backless benches below the judges' bench or up in the balcony. Margaret preferred the balcony, where like one of those birds in the belfry she could gaze down upon the proceedings.

She haunted the courtroom. As often as they were held that summer, which was nearly every day, she went to hear the plotters, said to have intended to burn the city to the ground, kill all the white men, and most astoundingly ravish, nay, *marry* their widows and daughters, defend themselves; they were denied legal counsel.

Her cousins with the little boys in tow accompanied her at first, glad to get away from their fretful, distracted mother and her colicky baby. But Margaret, the volunteer caregiver, soon turned over the supervision of them to their sisters, so absorbed did she become in the trials. (She made it up to her aunt in the evenings by ironing and sewing for her, tasks she liked for their mindlessness; she could think her own thoughts while she carried them out.) The girls soon grew bored with the court doings and wandered off to let their brothers climb trees on the Commons.

So Margaret had her days to herself. Day after day, she listened carefully to the justices' descriptions of what they called the "monstrous ingratitude of the black tribe," to their conviction that slavery among the Dutch and English of the city was generally softened with great indulgence. "Our slaves live without care, and are commonly better fed and clothed, and put to less labor than the poor of most Christian countries," the justices declared. "They are indeed slaves; there is no doubt of that. But they are under the protection of the law. None can hurt them with impunity. They are really more *happy* in this place than in the midst of the plunder, cruelty, and rapine of their native countries."

"They don't seem happy to me," she said to her uncle one evening.

"What do they know about happiness?" he said gruffly. "They're little better than animals."

"Animals are happy," she said.

He stared at her. "What makes you think that?"

"They look so, well fed, running free through the fields, gamboling where they may."

"Running free? Gamboling where they may? The fields are fenced," he snorted.

"I see your point," she said. The animals weren't free. They only thought they were. The slaves knew the difference. So how could they be happy? That was *her* point, but it did not seem fruitful to pursue it.

Every day, the justices expressed their indignation that, notwithstanding all the kindness and tenderness with which the slaves were treated, they were ungrateful. "Let us not forget that this is the second attempt this brutish and bloody species of mankind have made within one age," they cried, the now vividly remembered uprising in 1712 being the first. "The punishments meted out then, and the innocent blood spilt in the streets, should have been a perpetual terror to those that survived the vengeance of that day, should have been a warning to all that came after them." But apparently it had not been, ungrateful, silly, unthinking creatures that they were.

"I fear, gentlemen," intoned the justice Frederick Philipse, at the trial of Quack and Cuffee, "that we shall never be quite safe until that wicked race are under more restraint, or their number greatly reduced within this city. Bring in your verdict accordingly," he advised the jury, "and do what in you lies to rid this country of some of the vilest creatures in it."

"But how to rid the country of them?" she whispered to the woman sitting beside her. "Put them under *more* restraint?"

The woman stared at her.

"Make harsher laws?" she whispered.

"Are you a troublemaker?" the woman said. She didn't whisper. She gathered her skirts and moved away from Margaret to another part of the balcony.

Burn and hang and banish more of them? she wondered, wandering back through the pretty, tree-lined streets to her uncle's house after the proceedings. Or import fewer of them? That would be her choice, she decided, if she were in charge of making decisions.

She brought her lunch with her to the courts, and one day while she sat on a bench under a sassafras tree in front of the building ruminating over her bread and cheese, she saw her old friend Eliza! Eliza had broken her mother's heart by running away with her ferryman one dark night, never to return to live on the spar *kill*. Now here she was sashaying across the yard in front of the court on the arm of a man. A repellant memory stirred. Margaret had seen this man before.

She stared at the man, dumbfounded. He had noticed her before Eliza did. "Well, if it isn't Dutchie," he said, coming up to her with an insinuating grin on his ruddy face. "What brings you to the big city?" She felt that powerful contraction in her throat again, remembered the dog having his way on her leg.

"Margaret!" Eliza cried, breaking away from him.

"Eliza!" She jumped up and ran to her, putting her back to the man to shut him out of her vision. "What are you doing here? Where have you been all this time?"

They embraced. "How you have grown," Eliza said, standing back to look at her. "You are quite a woman now, Little One."

"And how you have grown," Margaret said. She was big with child.

Eliza laughed. "Five months gone," she said. "This is Danny. We are planning to be married."

Danny. She had never known his name. He grinned at her in a knowing way, as if he were privy to her deepest secrets.

She turned her back on him again. "I thought you were married," Margaret stammered. "To Cornelis."

"Cornelis ran away," Eliza said shortly.

"But Cuff said you were with child when he saw you."

Eliza looked daggers at Danny, who was laughing. "That was someone else," she said. "I learned too late he was married to another."

"You should have asked," said Danny. "What did you expect?"

Eliza ignored him. "Are you here for the trials, Little One?" she asked.

"Yes. I come every day."

"Then I shall come, too. Tomorrow. We will have a good talk. Catch up on all the news."

"Without Danny, I hope," Margaret whispered in her ear as they said goodbye. Eliza winked.

But she didn't come the next day, or for days to follow. Margaret moved down from the balcony to the floor of the courtroom, where Eliza could more easily spot her if she walked in, and looked hopefully for her every time the courtroom door opened.

On June 1, two days after Quack and Cuffee were burned at the stake, and while Caesar's corpse still dangled in the wind, the magistrates planned to examine Sarah, Mr. Burk's negro wench. And finally, that day, Eliza came into the court and found Margaret and sat beside her on the bench. She looked pale and wasted.

"Where have you been? What has happened to you?"

"I lost the baby," she said dully. "I made a drink of tansy and brought it off. And I got rid of Danny too. I hate him. He's a fool."

Margaret's head whirled. It was hard for her to take in how fast things happened in Eliza's life. Compared to her uneventful existence, Eliza's was a storm of lurid experience. Three lovers already, and only nineteen years old. And a child and now an abortion. *Where is that child anyway?* Margaret wondered.

"It's not my first with him," Eliza said. "I lost another when it was three months along. I guess I'm not fated to be the mother of his children, thank goodness. Or of any children, I hope." She laughed.

"What about the one you had?" Margaret asked. "When Cuff saw you?"

The judges scowled at them. And later, it occurred to Margaret that Eliza did not answer that question.

At the lunch break, they went outside. "You look so tired," Margaret said.

"I am tired," Eliza said. "I work like a slave."

"Why aren't you working today?"

"I don't have to this week," she said. "I got Danny to pay the room rent when I lost the baby. Though if I had told him how I lost it, he wouldn't have paid."

"How will you pay the rent with Danny gone?"

Eliza shrugged. "I'll have to steal something," she said. "And sell it to a fence I know."

Margaret was shocked again. "Steal!"

"You'd do it, too," said Eliza grimly. "If you had to."

"Maybe I would," Margaret said. "Life is hard without a family behind you."

"Family," Eliza snorted. "I came today because I know Sarah," she said softly. "She's been my family. She's been my good friend these four years. She took me into her bed when Cornelis left me up the creek."

"You slept in a bed with a slave?" Margaret was horrified.

"It's better than the street," said Eliza. "And I did more than sleep in the bed with her." She smiled at the memories. "She taught me the pleasures of my own body in Mr. Burk's garret."

Margaret was shocked again. "How could you?"

Eliza laughed. "Have you ever tried it?" she said.

Margaret blushed at the idea. "Of course not!"

"You might like it," Eliza said. "I did."

"I don't think so!"

"Her father was a white man," Eliza said. "It makes her wild to think of it—a slave to Mr. Burk because of a white man. When she's no darker than you or me."

The clerk banged on his desk for quiet, and Mr. Justice Chambers stepped up to the jury, gesturing toward Sarah in the witness box. "Mr. Burk's Sarah," he said, "is one of the oddest animals among the black confederates that you can imagine. She is a creature of outrageous spirit who, when she was first interrogated, denied knowing anything of the matter. But," he added darkly, pointing at her, "she is here today because I am convinced she does know of it."

At this, as the courtroom watched in fascination, Sarah threw herself into a fit of violent agitations, shaking, panting, and yelping. The fit reminded Eliza of Sarah's self-agitated pleasurings in the bed they'd shared, the panting, the cries, the yelps, the huge sighs of gratification at the end when her body shuddered from head to toe. To the consternation of the courtroom, she now foamed at the mouth and uttered a string of bitter imprecations. Margaret covered her ears with her hands to shut out the cursing.

"Remove her!" roared Justice Chambers.

Eliza chuckled. "She's putting it on," she whispered.

The histrionics ended as suddenly as they had begun. Sarah heaved a huge gratified sigh, and turned around to beam at Eliza, who chuckled again.

Then, on threat of death from Justice Chambers, Sarah confessed.

She arranged her shawl on her shoulders and addressed the bench. "Very well," she said. "One Sunday afternoon, about four or five of the clock, I was at John Hughson's house, in the kitchen, about five weeks before the fort was burned. A great many negroes were sitting round the table, betwixt twenty and thirty."

"And who were they by name?"

Judge and jury leaned forward as one to catch her words.

"Dr. Fisher's Harry, Bagley's Jenny, widow Schuyler's tall slender negro, Abeel's mulatto Tom, Niblet's Sandy."

"How long were you there?"

"I stayed there about an hour, and we drank rum," she said.

"Name more," the Judge said.

"And Mrs. Clopper's Betty, Robin, Mr. Clarkson's Tom, Old Frank, Philipse's Cuffee, Teller's Sarah, Vaarck's Caesar (hanged), Auboyneau's Prince (hanged)." And on and on, she went, naming them all, and telling how they sharpened their knives and said they would go and set fires along the docks.

"Comfort's Jack was for firing the fort first. But Caesar, the ringleader among the negroes, said no, the authorities would find them out if they did."

"And what did Jack say to that?"

"He said, '*what would you do?*'"

"And?"

"And Caesar said they would save the fort unto the end. First, every one was to set his own master's house on fire. Then they whetted their knives on a stone, until they were sharp enough to cut off a white man's head. They would kill the white men, they swore, and have the white women for their wives."

Margaret shivered.

But then, no sooner had she finished testifying than Sarah promptly retracted her accusations. "It is all untrue, a lie, lies," she shouted to the justices. "Everything I told you is a lie."

"She is outrageous indeed!" Margaret whispered.

Eliza smiled. "I can't help but admire her," she whispered back.

"She reminds me of you," Margaret whispered. "It is not hard to believe you are friends. You are one of a kind."

The clerk banged on his desk again. "Silence in the courtroom!" he shouted, glaring at the girls.

Sarah's retraction displeased the justices and the jury mightily. "Be informed that there is evidence against you, girl, on the mere account of your having been at a meeting when the plotters were talking of the conspiracy. You can entertain no hopes of escaping with your life but by making a confession and discovery of the whole truth of the matter," the Chief Justice said coldly and clearly.

At this, Sarah stood silent, as if taking stock of her choices. Finally, afraid for her life, she declared she would tell the whole truth.

Later, as the courtroom cleared out, Margaret overheard two judges complaining. "The outrageous creature must have had extraordinary qualifications to recommend her to the confidence of the plotters," one muttered to another, "for she is the only black wench of whom there is evidence of having been let in on the execrable project."

"They let her in on it because she's half white," said the other.

Eliza and Margaret went outside when it was over and sat under the sassafras tree. "Tell me now your story," Margaret said. "What happened when you got on the ferry that night?"

Eliza laughed. "I waited until they were asleep, and then I wrapped myself in my cloak and put a few things in my satchel, and I ran down the lane and jumped onto the ferry just as it came. I was mad for Cornelis. I had to go. I had to! I was all in a fever for him."

"And?"

"I saw your aunt's slave Caesar that night, and his friend Pompey. They were going to the city, too. It was a Saturday night."

"Caesar ran away at Pinkster one year and never came back to Tappan."

"Cornelis ran away that night, and he never came back either," Eliza said. "I looked for him everywhere for days, in the streets, on the Commons, on the wharfs, in the taverns. He was gone. The coward."

"But another time," Margaret ventured, "Cuff saw you. Cuff told my aunt that he had seen you, with a jack-dandy man."

"That was Thomas Pyke," Eliza said bitterly. "He deceived me. He has removed to Philadelphia."

"Is he the father of your child?"

"He was."

"Does he maintain his child?"

"His child is dead," said Eliza coldly. "I smothered her with a pillow no sooner than she was born."

Margaret gasped. She felt faint.

"What else could I do?" said Eliza. "Throw away my own life? I have plans for myself."

*   *   *   *

A month later, the jail being thronged with negroes judged guilty in the plot, and there being no room to put more, the justices submitted a list of names to the Lieutenant Governor to be pardoned and banished from the colony to Virginia. Burk's Sarah was the final name on the list. Eliza and Margaret cheered in their hearts to hear it! "At last, some justice," Eliza whispered. "This is what she was hoping for. She plans to slip away in Virginia and hire herself out as a servant to a proper white family. They will never know."

"Good for her. I am glad for her," said Margaret. "I have come to think that the plot is a figment of the blacks' imaginations, a wish to do what they are accused of plotting, but that they would never really have carried out. At my uncle's house, I must keep such notions to myself, though, for my uncle sharply rebuked me when I suggested it to him."

"It makes sense to me," said Eliza.

"I am so glad to have found you again," Margaret said. "Now at last I have someone I can talk to, who thinks as I do."

*   *   *   *

If there was justice of a sort for Sarah, there was none for John Hughson. From jail in the City Hall, he had announced he wanted to open his heart to the judges.

They fetched him from the jail. "I ask to be sworn on a Bible," he said.

The justices would not permit it. "You may speak," the chief justice said coldly. "But you may not be sworn."

Before he could open his mouth to protest, the recorder laced into him, reproaching him with his wicked life and practices, his debauching and corrupting of negroes, his encouraging of them to steal and pilfer from their masters.

"Why won't they let him swear? Eliza wondered.

"I am at a loss to say," said Margaret. "In the Dutch Church, if you swear an oath on the Holy Bible and then tell lies that are found out, you will be judged as guilty as if you had committed murder, and certain death and a future in hell will meet you. But if you are sworn and tell the truth, the sanctity of swearing on the Bible must give a strong impression of your innocence."

"So, then, I wonder," Eliza said, "do the justices not want to believe he could be innocent?"

"It seems so," Margaret said, "wrong as that may be."

Later, it was reported in the papers that Hughson's cellmates declared that they believed he spoke in earnest in wanting to declare his innocence, but that his wife had tried to discourage him from it. Margaret wondered about that, too. Why? To some mysteries in the cases that came to trial there were no answers. Why would his wife discourage him?

The recorder continued berating John Hughson with his wicked ways, with training his children up in the highway to hell, reminded him that he, his wife, his daughter, and his tenant Peggy had been convicted of a felony for receiving stolen goods of negroes. "Now, nothing remains but to pass sentence of death upon you for that crime and to appoint a day for your execution," he thundered.

Hughson shuddered.

And then the magistrates decided that the four of them, the Hughsons, their daughter, and Peggy, should be tried again, this time for their part in the horrible conspiracy. "If they're already going to be condemned to die," Margaret wondered, "why should they be tried on another crime, unless to furnish the court with information that could convict even more slaves?"

"You have answered your own question," Eliza said.

"It is clear," the recorder roared, "that you, Hughson, were a principal and head agent in this detestable scheme of villainy, the chief abettor of this execrable and monstrous contrivance for shedding the blood of your neighbors and laying the whole city in ashes."

Hughson shook his head and smiled softly. "I request again that I might be sworn," he said.

"Refused!"

"I knew nothing of the conspiracy. I am as innocent, along with my wife, my daughter, and Peggy, as a child unborn. Let me swear it on a Bible."

"You lie! It was taking place in your tavern! How could you know nothing of it?"

"Remand him to jail!" the Chief Justice roared.

"At Hughson's, they all say it," said Eliza: "There is no justice for the slaves or for poor whites either, like me. We're equally hated as the blacks by the better sort, like you."

They were walking north up Broadway, past Trinity Church toward Hughson's tavern. "You can be sure I do not hate you," Margaret said. "I love you, Eliza. I worry about you. You didn't used to be 'poor white'. Why don't you go home and start over again?"

She laughed. "Home!" she said. "That is my home, over there." She pointed to Hughson's at the corner of Crown Street on the Hudson River, where she rented a room. She no longer worked in Hughson's scullery. She stole for a living again, and very artfully, too. Her specialty was dry goods shops. She loved the bolts of fabric that she could carry away, one a night here, one a night there. But she spared proper Margaret the details.

As she wandered alone under the elms and the lime trees east on Crown Street, north on Nassau, east on John Street to her uncle's house, Margaret thought about what Eliza had said, that there was no justice, if you were black or poor and white. It was probably true, she decided.

✳   ✳   ✳   ✳

She conceived a sympathy for Hughson and his pathetic family, and she went to court with Eliza to hear him tried on the conspiracy charges, along with his wife, his daughter, and Caesar's woman Peggy Kerry. The charge was abetting and encouraging the negroes Caesar, Prince, Quack, and Cuffee to burn the King's house in the fort and the whole town, and to kill and destroy the inhabitants and to make themselves King (Hughson) and Governor (Caesar). "Preposterous," Margaret muttered.

"Quite," whispered Eliza.

"Gentlemen, of the jury," the Attorney General said, "such a monster will this Hughson appear before you, that for the sake of the plunder he expected by setting in flames the King's house, and this whole city, and by the effusion of the blood of his neighbors, he murderous and remorseless he, counseled and encouraged the committing of all these most astonishing deeds of darkness, cruelty, and inhumanity. Infamous Hughson! This grand incendiary, this archrebel against God, King, and country, devil incarnate, author and abettor of terror and devastation! What shall ye say of him?"

Then, Mary Burton, Hughson's indentured servant, witnessed against the prisoners. "With the reward in mind," Margaret whispered to Eliza. "Forty pounds and her freedom." She swore on her oath that twenty and thirty negroes at a time were at Hughson's tavern on any given Sunday, and that they talked always of burning the town and killing the white people.

"It is true what she says," Eliza whispered. "I heard them. I was there. But I believe that it was just talk on their part, brave but idle talk."

Hughson and his wife cried and bemoaned themselves, embracing and kissing their daughter, and protesting their innocence. But Mary Burton went on and on, and after she was finished, more witnesses were called and sworn, and a few were called to swear for the prisoners, but they were ineffectual. All four prisoners were found guilty and sentenced to hang.

A week later, Margaret went with Eliza to the execution of John Hughson, his wife, and Peggy Kerry, Caesar's woman and the mother of his child. From the cart on which the three were to be transported to the gallows, they all denied knowing anything of the conspiracy. Hughson had prophesied that at the last minute some remarkable sign would appear on his body to show his innocence, and the crowd's attention was drawn to bright red spots that appeared on his cheeks, for he was naturally of pale complexion. The people spoke softly together about the spots.

He raised one arm as high as his restraints would allow, and gazed back and forth over the crowd, beckoning with a finger, as if to summon his deliverer. None appeared. Even so, some in the crowd, even some of the jurors and men of the law, were disturbed. "Is he innocent?" they murmured to one another. "Is a man about to be executed for nothing? Are those two women to be executed for nothing? What will God have to say about that on Judgment Day?"

The masked hangman did his work.

The women's bodies were taken down and carted off for burial to a potter's field near the Fresh Water. But Hughson's body was left in chains, next to Caesar's and Prince's, which had been twisting in the wind since May 11. It was now June 12.

"Hughson was not content to live by the gains of honest industry," the lawyer William Smith railed, even after Hughson was hanged. "He must be rich at the expense of the blood and ruin of his fellow citizens, miserable wretch! His crimes have made him blacker than a negro." His corpse, hanged in chains, swelled, became monstrous in size, as if it strained to snap the oaken gibbet in two.

In his final report, Daniel Horsmanden noted that Hughson's cadaver was indeed "blacker than a negro's." In fact, the two cadavers had changed color: Hughson's had taken on a deep shining black, blacker than Caesar's, who alive had been one of the blackest of his kind, while Caesar's corpse had bleached out, turned whitish. No one could explain how black could become white, white black. Some were heard to mutter uneasily that perhaps the Bible was right, there was no slave nor free, for all are one in Christ Jesus.

That afternoon, along with most of the city, they attended while Albany, Curaçoa Dick, and Francis were executed as decreed. This made six hangings in one day, a record. But further trials were to come. Groesbeck's Mink, Pemberton's Quamino, Low's Wan, Becker's Mars, DeBrosse's Primus, Rowe's Tom, Kelly's London, Lawrence's Sterling, and Ten Eyck's Bill were taken into custody. "It seems to me," whispered Margaret, "that it will not end until all 2,000 negroes in the city are tried and sentenced and killed or banished."

The next day, they went again to the court to hear the King's case against Quash, Ben, Cowley's Cato, Vanderspiegle's Fortune, and Cato, alias Toby (Eliza's first partner in crime). The jury was called. This time Margaret knew one of the jurymen—at least by name and reputation. Elbert Haring, Esq., a prosperous baker and a man of property, was a cousin of Marytie's husband. She often walked past his farm on her way to the court, said to be the second largest farm in the city. It spread its curious windmill-shaped wings over the countryside between the wall and the Fresh Water. An alderman, a deacon, a church master, a good man supposedly, would he be swayed by the prisoners' protestations of innocence? Would any of the jurymen? He was not. They were not.

Some day, she promised herself, she would drop into his bakery on Bleecker Street and introduce herself. She would very much like to see the inside of his handsome house, which was adjacent to the bakery. She had heard Marytie say that it was a very fine house indeed.

"What do you think?" she asked Eliza, "I think the case against the plot is a plot in itself."

"Only the people in charge of it know the truth of it," said Eliza. "The people in ruffles," she added bitterly, thinking of Thomas Pyke.

What was true? The damning testimonies of the witnesses, or the prisoners' piteous declarations of their innocence? Her uncle was unapproachable on the subject. He owned one slave, and he wasn't about to lose her to any trials. He kept her under lock and key at night, especially now that they lived in the city. No frolicking for Bessie in the grog shops. And as for her distracted aunt, she hardly knew the trials were going on, though she must have been the only creature in the city that didn't.

*   *   *   *

The trials and the executions continued throughout the year 1741 and into the next year too, but they did little to restrain negro "nations" and "cabals," as the Governor termed them, from consorting with criminal gangs or with the "Geneva Club" to work their sinful purposes. The Geneva Club was described in the papers as a confederacy of negroes begun by Caesar and Prince and styled along the lines of the Free Masons ("which was looked upon to be a gross affront to the provincial grand master and gentlemen of the fraternity"), whose nefarious purpose was to help impudent, insolent negroes rob, pilfer, and steal whenever they chose. "Damn all the white people!" a Geneva Club slave was heard to shout. "If I had it in my power, I would set them all on fire!" He was arrested, of course.

The justices were convinced that what they called these "stupid wretches" had been seduced by Hughson to undertake their senseless and wicked enterprise, for "Gentlemen of the Jury," they said, "it cannot be imagined that these silly unthinking creatures could of themselves have contrived and carried on so deep, so dire and destructive a scheme, without the advice and assistance of Hughson, that never to be forgotten Hughson, who is now gone to his place, as did Judas of old to his."

Fourteen negroes and four whites had already been put to death, but every day brought new discoveries, new accusations. Mary Burton took the stand as often as she was called, which was often, and the slaves were induced to testify against each other with the promise of their freedom. Who knew if they were telling lies or truth? And why weren't they allowed legal counsel?

Her literature-loving schoolmaster Mr. van Blarcom had given Margaret a penchant for words, and she had never heard so many words in her life as at the trials of Quash, Ben, Cato, Fortune, and Toby. Especially when Justice Horsmanden spoke. He reveled in his own rhetoric, and she wallowed in it, too, voluptuously, she thought with a shiver. Her eyes were riveted on his grim face and his wig, especially the curious puffs that covered each ear, like rabbits' tails, but her ears drank up the exotic language coming out of his mouth.

He addressed Ben first. "Thou vile wretch! How much does thy ingratitude enhance your guilt! Your hypocritical, canting behavior at your trial, your protestations of innocence, your dissimulation before God and man will be no small article against you at the day of judgment, for ye all have souls to be saved or damned. Your spirits are immortal; they will live forever, either eternally happy or eternally miserable in the other world. And be not deceived, God will not be mocked, he will not be baffled, he knows all your thoughts and sees all your actions, and they that have done evil and die impenitent shall be thrown into the infernal lake of fire and brimstone, together with the devil and his accursed spirits. If you would not have this your portion, then confess your guilt, your horrid sins, and discover your accomplices, in this hellish conspiracy."

He proceeded without a pause to Quash. "And you, Quash, may you be upbraided with the like reproaches for your ingratitude, for you have had a very indulgent master, who has put great trust and confidence in you, because of your having better sense than the rest of his negroes. How vilely then have you abused his kindnesses, how vilely you wretches would drench your hands in the blood of your master and their families. You would destroy without mercy.

"As to you two Catoes, and you Fortune," he went on. "You appear to have been inferior agents, but your hearts are as corrupt and ripe for mischief as any of the rest. You have all alike taken that hellish, execrable oath, and equally bound yourselves in that villainous engagement not only to burn and consume your masters' substance, but to murder their persons...."

He finally tired of his linguistic excess. "It is a very irksome task to pronounce that sentence which the law requires of us, for we delight not in any man's blood," he finished piously. "But the law judges you unfit to live." Ben and Quash were to be chained to a stake and burned to death on the very next morrow in the morning, the Catoes and Fortune to be hanged by the neck until dead in the afternoon.

"What is his logic, burning for this one, hanging for that one?"

"It's just for the variety," Eliza said, "to keep the crowds interested."

Those cases only tired his powers temporarily, however; after a break he moved on with renewed enthusiasm to the next: the King against De Lancey's Antonio, Mesnard's Antonio, Sarly's Juan, Becker's Pablo, and McMullen's Augustine. Margaret was exhausted when she returned to her uncle's house and went directly to bed.

*   *   *   *

The plot of 1741 took on a new cast when the Governor reported to London that the hand of Popery was surely in it, for a Romish priest had been accused of having a deep share in the plot. Although this supposed Romish priest, John Ury, protested that he was no Catholic and no priest but a dissenting Anglican and an itinerant schoolmaster, his fluency in Latin made him suspect. He was brought to trial, and a letter from Governor James Oglethorpe of Georgia to Lt. Governor Clarke introduced at the trial was instrumental in his conviction, as was Mary Burton's solemn testimony that Ury had been a frequenter of Hughson's tavern.

Eliza reminded Margaret that it had been murmured at their trials that Mrs. Hughson and the red-haired Irish beauty Peggy Kerry were of the Roman persuasion, but the justices at that time had said it was of little significance what religion such vile wretches professed. "So why is it significant in Ury's case?"

"My uncle says they're worried that Spain and France are behind it," Margaret said.

Her uncle was right. Governor Oglethorpe interfered a second time, warned Clarke of a "villainous design of a very extraordinary nature" in which Spain had employed emissaries to burn all the towns in English North America. For this purpose, he warned, "many priests were employed, who pretended to be physicians, schoolmasters, dancing-masters and other such occupations." Ury, a schoolmaster, was duly hanged.

Now it was rumored that a number of the black plotters were, in fact, Roman Catholic Spaniards. "Black, yes," they retorted. "But free and literate, men captured on the high seas by an English sea captain and sold to rich men in New York." They were as angry as formerly free men could be at this turn in their fate. "We would like to burn down that captain's house, tie him to a beam, and roast him like a side of beef," they said, in public.

"Overthrow the English," Spanish-speaking persons were said to whisper to the plotters, "and Spain will come and free you from your bondage." Whites, ever fearful of a Roman Catholic takeover of the Colony, now believed such was imminent, whether by Spain or by France no one could say, and what did it matter? Either way they would be in bondage to Papist masters. But with the newspapers reporting weekly on England's impending war with Spain, Spain became the chief suspect.

And so it went throughout that long hot summer, until at a meeting of the Common Council on September 2, when the justices were exhausted by it all, when the masters were tired of losing their property to the stake and the gibbet, when Mary Burton began to intimate that some people "in ruffles" were involved in the plot—even as the aghast justices pointed out that several of known fortune, credit, reputation, and religious principle that she murmured of were beyond questioning—it was ordered that the treasurer pay to Mr. Moore, for Mary Burton's use and benefit, the sum of eighty-one pounds, which with the sum of nineteen pounds before paid by the corporation for the freedom and other necessaries to and for the use of the said Mary, made in the whole the sum of 100 pounds, in full of the reward offered.

Then, as suddenly as it had arisen, the taste for blood died down. Mary Burton, it was now begun to be thought, had taken to the witness stand with a little too much enthusiasm. When she began to implicate the high and mighty of New York, Daniel Horsmanden began to doubt her truthfulness. "The things you say cannot but stagger one's belief," he declared. And with that pronouncement, the trials petered out. Everyone calmed down. The great slave insurrection of 1741 was over.

"And when will the next one be?" Margaret wondered aloud to Eliza.

She clipped a ditty out of the *Weekly Journal*, a patriotic ditty about England's war with Spain and pasted it in the diary she had begun to keep since living in the city:

> *"Yet through all the mighty Ocean,*
> *The English cross shall honor find,*
> *Far as Wave can feel a Motion,*
> *Far as Flag can move with Wind,*
> *The insulting Monarch showing*
> *More regard shall humble be,*
> *The Sole Truth of Britain knowing,*
> *That her Brave men will be free."*

"It means Spain's monarch," she said to Eliza. "But there are other stirrings to be free it might apply to," she added in her prim way.

"I have stirrings of my own to be free," said Eliza.

"And what does that mean?"

"You will know soon enough," said Eliza mysteriously.

"I have decided that I must be against slavery and that I must declare in public that slavery is wrong and that I must convince other people, all the people I can reach, that it is wrong to take away the freedom of another," said Margaret.

"Good for you," said Eliza. "I can just picture you standing up in church and telling the people the truth about their precious lives."

Soon after this, Eliza announced that she was sailing to London to start a new life.

Margaret, bereft, expected never to see her again and cried when they said their farewells.

"You'll see me again." Eliza promised, embracing her. "And when you do I'll be in silk and brocade and on the arm of a handsome man—an officer of the Army will suit me very well, I believe."

"You are as resourceful as a hungry cat, so maybe I will see you again," said Margaret.

Eliza laughed. "Remember our promise," she said. "Friends forever."

PART TWO

CHAPTER 12

▼

CLOUDS

Marytie woke beside him one morning to find him with his eyes wide open, staring at the ceiling.

She sat bolt upright in the bed. She touched his bare chest. Cold!

"No!" she cried. "Oh! God! Come! Someone! Come!"

No one came, for no one heard her. Although it seemed to her that she was screaming, in fact her voice was inaudible. In any case, there was no one in the house to hear it, except a slave or two.

She scrambled over his body out of the bed box and looked at him from a standing position. He was dead.

So, you went first, as you wanted to, she thought dully. You slipped away from me in the night, left me behind. In June, in the year 1743, he was gone.

Better you than me, he had said once. I would be helpless on my own, *mijn lieveling.*

You would not be on your own! she had said. You would go to live with one of our children, or they would come to live with you.

And then she remembered. It came back like a bad dream. *"Ik ben ziek,"* he had mumbled, waking her.

"Slaperig," she had mumbled back. She was sleepy. *"Uitslapen."* Sleep your fill.

She had turned over, gone back to sleep, slept through whatever violence it was that had taken him.

She had failed him in his last moments. He had called out to her to help him, and she had chosen sleep. He had died alone because she wanted her pleasant cozy slumber! It is true what they say, then, she thought: One is born alone, and one dies alone.

She sat on the edge of the bed, rocking herself, keening: What happened? What had he suffered? What must he have thought of her, telling him to sleep his fill? Now you will sleep your fill, she thought bitterly.

Then it hit her. She would see him no more. Her beloved was gone.

*   *   *   *

She collected herself, gently closed his eyes, clambered over him again and lay beside him until the summer sun poured through the curtains of the *bedstede*.

She lay as close to him as she could, her lips pressed against his shoulder, cold as ice.

She herself grew cold as ice. She began to shiver uncontrollably. She pulled a jacquard coverlet up over her body, and his. Tears soaked her face. She dried them against the cold flesh of his shoulder. She had not been there when he needed her, her good man.

But he was gone and she could not lie there forever. After a while, she climbed over him a third time, wrapped her bed gown around her, and went to find Hagar in the smokehouse. There were things to be done, and she must do them, even though she was freezing cold. Hagar knew what had to be done, too. It was the same in Africa.

Together they straightened out the corpse before it stiffened, and then Hagar went to ask the *aanspreeker* to come and dress the body for the grave. He came and did his work and was gone in half an hour, and it seemed totally unreasonable and unacceptable to her that her husband should be lying in their dear *betse* dressed in his Sunday clothes with his green eyes shut, his body, like her own, as cold and clammy as a frog's, where the skin was uncovered: His face, his hands.

She lay beside him in the bed for an hour, murmuring to him in her mind those things she would have said had she been awake in his throes, while the housework and the cooking went on around her and the *aanspreeker*, in his black clothes, black shoes and stockings, black pantaloons, black cutaway coat (in June), and his black three-cornered *steek* with the long black streamer of crepe, went officiously about the neighborhood inviting all to the funeral.

Late in the day, she went out to the beehives to tell the bees he was gone, an ancient Dutch custom they had never forgotten to observe.

She buried her beloved under the spreading beechnut tree (*that* beechnut tree) in the same ground where five of their children lay. And all of Tappan and half of Hackensack came to the funeral feast to condole with her and her son and her two daughters and to celebrate his life that glorious June day under the locust trees.

A hundred guests were there, and the slaves rolled out casks of rum and Madeira wine, and others spread food galore on the tables and handed around the tobacco and pipes by the scores. Marytie's daughters and granddaughters distributed the mourning gifts, scarves for the pallbearers and gloves for the ladies. It was an idyllic day, despite the man lying in his grave, a day of family and the friends together, doing things in the old Dutch way.

Marytie ignored the goings on as much as she could and let her mind fill with memories of their life together, the long union of their spirits and their flesh, the hardships they had suffered, the children they had made together, and lost together, five of their eight. She dwelt on his tender way with her in her grief over them, his patience, her dearly beloved, his dearly beloved. He had truly been made for her and she for him.

*   *   *   *

The Lord giveth and the Lord taketh away. In more ways than one can count. He was no sooner in his grave than Aeltie discovered a lump in her breast.

"Up until that day, and even that day itself and for some days since," Aeltie said, "I haven't been able to take it in what such a lump might mean."

Marytie said, "Maybe it doesn't mean what you think it means. Maybe the doctor will cut it out, rid you of it."

"Maybe," said Aeltie doubtfully. "I have eight children to think of and only one of them married."

They drove together in the wagon, Jan and Aeltie and Marytie, to a barber surgeon in Hackensack. "I thought it would go on forever," she said bleakly. She meant that summer idyll, that family life, the ever-ripening fields, the rivers dancing with fish, the orchards dropping pears and cherries, plums, eight kinds of apples. The rosy healthy babies, the blonde *kinder* racing through the clover behind their hoops, the rich land to pass on to them, the promise of that dream of the new world they had dared to dream.

"It will go on," said Marytie. "You will be fine."

"I will hope," Aeltie said.

This surgeon had a technique for knocking his patients out with a smart smack to the temple with a wooden club, so that he could amputate on an unconscious subject. The blow had been known to be fatal on occasion, but not in Aeltie's case. He cut off the diseased breast before she came to and sewed the bloody flesh up with buckskin thread before it could swell.

He had spared her the pain of the surgery with his mighty clout. But the pain after it was unslakeable. And unbearable to witness, but Marytie witnessed it. She sat by her bed for three days and nights, suffering along with her, forcing her to drink a tea of the flowering tops of Lady's Mantle, for women's ailments, and a tea of its dried leaves, containing tannis, used to stanch the bleeding. Nothing could stanch the pain.

The surgery was useless. Schoolmaster's daughter, wife at eighteen, mother eight times in sixteen years, she was dead at forty-three. The cancer ate her up faster than a bobcat could devour a calf.

*   *   *   *

When Aeltie was no longer able to stand on her feet, Marytie left her own farm and all its appurtenances (it was too lonesome there without Cosyn anyway) and moved into her soon-to-be widowed son's house. Hagar and Hagar's two pesky children and Caesar's twins moved with her and slept where they found space, on pallets in the smokehouse, in the garret, in the lean-to, wherever.

Aeltie's two youngest, Sara and Rachel, were only ten and twelve. "It is not fair to have to see our mother die," she heard one of them complain to the other.

Granddaughters, Marytie thought bitterly, let me tell you: It is not fair to have to see one's spouse die, or worse, not see him die or hear him die. It is not fair to have to see one's children die, one's dearest friends die. And whoever promised that life was fair anyway? Granddaughters will learn that soon enough, she muttered to herself.

Aeltie, ever the schoolmaster's daughter, insisted, after the harvest was in, that they go to school as usual, the two youngest, though it made the house too still. Even Hagar's two and Caesar's twins quieted down, as if aware that death hovered, played by themselves in the barnyard.

It being January and the ground being frozen hard when she died, they stored her in her coffin in a corner of the barn, surrounding it with cakes of ice and mountains of hay to thwart the rats from gnawing their way through the pine wood and feasting on what was left of her flesh after the cancer had done its work. And there she stayed, until the ground thawed enough to dig her grave under the beechnut tree.

Who is to be matriarch now? Martyie had asked herself in despair, as Aeltie day by day declined. Who will follow me? Who will be that loyal attender to the family's welfare, that tenacious force holding it together, that optimistic pray-er and petitioner for its good? Aeltie's eldest daughter, Maria, was married. She was a Smith now, therefore not eligible. Marytie's own two surviving daughters were embedded in other families with their own needs.

There was only one possibility: the woman, as yet unidentified, who would become the wife of Aeltie's first-born son, Johannes Haring, now twenty-three, Marytie's grandson, reading law—and dallying with theology, it was said—in Hackensack. A studious fellow.

＊　　　＊　　　＊　　　＊

But Johannes Haring showed no signs of marrying. "He is more like our father than he is his own father," her daughters said. "Very cautious."

"And that is a good thing," Marytie said. She had gotten to know him again when he came from Hackensack during his mother's last weeks. Yes, he was very like his grandfather, her own Cosyn, retiring and careful, with the same coloring, the same soft wing of dark hair falling over his wide brow, the same seeing green eyes that seemed to turn up in every generation. His father, her son, was of the blond coloring, like her.

"He will be quite sure of a woman before he asks her to be his wife. Of that I am certain," Marytie said. "Although I noticed, Marretje, that he blushed when a certain person looked his way at Aeltie's funeral."

"And who would that person be?" Marretje asked.

"It would be none other than his pretty nineteen-year-old second cousin Margaret Blauvelt, my brother's granddaughter," said Marytie. "You remember her. She stayed with us for two summers."

"Of course. Didn't she set her cap for him back then?"

"That's what I recall," said Marytie.

Now she began to wonder if such a union could be brought about. The girl had fancied him when she was a thing of twelve or thirteen. Did she entertain a fancy for him still?

She had last seen Margaret to talk to during the trials in New York City, when Caesar was hanged. The girl had never come home from the city to live after that. She had stayed to work in the fine household of Elbert Haring, their cousin, keeping the books of his busy bakery on Bleecker Street. She came home to visit her family only from time to time. Was she a city girl for good by now?

Marytie began to think deeply about Margaret Blauvelt. In fact she began to be obsessed with her, couldn't get her out of her mind. From what she remembered of her when she was a girl, and from what she had seen and heard since, Margaret was a fine specimen of young womanhood in every way, good looking, strong, intelligent, healthy, and full of vigor. A good match for her best grandson, a good successor to herself. She prayed for it to happen.

*   *   *   *

About a year after Aeltie died, in April of 1745, Marytie's prayers were answered. The now beauteous, now passionate Margaret suddenly moved back to Tappan after four years in the city. She was not a city girl, after all.

No sooner did she reappear among them than she stood up in the church, her face aglow, her blue eyes flashing, her voice trembling with emotion, to make an ardent confession of her faith. "In the city, the Lord inclined his ear to me and graciously softened my heart," she announced in a loud, clear voice. "He granted me true faith in Christ to justify me, sanctify me, and preserve me forever in the fellowship of his Son. I am born anew."

Dominie Muzelius glowered at her from the pulpit, where he was about to launch into the long prayer, the same one he always gave, reading it from a book.

What a stroke of luck, Marytie thought, that her grandson was in the congregation that day! More than luck, a minor miracle! She stole a glance at him across the aisle. He was raptly watching the girl, his face aflush.

Marytie congratulated her great-niece afterward. And warmly hugged her. "I remember so fondly the summers you spent with me," she said. "And I am glad you have come to the Lord. I always knew you would."

"Thank you, Marytie," said Margaret, blushing. "I know, of course, that the idea of the new birth, of which I heard George Whitefield speak so many times, is unwelcome to *Dominie* Muzelius. He looked daggers at me as I spoke. Did you notice that?"

"Yes, I noticed," Marytie said. "But never mind him. He was born an ogre. Your confession means that you are now officially eligible to receive the supper of the Lord in this church and any other, and there is nothing he can do about it."

"Thank you," the girl murmured.

"Will you come to my son's house for dinner this afternoon?" she said. "The whole family will be there," she added. "My best grandson, too."

"Hmmm," Margaret said. "I would like that." She had learned from her mother that Johannes had left Hackensack, returned to Tappan. "His studies are over, they say," her mother said. "He is perhaps thinking of taking a wife."

It was the perfect time to look him over, see if he still made her heart flutter and her temperature rise.

He did, and she his.

And five months later, to Marytie's great delight, her grandson Johannes Haring married this tall, passionate, and pious blond and blue-eyed second cousin of his, this Margaret Blauvelt. And five months after that, converted by her piety, or her insistence, he too stood up in the congregation and confessed his faith. Margaret's best friend and second cousin, Willemptie Eckerson, did as well, also under Margaret's earnest missionary prodding. Marytie was overjoyed at all these developments. Willemptie was a niece, and one of her favorites, too. Her only regret was that Cosyn had not lived to see this miracle.

✳   ✳   ✳   ✳

But the miracle was shortlived, for no sooner was she a married woman than Margaret Blauvelt let it be known that she had no intention of moving into her father-in-law's house. She broke it to Marytie as gently as she could. "I want my own house, for my own outset," she said softly. "So, I've been thinking: Will you let us have your house, that no one lives in now?"

Marytie was aghast. "But, but that house is completely furnished," she stammered. "I left all my furniture, all my things, there when I came here to care for Aeltie."

She had left the place in such a hurry that she took nothing away with her but her clothing, and not all of that. An image of the garret came to her, still hung with ropes of peppers, parched corn, and herbs, baskets of nuts. The cradle where she had rocked her infants was muffled in cobwebs in a corner, and on the windbeams where mice scuttled after the corn were stacked as always the smooth pine boards saved for coffins. Her coffin one of these days, she thought wearily. "Where would your things go?" she asked.

"Mine would replace yours, and yours can go into the garret for another day," Margaret said.

"What other day?" Marytie stammered. "What other day do you mean?"

"It was just a figure of speech," Margaret said to her new husband. "You know that I do not want to move into your mother's house, most certainly do not want to live with her old-fashioned tables, chairs rushed by some dead old slave with cats from the salt meadow, that faded grisaille *kas*, the rope-strung beds, the battered sweet-gum cupboard."

"I understand," he said, "but …"

"And for the same reason, I don't want your grandmother's things either. I have my own new *kas*, my own new fruitwood bed, complete with bedding. I want to use them. I have my own sweet-gum cupboard filled with my own new linens and coverlets, and I have my pewter plates and redware bowls and majolica dishes, to deck it, my Dutch faience treasures, the dowry that my mother and father were years in accumulating."

"Of course," said Johannes. "I understand."

"And there's more," Marytie said to her son.

"What more?"

Marytie bit her tongue. She wanted to say that the girl was proud, she was tactless, she was a know-it-all, but she restrained herself to one specific: "She has turned up her nose at the books of Grietje's that were so precious to her and to me and to Aeltie, too."

"I'm sorry to hear it," he said.

He could see that the books were a sore point. Yes, Margaret Blauvelt made it plain that she wanted the *new* edition of *De Verstandige Kock,* recently published. "And as for the other books," Marytie went on, "she claims they are out of date, too. She has no use for them. She says she knows all she needs to know of home medicine and herbal cures, and she has her own ideas about childrearing."

He almost laughed. Spunky girl she was. Perhaps she would light a fire under that bookish son of his.

"And was it necessary for her to say she did not want to become stepsister to your half-orphaned children?" Marytie demanded. "Her new husband's young sisters and teenaged brothers can use a stepsister."

He sighed.

"And was it necessary to say that she did not want to live in a household with Hagar?"

The two of them had taken an instant dislike to each other. And Margaret to Hagar's little black urchins, too (Squall and Bawl, she had named them), much less Caesar's twin brats. "I have my own slave, given to me in childhood as a playmate, and I have trained her very well not to be sulky, like Hagar," Margaret said to Johannes

He could see that. She controlled Bett with a fine system of treats and rewards, held out like pippins to a horse, and she was as tame as a well-broken-in horse, too. But Margaret did not work her as hard as a horse, for she had her own ideas about slavery, he knew: It was a necessary evil. But it was an evil.

It made hard feelings in everyone's hearts when it became clear that Margaret Blauvelt wanted to live away from them, when she treated Aeltie's things with such disdain. "She has changed a great deal in her four years of independence in the city," Marytie's daughters said. They were taken aback by their cousin's outspoken opinions, this cousin of theirs who had been such a winning little thing when she visited those two summers so long ago. "The four years she has spent in New York City in the elegant household of Elbert Haring have altered her," Marretje sniffed. "She has taken on airs."

Marytie felt as if a trusted friend had waylaid her. She remembered the infamous comet that had come and lingered night after night in the sky, when she was a child. What is to become of us? she asked herself at night. What is to become of the family? Are we jinxed forever?

Margaret herself was like a comet, Marytie thought, fast and furious and heedless, full of light, no warmth.

CHAPTER 13

▼

MARGARET

There was, however, a saving grace to Margaret. She was not all light and no fire, by a long shot. It turned out, on Marytie's getting to know her again, that she still felt just as warmly as she had in the old days that slavery was wrong. Eventually, this renewed the old bond between them and linked them to Grietje and Aeltie, too, and the long talks they had once had on the subject. Even so, Marytie didn't expect that Margaret Blauvelt would turn the church on its ear over it.

But Margaret had not forgotten her decision at the end of the conspiracy trials in 1741, when she was a girl of sixteen, to make her views on slavery known some day. She had told Eliza she would do it, and she had been contemplating doing it for four years.

Now that she was a married woman and of the goodly age of twenty, she considered the time to be ripe.

She was always a careful dresser, vain about her appearance, and on the day she chose to speak her mind, a Sunday in the winter of 1745, she donned her best: a new blue dress of light wool that made her blue eyes even bluer and set off her heavy blond hair, worn in a thick braid down her back. The dress elongated her torso as was the current style, and the skirt was draped back to reveal her yellow silk petticoat scattered with embroidered flowers. She had bought the dress to console herself for a miscarriage, her first.

Without thinking to inform Johannes in advance of what she was to do—and that turned out to be a mistake—she raised her hand when the *dominie* had finished his interminably long and impenetrable sermon and was about to launch into his equally interminable prayer, to ask to speak. He glowered at her, but before he could refuse her, she stepped quickly out of her pew and turned her back to the pulpit to face the congregation. Faces turned to her with interest. They expected another rousing testimony to her born-againness, like the one she had delivered, all aglow and passionate, on returning from the city a year before. So they were surprised when she said, "I want to talk about slavery and the so-called insurrection of four years ago."

Eyes popped all over the sanctuary, including Johannes's, for in the four years since the trials, almost everyone had forgotten them. ("So-called?" people murmured.) Some had purposefully put them out of their minds as a distasteful episode in their history, others as a job well done that need not be dwelt upon further. Thus some in the congregation, about half, including *Dominie* Muzelius, who disliked the outspoken young zealot he considered her to be, glared at Margaret Blauvelt balefully and grumbled under their breaths as they caught her drift.

As she went on, some of the men began to hoot and stamp their feet in disapproval, and some of the women, too. The wooden floor and walls of the sanctuary resounded with their outcry, drowning out her voice.

But she held her own, waited till the commotion died down, and continued to set her points before them: "It was not proved that a plot existed at all. Or if one did, it was not as hellish as the justices presented it."

"The fires! The fires!" men shouted. "What about the fires?"

"Or do you think the burning of the King's house in the fort and the other buildings within the fort's walls was a coincidence?" Muzelius inquired, in a sneering tone.

"And all those many suspicious fires outside of the fort, after the burning of the King's house? How about them?" the people cried.

"The burning of the King's house and the other houses in the fort and eight other houses in all was one thing," she said. "It was not the same thing as burning the whole town and cutting off the heads of all the men and marrying their women." She had to shout to be heard over the uproar from the pews and benches.

"What about the testimonies?" someone called out from the back of the sanctuary. "Witnesses testified under oath. What about that?"

"What about the rewards offered for testimonies?" she asked.

Boos and hisses and stamping of feet greeted this.

"The plotters," she went on carefully, when they had quieted down again enough to hear her, "were not permitted the ways there are in the law to defend themselves against false testimonies. For one thing, they were not allowed legal counsel."

"They confessed! What about the confessions?"

"Were the confessions perhaps forced?" she asked.

Derisive hooting ensued. "Why bring this up now?" a man bellowed. "It was all forgotten."

"You can be sure *they* have not forgotten it, the ones who survived. In any case," she went on firmly, "the sentences were too severe, too cruel."

Here Marytie, her husband's grandmother, helped her out by standing up and joining in with Biblical citations. "We are to go forth and preach the Gospel to every living creature," Marytie said in a clear but wavering voice. She was seventy-five years old now, and frail, and she felt the cold these days. Had felt it ever since that day her husband died in their bed. She could still remember the stone-hard cold flesh of his body, his shoulder she had pressed her mouth to. She wore a woolen cloak almost year round now, even in the summer. "We are to Christianize the slaves. And a Christian cannot be a slave," she said.

Loud booing and hissing greeted her words. "Who says it?" men cried.

"The Bible says it," said Margaret. "'In Christ, there is no difference between bond and free.'"

The response was more stamping of feet. Several men jumped to their feet, knocking over benches with loud bangs and clatters, and charged out of the building.

But Marytie was not intimidated. "Remember Jeremiah," she insisted over the hubbub. "We are inviting God's wrath by holding slaves."

The slaves up in the gallery gazed down wide-eyed. They hardly dared look at each other. *This is all about us,* they seemed to say. They were truly amazed, and even frightened. *What if the angry ones turn on us?* they were thinking.

Marytie's older brother, Abraham Blauvelt, grandfather of Margaret, was still alive that year at eighty-three. He was one of a number of men in the congregation to remain silent, including Margaret's father, Isaac, Marytie noticed. But Marytie suspected that the silent ones were thinking their own thoughts, remembering Jeremiah indeed. ("You have not obeyed the Lord by proclaiming liberty, every one to his brother and to his neighbor. Thus the Lord will make you a horror to all the kingdoms of the earth.") She suspected they were silently mourning the dreadful predicament that it was so clear by now that slaveholding had cursed them with.

"'Slaves, be obedient to those who are your earthly masters,'" someone shouted. "Paul's letter to the Ephesians."

And at this, finally, Marytie's brother did stand and speak, in a voice creaking with age: "'Know that he who is both their Master and yours is in heaven, and that there is no partiality with him,'" he croaked, looking not at the shouter, but straight at the granddaughter who never ceased to surprise him. "The very same letter that you quote of Paul's to the Ephesians."

"Thank you, *Grootvader*," Margaret said softly.

"Paul's letter to Titus," shouted a neighbor: "'Bid slaves to be submissive to their masters.'"

"The same letter of Paul to Titus," Abraham countered, trying to project his failing voice: "'For the grace of God has appeared for the salvation of all men,' not just free white men."

"Hypocrites! Why don't you free your own slaves?" someone shouted.

The congregation fell silent at this, waiting for an answer. All eyes were upon Margaret.

"I have often asked myself that question," she said finally. She looked up into the gallery where her slave Bett and Sam, the overseer of their farm, were fixedly looking down on her. "I would like to free them, but it is not so easy," she added lamely.

"Hypocrite!"

Their anger chilled her, and she picked up her own cloak and wrapped it around her against their coldness. "I have a final point to make," she said. "You say the slaves should be grateful for their conditions. You say they are housed and clothed and fed at their masters' expense, that they are protected under the law, that they have their Sundays free. It is all true. But what is Sunday free when the other six days are not? They have everything, yes. Everything except their freedom. And until they do, we whites are at their mercy, not they at ours."

At that, half the congregation rose as one and stormed out of the church. Passing her, someone, a woman, pulled hard on her braid, yanking her head back so that she saw the rafters.

"Don't touch me!" she shouted, flailing after the woman. "Don't ever touch me again!" But the woman, a stranger, was gone in the crowd.

She was flushed and breathing hard. Her heart fluttered in her chest like a bird in a net. "Why didn't you speak?" she asked Johannes breathlessly, as they climbed into the wagon, with Sam driving. The other slaves went on foot, taking their time, Sunday their day off. "Why didn't you stand up for me?"

He looked angry. He spoke shortly. "I found your behavior unfeminine."

"Unfeminine!"

"For a woman to speak in public on such matters is not appropriate," he said stiffly. "You should have consulted me beforehand. You made me look like a fool, as if I do not control my own wife."

She stared at him. "But you feel as I do that slavery is wrong."

"It is for men to discuss," he said curtly. "It is not a woman's province."

For the first time in their one year of marriage she wondered if she might have set her cap for the wrong man, when she was a girl of twelve.

"If one cannot speak one's thoughts," she said, "why was it given to us to think?"

They drove home in silence.

He was a warm enough lover, though she had no point of comparison. But he was cold in some inner place she was not privy to, and it was not the first time she had thought so.

"A husband should desire to look deeply into the soul of his wife to understand her," she said to him fiercely as they arrived at their house She jumped down from the wagon, not waiting for his usual helping hand, and stalked into the house through the back door. "You are nothing but a bookworm," she shouted, over her shoulder. "You care for other people's thoughts, but not mine. Bookworm!" She slammed the door.

He stood stricken in the dooryard, his hands helpless at his sides. All that was left of her were a blur of blue dress and tossing wheat-colored hair. My wife, he anguished. My wife!

She went through the house in a fury and out the front door and down the lane to Willemptie's house.

"A lover's quarrel," said Willemptie. "Your first? There will be others."

"It was not a lover's quarrel," Margaret snapped. "It was a revelation of profound philosophical discord. I am hurt to the quick."

"Men are too busy to care about such things as our feelings," said Willemptie. "Understanding us is not their strong suit."

"I believe he understands me very well," Margaret said. "But he doesn't want to give me the satisfaction of my understanding that he understands."

"You make it too complicated."

"I need him to say he understands my thoughts," she insisted. "I need to have my views taken seriously."

"He is just a man, like any other," said Willemptie. "Let it be."

*   *   *   *

She had started out on married life as a haughty, and opinionated, young wife, but she soon had the starch taken out of her. In her first four years of marriage, strong, healthy woman that she was, she miscarried four times. When she finally brought one to term, a baby girl in 1749, she gratefully named her Aeltie after Johannes's mother. And meekly she asked his grandmother for the childrearing book she once had spurned.

So all was forgiven. "The Lord be praised," Marytie said, embracing her. "You have made me happy."

"I am happy to honor my husband's grandmother," Margaret said.

As she settled into the role she was destined for by her marriage to Marytie's eldest and best grandson, she took to wearing a tortoise-shell comb to secure her heavy blond hair away from her face on top of her head, as Grietje had and as Marytie still did, with Grietje's own comb.

Despite their slow start, five children were born to Margaret and Johannes in the decade from 1749 to 1759. They were: Aeltie, after her husband's deceased mother, Isaac after her father, John after her husband and his father, though she Anglicized it, and the twins Elizabeth and Abraham after her mother and grandfather and several favorite uncles. She was known to be unpredictable, so everyone was pleased that she kept to the old Dutch naming patterns, honoring first all four grandparents, and then dipping into the aunts and uncles, even though it meant for a great deal of confusing duplication among the cousins and second cousins.

By the middle of the century, the family had expanded so that first cousins had trouble remembering each other, and many second cousins had lost complete track of each other. If they attended church in another community, they might in some cases have never even heard each other's names. And, if they had had what Marytie and Margaret considered the misfortune to be born into one of those contrary families in the Tappan congregation, they didn't want to know each other.

Unfortunately both sides in the church feud were led by the same backward-looking Frederic Muzelius, a troublemaking, turbulent man, always writing to the authorities in Amsterdam to complain of the liberal bent of some in the Tappan church on the subject of "independency" from the mother church over the sea. "You think of yourselves as 'progressives,'" he sneered. "Your persistent quest for sovereignty maddens me."

"Why should it?" they asked back. "What is wrong with independence? What is wrong with wanting to govern ourselves on this side of the sea?"

He had announced his views to the congregation in 1737, when he was first called to them, when Margaret was a girl of twelve: "In ecclesiastical matters," he had said coldly, "know ye that I have subjected myself to the Classis of Amsterdam and in political matters to the Protestant Crown of Great Britain. And so must you!" He had even shaken his fists at them from the pulpit. "No talk of independency!"

Even at twelve, she had known he should not have spoken of religion and politics in the same breath. According to her father, the two were oil and water to each other. "They should be separate, and almost equal, with the government just slightly more powerful than the church," he had taught her, "but nevertheless with the state supporting the church's policies and endeavors, as the church must support the government's."

Her husband was of the same opinion and grew angry every time Muzelius repeated his views, which was annually on the anniversary of his coming to them. "These have been bad years for us, very bad years," Johannes said. "The church is in a mournful state by reason of his behavior and misbehavior."

"He is beyond the pale," Marytie muttered. "I feel like wringing his neck some Sabbaths."

"I feel the same," Margaret said. "I wish he would go away. Why can't we have a *dominie* who feels as we do?"

Marytie sighed. "We never had such troubles when *Dominie* Bertholf was among us."

The independency faction at Tappan was for uniting in an assembly, as they called it, forming themselves into an American body to govern themselves. They were also agitating for starting a college in New York or New Jersey, where they could educate and ordain their own clergy, rather than having to send them back to Holland. "It is expensive to cross the sea and back," they pointed out to the authorities in Amsterdam. "And it is dangerous."

Amsterdam grew concerned at the factionalism spreading in the colony, and two of their High Mightinesses arrived in New York in their black ermine-trimmed robes and their lace collars and their tall-crowned hats to hear the disputes with their own ears. *Dominies* from all the churches in the area, along with their elders and deacons, attended upon them in the consistory room of the Dutch Church on Garden Street. Both sides tried their best to convince them of their case. "The ship of one young minister returning from his ordination in Holland was captured by French pirates, who marauded from the waters around Cape Breton Island. They held him at sea for six months and suffered him to swab decks and climb the rigging to look for more likely victims of their trade."

"And a candidate for the ministry heading for his theological training in *patria* was drowned in a shipwreck off the coast of Wales. Why should we have to put our young men in such danger? Why is it not possible to educate and ordain them here, on our soil?"

Their High Mightinesses saw the point and began to agree, reluctantly. "There might be some merit in the idea of the American churches uniting fraternally to discuss your common goals and problems," they admitted. "But a loose union is one thing. Disregarding the rules of church order is another. You must tread carefully in this, be vigilant in preserving your subordination to the Reverend Classis of Amsterdam, never forget your Reformedness."

"How could we forget it? It is as dear to us as to you."

"We understand that you are sincere," their High Mightinesses said uneasily. "But we fear that the stirrings of independency will ultimately cause you to wander away into a dangerous congregationalism, overlook our venerable rules, the hierarchical nature of our church government, the decent and decorous and immutable Dutch ways of doing things as we have always done them."

"No one likes to give up power," Margaret said tartly, when she heard how things had gone. "We need to be free of those unnecessary foreign authorities dripping with ermine."

Amsterdam vacillated from year to year, afraid that allowing the churches in America to gather together in a formal body would lead to their cutting themselves entirely loose from the mother church, afraid that one step would lead to another and another. But then, too, they could see the advantages of allowing them to consult together ... as long as they kept in mind who was *baas*.

The problem always came down to Muzelius. Their High Mightinesses made a second voyage to New York. "Will you be so good as to tell us simply and purely the objections that you imagine would lie in such an Assembly?" they beseeched him.

He was an unsmiling man, sallow and pockmarked. "I took an oath to submit myself to the ecclesiastical authority of the Classis of Amsterdam," he said tersely. "I will not deny my oath."

"But if we say that you may?"

"I will not."

They sighed heavily. "Why not let yourself, in a friendly and brotherly way, dear Reverend Sir, be convinced that an assembly of the American churches, united for the preservation of doctrine and the edification of the flocks, is a good and proper thing? It is not a violation of your oath to agree with this idea. We are still the authority to which the churches in America must subordinate themselves, and we always shall be."

He shook his head. "An oath is an oath."

Their High Mightinesses called this assembly they had in mind by a Dutch name, *coetus*, a word the people had not heard before. "A *coetus* has no real power, you may be sure," they said, "for it is neither a consistory nor a classis nor a synod. It must be clear in everyone's minds that the *coetus* is only a novelty. It is there to give counsel in certain matters touching you, but it must be implicitly and explicitly agreed by one and all that it must be forever subordinate to the mighty Classis of Amsterdam of which we are the authorities." Again, they went away in their ecclesiastical finery with nothing settled.

"They are beginning to think their authority is not all it should be," said Margaret. "Or all it once was. In fact, they are beginning to see that change is in the air, on this side of the sea, and that they will have to deal with it."

And of course, inevitably, one thing did lead to another, as Amsterdam had feared. The *coetus*, an assembly of both factions, was allowed, finally, but it was only a matter of time before the progressives within it became dissatisfied with the limitations placed upon it and wanted to transform the body into a proper classis.

They wrote to Amsterdam to set forth their ideas. "We need real power," they wrote, "the power to educate American ministers on American soil and ordain them here too. We need a classis."

"Now see where it has led," said the Reverend Sirs, in their mahogany-paneled, tapestried meeting room in Amsterdam. They dripped with scorn at this preposterous notion. "How large an undertaking! What wonderful plans! A classis!"

"And a college, no less!" they said to each other. With all the acuteness it possessed, the Classis of Amsterdam was not able to imagine in what place, or by what authority, or by what means, or out of what treasury, such a university was to be established, or where its professor was to be found. "Let us not weary our brains with it," their leaders said, "but simply wait for the time when this new phenomenon shall appear in the American ecclesiastical heavens."

Muzelius's scorn for the progressives in the midst of his congregation grew by the year. He took every chance he got to rail from the pulpit about the effrontery of those who dared to think of independence. "You think yourselves equal to the

Reverend Sirs of the Classis of Amsterdam and the Synod of North Holland?" he sneered. "How dare you, liars and zealots that you are?"

To annoy them, he preached six Sabbaths in a row on one little *teckstje* ("Jesus wept") and invited them back to hear it a seventh time. He further tormented them by insisting that those they considered to be "unconverted"—that is, those quite content with having been born *once*, like himself—had a right to approach the Lord's Table. Marytie and Margaret were disgusted with him.

"Unfortunately, he has many followers," Johannes said. "There are many families among us who feel exactly as he does that their ecclesiastical allegiance is to Amsterdam and their political allegiance to the King of England."

"But the churches' subordination to the lawful authorities is not taken away by our uniting in a classis to sustain each other with counsel and advice," Margaret pointed out. "Or having a college to train our ministers. And in church matters we already recognize ourselves as subject to Amsterdam. And of course we owe our allegiance to the King of England. There is no doubt of that."

But the man remained intransigent. "And worse," Johannes confided to Margaret, "he begins to be habitually drunk now, along with his slatternly wife. He is in the tavern every night, and even some days in the morning."

"I have heard that his wife's housekeeping is as scandalous as his neglect of his office," she said. This was a rumor, for he and his wife never invited anyone on either side of the feud into the manse.

"Worst of all, he has become given to odious swearing and cursing, as if the devil himself had taken possession of his mouth," said Marytie. "It is shocking."

"No, worst of all," said Jan, "the other morning, after having given the Lord's Supper to his flock the very evening before, he was seen in the tap house, drinking and cursing, and playing at bowls."

"Now that is the last straw," said Margaret. "Johannes, you must do something."

"Yes," Johannes said. "It is time we act."

That afternoon, the elders of Tappan gathered around the big table in the *groote kamer* and composed a letter to their High Mightinesses in Amsterdam to complain of the scandalous behavior of the minister. "We must demand," Johannes said, "that he be charged to confess his sins from the pulpit and promise to do better."

They were all in agreement. "And if he will not desist, he must be relieved of the pulpit."

The Classis agreed, too, and from over the sea ordered him to reform himself.

He refused. He refused even to appear before a committee of the *coetus* to explain himself. He rejected all kindly efforts to heal the breach so as to preserve the church. The people despaired of ever getting rid of the monster.

*   *   *   *

The anti-authoritarian political spirit brewing beneath the surface, and the party spirit brewing out in the open, had their theological side as well. The progressives, whose parents and grandparents had been instructed in the faith by *Dominie* Bertholf, had been touched not only by his piety in their youth, but again in their middle age by the passionate evangelical ministers of the twenties. And then again, in their old age, in the forties, they were lifted up by the eloquent George Whitefield. His preaching of hellfire and damnation on the one hand and joyful devotion to God on the other, with conversion and the New Birth the necessary drama in between, renewed them once again

The other side scoffed at the idea that one must be "born anew," whatever that peculiar notion was. For them, belief, faith, rectitude, good works, dutiful church attendance, adherence to the prescribed rituals of the church were sufficient to ensure they would see the kingdom of God. They were outraged by earnest so-called New Lights claiming otherwise.

"If you don't mind, husband," she said one day, "I feel called to make peace between the factions. I feel *called*," she repeated. "So it is my duty. But this time I am informing you in advance that I shall speak in church."

He sighed. She was like a creek swollen with rain, he thought. She must do what she must do, go where she would go.

*   *   *   *

The next Sunday, again dressed in her best blue wool frock, she spoke. "I see it," she said, in her earnest, preachy way, "as a matter of two *styles* of worshiping, and I am sure that both are pleasing to God."

"We are not interested in yours views, Madam," Muzelius declared coldly. "You cannot know what pleases God."

She looked at him, up in his high pulpit. His long pasty, pockmarked face glared down at her. She was not afraid of him. She was imbued with a missionary zeal to win him over, and those in the congregation who followed him as well. "I will not be content, Reverend Sir, until you *are* interested in my views," she replied calmly. A stunned silence met her words. He flushed and looked fit to kill.

She turned back to the congregation. "It is not given," she said, with a confident air that the other side soon came to find maddening, "it is not given to everyone to be capable of understanding what 'unless one is born anew' means. It is given only to *certain ones* favored by God to understand it."

They were immediately challenged. "Certain ones?" they queried from the benches and pews. "What do you mean, certain ones, you audacious girl? Chosen ones?"

"*Certain* ones," she said. "I am fortunate to be one of them."

"What! How dare you consider yourself chosen?"

"Be not afraid," she proceeded. "God in his infinite wisdom will not reject those who have not experienced that light shining on the soul and warming it for Christ. He is a merciful God. He has promised that he will not snuff out a smoking wick or break a bruised reed."

"Light shining on the soul!" someone scoffed.

"Warming it for Christ! What license you take, woman, with your smoking wicks and bruised reeds!"

She ignored them again. "The good news is, those who have not experienced a warming of the heart for Christ might yet hope for abundant grace. And even work for it, by praying for it and reading the Bible and waiting for it to descend upon them like a dove. The good news is that a loving God will not abandon you."

"We do not have abundant grace? And you do? God would abandon us? Who are you?" they shouted at her. "Who are you to say what God would or would not do?"

Again, half the congregation rose and stormed out of the building. Friends of years, neighbors, even family members stopped speaking to one another that day over the issue of who was and who was not born anew and did not speak again for a generation.

"I had just the opposite effect from what I intended," she said ruefully.

*   *   *   *

Finally, in November 1749, twenty-two years after Muzelius came to afflict Tappan, the Classis of Amsterdam agreed that he might be censured by the *coetus* and suspended from preaching for three months. "We have had enough of your antics," they wrote. "At the end of the three months, you are to preach a penitential sermon, after which you will be declared Emeritus."

These things happened as they were supposed to, but at the end of the three months the unruly man refused to leave the parsonage for the house on Main Street rented for him by the congregation. He refused to leave the church land, where he still cut firewood and where he was seen to urinate upon a fragile bank of purple trillium, used by the people as an astringent and tonic. He refused to hand over the church records and all that belonged to the congregation. Afterward, it was suspected that it was he who had destroyed the *swart boek* of the slaves' baptisms, thrown it into the necessary or down the well, for it was never seen again, after that time, and his successor had to start a new one. He demanded a lump sum of money instead of the monthly pension the congregation had agreed to pay him. He refused to attend church. He was rude to his successor, Samuel Verbryck, a young man of good family, who was enthusiastically on the side of those who wanted to be independent of Amsterdam. Verbryck had to take up lodgings in a small rented house, unsuitable for a *dominie*, even so young and new a one, until the deacons managed to bodily dislodge Muzelius and his drunken wife from the proper parsonage.

The behavior of this so-called man of God made Margaret so angry that she felt like physically laying hands on him herself and throwing him out the door of the parsonage and kicking him down the front steps. It gave her pause, these violent thoughts. She couldn't help recalling the stories of how, twenty years before, Grietje Cosyns had wanted to spit in the eye of the land thief Lancaster Symes. It was the same wild anger against a recalcitrant man that raged in Margaret's heart.

Dominie Verbryck had to get used to being treated rudely, for over the next thirty long years, Muzelius was never to treat him with respect. He was warned time and again to change his ways, to stop preaching in private houses to the disaffected, thirty-eight families in all, to stop fomenting turbulence with his unchristian behavior. But every week came a new insult or injury. Margaret could hardly wait for Johannes to come home from the monthly consistory meetings so she could hear the latest outrage.

*   *   *   *

In their neighborhood, in the sad years when she was having miscarriages one after another, their friends and relations fell into the habit of gathering at Margaret and Johannes's house. It was their way of comforting them for their disappointments. In the cold weather they gathered in the *groote kamer,* where food and drink were always laid on the cherry table, and where there was a prodigious number of chairs. Someone had counted forty. In summer, they gathered in the *speelhuis*, under a ceiling of ripening grapes, with smoldering cattails to keep away the mosquitoes.

One warm September evening their cousins Abraham Haring and his son John came to call. The sun was setting in the west, and a full moon mounted the eastern sky over the Nyack hills. She was sad. From off in the fields, other people's children played their games in the day's last light, climbing trees, laughing, shouting, running about. She had had three disappointments in three years, the most recent just a month before, and she had begun to fear she was one of those women who would never carry a babe to term.

They sat in the *speelhuis,* sipping Johannes's Madeira and feasting on crisp and crumbling *krullen*

Abraham was Orange County's representative to the New York Assembly. He was the third in a row from the family to be its eyes and ears at the seat of government, following his father, Pieter, and his uncle, Cornelius. And just as Margaret could hardly wait for Johannes to come home from his consistory meetings to tell of the church scandals, she waited impatiently to hear what Abraham had to say about political affairs when he came home from the Assembly.

Which was not often enough. "We are glad to see you this evening, Cousin," she said. "But what keeps the Assembly so busy these days that you cannot come home more often?"

"King George's War," he said wearily. "The great and confusing war of the Austrian Succession raging in Europe in which England and France have taken opposite sides has begun to affect us here in America."

"And how does war there affect us here?"

"The Royal Governor of New York has proposed to mount an expedition to Canada to confront the French and their Indian allies on the New York boundary," he said.

"Confront them? Does that mean war?"

"Not if the Assembly has its way. It is almost to a man opposed to the undertaking. In fact, so intense is the conflict between us and the Governor, especially after he highhandedly committed artillery to New England's assault on the great French fort Louisbourg in May, that the Assembly voted to stay in session right through the harvest. It is just now that we have been able to break away."

"We've been counting," said Johannes. "You've been home about once in three weeks for the last six months."

"And my farm shows it," Abraham said. "It is going to pot this year. But then came Louisbourg. That great fort was thought to be impregnable with its thirty-foot walls bristling with a hundred cannon. It was France's Gibraltar. But a motley assortment of vessels and four English men-of-war overcame it in six weeks, much to the disgust of the Assembly. Yet even that victory did not make us change our minds. It is the economy that concerns the Assembly."

"The economy?" asked Margaret. "Not the French in Canada, and their Pope in Rome, and their Indian allies on the war path?"

"Yes, those, too. There is no doubt of that," Abraham said. "But the Assembly is of a mind to believe that New Yorkers do not want to wage a war on the frontier, pay for war, or disrupt their trade with Canada because of war."

"A toast to that," said Johannes, lifting his glass of Madeira.

Emboldened by the wine, Margaret asked a question of Abraham. "How do the other colonies feel?"

"The same," he said. "None of them wants war."

"You are a political man, cousin," she said. "So answer me this: if there can be an assembly of churches intent on independence, why not an assembly of the colonies for independence?"

Johannes looked sharply at her. "And where did you get that notion?" he asked.

She blushed. "From my reading," she said.

"And what exactly have you been reading?" asked Abraham.

"I have been reading *Two Treatises of Government* by Mr. Locke," she said. "To acquaint myself with political ideas. It is being published in the papers, and it is very fascinating."

"Yes, it is," said John Haring. "And what have you learned from the great Mr. Locke, as he is called?"

"That sovereignty belongs to the people."

"And so it does," he said. "The Dutch proved that." He laughed. "And Mr. Locke's Englishmen, too, more than once."

"And so it does indeed belong to them," echoed his father. "The people are sovereign. And I can assure you that the Assembly makes that amply clear to the Governor at every chance it gets. And I am also sure the same happens in the other colonies."

The church was the place to tell his news to his constituents, and that Sunday, Abraham stood up in the sanctuary and described how he had joined with those in the Assembly who opposed a motion to increase funds for the defense of the border. "We have opposed rebuilding the fort at Saratoga, and we have opposed the Governor's proposal to build six blockhouses on the frontier."

To the congregation, even those on the conservative side of the church troubles, this was welcome news, and it drew the two factions momentarily together.

They cheered when he described how he had voted against sending thirty militia-men to Saratoga and 450 of them to defend the northern frontier. They applauded and stamped their feet when he told them he had signed a letter to the English Governor. "The letter assured him in plain language that the circumstances of the colony of which we are the most competent judges will not suffer us to take one step further. His Excellency must know for certain that we will not allow war and the securing of our frontiers to involve us and our posterity."

"And what was the Governor's response to your letter?" Margaret asked, a little breathlessly.

"He was furious to be defied and denied. He railed that our behavior was disrespectful to him and thus must be taken as a disrespect to the fountain from whence he derives his Authority," Abraham said. "But we pointed out that that fountain is 3,000 miles away, and it is our pocketbooks and our children that would bear the costs of his ambition. In a rage, he dissolved the session. Otherwise, I would still be there."

The congregation cheered. "Change is in the air!" someone shouted.

"On that we can agree!" said another. The people cheered again.

"Amen!"

"When we reassemble," Abraham went on, "I intend to be one of those who deliver a unanimous and lengthy resolution of the Assembly to the Governor, asserting our body's undoubted rights and privileges to proceed upon all matters relating to the interest and welfare of our constituents, including going to war against the French or not going to war against the French. We shall tell him," he said, "in no uncertain terms that he is an enemy of the people whose stubborn plans to proceed with war are irregular and unprecedented. The people's prosperity is at stake!"

*   *   *   *

So thus it was that New York and New Jersey avoided war, and the 1750s as a result was a decade of prosperity. Indeed, European travelers passing through the country were amazed. They called it the garden spot of America, and they were only saying truth. It was a fine country dotted with handsome farmhouses and sturdy barns, rolling country, valuable meadows producing each year hundreds of tons of good green grass, waving fields of grain of all sorts, and all the vegetables and fruit one could name. Streams and rivers abounded in fish of all descriptions, and the forests were full of food for the table simply by aiming one's musket.

White men still toiled on the land, of course, and still with the help of slaves, now numbering about one to every five whites. But the white men had trades in addition to their farm income. Margaret's male relatives were tailors and tanners, farriers and wheelwrights, carpenters, coopers, and cabinetmakers, lawyers and merchants, bakers and blacksmiths, printers and masons.

"The slaves make it all possible, keep in mind," she told her children. "Their free labor is the principal foundation of our comfortable life."

"Yes," said Johannes. "They allow us the freedom to earn our livings or occupy our time in pursuits not so arduous as the endless cycles of plowing and sowing and mowing and threshing."

"And as a bonus," said Margaret dryly, "they are docile again." The hangings and the burnings at the stake in 1741 still sobered them in the '50s.

As for him, he did not need to work. Though he had studied surveying and the law in his youth, and then, not certain what profession to pursue, theology, which had led him to Hebrew, and Greek, and Latin, so that he was the most educated person in the community, other than the minister, he had not been obliged to have a trade or a profession to make life comfortable. He left to the slaves the tending of his fields, and the profits from his wheat and rye, oats, buckwheat, and barley he put at interest, and that is what they lived on. He much preferred to spend his days reading.

A bookworm indeed—she was right about that—he was adept at Greek and Latin, at home in the great epics of Virgil, in the Odes, Satires, and Epistles of Horace, and in the Iliad and Odyssey of Homer. He pored over his Hebrew Bible and Greek Testament, but his favorite was the literature of the fathers of the Reformation period, especially Melanchthon and Calvin. He had considered for a time studying for the ministry. But in the end he did not travel that road. He was content to read.

Margaret did not share his literary interests. She gravitated to a different literature, but he had come not to mind her independent nature, particularly as he had long ago conceded that he was incapable of stifling it. She read and reread Sir Walter Raleigh's *History of the World*, Locke on the role of government, serialized in the New York papers, the parliamentary debates in London, the proceedings of the Assembly, the course of the church wars, all reported in the papers. This reading caught her deeply up both in what he thought of as the politics of religious matters and the religion of political matters. As unseemly as he privately considered this reading matter to be, for a woman, he knew better than to forbid her. "My dear politician," he would tease her, when she spoke of the "role of the government" or the "sovereignty of the people."

"I am nothing of a politician," she insisted. "But I want to know these things, so that I may be *useful*."

"You are useful, my dearest," he said.

"I don't mean useful merely to my family," she said. "I want to be useful to society."

"Do you consider it a woman's place," he asked, "to be useful to society in the way you mean?"

"Do I think it's unfeminine?" she taunted him. "No, husband, I do not."

He flushed. "I'm sorry, my dear. I'm an old-fashioned sort of man. I can't help my thoughts any more than you can help yours."

"I forgive you," she said. "You are incorrigibly stuck in time. Still, I want to be useful in the way I mean."

✳   ✳   ✳   ✳

She was an idealist. They both were. In fact, her idealism was what had originally attracted him to her. Yet, she was not purely idealistic, as he had once naively assumed, for he had discovered that she loved her things, too, the English niceties (the gew-gaws, he called them) that flooded into New York and that she hankered after. "So many *things*, Margaret," he sighed. "Far more than we need, or should want."

She laughed.

"You baffle me," he said, "caring for salvation and ending slavery and envisioning an assembly of the colonies, but yearning for *stuff*."

Still, he had to smile to himself to see how readily she forgot her good causes when a ship came in.

"The *Lady Gage* is in from London," she reported to Willemptie, one summer day in 1756. "Let us go!"

The two tall, blond second cousins and best friends went twice a year to the city to take in the newest ladies' fashions and homewares, buy pewter cutlery, faience and redware plates and bowls, looking glasses, bed and table linens, had them packed and shipped to Tappan by sloop. This day, they fingered bolts of brocaded silk and Chinese damasks, stays of baleen boning lined with satin. They lingered at Stephen Rapalje's store near the lower end of the Fly Market, surrounded by fabrics, calicoes of many sorts, cambrics, lawns, English and Indian taffetas, broadcloths, shaloons, Irish poplins and linens, mohair, silk. They stared in astonishment at the gowns in the shop windows, extraordinarily wide at the hips and undergirded by hoops. They still wore the dome-shaped skirts, with cone-shaped bodices, of the 1740s. "I could never wear such a gown," said Margaret. "I would feel a complete fool, as if I were sitting on a giant pumpkin."

She bought herself purple mitts from an assortment just unloaded from the *Lady Gage*, and a box of fine spermacetia candles. They passed up shops selling loafsugar, tea, and wine, lemons, limes, and spices. These items they could easily acquire in the markets at Hackensack and at the store at the Slote, which was no longer owned by Margaret's family but now by Willemptie's husband Casparus Mabie and his brother Abraham. She splurged on a pair of silver buckles for Johannes's shoes (a shocking eighteen pounds). He was aghast when she presented them to him that evening. "I shall wear them, year in and year out for as long as I can could walk on my feet, to get their worth out of them," he declared.

She laughed.

In the country, the peddlers who passed her way in Tappan with their wagons full of trinkets knew they were always welcome at her door. From such a peddler she acquired two copper candle sconces to go with the copper candelabra that had been Marytie's. And she hinted to Johannes at a new house, too, or at least an expansion of Marytie and Cosyn's house, now twenty years old, where they had lived since they married, and new furniture to fill it. But Johannes, always prudent, ruled against these ambitions. "There must be a limit to our spending," he cautioned, "for the outflow of our silver and gold on mere goods will cause us, if we are not careful, to betake ourselves to all possible arts to make our remittances to British merchants."

"You are right," she said meekly. She contented herself with studying the mansion houses of rich American merchants springing up along the Hudson River, even on the west shore of it, with their five-bay façades and their pedimented doorways, formal rooms downstairs on either side of a center hall with doors at both ends to let the breezes cool the house. And the impressive houses on the Green in Hackensack, with stone walls three feet thick, and rooms finished in fine paneling, fireplaces adorned with Delft tiles. To these houses, periaugers and sloops, bateaux and yawls, sailed up and down the Hackensack and into deep tidal creeks to docks and stores and mills, off loaded their European wares and took on their cargoes of grain and timber for sale in New York.

"How Abraham and the Assembly were right," he said. "War would be fatal to our prosperity, our economy."

"Why would England want to war with France anyway? Why would anyone want to go to war?"

"The English are of a warlike nature," he said. "They seem to require war to be at ease with themselves. They warred with the Dutch nation three times in the last century."

*   *   *   *

"Bestir yourself from your reading and let us drive to see Dirck Dey's new house," she cajoled, one fine day.

He couldn't refuse her. He loved her more with every passing year. After twelve years of marriage he was even getting used to her.

He put his book aside and drove her in their new riding chair to see the elegant Georgian plantation house built by Dey in Preakness, the first one of its kind west of the Passaic River. Two stories tall, with five windows on the front façade on both floors, it was of soft rose-colored brick, and its slate roof was the first they had seen. "It is very genteel," she said wistfully.

The word *genteel* was bandied about these days. "*I* want to be genteel," she said on the way home along the bumpy rutted road.

"I thought you wanted to be useful," he teased.

"Why not both?" she retorted.

"We are genteel," he said. "We don't need to show it off."

"I suppose so," she admitted.

In their rural way, of course, she knew they were. They belonged to the small prosperous minority in the community that could live comfortably on the proceeds of the money they had put at interest.

"We have plenty and some to spare. But it doesn't mean we can be spendthrift," he cautioned. "It's not our way."

"You are right," she said.

Still, it didn't mean she couldn't read books that instructed her in the amazing new refinements, how fashionable women dressed, conversed, behaved, decorated their houses, even though it made her dissatisfied with her own. She gazed upon the elegant townhouses in the city and the merchants' country houses springing up on the Hudson, large, two-story houses with grand staircases with turned balustrades and swirling rails. Their big windows and high ceilings made her sturdy farmhouse seem dark and cramped, especially on a gloomy day.

But a grand mansion in the English style was not in her future. That was clear to her when she walked one day with Willemptie from Comfort's dock near Trinity Church on the Hudson through the pleasant city streets shaded with beech and locust and lime trees, and elms, to view the mansions on the landfill on the East River. "If I were a city house," she mused, "I would have to be one of the strong and neat brick houses, in the old Dutch style, gable on the street side, a balcony on the roof with views of the water, the roof shingled in white cedar. Within, my walls would be whitewashed above and covered with framed pictures, wainscotted below, the woodwork a bluish gray color."

"I wonder why it is," said Willemptie, "that we have been legally English for eighty years and yet we still keep to the Dutch ways?"

"It is because we hate the English," said Margaret. "We hate them because of the wars they put us to in the old days. We have not forgotten those. And because they made laws to keep us from our markets, and because they came here and took our colony. And because the English governor took our land into New York. And because the Englishman Symes came and took it again. We have many reasons to hate them. Of course we hate them. We always will."

Willemptie sighed.

"So that is why," Margaret said, "that is why, if I were a house I would have to be a Dutch house. Not a house such as this," she said, stopping in front of Elbert Haring's house on Bleecker Street. She knew the handsome house well, for before marrying she had lived in it for four years when she did the accounts for Elbert's bakery. "It has stylish moldings and panelings, Willemptie, and is chock-full of mahogany chairs and tables, gilt-framed mirrors, walnut tea tables, gleaming brass andirons in the style called Georgian after the King. And you should see the equipage of tea drinking in that house: the silver teapots and the long-handled silver mote spoons for clearing the tea spout and little short-handled English silver spoons for ladling the tea into the English porcelain tea pot. Indeed, I would have to give up my very Dutchness, wake up some morning as an entirely different person, an *English* person, to be matched to a house such as our Elbert possesses."

Although the elegant trappings of the genteel life were readily available in the shops of the city, they were beyond the reach of her husband's ambitions and, she had to admit, of his nature and her own. She could observe the fast-changing world full of novel refinements and varied and rich commodities, observe it, admire it, wonder at it. But something within her restrained her from too dearly wanting it.

"We have our own ways," Johannes said. "And they are good enough. Content yourself with a little redecorating."

"I shall," she said.

She had the slaves paint the white plaster walls of the *groote kamer*, which served as parlor, dining area, and bed chamber, a vivid yellow, the color of egg yolk, to bring light into the room, and the wainscoting and woodwork a rich reddish brown, and she had them scour the tulipwood floors until they gleamed nearly white. She covered the gate-leg table where they took their meals with a brilliant new turkey carpet whose figures were illuminated by the candles in the copper candelabra and the copper sconces.

She banished the last of the old-fashioned chairs (Marytie's chairs) to the garret, replaced them with new fiddlebacks with Turkey-work woven wool seats. She hung blue and white linen curtains at the windows and a red-fringed chimney cloth over the manteltree and polished the old Dutch andirons until the brass gleamed. Her sweet-gum *kas* was stocked with linen sheets and damask tablecloths and napkins and jacquard coverlets and chimney cloths and curtains in quantities she knew she would never need, and she lovingly arranged and rearranged her treasured faience plates and bowls along its massive cornice. Her boxed feather beds were plump with pillows and bolsters and coverlets and hung with bright curtains. She was content with it. And if it was Dutch, well, so be it. So were they.

*   *   *   *

The topic of war came up again in the Assembly. The papers were full of it.

"Why would anyone want to go to war?" she asked of her cousin Abraham, when he came to visit.

"No one does," he said, "except the King and Parliament and the King's appointed governors. They are raring for it."

The King and Parliament and the governors got their way. In the summer of 1757, news arrived that England and France had gone to war. And the war went on for seven years. As it finally ended, in 1763, the Dutch churches in New York City called to their pulpits a Scotsman, Archibald Laidlie, the first English-preaching *dominie* in 135 years. Yes, change was in the air indeed.

Now, when picnicking under the trees after church, at baptisms and weddings and funerals, at barn raisings and harvest festivals and knitting bees, the topic inevitably came up of the parallel between the troubles in the Dutch churches wanting to be independent and the troubles brewing in the colonies with the King and Parliament of England.

"Will the colonies ever dare think of independence as the church has?" people wondered aloud in the taverns and around the laden tables under the trees between the morning and afternoon services.

"*Will* we ever gather into an assembly of colonies to show our strength? What is your opinion?" Margaret asked Johannes.

Drawing on his clay pipe, he gazed thoughtfully upon her, his tall, comely, blond, sturdy, healthy, independent-minded wife. "Somehow," he said, knocking the tobacco from the bowl, "it no longer seems possible that we will not."

CHAPTER 14

▼

DEFENDER

Change was coming, that was clear. Except for one thing that never changed. From the beginning, as each generation came to learn anew, they could count on trouble with the land.

John Haring sighed heavily. Thirty years old in 1769, and toying with plans to run for his ailing father's seat in the New York Assembly, he stared out the window of the room in his father's house that he used as his law office. He had not had a client in weeks, and except for writing a few wills and deeds here and there, his practice could be said to be moribund. There was little to occupy a lawyer in sleepy Tappan.

It was time to move on, as his father was urging him to do, move on to take up the Orange County seat in the Assembly. It was the land problem that was holding him back.

"Go to visit Mary," his mother suggested after church that morning. She was eager for him to marry, and she knew of his feelings for his second cousin, Mary Haring, Elbert's daughter.

"Yes," he said vaguely. "Mary."

"You sound as if you have forgotten who she is," his mother said.

But he had not forgotten Mary. He hoped to make her his wife some day, though she had no idea of this as yet.

Her mother was eager for the match, too. Mary was eighteen, young for him at thirty, but of a marriageable age even so. But her mother, though she knew his intentions and looked kindly on them, did not consider the time ripe for a proposal of matrimony. The girl, who was determined to be "of use" to the world (a ridiculous notion, in her mother's opinion), had recently thrown herself into missionary work and under the direction of *Dominie* Laidlie's wife spent her mornings laboring among the impoverished and bedraggled of the city both for their material benefit and their eternal welfare. She labored on behalf of impoverished white people, that is. But it was whispered that she was also for the abolishment of slavery.

"She has committed herself to Mrs. Laidlie and her missionary work in the huts and hovels of the city. But I am hoping," her mother had added, "that when the heat of July and August arrives to cook the city's normal stink into its foul summer stench, her interest in her so-called work will decline in proportion to the reek. And I am hoping that the decline will be permanent. Then will be the time for you to broach marriage."

He often went to the city to call upon her family of a Sunday afternoon. The two families were close. Her father, his uncle, had already appointed him one of his executors, and John Haring had more than a passing interest in his uncle's affairs, for Elbert owned one of the largest properties in the city, a farm of 200 acres and on it several valuable houses and a prosperous bakery, and of course he had slaves aplenty, fine furnishings, livestock, and substantial sums at interest. A woman's worth was not something to overlook when choosing a wife.

They strolled into the garden and sat together in the shade of the grape arbor. Near them a slave raked leaves off the walkways of crushed oyster shells, while in the distance others bent over their hoes in the vegetable garden. He saw that she frowned. Their servitude caused her pain, it was known.

He sighed.

"That is the third sigh I've heard from you this day, John," she said. "What is on your mind?"

"Trouble with the land again."

Now it was her turn to sigh. "And what might it be this time?"

"It is rumored," he said glumly, "that the royal commission appointed to settle an irksome boundary dispute once and for all is about to announce its decision. Perhaps this very week."

"And?"

"And I fear the decision might not go well for us in the country."

He wished he could reach out to take her soft little hand in his own, but he knew he must not. He must content himself with admiring her pretty face, her curling blond hair, her intelligent blue eyes, her careful dress. He liked to think she had chosen her gown and petticoat and blue damask shoes with him in mind this day.

She cocked her pretty head at him. "And why is that?"

"As you know, we have long had troubles in the country with boundaries," he said.

"I know there has been an especially long and vexatious dispute over the boundary between New York and New Jersey," she said. "Is that what you refer to?"

"Yes. It is finally, at long last, now coming to a head."

She was silent for a moment, recalling what she knew of the land troubles. "The land is cursed, some say."

"Some say it."

"Do you agree?"

"I agree that there has been a long history of trouble," he said. "From the beginning, even before we could settle on it."

"When four of our leaders died, all in the same month."

"Yes. Including our great-grandfather."

"Yes," she said. "That dreadful accident."

"The currents are swift and strong in the Hudson."

"Dreadful," she repeated sorrowfully. Their hearts swelled with sadness at the thought of the men's fright and panic, their great-grandfather's death by water in the icy cold Hudson, the horror when the news reached the families, the other deaths coming on the heels of his.

She took her lace handkerchief out from the embroidered pocket around her waist and dabbed at her eyes. He took out his own handkerchief from his pocket and flicked a bee away from her bodice with it. Her gentle heart pleased him. *I love you,* he wanted to say, fiercely.

"And then some of the other leaders dropped out."

"Yes. They were frightened off by a comet at around that time, and the deaths convinced them to desert the plan."

"Cowards," she murmured.

"Yes," he said. "It was the sons of the four who died who ended up having to clear and plant the land, and they were young, too."

"Our grandfathers, yours and mine, were among them. I have heard the stories many times."

She pleased him to the core! *We have so much in common, my dearest!* he wanted to say. "And they had no sooner begun to clear it than the English Governor declared the land to be in New York, not New Jersey," he said, sighing.

"And I have forgotten why that mattered."

"It thwarted their plans for trade. Once the land was in New York, they had to pay New York custom to sell their market goods."

"The *English*," she said scornfully.

"And then in the next generation another Englishman came and claimed the best part of the land as his own. Successfully, too. The five surviving owners had to pay through the nose to retain what was lawfully theirs. And we are still paying for it."

"How can that be so?"

"It diminished our fortunes then, and the effect ripples on. It cannot be made up."

"When my father speaks of Tappan," she said, "he always says 'land so fair, peace so rare.'"

"That is the saying."

They were silent for a moment, gazing at each other. *We have so much in common!* she thought. He was a handsome man, dark haired and green eyed, unlike most of her blond, blue-eyed relations. A serious, a thoughtful man. Her married sisters teased her about him after his Sunday visits, hinting that he would one day pay court to her. Or that he was already paying court to her.

Will we marry? she wondered. And why not? He was considered the most promising man of his generation in the family. And she did not regard herself as too young for him. So why should they not marry? But my endeavors! she thought with a pang. It would be a great disappointment to Mrs. Laidlie if she deserted her work among the poor and unchurched. The wretched of the earth needed her. She could not marry until she had done some good for the world.

She blushed at her thoughts and changed her mind's subject back to his subject, the land and its troubles. "Slavery has been another trouble of the land," she said. Slavery was a pet topic of hers. She wondered what his opinions were of it. She could not marry a man who tolerated it, that was certain.

"Ah, yes. If they had not had the land to clear and plant, they would not have needed slaves, nor would we today." What had made her blush? he wondered.

"But then how were they to live without land, thus without slaves? How are we, even today? People cannot imagine how."

"Mary," he said, yearning to take her in his arms and kiss her. "We will learn how, someday, somehow. If we know what's good for us. The slaves want their freedom, and in the end they will have it, if we give it to them or not."

"I believe they must be free," she said softly. She was about to blurt out that she was glad they were of like mind on the subject. But something stopped her. It would be forward to draw attention to such an intimate thought, a thought linking them in mind, if not in body. She blushed again, at the image of being linked to him in body.

"Yes," he said. "In the end they must be." *I am smitten!* he thought. He could hardly remove his gaze from her comely intelligent face, longed to take in his her little hands beneath the lace ruffles on her sleeves. But no, though he was love-struck, he must restrain himself!

"Let us look at the garden," she said, standing. "Come." She took his arm, and now it was his turn to blush at this gesture that seemed to him so wifely. He swallowed hard and turned his face away so she could not see his agitation.

They wandered beyond the arbor into the garden, strolled along the oyster-shell walks, admired the tall nodding delphiniums and phlox, the fragrant stock, the big pink cleomes trembling on their stalks.

He cleared his throat. "The cause of the boundary dispute between the two colonies was imprecise language in the original document of 1664," he said. "Or am I boring you?"

"Oh, no, not at all! I like to hear it."

He brightened. It was a topic he knew intimately. He continued: "The sticking point was that the document read that the southerly end of the boundary line was 41 degrees latitude on the Hudson River, and the northern end of it was at the northernmost branch of the Delaware River at 41 degrees and forty minutes of latitude."

"And?"

"And the trouble was, no tributary of the Delaware River wandered anywhere in the direction described."

"But since they knew the degrees and minutes, couldn't they agree?"

He smiled. He admired her quickness. If only she had not gotten caught up in this quixotic pastime of hers, ministering to the destitute and the hopeless. He was thirty. It was time to settle down! Suppose, he thought, a radical idea suddenly popping into head: Suppose I were to offer that she might continue with her "work," as she calls it, after marriage?

Whoa, he thought to himself, slow down. Don't scare her away. He put the idea out of his head.

"No, unfortunately, they could not agree," he said. "Over the years, the royal governors appointed commissioners to attempt to reach agreement, but none could. The settlers resorted to violence whenever it was proposed to reconcile the matter. They were determined to assert their right to be New Yorkers, or New Jerseyans, as they perceived their advantage to lie."

"And the wise men went away, scratching their heads over it."

"Yes," he said. She was so bright, so quick, so the very one for him.

And then he could stand it no longer. "Cousin?" he said, turning to her on the oyster-shell path.

"Yes?"

"Mary?" He went down on one knee before her. "Mary, is it possible that we could sail together in our own boat?"

Her lovely face flushed. "Sail in our own boat?" she asked.

"I'm sorry," he said. "It was my clumsy way of meaning marriage. I mean, will you do me the honor to be my wife?"

"Oh!" she said.

He was furious with himself. Why had he put it in such a lame, ridiculous way! Sailing our own boat!

"I am honored, Cousin."

His heart leaped.

"But ..."

"But?" His heart sank.

"But," she faltered, "but there is my work with Mrs. Laidlie. I have joined her in trying to alleviate the misery of the poor and helpless of the city. She would be enormously disappointed if I should desert her. And so would *they*. They already look forward to seeing me. And hear me talk of their improvement."

He could see how devoted she was to her ... work. But where there is a will, there is a way, he thought. He wanted her! He had to have her! "It would not be inconceivable to me that you should continue with your interests after marriage," he said, rather stiffly.

She stared at him. "What an idea," she said wonderingly. "A married woman with interests outside of her home?"

"Mrs. Laidlie is a married woman," he said.

"So she is."

"I have taken the liberty of speaking to your mother," he said, "and she has spoken to your father. They approve of our marrying. Perhaps they will approve of your continuing with ... Mrs. Laidlie after we marry." It was hard for him to utter the word *work*.

She clapped her hands. "Then," she said, "if I can have it both ways, it will be my great honor to be your wife, John Haring!" She extended her hands to him and helped him to his feet. "The novelty of it," she murmured, almost to herself. "Married and continuing my interests.... I can hardly believe it. Wait till I tell my sisters!"

He laughed, much relieved. He led her to a bench under a lime tree, and they sat close together side-by-side, so close it seemed to him a kind of bundling. "You have made me the happiest man alive," he murmured into her little pink ear. "I have loved you for two years."

"And I you, Cousin," she said, looking into his eyes. "We shall be happy together."

"I cannot believe my good fortune," he said.

*   *   *   *

The next day, the trouble John Haring had been expecting exploded in his very lap. The commission announced its binding verdict—by which New Jersey to its dismay lost over 150,000 acres to New York.

In Orangetown, to the stupefaction of him and the rest of the inhabitants, 150 families, including at least twenty-five households in the Haring family, now found themselves in Bergen County on the New Jersey side of the border. Their beloved Reformed Church in Tappan and the Tappan courthouse were still in New York, but they themselves no longer were. "We are dismembered from the colony and exposed to utter ruin," they cried, running to each other in the lanes, in the fields, in the churchyard, in the taverns, wringing their hands, some tearing their hair.

Their lamentations were loud and long. "It is Governor Dongan all over again!"

"It is Lancaster Symes all over again!"

"How could this happen to us?"

"How are we not in control of our own land?"

"How are we not in control of our own politics?" said John Haring, for to him it was first and last a political matter. For generations, men of his family had represented Orange County in the New York Assembly. But now, by a stroke of the pen, his father, Abraham—though sick of body still the county's duly elected representative—was ineligible for the office he had held for a quarter of a century. Thus the family was cruelly cut off from its loyal constituents and from the political allies and benefactors they had cultivated in eighty years of service. Utterly ruined indeed, it seemed.

He sought the advice of his uncle and soon-to-be father-in-law. "With an election for the New York Assembly coming up this very year, should I fight back? Shall I run for my father's seat in the election?"

Elbert looked puzzled. "How can that be? You now live in New Jersey," he said.

"Yes. I shall have to build myself a house on the New York side of the new boundary. A nice parcel of land there is earmarked for me in my father's will."

"It will be a vicious election," Elbert said doubtfully. "The Livingstons in the country are already stirring up the Presbyterians and the Dutch, and the DeLancey faction in the city is marshaling the Episcopalians."

"They are," John said. "And the Livingstons threaten mayhem—bloodshed, even, if there is foul play on the part of the DeLanceys."

"The foul play has already started," said Elbert. "The DeLanceys are sending their agents into the countryside, stirring up the tenants and small farmers against the Livingston land hogs, as they call them."

"I know it will be vicious," said John Haring. "But I think I can win. If I build my house, and stand for election for Orange County, I believe the people will elect me."

"What about Mary?" Elbert asked. "Would she like living in the country? She is so devoted to Mrs. Laidlie and her efforts to help the poor."

"Our *dominie's* wife, Mrs. Verbryck, also engages in good works," said John. "She would welcome Mary's assistance."

"Well, in that case," Elbert said. "It will have to be between the two of you."

"I shall persuade her," John said.

"She is fond of the city," Elbert said.

John smiled. "If I win the election, we will occupy my father's house in the city when the Assembly is in session. I believe Mary will not mind having the best of both worlds. That seems to be in her nature," he added.

He built his house in Tappan, and stood for his father's seat, but his trouble and expense came to naught. He did not win the election, for the DeLanceys practiced vote fraud. He went to court to have the results overturned, but this was unavailing.

It was a double blow, a blow to the 150 families so ignominiously dispossessed of their colony. And a blow to Tappan as well. Not only was it bereft of twenty-five households of its leading family, but it had lost its voice in the Assembly, probably for good.

"I am not so sure about that," said Elbert. "If the English persist in squeezing us as they are doing, it may be that even the New York Assembly's days are numbered."

*   *   *   *

In the same year that their cousin lost this important election, Margaret Blauvelt began to keep her eye on Cathlyntie Mabie, with her eldest son John in mind.

Cathlyntie was the daughter of her best friend and second cousin Willemptje Eckerson and Casparus Mabie, a prosperous merchant and tavern-keeper in Tappan. As a baby Catie had been as bright as a bee, curious and adventurous, and comely, too. Anyone could see that she would develop into a vivacious merry girl full of ideas, and fair of face, like her mother, and she was.

"She is just the right age for John," she gushed to Johannes.

He laughed. "The two are but ten and twelve," he said. "Aren't you counting your chickens?"

"Not at all," she said. "It is common sense. Her father owns the best house in Tappan. As our John is to come one day into an inheritance that is nothing to sniff at, why shouldn't they join their fortunes?"

He chuckled again

"What is so funny?" she said crossly.

"The girl is one of eight children. She has older brothers. What makes you think she'll get the house?"

"I will work on it with Willemptie," she said. "Willemptie will see the logic in it."

He sighed. "I suppose you are already entertaining delightful fancies of the young couple presiding over the most prestigious site in town, raising a brood of healthy *kinder* in that commodious eight-room house, and of Cathlyntie taking up the role of matriarch when you are gone."

"You are not far wrong."

"And am I wrong in suspecting that some additional long-range planning underlies your fancy?" he said.

"You are not wrong," she said. "You know me too well, husband. But it is only sensible to think ahead."

"And what is the long-range plan, may I ask?" he inquired.

She took a deep breath. "I have it all worked out," she said. "Once John and Cathlyntie are in possession of Casparus's house, then we can settle our old farm on Isaac and our new farm on Abraham." Abraham was a twin; the slow one, they called him. The "new" farm was the house that Cosyn and Marytie had built in 1737, where she and Johannes had lived since they married. The old farm had been Jan and Aeltie's, built in 1704.

"Always thinking," he said. "You are ever the schemer."

"Is that such a crime?" she asked tartly.

*　　　*　　　*　　　*

These fine plans for the future did not take place. Ten years later, John and Cathlyntie at twenty-four and twenty-two indeed married, in 1779, right in the middle of what was being called the "American Revolution." But Casparus Mabie, six years earlier, had sold his house, that convenient stone house, four rooms on a floor, with a good barn, garden, and sundry other conveniences, to his cousin, the rich widow of Elbert Haring of New York City. After living in it for a few years, Mrs. Haring tired of the country and sold the house to Frederick Blauvelt, who wanted it for his only child, Elizabeth, the wife of Cornelius Mabie, Cathlyntie's brother.

"So, you see," said Johannes. "There it is."

"So, I see," said Margaret ruefully. "So much for well-laid plans."

John and Cathlyntie had to make do with a little house on land north of the church that he was eventually to inherit from his father, land on which also stood an old stone barn from an earlier period and the usual outbuildings and sheds, smokehouse, icehouse, hay barrack, all of which had seen better days. Because of the uncertainties of life and death during that terrible time and terrible place in what came to be called the neutral ground, because neither the British army nor the Continental army could hold it, though both fought for it, they thought it wise to invest their labor in a modest property, which theirs certainly was. In hives behind the house, Cathlyntie would keep bees. But this is to get ahead of the story.

*　　　*　　　*　　　*

In 1763, the Seven Years' War between England and France ended, and new developments were occurring that did not sit well with the people. In Tappan, Margaret and Johannes's house was one of the places where they gathered to hash out the new developments.

Margaret encouraged their company, laying out her best *zoete koek*, spiced sweet bread, which Marytie had taught her to make, and her small seed cakes and her *olie-koecken* and urging Johannes to be generous with his cider and rum and Madeira. "Give them food and drink, and they will come back," she said, "and I like them to come. I am discovering these days that I like political conversation almost more than talk of slavery."

"Or even of salvation?"

"Yes," she said. "Even that these days."

"For shame," he teased.

"It is time," she said. "We have been chafing at British taxes and laws and civil restrictions for a hundred years."

The company agreed with her. "Yes," said John Haring one night. "But in fact, we have had it good, if we speak the truth. For a hundred years, England has been so preoccupied with her wars in Europe that we have got away with all sorts of sins. We have happily committed customs fraud, smuggled as we pleased, shipped our goods where we wished, issued paper money as we needed it, and even began to manufacture cloth, ignoring the laws designed to force us to buy cloth of British manufacture. We have prospered mightily."

"But now that is changing," said Samuel Demarest. "Now that the French threat has been removed from the continent, Mother England has decided to train her attention on us, tighten her control over our economy and our defenses, and levy taxes to pay off the expenses of her wars. Thus the brilliant Stamp Act."

"A fatal mistake," said John Haring. "For I believe the stamps will have the effect of uniting us in a common purpose."

"Stamps are a folly. They will be the ruination of America! The bells will toll in mourning when the stamp ship arrives in port, and eager soldiers will spike up the cannon in the fort for action, you can be sure."

"Stamps are a new idea but a bad idea. Uniting is not a new idea, but it is a good idea," John Haring observed.

"Unacquainted as I am with politics," she ventured (having learned to defuse in this deferential way any prejudice against a woman speaking out on such matters), "did not Benjamin Franklin propose ten years ago that the colonies unite?" All those years she had kept, pressed into her Psalm book, a copy of his cartoon "join, or die" that she had cut from a New York paper.

Johannes looked at her in that sharp way he had when he suspected she was to begin speaking her mind. "Yes, wife," he said. "But union was a Dutch idea before it was Franklin's."

"And Franklin well knew it," said John Haring. "He much admired how the Dutch provinces united to protect themselves against their common enemy."

"Protestant England is as much a threat to us as Catholic Spain was to the Dutch," said Samuel Demarest, a Frenchman.

"Even an Englishman as I am can grow excited at the thought that the colonies might imitate the Dutch system," said Edward Blake. "And join lest we die."

"What union can do for us we need only look to those United Provinces to know," agreed Thomas Jewell, a Scotsman.

They were all in agreement, whatever their nation of origin. "It is plain as a post," said Gardner Jones. "United we could, as a legal, regular, and firm confederation, lay a sure and lasting foundation of dominion, power, and trade."

"A toast to union!"

They all quaffed deeply.

Samuel Demarest set down his tankard so hard that its contents splashed upon the table. "Then what is taking us so long?" he demanded. "We detest how the British require us to now purchase and affix stamps to all legal documents and licenses, even to newspapers and almanacs and playing cards. We detest it. Why should we obey them?"

"It is hard to imagine what they could be thinking of," Johannes said. "Charging us twenty shillings for stamps to a liquor license, five shillings to have a will probated, two shillings to put an advertisement in a newspaper!"

"Especially when the economy has gone into decline," said Demarest. "They must imagine we are unmindful of our ancient rights and privileges. What right have they to tax us unless we sit in Parliament and have our say?"

"I am curious. What do the English estimate they will raise by the Stamp Act?" asked John Huyler, among the men and women gathered one night around the fireside at Yoast Mabie's house.

"They estimate they'll raise 60,000 pounds," John Haring said.

"I predict they will raise hardly a shilling, if we refuse to buy the bloody things," growled Samuel Demarest.

"Let us refuse to buy them, then!" Huyler said.

Demarest's prediction was correct. The Stamp Act raised hardly a shilling, because the colonists refused to buy them. But it did raise questions. "What are the limits of British power?" men and women began to ask each other in taverns and churches, in *groote kamer* and *speelhuis*. "What are the limits? Where does it stop?"

The heady talk, coming from every direction, evening after evening, made her brain spin.

"For hundreds of years, haven't Englishmen had a right to be taxed only by their own representatives? And haven't we been Englishmen for a century and more?"

"In fact, where is it written that we should be taxed at all, unless we have direct representation in Parliament?"

"I predict that the idea that we might demand an end even to the low taxes we pay, compared to the long-suffering English, who pay twenty-six times more in taxes than we do, and are nowhere so prosperous, will be greeted in London with derision," John Haring said.

"Let them deride!"

"Derision will only encourage us!"

In New York, as in Boston, and all through the colonies, men described by one royal governor as young, hot, and giddy began to call themselves the Sons of Liberty and put forth the idea of forming a "congress" and petitioning the King and Parliament to repeal the Stamp Act. The people rose in a body in every colony to resist the hated legislation, with representatives of nine colonies famously gathering in New York in the Stamp Act Congress.

The petition went nowhere. In London, the Congress and the Liberty Boys were ignored.

But in America, the colonists cheered when the Sons of Liberty in New York ran the stamp master out of town and looted his house. They cheered when a thousand merchants signed agreements promising not to import British goods. They would nonimport with a passion. And they roared their approval when Parliament, a year after it passed it, revoked the despised Act. They had got their way!

It was not noticed at first, or perhaps it was simply overlooked, because it was so absurd, that the same day Parliament revoked the Stamp Act, it passed another act, a presumptuous, outlandish piece of legislation called the Declaratory Act.

"What exactly does it declare?" Margaret asked, when John Haring brought them news of it.

"It declares that the colonies will always be subordinate to King and Parliament and that Parliament has a right to pass any act it pleases to bind the colonies and people of America," he said.

"Whatever makes them in London think it could be acceptable to us?"

"I am at a loss," he said.

"Things are coming to a head," Margaret murmured.

"But we do not, cannot, imagine ourselves declaring independence from our King and Parliament," Johannes protested.

"I am not so sure that we cannot," said John Haring.

Yes, husband, speak for yourself, Margaret thought.

"It is better that we behave like dutiful children, who have received unmerited blows from a beloved parent," Johannes said. "In time, the good parent will see the error of his ways."

But the beloved parent was having none of it. Parliament ordered the royal governor of Massachusetts to dissolve the legislature and sent two regiments of British troops to Boston to quell the upstart children.

And then came the Tea Act crisis. Parliament had granted the British East India Company a monopoly on all the trade between India and the rest of the empire. The Company owned 17 million pounds of Indian tea, which Parliament heavily taxed. Stored in English warehouses, it was sold to English wholesalers, who sold it to American wholesalers, who sold it to local merchants for sale to the consumer. This long chain of command caused the price of the tea to be high. So the colonists bought Dutch-grown tea smuggled in from Indonesia. The quality was just as good, and it was half as cheap.

In 1773, the British prime minister remitted the main tax on England's tea, retaining only the three-penny Townshend Act tax—"in order to remind the colonists of Parliament's right to tax as it pleased," he said—and the government began selling the tea directly in America through American merchants acting as English agents. English merchants and American wholesalers were left out of the picture.

Although the idea was to reduce the price of the tea and raise the demand for it, and thus undercut the demand for the smuggled Dutch tea, the colonists understood the logic differently. "If Parliament can grant the East India Company a monopoly of the tea trade, it can do the same with any part of American commerce," men pointed out in the taverns and houses where they gathered nightly to talk it out.

"And if our trade can be taxed," Johannes said, "why not our lands, why not the produce of our lands, why not every thing we possess or make use of?"

"Who can call anything his own that can be taken away at the pleasure of another?"

"In that case, why would we not be slaves to English masters?"

"We *would* be slaves to English masters," Margaret said. "In my humble opinion, we must not let that happen."

Opposition was unanimous. American sea captains refused to transport the tea from London to American ports, and when some of it did arrive the merchants chosen to sell it in America were harassed just as the stamp masters had been, and run out of town, too, their houses looted after them.

When the tea ships arrived in New York, the authorities refused to allow them to be unloaded. "In any case, they could have been unloaded only at the point of the bayonet and the muzzle of the cannon," the governor glumly reported to Parliament after the tea ships in New York harbor had slunk back to England.

But in Boston harbor, a band of colonists disguised as Indians and witnessed by a crowd of thousands, boarded three tea ships and dumped the tea chests into the drink.

In New York they cheered for the Boston Tea Party in 1773, when news of it came at Christmas time. "Our rights," they cried in the streets, most of all they remembered their rights, particularly their right to representation in Parliament in return for paying taxes to the King. "Our ancient rights and privileges!"

Parliament, not getting the drift, responded by passing three Coercive Acts. The first closed Boston harbor until the tea should be paid for. The second provided that court cases be moved out of Massachusetts if the royal governor felt that a fair trial could not be had. The third revised the colony's charter, strengthening the power of the governor, making his council appointive rather than elective, and diminishing the power of the town meetings.

The colonists called them the Intolerable Acts.

In the spring of 1774, the Sons of Liberty suddenly remembered Benjamin Franklin's aborted plans for confederation and the cartoon that had moldered in Margaret's Psalm book for now twenty years. "Let us propose that the colonies appoint committees to correspond with each other and take joint action against the injustices they perceive," said the young hothead John Morin Scott. "Let us form the New York Committee of Correspondence and show the way to the counties to appoint their own committees to address their grievances against the King and Parliament."

On July 4 of that year, the freeholders and inhabitants of Orangetown did just that, met to appoint their own committee. In the evening, with the July sun still high in the sky, they gathered at Yoast Mabie's house in Tappan, and as other towns and counties were doing, drew up a set of Resolutions, unanimously agreeing that they were and ever wished to be true and loyal subjects to His Majesty George the Third, but urging that the offending acts be repealed.

"Have we made it clear that we are most cordially disposed to support His Majesty in every constitutional measure as far as lies in our power?" Abraham Lent asked the gathering that night.

"Yes, we have made it clear," said Thomas Outwater. "We wish to be loyal to the King, but at the same time we cannot see the late acts of Parliament imposing duties on us and shutting up the port of Boston without declaring our abhorrence of measures so unconstitutional and so big with destruction."

"We have our perfect right to use every just and lawful measure to obtain a repeal of all acts destructive to us," said John Haring. "And it should be our unanimous opinion that the stopping of all exportation and importation to and from Great Britain and the West Indies will be the most effectual method to obtain a speedy repeal."

"But we have spelled out, remember, that it is our most ardent wish to see concord and harmony restored to England and her colonies," Peter Haring cautioned.

"That is important. We must strive to restore harmony between us. But we nevertheless shall appoint five of our number to be a committee to correspond with the city of New York and to agree upon such measures as they should judge necessary in order to obtain a repeal of said acts. Shall we, or shall we not?"

"Shall! We shall!" The gathering cheered and stamped their feet and toasted concord and harmony.

"Amen to our committee!"

"Amen!"

Ten days later the Orange Town Resolutions, signed by Abraham Lent, John Haring, Esq., Thomas Outwater, Gardner Jones, and Peter T. Haring were published in Patriot John Holt's *New York Journal* for all to read.

*   *   *   *

In September, two months after he was appointed to the Committee of Correspondence that signed the Resolutions, John Haring went to Philadelphia as a delegate to the First Continental Congress, where he joined the others in demanding that the British overhaul their empire.

"Imagine it! Overhaul the Empire!" Margaret marveled to Willemptie.

"It sounds like an excellent idea," said Willemptie. "It doubtless needs overhauling."

"I have heard that the Congress envisions an American government," Margaret said. "Our own confederated government consisting of a president appointed by the King and a council chosen by the colonial assemblies to manage their affairs and be possessed of the veto power over parliamentary acts affecting them."

"Possessed of the veto power?"

"Yes!"

"But, no, on second thought, even that is not good enough!"

"If taxation without representation is tyrannical, so too is all legislation coming out of Parliament!"

Such sentiments were suddenly on lips everywhere. "Parliament has no inherent right to control the American colonies," Gardner Jones declared. "The foundation of all free government is the right of the people to a free and exclusive power of legislation in their provincial assemblies."

"The people are sovereign! The people must consent to be governed!"

"Remember John Locke!"

"Let us disallow British goods, disallow British exports of every shape and manner on American shores."

"Let us remember Benjamin Franklin's snake. United we will live. Divided we will die."

"Parliament has introduced new levies on glass, lead, paint, paper, and tea," John Haring reported. "We colonists should follow our own model and enact another nonimportation agreement against British goods."

"Yes! The first was successful. Let us repeat it!"

"We shall plight our faith and honor to each other and to our country," they solemnly swore. "We shall discontinue all commerce with Great Britain and we will encourage the improvement of our arts and manufacture at home."

*   *   *   *

"Ladies," Margaret said to her friends and female relations, "it is time. If there be Sons of Liberty, why not Daughters of Liberty?"

They gasped.

"Unacquainted as I am with politics," her cousin Rachel ventured, "can a woman be a Patriot?"

"Of course, my dear," Margaret said. "Shall we not be Patriots, we shall be slaves."

"How shall we be daughters of liberty?" the women asked uneasily.

"We shall not buy British goods. We shall not drink British tea. We shall wear homespun. And we shall spin it ourselves," Margaret said. "You are invited to my house tomorrow morning with your spinning wheels, and we will spin for America and for no stamps."

Wagons pulled up in front of her house the next morning, and eleven women and their spinning wheels took over the *groote kamer*. "A good spinner can spin two and a half pounds of linen in a day," Margaret announced. "We are all good spinners. We can spin twenty-seven pounds among us for the cause this very day. And we shall wear tow and homespun and be proud of it. No more British finery, ladies, be it come to war."

*   *   *   *

And it came to war. In April 1775, fighting broke out at Lexington and Concord.

A column of Royal infantry, marching to take the military stores at Concord, killed several farmers at Lexington along the way.

At Concord, they destroyed some military supplies, exchanged shots, and hastily retreated toward Boston, sustaining heavy losses.

In Boston, the Sons of Liberty took over the city, seized muskets, powder, and shot, closed the customhouse, and lay siege to the city. The war was on.

And through New York passed the great man himself one fine day in June of '75, bound for Boston to take command of the troops besieging the British commander in chief General Thomas Gage, his old ally from Fort Duquesne days.

Hearing that the Champion of Liberty was to appear, Margaret and Johannes and Willemptie and Casparus and a few other friends and relations wasted no time. The men grabbed their hats and the women their shawls and bonnets and caught the first ferry they could down the Hudson to Comfort's dock on the west side of lower Manhattan. They rushed through the streets of the city to Broadway and Hull's Tavern, where it was rumored he was to spend the night. There they stationed themselves before the door, to see him up close.

Under military escort, with flags flying, church bells ringing, and militia fifing and drumming, cheering crowds adored him all the way up Broadway from the barge that had conveyed him over from Philadelphia.

When, tall as a tree, he alighted from his carriage at Hull's Tavern, his calm demeanor and his stately bearing, his brilliant blue and buff uniform and his amazing tricorn, plus the knowledge of what he had already suffered on their behalf in another war and the premonition of what he, and they, were to suffer in the new war, caused hearts to nearly explode with emotion and agitation. All well knew by what Providence he had survived at the first battle of Fort Duquesne, when two horses were shot out from under him in two separate incidents, and at the second battle, when he inserted himself between two American forces mistakenly firing on each other, to knock their muskets out of play with his sword. All knew of his determination that America be free. With trembling hands, Margaret removed her bonnet.

"Speak! Speak!" the crowd cried.

The afternoon sun was in his eyes. He turned from it and spoke to them. "The once happy and peaceful plains of America are either to be drenched with blood, or inhabited by slaves, and a virtuous man cannot hesitate to choose blood," he said. "We are all virtuous men, and women. We shall choose blood."

Margaret was beside herself with nervous fervor, her heart banging and clashing in her chest at the sight of him, her throat closing and opening as if she was about to burst into tears. She opened her mouth to gasp for air. Only days before, a Tory plot organized by the royal governor and the mayor of New York to blow up the Patriots' powder magazines, burn the city, burn the wooden bridge at the north end of the island to the mainland, and assassinate the great man himself had been uncovered. Thomas Hickey, the General's own body guard, was accused of being the chosen assassin. Thomas Hickey was even this very day in jail awaiting his execution.

One of his aides, noticing the Tappan people near the doorway, whispered something to him, *the Dutch farmers of Tappan*, and he looked their way with interest. "I am not much familiar with the Dutch," he murmured. He had in fact never seen them, the country people, before. He was a Virginian. He had heard they were of an independent turn of mind—and hated the British, for many good reasons.

His eyes fell upon a woman of striking appearance in their midst—he liked comely women—one with a strange old-fashioned comb twisted into her blond hair, securing it up off her handsome face. She held her bonnet to her breast, was gazing intently at him, her lips parted, her face flushed, her eyes missing nothing, her thoughts speaking to him loudly, strongly. She had an intensely ... *expectant* look about her, a deeply *communicating* look, he thought, as if she were willing him not to disappoint her in something. And what thing could that possibly be but one?

This handsome, this intent, this ardent, this political, patriotic, yes, this radical Dutch woman was conveying to him from the depths of her soul that she shared his own radicalism, his conviction that Americans should not beg the King or Parliament for their natural rights, even if it meant that they would have to go to war and stain the peaceful plains of the continent with their own blood. With every fiber of her being, she was willing him to succeed.

How could he not succeed? *Yes,* he answered, from the depths of his own soul. He was damned if he disappointed her! And her sisters.

With his eyes fixed upon her face, he lifted his hat to her and entered into the tavern. As he passed her, she bowed her head and put her fingers to her eyes as if, he thought, to press back tears. He had a feeling he would see her again, perhaps even hear from her. Women, total strangers, wrote to him on all sorts of matters.

Back in Tappan, they found the militia drilling on the Green across from the church, and Margaret and all of her friends and relations had no idea how much blood would be spilled on their peaceful plains before it was clear where the blood would get them.

CHAPTER 15

▼

WAR

The day they began to find out where it might get them was the twelfth day of July, 1776. That bright and sunny day, Admiral Lord Richard Howe arrived at Sandy Hook with a mighty fleet to reinforce his brother Sir William Howe's smaller fleet, which had been anchored off Staten Island for a fortnight. Now there were so many formidable British warships and supply vessels in the narrows between Staten Island and Long Island that people likened their masts to a forest of pine trees.

On that day also, the fateful twelfth of July, just a few hours after Admiral Howe's appearance on the horizon to cannonades of salute guns and clouds of black smoke, Sir William launched a squadron of five ships across New York harbor and up the Hudson. When the squadron hove into view, around the tip of Manhattan, Margaret happened to be on Vesey Street, near St. Paul's chapel, at the house of her daughter Aeltie, whose second child was due any day. Aeltie and her husband Cornelius rented this little house, while Cornelius tried to succeed at growing tobacco in the Out Ward, beyond the wall.

Margaret shivered. "Things are happening too fast," she said to Aeltie. First the arrival of Sir William at the end of June, while she was still in Tappan. Then on the fourth day of July, with all the state and solemnity the circumstances admitted, the Continental Congress declared the colonies to be free and independent of England. And now eight days later, the arrival of the great fleet, news of which flew through the city, and the ominous advance of the squadron.

All week, as the news of the Declaration of their colonies' independence spread, in every town in the land, the citizens with the loudest voices stood on the highest porches and read it in their ringingest tones, accompanied by acclamations and illuminations and fifing and drumming and volleys of musketry. "The people are now convinced that our enemy has left us no middle way between perfect freedom and abject slavery," Johannes said sadly. "And therefore war is inevitable. I do not wish you to go into the city, Margaret. It is not safe."

"They are ready for anything, even for war," Margaret agreed. "But you know I have to go, my dear. Aeltie is expecting me."

They had been married for thirty years. He knew her all too well. "I know I can't stop you from going," he said. "You always do what you want to do."

"What I have to do," she corrected him. "She cannot manage without me."

He drove her in their riding chair to the ferry, and after ushering her on board and settling her in a corner with her valise he sat beside her for a moment with his arm around her shoulders. He lifted her face to his, tipping up her chin. "Good-by, my dearest love," he whispered to her, his steady green eyes fixed on her features, as if to memorize them. "Keep yourself safe." He had a portent that trouble lay ahead for her, for all of them. For the country.

"I will be fine, *mijn lieveling,*" she said. "Do not worry. If they evacuate the city, we will come home post haste."

He gave her a packet of gold and silver coins. "In case of emergency," he said. "It will be enough to get all of you home by the swiftest method."

She tucked it into the embroidered pocket she wore around her waist. "Don't worry about me," she said. "I will take care of myself and my family."

Then, in the city, in the middle of the momentous week, on the evening of July the ninth, just after she had settled into Vesey Street, word spread that a boisterous mob of militiamen and Patriots was on the Bowling Green pulling down the lead statue of King George III on his mighty steed.

They joined the exuberant crowds trekking to see this feat. Aeltie, huge with child, waddled beside Margaret, the both of them trying to keep up with Cornelius and little David streaming ahead with the crowd. They arrived just in time to see the huge statue of King and horse land with a resounding splat on the Green. With loud cheers and huzzahs, men then merrily loaded the statue on a farm cart and marched it all the way up Broadway.

"To the top of the island," they shouted.

"To put the King's head on a spike!"

"And melt his body down for Yankee musket balls!"

"We will show the British what we mean!"

"The Green brings back memories to me," Margaret said, recalling. "I came here in 1740, when I was a girl of fifteen, to see another George. George White-field. He preached at this very place."

"Was he the one who wanted to free the slaves?" Cornelius asked.

"He wanted the Gospel to be taught to them," she said, "for their salvation. He preached that a Christian couldn't be a slave."

"He stirred them up pretty good," said Cornelius. "The next year they burned down the Governor's house in the fort and eight other houses."

"They were accused of plotting to burn the whole city," she said. "But I came not to believe it. I came to think it was all boasting, brave talk. I was living near here with my aunt and uncle. I went to City Hall all summer for the trials." She thought of Eliza and how she had seen her that day on the Green, and how they had gone together to the trials. And how when the trials were over Eliza had left New York in search of a better life in London. She had often wondered how the girl had fared. (*The girl,* she thought, amused. *She is fifty-four years old by now!*)

"Did they hang them?" Aeltie asked.

"They hanged them, and they burned them at the stake. By the dozens. The authorities were very severe." She shivered to recall the savage punishments meted out. "Their only crime was wanting to be free."

"Well, they're free now," Cornelius said. "Aren't those two over there from Tappan?"

She glanced to where he indicated. "Indeed," she said. "They are Phoebe and Toby. They belong to Jacobus Bogert."

"I've seen a few others that I recognize, too," he said.

"Yes," she said. "They are all deliriously happy to welcome the British to New York."

"And why wouldn't they be? Sir William Howe has promised to give all slaves deserting the rebels their freedom."

"And the young healthy ones have been deserting in droves ever since, leaving the old and the worn out behind on the farms. I don't know how we will manage."

Well before he arrived, with 10,000 men, determined to take New York City, Sir William had been anticipated, and the authorities had set the city's slaves and servants and soldiers to digging trenches and erecting fortifications on Governor's Island, on the heights of Brooklyn, at Red Hook, at Paulus Hook on the New Jersey shore, and on Manhattan Island. But now that the slaves had run away to the British, soldiers and white civilians had to do the heavy work.

They walked home that July evening from the pulling down of the King. "What a sorry sight the city has become," she said. As a result of the expected military action, the militia had set up gun batteries everywhere, spoiling the pretty, tree-shaded cobbled streets. Creaking baggage wagons and neighing horses made a clamor and a commotion, and everywhere one turned the streets were full of horse manure and noisy, rowdy soldiers leering at young women on every corner. "Those young women would be better advised to stay indoors," Margaret said, stepping around a clump of steaming dung.

"They appear to enjoy the attention," said Cornelius. "They are ready and waiting for the excitement of war."

"Yes," said Margaret. "If they are ready to topple the King and raise his head on a spike in front of a low tavern and melt down the rest of him and his horse for musket balls, they are ready for anything."

"I think we are about to find out where all of it is leading," he said. "I feel it in my bones tonight. We are now embarked on a most tempestuous sea."

The next evening, the tenth of July, a Wednesday, they went to the Dutch Church in Garden Street to hear the Patriot minister John H. Livingston preach. "Life is very uncertain now," he told the congregation. "Seeming dangers are scattered thick around us, and plots against the military abound. It is whispered that there are plots against the Congress, too, and as we know too well a vile assassin has even conspired to murder our Great Chief."

The congregation murmured uneasily, and a shiver ran through the sanctuary. Some looked nervously over their shoulders as if expecting to see a vile assassin enter into their midst with slaughter on his mind. "Let us prepare for the worst," he said. "But let us also support our freedom and independence with our lives and fortunes and with all of our force."

"How do we prepare for the worst?" she asked, walking back to Vesey Street. "And what is the worst?"

"Mayhem beyond compare, I believe," Cornelius said glumly. "It will not be pretty."

"Maybe we should go back to Tappan for the birth?"

"I can't leave my tobacco," he said.

On the twelfth of July, Friday, at about three in the afternoon, when word began to spread through the city that the five British warships had left their anchorage off Staten Island and had begun to sail toward Manhattan, Margaret shivered again. "It is starting," she said. "Now we will soon find out what the worst is, for sure."

With a strong wind behind them and a favorable tide, the warships with their bulwarks sandbagged crossed the harbor easily, dodging cannon fire and mortars from the American batteries. Troops fired upon them from Red Hook, Governor's Island, and Paulus Hook, which it passed at four in the afternoon, but Howe, in lordly contempt of the mostly ineffectual efforts against him, did not bother to return fire until the squadron reached the shores of heavily populated lower Manhattan.

Then he bothered, attacking with all the vengeance the British navy could summon. The cannon fire was frighteningly loud. Birds of all species rose from the trees in a great flutter of wings and flew as one flock north, cheeping and cawing, away from the fury. Margaret and Aeltie's little family took shelter from the cannon fire in the cellar of the rented house on Vesey Street. Above, they could hear terrorized women and children who had no cellars for refuge from the bombardment pound past the house, fleeing frantically through the crooked streets to the east side of the island to avoid the fire. Their panicked shrieks and cries as they ran every which way hither and thither filled the air, along with dogs barking, horses neighing, chickens squawking, men shouting, muskets firing, bombs bursting.

By half-past four the fast-moving squadron was at Fort Washington at the northern tip of Manhattan, and official criers appeared in the streets to announce that General Washington had ordered all women and children to leave the city immediately, in case the vessels turned around and sailed back down the river to do their mischief, or before General William Howe's army invaded by land, which it was at any moment expected to do.

Margaret and Aeltie and Cornelius and the child clambered out of the cellar, hastily packed a few effects and fled to the Hudson River, along with scores of others with the same idea: to find a boat, any boat, to take them to security across the river. Margaret lost a shoe in the process, but she didn't stop for it. Half hopping, half running, she hustled her hugely pregnant daughter through the cobbled streets with one thought on her mind: get out of the city.

They piled into the first vessel to come along, a large leaky rowboat whose owner conveyed them for a fancy price to Paulus Hook on the west shore. From there they hied themselves to Tappan in a crowded stagecoach. It was slow going, for the roads were thick with carts, wagons, horses, carriages, coaches, wheelbarrows, and weary walkers all heading away from the dangerous city, toward what uncertain future they knew not.

And thus it was that, at about eight in the evening of that innocent July day, a Friday, with the sun still blazing above the Nyack hills, and the sky as blue as the river, and the river dancing with saucy whitecaps, they reached Sneden's Landing in time to see the squadron of British warships appear ominously in the Hudson and parade themselves about in the wide Tappan Zee. It had been mortifying to those of Patriotic bent along the route to see the tall vessels with their enormous areas of canvas sail steadily north, undeterred by the fire from the American batteries, shelling with impunity the solid sandstone farmhouses and elegant merchants' mansions on the river's banks. For thirty miles they inexorably advanced, until they forced the passage, put themselves into position to prevent the American line of supply from moving down the Hudson.

As she stepped down from the coach at the Landing, she spied Johannes in the crowd and ran to him. "You are home, thank God," he said, taking her by the arms, scrutinizing her face, as if for changes in it, damage. "I have been so worried. Are you well?"

"The city is in turmoil," she said breathlessly. "Refugees are fleeing by the hundreds, thousands perhaps."

"It is clear what it means, of course," he said.

"All know it." It was the setting into effect of Sir William Howe's plan to cut communication by water between the northern part of the province of New York and George Washington and the American forces in their hastily thrown up fortifications in the lower Hudson.

"He is convinced of the absolute necessity of the British being in possession of the upper Hudson in order not only to cut off our channel of supply to the lower river, but also to sever New England from the southern colonies. He had to take the risk of passing between the batteries on shore."

"And small risk it has been for him," Margaret said, "considering the range of our fire. Look! The squadron keeps itself a mile away, and our musket balls fall into the river."

Word of the squadron's appearance had spread like wildfire. In great panic, the inhabitants of the villages along the river flocked to the shore to gaze at the sight of the frigates *Rose* with her twenty guns and the *Phoenix* with her forty-four, a schooner, and two tenders slicing about in the saucy waters of the Tappan Zee as if they owned it. "It seems the war is on," said Johannes glumly. "And the young slaves have all run away from us. Who will do the planting?"

Margaret shivered, even though the evening still bore the heat of the day. "Maybe you will have to do it," she said. "You and our three sons."

"Our sons will be going into the militia," he said. "I will be the one to do the planting. Sam and I. And I have never liked planting and all that goes with it."

Although she should have been expecting it, the thought that her sons would be going into the militia came as a shock to her. But of course they would. It was the law. And they would want to in any case serve their country, Isaac, John, and Abraham. "Let it be over quickly, and let us prevail," she said.

She turned back to the river. The *Phoenix* and the *Rose,* the schooner *Tryal,* and the two tenders carried 400 men in all. As it sailed in stately pace past the Palisades toward the wide Tappan Zee that first evening, the squadron spied a periauger with three aboard. On shore the people watched as the *Rose* sent out an armed barge and took the three onto her, an unlucky butcher well known in the area, his teenage son, and his assistant, trying to make their way from the city to Sneden's Landing to buy livestock as they did every week. "It is coming home very swiftly," she said. "We know those unfortunate people."

The squadron with the periauger in tow dropped anchor off Nyack, in the widest part of the Hudson. "Its sails and riggings are in tatters. Its hulls are full of shot."

"That doesn't mean anything," he said. "The ships are still perfectly seaworthy and the damage to them easily repaired. The crews are already at work."

"My water has broken," Aeltie said.

"We must go," Margaret said. "We should not be here. Let us go home." Hurriedly, they climbed into the wagon behind Johannes and drove west to Tappan, and then on to the farm, another two miles to the northwest of the village.

*   *   *   *

That night, Margaret's cousin, Colonel Johannes Blauvelt, chairman of the Orange County Committee of Public Safety, ordered the rag-tag Orangetown militia to take post along the Nyack shore to ward off the dreaded expected attack, perhaps that very night it was feared, certainly by daybreak. Then he ordered all the women and children inland, out of harm's way.

As they approached Tappan, Margaret found that not only were local women and children obeying his command to flee inland to the village, but the stagecoaches full of refugees from the city had emptied their human cargo in front of the courthouse in the center of Tappan and returned to the city for more. The people wandered about in the dark whimpering and moaning. A woman ran up to Margaret. "Take me in!" she cried, grabbing her by the arm. "I have four little ones. Please! Give us shelter!"

She took the woman in, Mary Bacon and her four little ones. All the families did the same, even those suspected of Tory leanings, even those lukewarm so-called Patriots wishing to stay neutral in the business. "The house will be very uncomfortably overcrowded," she said to Johannes, "with us and the refugee family and Aeltie's family. But we must do all we can."

"Aeltie and her family are refugees, too," he pointed out.

"And so they are," she said sadly.

As it was summer, the slave woman Bett and her three children sheltered in a cabin at the edge of the first planted field from the house. In cold weather, they lived in the garret of the house, which they were accustomed to treating as if it were their own to come and go in as they pleased, and in some sense it was. Now they milled toward the house to stare at the new arrivals, the little ones all whining and whimpering, and Aeltie moaning in labor in Margaret's bed.

"It is total chaos, and I have never been one for chaos," Margaret muttered. She climbed into the garret and dragged the cradle out of its corner and handed it down the stairs to Cornelius. She dusted it off, readied it for the baby with clean towels and swaddling cloths. It was a large pine cradle, covered in leather and studded with brass tacks; it had come down to them from Johannes's great-grandmother, Grietje Cosyns.

Now Aeltie's moans were giving way to shattering screams. Cornelius had tied a rope to the foot of the bed where she labored, and as each pain wracked her pelvis, Bett helped her pull on the rope to make the baby come. She shrieked in her travail. The baby would not come. Margaret, feeling sick to her stomach, wiped her daughter's brow with a wet towel, tried to comfort her.

At last, at midnight, the midwife arrived. She thrust her none-too-clean hands into Aeltie's birth canal and pulled on tiny legs, and Aeltie with one final ear-piercing scream delivered into her hands a baby boy, still born. The midwife cut the cord, which was around the baby's neck. "It strangled him," she said.

Grimly, Cornelius went back up to the garret to get a tiny coffin; there were always two or three made in advance, just in case. He laid the baby in it and paid the midwife. She went away to sleep in a corner until morning came and she could go on to her next job. He lay down beside his exhausted wife, the coffin on the floor beside the bed, alongside the empty cradle. Aeltie wept.

Margaret threw a pallet on the *stoep* and lay down under the stars beside Johannes, with a smudge pot burning to keep away the mosquitoes. Sleep eluded her. She lay awake all night, worried sick for what the future held. In the morning, she turned to look at him, lying awake also, on his back staring up at the dawning sky. "It is well the baby did not live," she said. "Life is not going to be pleasant for the living, I suspect."

"It is going to be very unpleasant, I fear," he said.

*   *   *   *

Colonel Hay of the Orange County regiment of the Continental army called out his 400 men that Friday in order to prevent the enemy from landing and committing depredations upon the inhabitants. On Sunday, Margaret's cousin Colonel Abraham Blauvelt reported to the congregation at the morning service that Hay's 400 men had now been on duty for two days and nights. "They are greatly fatigued," he said. "Besides, they are uneasy that they will lose their harvest by staying longer, for the grain is ripe to gather. He fears they will be going home."

"But Hay's men are our main defense!" the people cried. "How can he let them go home? What are his plans?"

"He has begged for reinforcements from General Clinton's brigade to relieve them, and two or three armed boats."

"Will these be forthcoming?"

"I cannot say," Abraham said glumly. "Colonel Hay may be on his own, for all we know. And we on our own as well."

They went out into the fields at night to see the beacon fires on the hilltops, the means by which the militia sent word to the forts in the Highlands of the dangers besetting them. "They have sent men on horseback as well, to beg for reinforcements and ammunition," Abraham reported the next Sunday, "but those forts themselves are in danger and not willing to give up any of their defenses."

John Haring was in the congregation. "There's worse," he said. He had been made a Brigade Major in the Continental army under General George Clinton and was well informed. "It is now obvious that the army, encamped on Lake Champlain, is endangered, for if the squadron could make it through the shore batteries to the Tappan Zee, what is to stop the rest of the Royal Navy from sailing all the way to Albany and on to the Lake?"

The squadron still dallied ominously in the Tappan Zee.

"What are General Washington's plans? What is he doing to defend us?" the worried people asked Haring. They were convinced that he was in direct communication with the commander in chief, but that discretion prevented him from admitting it.

"His plans are uncertain. He is alarmed at the possibilities for mayhem and failure on every front. He fears the army aboard the five vessels in the Tappan Zee will attempt to go ashore and make their way over land to the mountain passes north of here to attack Fort Constitution and Fort Montgomery. He is sure, too,"

Haring added, "that the vessels bear stores of arms and ammunition to supply Loyalists across the river and up into the Hudson Valley, of which there are very many. I overheard him refer to them in disgust as 'brave hearts.' Those self-styled 'brave hearts' he called them, who are so sure victory will be to the British."

"But what are his plans?" they persisted. "To defend *us*? Us, here in this place?"

"I'm afraid our defense here is not uppermost in his mind," said Haring. "You will have to defend yourselves as best you can. On both shores of the river," he added, "Loyalists and Patriots are working feverishly to build fortifications, the Loyalists to protect the squadron on the one hand, the Patriots to attack it on the other."

"Are you saying we should be building fortifications?"

"It would be good," he said.

"But with what labor? Every man from sixteen to sixty is in the militia, and the slaves have run away."

"Could you look to your neighbors to the west to help?" he said. "This very day in Dutchess County, the Connecticut militia helped suppress a Loyalist uprising of dangerous proportions."

"The people to our west are as anxious as we. We want to know, what is *he* doing? What is *he* doing to protect us?"

"His main purpose must be to protect his army," said Haring shortly.

They gathered at Margaret and Johannes's house, around the table under the grape arbor. The men smoked their pipes and drank coffee from the Dutch East Indies. They had sworn off English tea from India, of course. When the coffee was consumed, they turned to Johannes's Madeira and rum or beer. The cider barrels were empty and would be until the orchards ripened and the apples were pressed.

The women, needles clicking, knitted, as long as there was light to see. Margaret insisted that they spin and card, knit and sew, without stopping. "Winter will come. The men will need warm socks and shirts, hats and mittens. We must keep at it."

"It will be over by winter," Mary Burton muttered.

Margaret shot a look at her. "A woman can spin four skeins a day, or six if someone cards for her," she said.

But ever since the squadron had taken possession of the Tappan Zee, the women were distracted from their spinning and carding and knitting. "They can hardly bear to pry themselves away from the shore in the day time," she complained to Johannes. "They watch the vessels as if to watch them is to contain them."

"He is taking every effort to impede the squadron," John Haring was saying. "He has ordered the forts in the Highlands to build up their defenses. He has sent an engineer to help them with the fortifications. But unfortunately he cannot afford to supply them with troops or cannon, though they have begged for these."

"Nor can he spare whaleboats to the militia so that we can get close enough to the squadron to fire upon it," Abraham Blauvelt added.

"But at least," said Haring, "he intends to order the militia in western Connecticut to come to your aid to move as many stores and provisions as possible inland, away from possible capture. They will be safe in the swamp on the other side of the Hackensack."

"Safe in the swamp?" she said. "Pray tell, how are we to get at them if the rains come and flood the swamp, as they do every year?"

"It is thought to be the safest place we can tell them of. And the rains won't come until September."

"September will be here soon enough," she said.

"He is doing all he can under supremely difficult conditions," Haring said. "At the passage below West Point across from Fort Montgomery, he has ordered the men to collect large piles of brush to ignite to illuminate the squadron should it attempt to sail into the Highlands on a dark night to take the Fort by surprise. And, too, he has ordered Fort Washington, which failed to stop the squadron, to be strengthened, and a sister fort begun on the Palisades, opposite it, to be called Fort Lee after his General Charles Lee."

This news calmed the people's fears somewhat. "So, then, he is doing all he can?"

"Yes," said Haring. "He is doing all he can. Now his generals have hatched a scheme to sink a line of ship hulks and timber cribs weighted with stone in the river between Fort Washington and Fort Lee to prevent the squadron from moving back down the river or more ships moving north to join it."

By the end of July five galley ships borrowed from Connecticut and Rhode Island and furnished with heavy guns were at New York. Two of them lay in the *Spuyten Duyvil* at the north end of Manhattan, there to waylay the British should they attempt to pass up or down the river.

Still, for four days, the squadron went freely to and fro in the three-mile-wide Tappan Zee, flaunting themselves, and every day Margaret and her household and scores of others flocked to the shore of the Hudson to watch the vessels tack and come about and tack again. The Orange County militia, 180 strong, patrolled the shore along the river road, and declared they would sink the entire English Navy if it attempted to pass out of the harbor of New York.

"Precious little chance of that," said Margaret. "They know how to keep themselves well out of the range of our muskets."

"But at least they serve to keep the men aboard them from coming ashore for provisions," Johannes said.

On the fourth day, the five ships hove to and sailed north, beyond the hook the Dutch called *verdrietige* (tiresome, because it took so long to tack around it) into Haverstraw Bay. The inhabitants along the shore saw what was coming: a landing on the north side of the hook to seize their cattle and sheep and stores of grain and pork and molasses and rum. The frightened people drove their livestock off into the interior for safekeeping, and when the tenders anchored by the dock of one Captain Keirs, they fired on them and forced them to turn back out into the Bay.

The militia now straggled northward along the river road to Haverstraw, keeping the squadron in its sights, while a detachment of eighty men supplied by General Clinton from Fort Montgomery headed south to reinforce them.

Clinton himself came down from the Highlands to study the situation. "My God, it is untenable," he shouted. "An undisciplined rabble is firing at ships a hopeless mile away. For every useless shot they fire, the frigates methodically return cannon fire!" In short order, he reorganized the militia and caused the last stores of food and ammunition to be removed inland, and the cattle and sheep to places of safety.

As the people on shore watched, one of the tenders made a break for the north, but it was stopped in its own wake by a thirty-two-pound shot to its stern from the battery at Fort Montgomery. It beat a retreat, and then it noticed, tucked into the hillside, a little frame house. It belonged to one Jacob Halstead. A poor and hapless farmer, half blind, Halstead had hurried into the woods with his cattle when the tender first sailed past his rocky river frontage that day. Now the tender anchored and sent an armed barge ashore to plunder his garden and to take a calf that was too weak to have been driven with its mother into hiding.

The next day again, the *Rose* and the *Tryal* sailed up the river and anchored off Jacob Halstead's riverbank. Again he ran off into the woods, but this time he thought to take his musket with him, and when the men from the ship knocked at the door of his house, he fired on them from his hiding place, chasing them back into the river to the barge, which they hastily rowed out to the vessels at anchor.

This time with the *Tryal* covering them, they approached the shore again, now on three barges, which all successfully landed. The men surged ashore and fell upon Halstead's scrawny hogs, eighteen in all, and killed them for pork for the ships and then merrily set his house on fire to teach him a lesson for shooting at them. From the woods, his ammunition gone, he watched the flames consume the frame building in a matter of minutes. Later, Margaret would learn from her cousin Abraham that he ended up living in a cave in the woods, eating roots and berries and nuts, and dying of cold that winter.

The inhabitants were enraged by the actions of the British in destroying poor Halstead's house and farm and killing his hogs. "We keep careful guard on shore," Colonel Blauvelt said wearily. "But we lack cannon and whaleboats to repay the enemy for their dastardly destruction." They could only play defense as the *Rose* and the *Phoenix* moved from place to place on the river, much faster than they on shore could track them when the wind and tide were in the ships' favor.

*   *   *   *

It was a hot and moonless night. The river slapped lightly against the *Rose's* hull. Private Eli Cole, an American prisoner, slipped out of his boots and jacket and soundlessly let himself down the side of the ship. He struck out as quietly as he could for Stony Point. Although it was only a mile away, and the tide and current were with him, dawn was breaking as he clambered out of the water and up the embankment formed by fallen rock. An alert militiaman on guard spied him. "Halt!"

"Don't shoot," said Cole, holding up his hands. "I'm an American prisoner escaped from the *Rose*."

"Show me your papers."

"The British have them. I have only the clothes you see on my back."

"March!"

The militiaman marched him south along the river road to Colonel Hay in Haverstraw for interrogation.

"The British are highly mortified to find themselves prevented from their wanton aims by what they call the ragged militia on shore," Cole reported, standing before Hay barefoot and wet.

Colonel Hay laughed out loud.

"Particularly, that they are prevented from plundering the farms for the Navy's mess."

The Colonel laughed again.

"A Loyalist delivered cabbages to the squadron in a canoe," Cole went on, "and they hoisted a dead bullock onto the *Rose*, plunder from a foray upon the Westchester shore, but that is all they have been able to secure."

"A few cabbages and a bullock are hardly sufficient to feed the 400 men lying in the bay," said Colonel Hay with satisfaction. "They must surely be grumbling and worse about their provender, or lack of it. And what are they doing for water, I wonder? The river is salty for a hundred miles from the harbor."

"They are running out of it, Sir," Cole said.

"Provide him with shoes and a musket. And papers," Hay said to his adjutant. "And raise him to Corporal."

On July 25, almost two weeks to the day from when they had arrived in the Tappan Zee, the squadron left Haverstraw Bay and returned to the Tappan Zee, anchoring off Sing Sing on the eastern shore at night, tacking ominously hither and thither by day.

For two weary weeks, Colonel Blauvelt and his little battalion followed the *Phoenix* and the *Rose* from Nyack to Haverstraw and back to Nyack, down to Tappan Landing at the Slote, and on to Sneden's Landing. The men slept in the woods at night, or in swamps, and patrolled by day.

With his lieutenant, also a cousin, Harmanus Blauvelt, Abraham galloped by to visit Margaret one afternoon. They were exhausted, hungry, thirsty, dirty, a sad sight in their torn blue rifle frocks and soiled leggings, once white. "I shot just now, on my way here, at an American deserter trying to make his way on a log to a British armed barge in the river, but I missed," Abraham said, collapsing onto a bench on the *stoep*.

"I am sure the men are worried about their crops?"

"Yes, they fret over who will do the harvesting."

"What about my sons?" she asked fearfully.

"We are all in the same boat," he said. "All weary to the bone. They are with Harmanus."

"Last night," said Harmanus, "my men, your sons included, engaged with a company of British who landed from one of the ships to plunder farms and steal cattle. We lay concealed in the woods, until all the British on the barge had landed, and then we rushed upon them and took them prisoners, while cannon balls from the *Phoenix* and the *Rose* whistled about our ears and wounded us," he said. "I have just come from marching the men to Tappan and locking them up in the church until the jail can be enlarged."

"And my sons?" she asked him. "Are they good soldiers?"

"Yes," he said. "They shoot straight."

"Let us have some soap, Cousin," said Abraham. "We will go to the creek to wash our stinking selves."

She brought the soap to them and towels. "I can give you these clean shirts, too," she said. "And leggings. But I have no rifle frocks to spare. Only two set aside for my sons when they come."

They took the soap and the clean clothing and galloped off.

"Women, we must spin again," Margaret said, when the men were gone. "Even though it be so warm. Even though we would prefer to be at the river to curse our enemy, we must be spinning." She and Aeltie and daughter Elizabeth and her cousin Rachel and Willemptie Eckerson and Willemptie's daughter Cathlyntie Mabie and all their women friends, even those known or suspected to be of Loyalist persuasion, even Mary Bacon, knew it. They bent to the wheel, made blankets for the soldiers that hot and steamy July, knitted mittens and socks with the coming winter in mind.

✳   ✳   ✳   ✳

The three of them, Margaret, Johannes, and their cousin the Colonel sat one night in the gathering dusk in the summerhouse speaking in low voices of Abraham's latest news. "There are across the river fourteen companies consisting of about 700 men," he whispered. Mary Bacon hovered close, taking clothes off the line. Margaret, her back to Mary, put her finger to her lips to indicate to Abraham to speak low.

Margaret had suspected from the start that she sheltered a Loyalist. Mary Bacon spent part of each day walking about the neighborhood, and Margaret believed she was collecting intelligence for the British, spying on Patriot households. "She listens to everything that passes between us," she whispered, "and between us and our friends when they drop in of an evening with the news, as now."

"Yes. Her ears are always flapping," Johannes muttered in a low voice. "We must be careful."

"The Great Chief believes the squadron is scarce of water," Abraham said softly, "and that it is necessary for us to keep a vigilant guard to prevent their obtaining a fresh supply."

"Mary," said Margaret, "Will you be so good as to refill this flagon of Madeira from the cask in the barn?"

Mary's eyes narrowed in annoyance. She took the jug and walked away toward the barn.

"How many men are now guarding our side of the river?" Margaret inquired softly, when the woman was out of earshot.

"Near the Slote, 300."

"And across the river?"

"Another 300," he said, "and 200 at Peekskill—though they are unarmed."

"What good are they then?" Johannes asked. "Unarmed."

"Not much good," Blauvelt admitted.

"How many does General Clinton have?"

"He expects about 1,700 men. He has ordered in the troops from Kingston, but he has no idea how they will be supplied with ammunition, tents, and provisions."

"Are they armed?"

"Yes."

"How *will* they be supplied?" she worried.

"The New York Convention has appointed Commissaries. They are in charge of getting supplies to him."

"It is all so fragile," she murmured.

Margaret caught a glimpse of Mary returning from the barn with the flagon. "Shhhh," she whispered.

"Get rid of her if you can," said Abraham. "The sooner the better."

"Yes," Johannes said.

"Yes," said Margaret. "Tomorrow."

The next day, Mary Bacon went into the city "on some business of her own," she said coolly, leaving her four children in the care of Bett and setting out on foot for the next city-bound boat to stop at the Slote. As soon as she was out of sight, Margaret hitched a horse to a wagon and set out on a different route. It was her plan to find a Tory household with Patriot refugees that would take Mary and her brood in a trade. She knew just where to start looking, and if she had no luck there, she would not have far to go, there being many Tory households sheltering Patriot refugees quartered on them by the militia and none of them happy about it.

She went first to Mrs. Sneden, whose sons ran the ferry from Sneden's Landing to Dobbs Ferry, on the east shore, and who were widely suspected of a treasonable correspondence with the warships of the King's Navy lying in the river. As she expected, Mrs. Sneden readily agreed to the exchange, and back at the farm with Bett's help Margaret loaded Mary Bacon's possessions and four children into the wagon and deposited all with Mrs. Sneden. In turn, she took Helena Westervelt, a refugee Patriot woman and her four who had been quartered at Mrs. Sneden's by the militia, into her now more secure household.

Mary Bacon's fury knew no bounds when she returned to find her children and her possessions moved out. "You thieving whore!" she screamed at Margaret. "Is that the thanks I get for my hospitality?"

"You poaching strumpet!"

"Watch your language," said Margaret coolly. "Or I'll have you arrested for slander. And after that for spying for the enemy. We all suspect you, you know. And the punishment is death by hanging. Do you fancy that?"

"I have a good mind to pull out every hair on your damned head!" Mary shouted.

"Lay a hand on me and you're a dead woman," Margaret said.

"Bitch! Bitch! And triple Bitch!" Mary Bacon screamed, as she skulked away to Mrs. Sneden's house.

"Just a little cat fight," Margaret said breathlessly. "We are well rid of her."

*   *   *   *

On August 3, a great battle suddenly erupted in the river off Nyack. All Tappan rushed to the Hudson shore to see it. Without warning, the galleys in the *Spuyten Duyvil*, now six in all, had sailed up to the British squadron and begun firing upon it. For an hour and a half the battle raged, with the smoke of cannon fire visible all the way down to Fort Washington and the cannon detonations audible on Staten Island, thirty miles away, it was later reported.

"It was as hot a fire as perhaps ever was known," one of the sailors gloated afterward, in the tavern in Tappan, where they celebrated. "But never did men behave with more firm and determined spirit than our little crews."

"We lost only two men dead and suffered fourteen wounded, some later sure to die of their wounds, though," said another, "for one poor sod lost both his legs."

"Oh, the despicable bawlers! It could only have entered into such dastard souls as theirs to believe that the brave Americans were cowards and would run away from them."

"We look forward every man Jack of us to giving them another drubbing! We want another chance to fight those pirates, before they leave our river, which God prosper."

The hulls and riggings of the six galleys, low one-decked vessels equipped to be rowed or sailed, were damaged beyond repair, oars, tackles, and breechings vanished, and on one her bow guns and her thirty-two pounder split and disabled.

"You behaved extremely well with great spirit and bravery," John Haring said. "The damage done the galleys shows beyond question that you had a warm time of it. We can be proud of you and you of yourselves." He reported the same to General Washington. "The men fought for two hours an enemy four times their force," he wrote.

*　　*　　*　　*

Soon after this river battle, Colonel Blauvelt galloped up to the house again one evening to report the latest. "They are deserting me," he said breathlessly, climbing off his horse. "I have now only a hundred men left in my battalion. My challenge is nearly impossible." He hitched the horse to a fence post. "With a hundred men I have to guard seven miles of shoreline, which means they are in constant motion. It gives them no time to take care of their farms."

"Come have some refreshment," she said. "John Haring is with us."

"What will you do?" Haring asked.

"I don't know," Blauvelt said glumly.

They sat at the table in the *speelhuis*. "And how are my sons?" she asked.

"I have not had word of them," he said. "They are still with Harmanus."

"It is all so worrisome," she said. "I can hardly sleep at night. What *will* you do?"

"The Convention has ordered me to enlist more men. I raised a company in the north part of the county, but after one day it was ordered to Westchester. I am at my wits' end."

Johannes joined them. "How will your hundred remaining men get their grain in the ground?"

"I do not know," he said. "It is August, time for planting the winter wheat."

"Have you protested to the Convention?" Johannes asked.

"I wrote to tell them that they should not be surprised that men are reluctant to enlist, for no one who has the feelings of a man would choose to leave his family exposed to the fury of a cruel enemy."

"I don't suppose they will be much swayed by that touching argument," Johannes said dryly.

"Further, it is reported," Abraham went on, "that General Washington has ordered fire ships to be built in New York. The war is heating up."

"What are fire ships?" Margaret asked.

"Boats fiendishly designed and fitted so that they can sail close up to the British squadron and set it on fire," John Haring said. "They are devilish inventions. Along both port and starboard bulwarks, the men construct troughs six inches by ten laying a half-inch of gunpowder into each. This they cover with a layer of straw soaked in brimstone, and then on top of this they lay a layer of rosin-soaked twigs and branches. On the decks they stack barrels of pitch-pine fagots side by side, and arrange melted rosin and bundles of branches soaked in rosin on every foot of space to the gunwales. They raise sheets of canvas soaked in turpentine into the rigging."

"Fiendish indeed," she said.

"The very devil's design."

*   *   *   *

In the late afternoon of August sixteenth, two such devil's designs, the hundred-ton sloop *Polly* and a schooner of six tons, the *Mary Ann*, rendezvoused with three galleys lying in the *Spuyten Duyvil*. Under cover of a dark and rainy night, the galleys towed the two fire ships and their officers and crews of nine—six on board to do the dirty work and three in the escape whaleboats lashed to their sterns—to the eastern shore.

The squadron, unaware of what was about to happen to it, lay at anchor in the river off the Tory Frederick Philipse's handsome manor house on the east shore, or at least that is where the Americans expected to find it. But the squadron was tipped off of trouble to come, and during the evening it moved, under cover of the moonless night, over to the Jersey shore, under the Palisades. On this shore, just above Sneden's Landing, the inhabitants, already informed of the action to come by spies from New York, gathered in the dark and the rain to watch the conflagration just below them on the Tappan Zee. The awful and certain destruction awaiting the enemy was enough to awaken fear and terror in the stoutest heart. Margaret's heart was stout, but it beat now as if it would explode.

The Americans in the *Polly* and the *Mary Ann* had orders to fire the *Phoenix*, but the British tender *Charlotta* stood in the way, and the ensign in charge had to throw the grapnels to her instead of to the *Phoenix*. In an instant, he fired the rosin-soaked troughs of the *Polly*, and both it and the *Charlotta*, now grappled to it like a cancer, burst into flame, the fire leaping from troughs to bundles of rosin-soaked hay and branches to the barrels of melted rosin to the turpentine-soaked sheets to the *Charlotta* and its panicked crew.

"We must jump," shouted the ensign as he and three of his crew on the *Polly* saw that it was impossible to make it to the whaleboat tethered to the *Polly's* stern. "Jump!" the people watching from the shore heard him shout. The four jumped together into the river to save their lives. The flames that lit the sky that dark and dreadful night could be seen on Staten Island. The four men were never seen alive again. Their bodies washed up on the shore in various places over the following week.

The *Mary Ann* grappled the *Phoenix,* but took her on the leeward side. Alas, the wind was not strong enough to blow the flames upon her, and she escaped up the river.

The next day, Lt. Loudon and two men towed the wreck of the *Charlotta* into shallow waters and removed from her her guns and cutlasses and grappling irons and chains and whatever else they could salvage. And out in the river, Captain Parker of the *Phoenix* and Captain Wallace of the *Rose*, conferring, decided that they could no longer take the risk to the squadron from the intrepid American marine force by lingering any longer in the cursed Tappan Zee. Besides, their supplies of powder and shot were depleted, they could not obtain provisions or water, or contact the Loyalists on shore, and they did not like the looks of the obstacles being sunk below Fort Washington to prevent their rejoining the fleet off Staten Island. They hauled anchors and left.

When she got home that night of the fire-ship engagement, Margaret was suddenly sure she must hide her plate. But where? To bury it would require getting old Sam to dig the hole. Then what was to prevent him from digging it up when their backs were turned and running away with it? Johannes had already laboriously raised the hearthstone to hide their gold and silver coins, swept ashes over it, tried not to look at it. But the plate was too large and bulky. It had to be buried.

"We shall send Sam and Bett to Hackensack for supplies," he said, "and while they are gone, you and I will dig the hole."

When the slaves were gone, they went out into a well-turned and loamy field that was to lie fallow the next year and dug a deep hole in the loam and laboriously buried in it a metal chest of plate with, on top in baskets covered with tow, two pieces of Margaret's best faience. They planted an insignificant looking bush to mark the spot and scattered hay and leaves around the bush to hide the signs of the fresh digging. But afterward, as she gazed around her house, she saw plenty of her beloved treasures for looters to fall upon.

In late August came bad news.

CHAPTER 16

▼

DESPAIR

In mid-August, Colonel Abraham Blauvelt, fresh from New York, leaped off the ferry at the Slote, rented a horse and, blue linen rifle frock flying, galloped at top speed three miles west on the plank road to Tappan. Along the route, the people heard the galloping hoof beats and saw him tear past and knew it meant news. It was the signal to flock to the Tappan church to hear it, and he went up into the pulpit to tell it: "A great battle is imminent," he announced when they were gathered. "General Washington has warned the New York Convention meeting in White Plains of it."

A collective shudder passed through the sanctuary. In the pews and on the benches, husbands and wives gripped each other's hands. Children moved closer to their parents. Old folks looked grim. "How bad will it be?" someone called out.

"It will be bad. Manhattan must prepare to be the scene of devastation," he said gravely.

"How bad?"

"So bad that the General has issued a proclamation recommending that the inhabitants leave the city at once. Further, he has ordered the infirm and the indigent to be removed to the countryside. We must prepare here to be inundated with refugees."

"We are already inundated with them," the people murmured. "Where will we put more? Every house is full."

"Especially the sick and the old. Who will care for them?"

"You must take them in, however inconvenient," Abraham said, "and however sick they may be. You cannot do otherwise. In the same way, New Yorkers must take General Washington's recommendation seriously and leave the city. If you have relatives there, insist on it. The British are far stronger than we."

"They are not invincible," John Perry protested.

"No, they are not invincible," Abraham agreed. "General Lee demonstrated that in June by repulsing the enemy's attack on Charleston. But just over the water on Staten Island is gathered the hugest expeditionary force Great Britain has ever deployed, perhaps the largest the world has ever known."

John Haring stood to speak. He was passing through Tappan on his way to Kingston to collect lead window weights from the people to melt down for bullets. "You are right, Abraham," he said. "We cannot afford to be nonchalant. New York is not Charleston. And, as you have read, people, it has been reported in the papers that a frightening twenty-seven regiments of the line, four light infantry battalions, a regiment of light dragoons, 9,000 Hessians, a regiment of 800 fugitive slaves, and 10,000 sailors are arrayed on Staten Island against us."

"The British mean business," said Thomas Blanch, standing. "They have 33,000 men in all, trained and experienced, supported by thirty warships, twenty frigates, and nearly 400 transport vessels. They are determined to put us down."

"Far be it from me to know all the facts," said Margaret, standing, "but we have six fire ships lying in wait to destroy Admiral Howe's fleet, should it approach. Do you not think our army and the fire ships are striking terror in British hearts, just as the British are in ours?"

"Cousin," said Colonel Blauvelt sadly, "General Washington has a mere 19,000 troops, and they are not well trained and not experienced. And he has spread them out, as not he nor anyone knows where General Howe will decide to strike. Half of them are encamped on Brooklyn Heights, a quarter in Manhattan, a quarter in New Jersey. In effect, we are on our own here, with only our militia to protect us. And heaven knows they are poorly trained and inexperienced, too."

The gloom and dismay in the sanctuary were palpable. "Then we should not take comfort in our fire ships and our brave men?"

"No. We should not, Madam, and we must not," said Thomas Blanch. "They have only to elude the fire ships, take Brooklyn, and the war is over. We are finished, and our dream of liberty, too. Do not have faith in the fire ships."

"What shall we have faith in then?" she queried, her heart pounding in her ears. She sank back to the bench and pressed herself against Johannes for support. Since it was not a worship service but a community gathering for a public reason, they were not sitting in their accustomed Sabbath places, women in pews on the east and west sides of the house, men on benches down the middle, but rather together, side by side. He put his arm around her shoulders. "We will be safe on our farm," he whispered. "It is far enough out of town that they won't find us."

"Have faith in Providence," said an old lady from the back of the church.

"When is it thought they will strike?"

"They can come at any moment," John Haring said glumly. "They can come whenever they decide to. They are ready for it."

"Why do they delay?"

"No doubt they have their reasons. Which are not for us to know," he said, "although you can be sure we have many spies among them who attempt to determine their plans. For the moment, I advise you to make sure your larders are full and medicines and bandages are at hand."

The people gave out a low moan, and some began to weep. Small children, catching the atmosphere, whimpered anxiously. Women trembled. Men stared bleakly out the windows of the sanctuary as if to discern the unknown beyond.

The people left the church and filtered into the tavern to hash it over. "When?" they asked. "When will it be?"

"Assume that the time is at hand," Haring said bluntly.

But as it happened, the time for the enemy to strike was not quite at hand. Nature, or something even more mysterious, intervened. Perhaps it was Providence, the people finally said.

*   *   *   *

In the early evening of August 18, two days after Colonel Blauvelt had delivered his alarming announcement of the impending battle, the summer skies over New York and New Jersey grew dark, as if at an eclipse of the sun. Colonists, British, Hessians, Patriots, Loyalists, white, black, slave, free, men, women, children, all shrank in terror from the tremendous black thundercloud that rose in the west. Rain began to pour out of the skies as it never had before in memory, and the monstrous cloud burst open with a deafening crash, like the roar of a thousand cannon. Lightning came down out of the sky in sheets of fire. "The hand of God," people murmured. "It is the end of the world. Armegeddon."

For three fearsome hours, the cloud lingered, pivoting slowly around and around in the sky like a wheel guided by an unseen hand. People cowered in their houses, weeping, praying, expecting Christ to appear in his glory to separate the wheat from the chaff, for eternity. "And what if we are the chaff?" they asked themselves and each other. "What if we are?" They recalled all their sins and wickedness, fell on their knees, overcome with fear, moaning, begging forgiveness.

"Get up," said Margaret crossly to the cowering women in her household. "It is not the Last Judgment. It does not mean the end time has come. Get up and get busy. We have twenty mouths to feed in this house three times a day, not to mention the slaves, storm or no storm."

"But what does it mean?" the terrified women begged, trembling.

"I tell you, it is not the Last Judgment," she said again, firmly. "It is an Act of God to warn the British to desist from interfering in the cause of liberty."

In Hackensack, a Loyalist was struck deaf, dumb, and blind, although he had no visible injury, and on Long Island, a group of men, all of them disaffected to the Patriot cause, were transformed into smoking black cinders by single bolts of the terrible lightning. "You see," said Margaret triumphantly, the next day, when she heard of these things. "I was right. It was an Act of God. Be comforted, sisters."

As news trickled in in the days that followed that many more British and Loyalists were incinerated, killed, or maimed than Patriots, the people began to share Margaret's opinion. "It was no ordinary storm," they murmured. "It had a hidden meaning, a secret purpose."

Dominie Verbryck in Tappan agreed. "It was a phenomenon launched by an invisible arm, from the mysterious depths of the heavens, for reasons not clear," he told his flock. "But we may safely interpret it as a warning from the Lord to those who would force the Monster Tyranny on a people wishing to be free. It was sent to discourage those who would enslave us."

"*Dominie*, be aware that you can be taken by the British and imprisoned for such views," shouted Frederick Muzelius from a back pew. "Or worse."

"And you for yours, Mr. Muzelius," Verbryck replied calmly. "By the Americans."

For a while, a short while, the awful phenomenon did discourage the enemy, for all around their encampments men had been struck dead in their tracks and burnt to crisps. They too considered the frightening preternatural event as a warning from on high.

But on the twenty-first, General Howe recovered his will and stirred at last, and it began, the first battle since Charleston in June, and the first since the Declaration of Independence was read in Philadelphia six weeks before: the Battle of Brooklyn.

The fire ships never had a chance to burn the British fleet of 400, protected by thirty-three men-of-war, much less defeat Howe's army of 24,000, with more artillery than had yet been marshaled, even on the Continent, perhaps ever in history, it was said. People murmured in awe at the figures reported in the papers.

That day, in flat boats, Howe crossed the Narrows from Staten Island to Gravesend Bay and landed 15,000 men on the shores of Brooklyn. Behind him on the twenty-second, Lt. General Henry Clinton landed the Grenadiers and 4,000 light infantry, and the same day, General Howe landed a second division on the same beach and marched to the village of Utrecht in Brooklyn, where he established his headquarters.

Lord Cornwallis commanded an advanced post three miles away. Six regiments of Hessians embarked from Staten Island to join Howe.

At his headquarters in upper Manhattan, a grave George Washington spoke to his generals and officers. "The enemy have now landed," he told them, "and I fear we face what may be the largest battle we will ever fight. The hour is fast approaching on which the honor and success of this army and the safety of our bleeding country depend." He invoked Bunker Hill, and Charleston: "Remember what a few brave men contending in their own land and in the best of causes can do against base hirelings and mercenaries," he urged. The men were as grave as he was, going to their death, for all they knew.

In the city, John Haring received two militiamen, Samuel Demarest and John Huyler, sent from Tappan to observe the battle, to obtain the latest news, to estimate the chances of success, or failure. "Our troops rally in high spirits," he assured them. "Let the monster tyranny have at us if it dare. Tell the people of Orangetown that we will resist the enemy to our last breaths in the name of our freedom."

The two men were skeptical. "Our troops are living in tents around the earthen batteries on the heights of Brooklyn, and they are outnumbered seven to one," Demarest pointed out.

"And thousands of them are too sick with putrid fever to engage," Huyler said. "Their drinking water is contaminated, and the fever is spread by infected lice. How can they fight?"

"There are 3,000 capable of fighting," said Haring, "and those 3,000 will keep their commander's words in their hearts and contend like tigers for their own land and for the best of causes. I am sure of it."

*   *   *   *

Neither of the two militiamen had Haring's confidence that the Americans would persevere, but they stayed in the city for a week to bear witness, as their commander had ordered them.

"It was not easy to gather the facts," they reported on their return to Tappan a week later, "for when the great battle was over yesterday, and the successful evacuation of the Americans from Brooklyn was complete this morning, it seemed that the battle was both won and lost."

The inhabitants, gathered to hear them in the Tappan church, hung on their every word. "How won the battle? How lost?" they asked. "Give us the news."

"We will tell you the good news first," Demarest said, "how it was won: On the night of the battle, the Americans were guarding the Gowanus Heights, the Flatbush Pass, and the Bedford Pass. Then General Howe, who had 20,000 troops to our 3,000 well enough to fight, ordered his second in command, Sir Henry Clinton, to make a night march. Four thousand of Clinton's troops pushed and pulled fourteen pieces of field artillery from Flatlands six miles northeast across Brooklyn to the Jamaica Pass, which intelligence had told him was unguarded except for five American officers on horseback. It was a feat beyond compare."

"It was a sneak around our left wing intended to encircle and trap our troops, a brilliant sneak," said Huyler. "And it worked. Howe himself followed two hours later, with 6,000 men and fourteen cannon. General James Grant marched leading a column of 5,000. By dawn they had secured the pass. Our troops panicked and fled before the onslaught, abandoning their positions as the Redcoats advanced."

"But where did they go?" Johannes asked. "Where could they go? Into the sea? And you say the battle was won? How is this good news?"

"They took refuge in the earthen fortifications on the heights of Brooklyn," said Demarest. "Maryland sent 400 troops to aid us, but they were of little help. At Gowanus, 9,000 Redcoats and two companies of Tories from Long Island pursued the Marylanders under the Command of General Stirling across the Gowanus Creek and right up to the walls of the fortifications."

"And how many did we lose?"

"When the dust of the battle cleared, we counted 200 dead and 900 captured, wounded, or missing. Of the 400 gallant troops from Maryland, all but eight were captured. The British lost 400 killed, captured, or wounded."

"What of George Washington?"

"He was in despair," Demarest said. "Fully expecting Howe's fleet to pass between Governor's Island and Red Hook and take Brooklyn Heights and his men in the forts there from the rear, he had to assume that the war to make America independent was to be terminated in its infancy."

"But you said we had won the battle."

"Yes, there is good news to tell," said Huyler jubilantly. "We did win. And once again, nature intervened to assist us, this time in a drenching wind and rainstorm from the northeast. Again Howe decided to wait out the weather. Our troops, trapped in their fortifications, were stranded, he believed. In some parts of the American lines, he knew, the men were waist deep in water."

Demarest laughed out loud. "It was reported by one of our informants that Howe said to his adjutant, 'Where is Mr. Washington to go in this climate?' He judged the weather to be one of our peculiarly American storms out of the northeast that last for three days, and he went back to playing whist in his tent."

"But he was wrong," Huyler said. "It lasted for only two days. And no one was more astonished than General Howe when he learned that during the night of August 29, with the storm abated a day sooner than he had counted on, and the harbor lying under cover of a thick fog, George Washington and half of the Continental army had escaped from Brooklyn across the East River to Manhattan. They were gone, under his very nose. He had missed his chance."

"Thank God," the people cried. They clapped and cheered and stamped their feet, shouting, "Long live George Washington! Long live our rights and privileges! Long live our freedom!"

"There is more," Huyler continued. "At ten in the night, the American regiments began to march, in a silence kept on pain of death, from their forts to the ferry landing. General McDougall was in charge of the embarkation. General Washington oversaw all. On horseback he cantered quietly, as quietly as a horse can canter, from forts to landing and back, again and again, until all the men were safely in boats, their oars wrapped in cloth to muffle the sound. They could not use sail. They had to row. The wind continued strong from the northeast."

"Our side was aided by brave mariners from Massachusetts," Demarest said. "Without them, the evacuation would not have been possible. Washington had ten flatboats. As quiet as mice, those mariners made repeated round-trips on the flatboats from Manhattan to Brooklyn and back again, transporting cannon, horses, artillery, wagons, provisions, baggage, and countless barrels of flour and salt pork to safety on Manhattan. The men, hauling their baggage, tents, and gear, piled into every vessel they could find."

"Then the wind dropped," Huyler said. The people were sitting on the edge of their benches in fascination. "The mile-wide East River became almost preternaturally as smooth as glass. Then, in the wee hours of the morning, the wind kindly came up again, from the southwest, and the men raised the sails on every vessel equipped with them. A dense fog rolled in on the southwest wind."

"A providential fog," the people said.

"Yes," murmured Margaret.

"Yes," Johannes said, taking her hand in his. "It was a miracle."

Samuel Demarest took up the story. "We learned that a wakeful Tory woman had caught on to the activity during the night and sent her slave to inform the British. But Hessian soldiers captured the slave as a runaway, and they could not understand his protestations, for he spoke only Dutch. And we learned that a British sentry had noticed at midnight that the rebel breastworks were empty, but for some inexplicable reason he neglected to sound an alarm."

"The storm abating, the fog, the Hessians and the slave, the British sentry's neglect of his duty," Margaret said. "Isn't it clear whose hand is in it?"

The women were of this mind, but their men folk put a different light on it. "The British army under General Howe had the whole American army in its power, yet let it get away," Thomas Blanch said. "Why?"

"It is rumored," said Samuel Demarest, "and this is hard to believe, but it is rumored that Howe and his brother the Admiral are secretly on the side of the Americans."

"Is that possible?"

"People say that General Howe is either our friend or no general worthy of the name," Demarest replied.

"Consider it: How we escaped from Brooklyn is more than surprising," John Huyler said, "for had they pursued us to our fortifications as by military logic they should have done, we would have surrendered of necessity. Or had they attacked us from the sea, not a man of us could have escaped, and the war lost."

"The Howes on our side?" the people murmured as they drifted away to go about their work. "What a calamity for the enemy, if true."

"And what good fortune for us!"

"Gather in the tavern this evening. There is more to hear from Bergen County," Demarest called after them.

That evening, James Christie and Abraham Brouwer, Patriot spies from Bergen County, who had also been in the city during the battle and the evacuation, joined the Tappan people at the tables in the tavern, where by lantern and candlelight they smoked and drank and listened to the tale.

"By eight this morning," Christie reported, "gleeful Patriots in Manhattan were trumpeting the astounding feat of the evacuation, which was accomplished in every sort of vessel that could be commandeered, rowboats, canoes, barges, sloops, skiffs."

"Our giving of the slip to them must have aroused a profound dissatisfaction in the enemy," Johannes said in awe.

"Indeed it must have. It was a flawless evacuation, a most fortunate retreat."

"Then," said Thomas Blanch, hopefully, "you are saying the war is ended, and we have won?"

"If only that were true," said Adam Brouwer. "Some were so certain of victory this morning that they declared it from the rooftops as one of the greatest achievements in the history of warfare. They did indeed announce the Revolution to be saved, the cause of liberty preserved. But unfortunately, it soon appeared otherwise when our men began to straggle through the streets of the city."

"They were as if in shock," Christie went on. "Exhausted, sick, injured, hungry, wet, cold, and discouraged. Before noon this very day, 6,000 of the 9,500 who were evacuated only last night deserted the Army. They have gone home to tend to their fields. To them, there seems no point in fighting on. From their view, the Revolution is not saved. It is over. British might won the Battle of Brooklyn as if it were child's play."

"We withstood the British onslaught of cannon balls and shells amazingly well," said Brouwer glumly. "Our Army fought off charges from an enemy far superior in numbers and experience, but it was not enough."

Along with all of Patriot fervor, Margaret grieved to hear the news, and all the more so as she could not help but imagine the thoughts of the defeated leader, the symbol of his country and its will to resist, imagine him now cast into deepest despair. Her prayers had gone unanswered.

"Has everyone despaired then?" Johannes asked, in a quiet voice.

"Not at all!" said Brouwer. "Rather, every able-bodied Patriot male left on Manhattan and some females too and not a few children have joined together to throw up fresh defensive works on the shores of the island. What is left of the Army is busily larding the Hudson and East rivers with sunken obstructions as we speak, and they are preparing fearsome new fire ships. The fight is not over yet."

The Americans had a good two weeks to do these things, before General Howe, to the strains of stirring music and the peals of thundering guns, landed a division of troops, the Light Infantry, the British Reserve, the Hessian Grenadiers, and the Chasseurs, on the east shore of Manhattan, at Kip's Bay. Fire and murderous shot and rolling volleys of smoke vomited forth from the guns.

It was September 15. "But is it not curious that he gave his enemy two weeks to prepare their defense works?" Margaret asked.

"Very curious," said Johannes. "One must wonder."

*   *   *   *

When the cannon fire began, General Washington was at his writing desk in his headquarters at Robert Morris's fine mansion on Harlem Heights, where he could be close to Fort Washington and the main body of his army, which was posted between the Heights and White Plains to the north. As soon as a messenger arrived with the news, he ordered his aide to have the grooms saddle up his great white English charger Nelson, and he galloped at a clip the several miles down the Post Road to Kip's Bay. "Besides my beloved Mount Vernon," he called to John Morin Scott, who galloped alongside him, "I love nothing better than a good battle."

But at Kip's Bay, to his surprise and mortification, he found his troops, faced with fifty or sixty Redcoats firing grapeshot, running away in every direction and in the greatest confusion. Though he used every means in his power to rally them into position, including ordering two of his generals to cane and whip them, his attempts were ineffectual. Even though he himself drew his sword and slashed out at them, they fled.

The next day, John Morin Scott passed through Tappan on his way to West Point. Word of his arrival sped through the village, and all gathered in the church to hear his account of the engagement—or lack of it. "The disgraceful conduct of the troops severely discountenanced the commander in chief," he said. "The men flew away into the cornfields without firing a single shot, notwithstanding the pistols he cocked at them, the imprecations he hurled, or all the solicitations, prayers, and it was finally observed, even the tears the great man shed. They ran as if the devil was in them," he added in disgust, "and left His Excellency to shift for himself. He threw his tricorn on the ground and shouted a great shout."

"What did he shout?" Margaret asked.

"He shouted, 'Are these the men with which I am to defend America?'"

"It is a day of ignominy," Margaret said bitterly. "We should be deeply ashamed of our cowardly countrymen."

And deeply embarrassed for *him*, she thought, her hero, whom she had looked upon and he upon her in that crowd that day. The memory of that brief encounter was fresh in her brain. She harkened to it often: he, tall, elegant, and full of virtue, alighting from his carriage, truly His *Excellency* in every respect, actually noticing her, raising his hat to her, a mere Dutch housewife. She had been overcome with awe to stand in his presence that day. She remembered how she had searched his brave, calm features, commended every detail of them to her memory, signaled him one thought, one commission, from the depths of her soul: *Starve the Monster Tyranny! Starve the Monster Tyranny!*

He had understood her silent message, she believed, and had sent a silent one back to her. His face, his form, his dignified hauteur, his sacrifice had given her that day the conviction that he would not disappoint her, nor she him. If she prayed hard enough, she believed, she could pray him to success in the service of his country, and that is just what he counted on her to do. It was a presumptuous notion, she knew, but she believed it: She could *will* him to succeed so that the country might be free, and she *would* will him to succeed. And he would not be in the least surprised at her success in his success. She kept these bold thoughts to herself, did not share them even with Johannes.

"General Greene is of the opinion," Scott went on, "that the great man was so vexed at the infamous conduct of the troops that, marooned within eighty yards of the enemy, he had put his life in danger by staying his ground and exhorting them to turn and fight."

At this, she was even more disturbed.

"It is said that he was in such mortal danger that day," Scott continued, "that an aide saw fit to seize the reins of his horse and turn him northward, lead him away from the enemy over ground strewn with the deserted arms, knapsacks, coats, hats, and canteens of his sorry army lest he be shot to death."

That evening they sat together under the grape arbor in the last light of day. "If it is true," she said, "that he risked his life among the cornfields of Murray Hill, while his men panicked and ran, it is disturbing. Because, if he loses his life, who will lead us away from English oppression to our dream of liberty?"

"It seems that the great man you have so much faith in is rather rash and unpredictable," he said teasingly.

"Johannes. He is a very great man," she said huffily. "And I do have faith in him. And you must too."

"I do," he said. "I do, my dear."

She was mollified. "Do you remember that he has said that, if his men stood by him, he was resolved not to retreat while he had life?"

"Yes, I do remember that. And he proved again that he is fearless even in the face of death, even though his men did not stand by him," Johannes admitted. "He is a remarkable man."

"But is that a good thing, or not?" she wondered. "To be fearless in the face of death? I think perhaps not. It is perhaps the better part of valor to retreat while one has life."

The lines came to her, written by a slave woman in New England and published everywhere: "Proceed, great chief, with virtue on thy side./Thy every action let the goddess guide./A crown, a mansion, and a throne that shine,/with gold unfading, Washington! Be thine."

"I want him, with virtue on his side, to survive to be our great chief after the British are chased away," she said. "I want him to be the author of our liberty, not to take rash chances in a meaningless cornfield."

"We all want it," he said. "We want it with our whole being."

"But then again," she mused, "Why didn't General Howe march across the island east to west to trap the thousands of Americans fleeing their way north up the Hudson shore?"

"Everyone wonders," said Johannes. "It is perhaps true that he is secretly sympathetic to the American cause."

"And why didn't the English soldiers kill him, if he was only eighty yards away from them? The range of a musket is eighty to a hundred yards. What stopped their fire?"

No sooner had she framed the question, though, than the answer was clear to both of them: Divine Providence had stopped their fire. "God is on our side, Johannes," she said joyfully. "He is on our side."

"God is the author of liberty and property and no stamps," he said. "And so he and we must be on the same side." He put his hand on hers and in the gloaming gazed into her familiar and dear and still handsome face, aging so gently. "*Mijn lieveling*," he said.

"I love you, my dearest heart," she said. "We will come through all this."

She had, of course, set her cap for the right man at age twelve. She could imagine herself wed to no other.

"Don't forget how John Jay put it," he said. "Americans will never submit to be hewers of wood or drawers of water for any nation in the world."

"Especially the Royal Brute of Great Britain, so called by Thomas Paine," she said.

*   *   *   *

But if God was on their side, he was miserly with his favors. The British were now in complete control of Manhattan, and everything was in pandemonium in the city as more hundreds and even thousands of residents packed their belongings and fled across the Hudson. Margaret's heart filled with rage when she learned from exhausted refugees arriving in Tappan, dirty, disheveled, and frightened, with their bedding strapped to their backs and pots and pans dangling from their waists, that a Tory woman had pulled down the American flag on the fort and that another Tory woman had trampled it under foot, then helped to raise the King's flag. The refugees brought tales of looting and pillaging in the city, of "GR," George Rex, painted on the forfeited houses of known Patriots, of Americans imprisoned in Dutch churches and English sugar warehouses.

"The people will be losing hope," she said, in despair despite herself.

"Are you?" Johannes asked anxiously. He counted on her faith to support his own.

"No," she said, but she was, she feared, though she would not admit it to him or anyone.

There came a few days later, though, from Harlem Heights a ray of hope, and news of it soon flitted over the Hudson to Tappan. There on the tip of northern Manhattan, General Washington had roused his men to repulse the Redcoats. Modestly, he described it as a "brisk little skirmish," but it was the first success for his troops since Bunker Hill, and it brought new heart to Patriots everywhere.

Five nights later, a great fire swept through the city consuming everything in its path. From Harlem Heights, where he watched the night sky, it appeared to him that the heavens themselves were in flames.

By morning, Trinity Church and 500 houses, some counted a thousand houses, from Whitehall to Barclay Street, a distance of a mile, lay in embers, Aeltie's rented house on Vesey Street among them, all of her family's possessions gone up in flames, except what they had taken with them when they had fled the city in July.

"Was it arson?" they asked in the taverns and the churches.

"No one knows."

"Perhaps someone knows. Perhaps Providence, or some good honest fellow, has done more for us this day than we were disposed to do for ourselves."

"If Providence had something to do with it," Margaret said to her household, "there is hope. Let us rejoice in it!"

The British put out the story that it was rebel arsonists, secreted in houses in the city, who had set fire to several places at one time, between midnight and one o'clock in the morning.

*   *   *   *

After the Great Fire, so many homeless fled the tumultuous city to Bergen and Orange counties every day, both Tories and Patriots, that in Tappan every house and hovel was bursting with humanity. They flocked to Tappan, because it was thought to be safer than Hackensack, where it was rumored the British army would make its winter encampment.

Margaret took in another family fled from the city, the homeless wife and children of General John Morin Scott, and she soon regretted it, for Mrs. Scott was overwhelmed with distress at having to be separated from her husband and lodged in a back room in a curious Dutch farmhouse in the countryside with her children whining and whimpering around her. She herself whimpered without ceasing, helpless to know what to do, how to care for her dear ones. She sent a messenger to find her husband in the city with a letter begging him to come and comfort and advise her.

"There is no time," he said. "I have no time for this!" But he sailed to Tappan Slote, rented a horse, asked directions to the house, and galloped to it. He was in a great hurry to get the next tide back to the city. He admonished her to carry on. "You are much better off here, my dear," he said, looking around at the colorful, though crowded *groote kamer* with beds and pallets in every corner. "You cannot imagine what the city has become. The Redcoats and Hessians have broken into any and all houses left standing after the fire and quarter themselves in comfort."

"Necessity knows no law," Johannes said grimly.

"And revolution no niceties," said Scott. "They cheerfully soil fine silk and wool upholstery with their muddy boots, tear up fences and parquet floors for firewood, keep their horses and their dogs in the gardens, where they trample and manure once-tidy beds and borders. You are better off here, wife, in the country with these kind people."

She mopped at her eyes. "I shall try to accept my fate," she murmured, sniffling.

"Your husband is right. It is better you are here than there," said Margaret, although she heartily wished she had not taken this family into her house.

"Do you bring any good news?" Johannes asked.

"Yes, I bring good news," Scott said. "General Washington has escaped over the Hell Gate from Manhattan into Westchester. So he is safe, too. For the moment."

"I am no military expert, needless to say," Margaret said. "But why didn't General Howe burn that wooden bridge over the Hell Gate when he had the chance, earlier in the summer?"

"You may well wonder, Madam," said Scott. "Even generals wonder."

"Everyone will wonder when they hear it," Johannes said. "Why did he let him escape once again?"

"I'm convinced Providence had a hand in it," said Scott. And then, "I must be gone," he said. "The tide waiteth not." He downed the last bit of Madeira in his glass, heartily embraced his wife, and left, his sword clanking at his side. The unhappy woman crawled into her bed, moving her children around to make room. She wept quietly.

"I m sorry for her," said Margaret. "But to say the truth, no one in the household would be sad to see her leave."

*   *   *   *

John Haring, who now represented Orange County in the Provincial Convention of the State of New York, received orders to attend on General Washington in White Plains, where he was headquartered in an old Dutch farmhouse. He saluted him, and Washington returned the salute. "It is now necessary, Major," he said, his tall frame dwarfing the small room he had made his office, "to ask the New York Convention to procure four large sloops to convey the sick and wounded from New York City to Orangetown. The fatigue of traveling that distance by land would be more than the afflicted could bear. Moreover, we fully need our wagons for transporting baggage, tents, and provisions for the troops. Kindly make the arrangements at your earliest convenience. I have ordered my chief medical officer to Tappan to meet with you," he added.

"We are to locate a hospital site in Orangetown," this officer told Haring upon his arrival in Tappan.

Haring shook his head. "We could make a diligent search," he said, "but I know of no suitable place in all of Orangetown, and I am familiar with its every corner, without turning hordes of distressed persons out of doors. The Tappan Reformed Church is the only option."

"Then so shall it be," said the medical officer.

They ordered the benches and pews removed, and the sloops began to convey the wounded, and the sick, many with smallpox and typhus, from the city to the Slote, where soldiers and medical personnel transferred them to flat-bottom boats and little periaugers and poled or sailed them up the *kill* to Tappan.

The women of the neighborhood, their faces masked against the poisonous breaths of the sick, were their nurses. They carried food and drink to them every day, changed their bloody bandages, tended the worst to the death and saw them buried in the cemetery behind the church. Slaves, the old ones who hadn't run off to join the British as the young ones had, washed and mended their clothes, bloody and muddy and rent with bayonet slashes and musket holes and powder stains.

When they weren't attending the wounded, the women busied themselves knitting socks and mittens for the militia and making linsey-woolsey blankets, felt hats, woolen cloth. Winter was coming. Margaret's fingers bled from the spindle. She soothed them with sheep's lard.

On the 27th of October with a nip in the air came the bad news that Howe had routed Washington in White Plains. Captain James Smith's company of Orange County militia was with him there that day. In the evening, Margaret's cousin, John Blauvelt, a lieutenant in Smith's company, galloped up to the house to report that, in a hot battle, one of their best friends and neighbors, Abraham Onderdonk, was killed by a cannon ball. "It separated his head from his shoulders," he said, shivering at the memory. "Two other men fell within a few of feet of him. Their legs and arms were severed from their torsos. The hills were smoking as if on fire, bellowing with cannonade and the fire of field pieces, howitzers, and mortars."

"God help us," she said.

"The very air seemed to groan," he went on. "The bursting shells echoed off the hills. Fences and walls were everywhere destroyed, and legs and arms and bodies and Abraham Onderdonk's head lay on the bloody ground."

"It is going to be worse, much worse than I had possibly foreseen, than anyone possibly foresaw," Margaret said.

"It is perhaps hopeless, even now," John Blauvelt said.

But even as he said it, something within her said *No*. No, it was her duty, her sacred role, not to give up hope. It was her duty to pray and will him to succeed!

"Though White Plains was no victory," John Blauvelt went on, "His Excellency is said to feel himself and his men, minus 175 dead, fortunate, for they killed more than that of British and Hessians, and they got away. Plus, his generals suspect that Howe will now lie back to lick his wounds."

"So you see, Cousin," said Margaret. "We are right to hope. We are not lost yet."

*   *   *   *

Leaving half his army in Westchester, Washington retreated with the other half across the Hudson to the safety of Fort Lee. But alas, from there, he soon had to watch in sorrow and in anger as, two weeks later, on November 16, 20,000 Hessians and Redcoats took Fort Washington directly across the river and marched 3,000 American troops off to prison.

"Let every man of them be publicly hanged," urged a prominent Tory.

"That, of course, would take too long and is too much trouble," said a cooler head.

"Yes. Suffice it to let them dwindle and die in the hellholes the British call prisons," Margaret said bitterly.

With Fort Washington gone, George Washington, admitting that Fort Lee was useless in obstructing the passage of the Hudson without the assistance of its sister fort opposite on the east shore of the river, moved to save what he could of supplies and provisions, for the ten acres of Fort Lee in its brief existence had become an important supply depot. "Put the word out around the countryside," he ordered his generals, "that wagons and drivers and horses are needed to transport the powder and fixed ammunition over land to safety in Passaic, Springfield, Bound Brook, and even as far south as New Brunswick and Princeton. These precious items are too valuable to transport by water. It is only a matter of time until Fort Lee is next." He was sure, and had been assured of it by his generals, that Cornwallis would come ashore on the beach at Nyack and march south to take Fort Lee.

From his headquarters in Hackensack, four miles west of Fort Lee, he gave orders to General Nathaniel Greene to strip the northern New Jersey countryside to prevent Cornwallis, when he came, from foraging upon it. "Send the livestock into the swamps and woods," he ordered. "Remove hay and grains, disassemble fences and conceal their pieces so they cannot be used for firewood."

But at noon on the twentieth of November, Margaret's son Isaac, garrisoned at Sneden's Landing, galloped up to the house to report the unthinkable: "The enemy has come ashore," he shouted from the dooryard. "Two divisions of them, south of Sneden's Landing, at Huyler's Landing. A smart firing was heard below Fort Lee."

"What are you saying?" Margaret cried in disbelief. "What is the good of coming ashore at Huyler's Landing? It is a sheer cliff to the Fort!"

"They have done it, Mother, they have done the impossible. And I must be away. I have to spread the word. My orders." He was gone in a whirlwind of dust as quickly as he had come.

They stared at each other. "If they can do that, they can do anything," Johannes said.

"We are abandoned," she said.

"Yes. And now we are about to be surrounded by a brutal enemy."

"And we have not yet done the slaughtering and butchering. What will we eat this winter? There are twenty of us!"

"I will start it tomorrow," he said wearily. "Sam and I. And Abraham."

They had come on twenty flatboats, several thousand troops, all unseen, for the area was unguarded and unpatrolled, it having been thought not only by General Greene, but by all of the American generals, that the nearly perpendicular Palisades and the narrow twisting roads up them were impossible for troops, horses, and wagons loaded with cannon and ammunition and provisions to scale.

In a tent on the Green in Hackensack, Washington, sitting at his writing table, demanded an explanation of him.

General Greene, standing before him, was abject. "Your Excellency, I was determined to repulse the British should they attempt to cross the Hudson," he said. "But believing that the cliffs were impossible to scale, I regret to say that I left the roads up them undefended. I expected the enemy would try to land instead at Nyack or Haverstraw and attack over land. Thus I ordered the Orangetown militia to patrol the Nyack shore, 500 men to Sneden's Landing, and another 500 to the mountain passes leading to the Hudson Highlands to foil any movements of the British southward, but they came up the cliffs, a feat too daring to contemplate."

"You badly miscalculated," said Washington coldly. "You may have lost us our liberty forever."

"Your Excellency, I consulted with General Wayne," pleaded Greene in his own defense. "He also believed as I did that the mountain roads up the Palisades to the plateau were practicable only for a sled and two horses from the edge of the mountain to the water. He assured me that one-half mile of the cliff is too steep and narrow to admit of a common carriage, the descent being on an average one foot in five. Further, we agreed together that the area at the bottom of the mountain is far too small for handling supplies satisfactorily."

"It was not too small, as we now know," said George Washington through clenched teeth.

He fumed so vividly to have been so poorly served, and by one of his favorite generals—the one he had decided would be the best to replace him if it should come to that—that Greene could almost imagine smoke uttering from his nostrils.

Things got worse for General Greene. In a second breach of military diligence, not wishing to incur the wrath of the inhabitants, he had chosen to ignore his commander's order to send the livestock into the swamps and woods, strip the land of hay and grains, and disassemble the fences, so that the British, when they did scale the Palisades to Fort Lee, found the Hackensack valley a veritable granary, a teeming cow pasture, a trove of split rails theirs for their cooking fires.

An aide informed him that the commander in chief ordered him to appear before him again in his tent on the Hackensack Green, where again he turned on him with cold fury. "You disobeyed my order," Washington said fiercely.

Again, Greene was abject. "I will make it up to you," he said miserably. "I promise."

"Promises," said Washington, cold as ice. "Due to your insubordination, the unhappy affair of Fort Washington has been succeeded by further misfortunes. The enemy now hopes to enclose our troops and stores on the narrow neck of land between the Hudson and the Hackensack rivers."

"I am sorry," Greene murmured. "I am mad, vexed, sick, and sorry."

"Finding the enemy's numbers greatly superior to mine, there is nothing to do now but direct my men to remove west of the Hackensack," said Washington. "By doing so we must leave a very fine country open to their ravages, and a plentiful store house from which they will draw their supplies, thanks to your disobedience."

Greene backed out of his wrathful presence and slinked away, mortified. "Clearly, I overrated him," he heard Washington mutter.

The landing of the British under Lord Cornwallis was complete by nine in the morning, and by one o'clock in the afternoon they were up the Palisades and at Fort Lee. General Greene, at the Fort with his troops only to get off the stores, not to defend the redoubt, had been warned of the landing by a Patriot farmer and immediately ordered its evacuation. His men left behind 146 cannon, 2,700 muskets, 400,000 cartridges, shot and shell, tents, entrenching tools, the entire stuff of an army. When the British arrived, they found the place deserted, 300 tents abandoned, the campfires still burning and food simmering in the cooking pots, fifty loaded cannon, hundreds of barrels of flour, considerable parcels of baggage and ammunition, provisions, and stores. "And some copies of Thomas Paine's *Common Sense* lying in the mud," John Haring reported glumly.

A Tory went about Tappan boasting that, had not that cursed farmer warned Greene of Cornwallis moving toward him, every man in the garrison could have been taken prisoner. "On the appearance of our troops, the rebels fled like scared rabbits, and in a few moments after ours reached their entrenchments, not a rascal of them could be seen," he gloated in the tavern frequented by the Tories—and by Patriots spying on them.

Greene and his troops fled over the Hackensack River so as not to be trapped by Cornwallis in the territory between the Hudson and the Hackensack.

Inexplicably, Lord Cornwallis decided, like Howe before him, to take his time. His army rested for the afternoon and that night slept soundly in the abandoned tents of the Americans, their fires burning brightly in the moonless night.

When he bestirred himself in the morning and ordered his troops to march, Cornwallis found the roads from Closter to Tenafly to Liberty Pole to Englewood littered with abandoned muskets and knapsacks, thousands of cattle and sheep brought there for the use of the rebel army wandering about, the cows and ewes unmilked and bellowing in pain, and, on the road to Hackensack, both heavy and light artillery abandoned on their traveling carriages by the fleeing army.

He was awed at these signs of the haste and disorganization of the flight. "Surely, an army not worthy of the name," he was heard to murmur. Still, he did not hurry. Even if Washington had crossed the Hackensack, which Cornwallis's spies had reported he had, now he was trapped between the Hackensack and the Passaic, easy prey.

*   *   *   *

The next day, stirred by prospects of victory, a mob of British officers and their servants, soldiers and their women, jubilant Tories, and a dozen cheering slaves sacked the house, near Hackensack, of the Patriot minister Dirck Romeyn, raided his barns, and stole his cattle and all his furniture and clothing. He made his escape and, stopping in Tappan on his way to safety in New Paltz up the river, held "church" in the parsonage of Samuel Verbryck—the actual church now filled with the sick and wounded, and Verbryck himself fled to Clarkstown to escape capture on account of his vociferous sermons in the cause of liberty.

Romeyn described to the congregation, some seated on chairs and benches in the *groote kamer,* the rest standing around the periphery of the room, how he had looked out of his window that dark, cold, rain-swept night when Greene's troops marched into town on their retreat from Fort Lee. "They marched two abreast. They were ragged, some without a shoe to their feet, and most of them wrapped in their blankets."

Men sighed, women cried and wrung their hands, all mourning for the ragged, shoeless troops, mourning to think that the cause of liberty seemed to have ended so soon, so ignominiously.

"I tremble to think that at least some of the British success is due to the Tory guides and traitors all around us, and our own runaway slaves, too," said Johannes.

"Yes," said Romeyn. "It is disgusting to think it. Our own former friends and our own slaves leading the hunters to their prey, our own Army, now vulnerable in our own river valleys."

One of those traitors was a favorite young cousin of Margaret's, a lad she never would have suspected of desertion. His mother, her aunt, was beside herself with anxiety. "Do something. Do something! Help us!" she begged Margaret, coming to her door in the morning. "He has received a sentence to death for it."

Margaret, distraught, wandered the frost-covered fields, asking herself, *What can I do? What can I do? How can I save the poor fellow's life?*

Then, as clearly as the sound of a cowbell coming to her over the fields on that cold winter's morning, the answer came to her. She went back to her house, sat at her desk, and wrote a letter to the great chief himself. If a slave would write a poem to him, she would write a letter.

Of course, he knew not who the writer was who signed herself Margaret Blauvelt, but the letter was from Tappan, and Blauvelt was a Dutch name. The Orangetown militia was loaded with Blauvelts. A Colonel Blauvelt commanded them, he knew. A good man. A solid Patriot. He recalled the woman he had noticed among the "Dutch farmers of Tappan," who had been pointed out to him in the city on his way to Boston. It seemed so long ago.

It was long ago, he realized, staring out of the window of the room where he dictated the day's orders. Snow was falling. That had been summer. He had been on his way to Bunker Hill. He was stopping at Hull's Tavern for the night. The one with the intense expression on her face, those impassioned eyes, telling him what she expected of him, that old-fashioned comb in her blond hair. Could she be the writer?

Whether she was or was not, he could not know, but he wrote back to whomever it was: "Madam, I am sure he is a bad man, but out of respect for your concern for an ill-advised relative I grant your request."

She read the short note over and over again, pressed it to her bosom for a long moment, and then put it for safekeeping in her Psalm book.

They freed the boy, but in a day he deserted again. He was immediately captured and taken by his commander to the hill behind the tavern and shot through the head, a traitor to his country. Margaret's aunt threw herself on her precious boy's body and beat the bloody snowy ground with her fists, sobbing. Margaret could not console her, though she tried mightily.

*　　　*　　　*　　　*

Margaret's two oldest sons, Isaac and John, with the Orangetown militia, guarded the river from two small eminences above the ferry at Sneden's Landing. Johannes and their third son, the twin, Abraham, sixteen, not one for war (he professed, much to her consternation, to want to be "neutral"), had the day before the hasty evacuation of Fort Lee harkened to General Washington's plea for men to move the army's stores out of harm's way. "The butchering will have to wait," Johannes said. "This is more important." They hitched up two horses to the wagon and, with a large ham and bread and a wheel of cheese and a jug of cider to sustain them, set out. "It will be a week before we are back," he said. "Be well. Be safe, my dearest."

"You be well," she said. "Be safe." They embraced, both thinking it might be for the last time.

She trembled for their lives, for a bad element was inserting itself in the area, and people were afraid on this account in every Patriot household in the vicinity. No sooner had the British crossed the Hackensack and encamped on the Green in front of the Hackensack Reformed Church than they were joined by jubilant runaway slaves and hundreds of Irish, Scots, and Germans from the Ramapo Mountains, iron workers lured by the Loyalist offer of five guineas to join the cause—and arms and smart green uniforms. They called themselves Greencoats and were led by one of Tappan's own Dutch Patriots, turned Tory, Abraham van Buskirk, now calling himself simply Buskirk, as if to erase his Dutchness along with his politics.

He and his unsavory crew soon busied themselves recruiting young and old, taking Patriots into custody by day, robbing and plundering at night. A thousand of them remained to torment the Americans when Cornwallis moved on his way after "Mr." Washington, as he persisted in calling him, and his ragged troops. Over the Bergen meadows, he pursued, over the Passaic River, on to Newark, Elizabethtown, New Brunswick, and Trenton, and at Trenton he made camp, while over the Delaware to Pennsylvania his barefoot quarry hurried. In droves Americans all along the way took up Sir William Howe's offer of pardon and signed an oath of allegiance to King George III that protected them from molestation by Tories, the British army, and the hired Hessians.

Patriot hopes had reached their nadir.

She felt a need to see for herself what was happening in Hackensack. She left the women and children in the house with instructions to keep the doors locked, and though the ruts in the roads were so deep at this time of year that the hubs of her wheels were level with the tops of the ruts, she set off in her elegant riding chair for her cousin Rachel's house, five miles to the south. Sam rode beside her for protection. She was glad to have him, although in truth she felt protected by her own oath of allegiance—to a higher King. That King would not let harm befall her, she believed. But just in case, Sam carried a loaded musket and was a good shot, old as he was. And she had a sharp little sword, a rapier that had come down to them from her husband's family, buckled around her waist.

Driving her coach through the forest, dappled with sun and alive with twittering birds, even in November, and fragrant with pine, a kind of calm overtook her, the calm of being alone, away from the demands of her hectic household. And in the calm, thoughts of *him* came to her, the tall calm general, that aloof and, many believed, divinely guided leader of their cause, who had looked at her that time in that crowd, and passed something to her that she would never forget as long as she lived: *He was damned if he would disappoint the country.* That was what he had seemed to say. And he would not disappoint the country, she was certain. With virtue on his side, a crown, a mansion, and a throne, the people's throne, were his.

A pang of envy for the slave poet woman who had written that ode to him struck her, for he had written back to her. It was said to be the only time in his life he had written directly to a slave, no doubt because most were unable to read, but there was also something else. He *admired* that slave woman, admired her, she knew, because he shared her love for "Columbia's scenes of glorious toils, while freedom's cause her anxious breast alarms." Margaret felt a dull ache in her own breast, an aching wish for something she knew not how to name. She had written him a letter. But an ode, *poetry,* was beyond her!

This thought made her frown. Why should it be beyond her? I shall learn about poetry, she decided. When he returns from his mission to Princeton, I shall ask Johannes to teach me all about odes.

In the meantime, she quickly saw that poetry was not a subject to bring up in Hackensack.

"Everything in Hackensack is in utmost confusion," Rachel said. "The militia refuses to do its duty and is threatening to turn to the British, for General Howe promises them peace, liberty, and safety, and that is all they want, they say, peace, liberty, and safety."

"Liberty!" Margaret scoffed. "Liberty from the English? What is to be done with such men? They are a vile generation."

"Cousin, the country is greatly alarmed at having their grain and hay burnt," Rachel said meekly. "Many think that to war is a mistake."

"This war is a mistake only for the enemy," said Margaret grimly. "We must and we will win it."

A few days later, back at home, with Rachel and Rachel's four in tow, for it was clear they were no longer safe in tumultuous Hackensack, she found her men folk still gone and the house bursting with women and children: daughter Aeltie and her croupy son, daughter Elizabeth, Mrs. Scott and her whining children, Helena Westervelt and her brood, and now Rachel and her four. "We are too many," she said, helplessly. "How can we feed so many?"

Her strapping militiaman son John, who was single and could eat like three men, stopped in for a square meal whenever he was in the neighborhood. And even her married son Isaac packed his saddlebags from her larder when he got the chance. And Bett and her three offspring were always under foot and always ready to eat.

It was domestic bedlam. There were now five families to feed and clothe and care for. The house, built to house one, strained at its corners. "I want privacy!" she railed. "I want to take a bath without twenty people milling about me!"

But even amid this teeming humanity, she no longer felt safe, as she had on the road to Hackensack, no longer felt protected by a benevolent heaven. For things had changed. In Hackensack, in the very neighborhood where His Excellency had headquartered before retreating with his army over the Delaware, vicious Tories, neighbors and even relations, and former slaves drunk on their success in destroying *Dominie* Romeyn's comfortable house, had begun to break into other Patriot homes at night to plunder them, smashing redware and faience with abandon, hurling looking glasses and clocks against walls, prying open locked chests and cupboards with their bayonets. She was now quite terrified, but she dared not show it to her household, though she took care to lock the doors and windows at night and to keep them locked even in the daytime. She slept with a loaded musket at the foot of her bed.

At last Johannes and Abraham returned from their travels, bone weary and dirty. "I worried about you every minute," she said.

"I am exhausted," he said. "And now I must butcher. And twice as many hogs as usual, to feed this crowded house," he added. "And we will need at least three horned animals. One carcass of beef will not last through January."

She pitied him. Butchering was far from his favorite thing, slaughtering and dressing fat porkers, dissecting the salted pork, hams, and shoulders for smoking, stashing them into casks in pieces of a size to serve the gathered, cutting the side pork for bacon. And it was not her favorite thing, either, packing sixty pounds of sausage into jars, forming the clippings and trimmings into souse, and filling earthen pots with lard. And then the cows had to be slaughtered and dressed, a quantity salted to be boiled, ribs hung to be cooked fresh, pieces reserved for smoking, head cheese to be rendered and pounds of the trimmings and clippings sewed into bags made from tripe and packed in vinegar to be sliced and fried for the table. It was endless, and dirty, and smelly, and necessary.

"At least you are safe."

"I predict that Tappan will not be safe for very long," he said glumly. "The village is an obvious target."

And in early December, on a cold rainy day, he was proved right. Isaac galloped up with the news. "The Peek brothers with a force of Tories are marching up the Schraalenburg Road to attack Tappan," he cried from his horse. "They are heading for the Green to chop down the Liberty Pole. Keep inside. And keep the doors locked. I am going to warn Colonel Malcolm." He was gone in a trice, wheeling around in the dooryard and galloping off to Colonel William Malcolm and his New York State troops encamped on the ridge between their farm and the Tappantown center.

Margaret knew the Peek brothers well. Jacobus Peek's sister Elizabeth, born the same year as she and a good friend, was married to her cousin Johannes Blauvelt of the Orangetown militia and was the widow of another cousin, Cornelius Smith. Their father was a well-known and vehement *conferentie* partisan, but the sons had seemed to be on the American side, until now. Now they showed their true colors. "I will do no such thing," she muttered. "Stay in the house, indeed. Johannes, let us go to see the fiends do their dirty work."

"But the butchering," he said.

"You can start it tomorrow," she said. "It will get done."

They drove in the farm wagon south down the muddy lane and then east over the ridge, past the encampment, which was alive with Malcolm's troops donning their blue woolen rifle frocks and their hunting shirts of deerskin, fastening their leggings under their boots, loading muskets, getting into marching formation.

"They had better hurry," said Johannes. And he was right.

At the village when they got there, Tories with bloodthirsty cries were already chopping down the liberty pole. Others, screaming imprecations, were breaking into houses, plundering them, smashing what was too big or too heavy to carry off.

With war whoops, Colonel William Malcolm and his New York State troops fell upon them and chased them away, but not before they had abducted an old man and stolen a horse and a team of oxen and plundered private property, people's favorite things.

"These turncoats," she said bitterly. "These former Hackensack friends! May God punish them in hell for eternity for what they have done here!"

The weeping and lamentations of the inhabitants of the once idyllic hamlet were terrible to see. She wept with them, wringing her hands as she alternately ran and trudged, ran and trudged through the mud and snow, from despoiled house to despoiled house, trying to comfort the terrified inhabitants. *This land is our land!* she thought. *How can they do this to us?* And then she recalled the day so long ago that she had stood up in the farm wagon and reminded the heavens of it: "This land is our land!"

At the end of the day she stood on the wrecked, muddied Green and cried aloud again to the heavens, this time shaking her fists at the skies. "Stop the mayhem!" she cried. "Stop this ruination and mayhem! Stop it now!"

"Margaret," he said, shocked.

"This land is our land," she wept.

He put his arms around her and tried to calm her, but she was inconsolable. He led her to the wagon, and she wept all the way home, sobbing to the leaden skies, not even bothering to cover her face.

"The problem is, it's their land, too," he said.

A week later General Heath retaliated by attacking Hackensack. "I took sixty prisoners, and all the stores of flour, rum, and cheese the lovers of King and Parliament were readying for shipment to New York," he reported that night, around the table.

"They will be back," Johannes said. And they were, raiding the homes of all the Patriots they knew, smashing and looting with abandon. But not their house.

*   *   *   *

Their house, which the 1769 boundary settlement had cast into Bergen County, was a safe distance, they liked to think, from Tappan, now a daily target. For this reason, and because it was warm and inviting with its egg-yolk colored walls and its gleaming copper sconces, and because she welcomed company and because Johannes was generous with his Madeira, it had become an evening gathering spot for army and militia officers and their friends and neighbors, as it had been in the old days of the Stamp Act crisis. Here they could, in safety, exchange reports of troop movements and numbers without fear of being spied upon by Tory eyes and heard by Tory ears and share news of Tory depredations. The women, Margaret, Mrs. Westervelt and Mrs. Scott and Aeltie, Elizabeth, and Rachel joined the men when the children had been stowed in their various sleeping places around the house.

John Haring and his pretty wife Mary, who had rented out their new house and moved into the Tappan parsonage when *Dominie* Verbryck thought it wise to flee to Clarkstown, were frequent visitors. "Every man and woman within a large circle of this place are constantly distressing me with their fears and apprehensions of the enemy and the Tories," Haring sighed one evening.

"That is because they know the Tories know the country so well they could guide the troops anywhere," Johannes said.

"They say that a great number have gone over to the enemy," Margaret said.

"More than we know," said Haring. "The falling of the two forts and the flight of General Washington have caused a mass going-over to the enemy. And worse, have unleashed among the people what I believe can only be called a civil war. A terrifying civil war within this terrifying war of revolution."

"Oh, why are we so plagued?" Mrs. Scott cried.

"It's becoming a war of families, a war of cousins against cousins," said Johannes.

"Yes. The same families that left the Tappan church twenty years ago are flocking to the Tory side," Haring said, "while those who stayed are going in droves to the Patriots."

In the war within the war, families everywhere in the neutral ground were split down the middle. "It is whispered, as Washington and his ragtag army, now sorely diminished in numbers, retreat toward Pennsylvania, that one out of every three Americans is disaffected to the American cause," Haring said. "And if they are Dutch Americans, it can be counted on that every last one of the disaffected is on the *conferentie* side in the church wars."

"It's all about allegiance, isn't it," Margaret said wonderingly. "It's as if that one idea—allegiance—has unleashed a violence so powerful that it threatens to destroy all we love, all that both sides love and hold dear."

Allegiance to Amsterdam, or to America. To London, or to America. To the King, or to Congress.

"It is an idea as powerful as the idea of liberty itself," Johannes said. "And it reduces us to low and vile behavior. Cousins spy on cousins, and in some cases I have heard that brothers spy and even fire on their own brothers."

"Give thanks that our immediate family is not so disrupted," Margaret said.

"But the wider one is," said Haring glumly. Several of his cousins and uncles had gone over to the Tory side, and he had to be circumspect, careful of what he said, because he was suspected by some of them of being a spy for George Washington, his secret informer in Orangetown.

"Yes," said Margaret. "Word has come that, convinced the American cause is lost, my cousin Theunis Blauvelt ran off to join the British the moment General Washington retreated across the Hackensack."

"Was he a member of the *conferentie* church?" Haring asked.

"Yes, and way before the war began he married in it the daughter of a violent Tory."

*   *   *   *

Another reason to keep her doors locked: The Commissary General of the Continental army had, without asking permission, sent 3,000 pounds of lead and bullets packed in casks to her house for safety, where troops concealed them in the cellar. But although this transfer had been effected surreptitiously in the middle of the night, she could not be sure that no one had seen and told. Spies were everywhere.

"There are ten tons of lead secreted at Tappan," General Scott told them on a visit to his wife and children. "And you have a ton and a half of it in your cellar, I am told."

She was shocked that he knew. She did not want to talk about the lead, wanted to forget about it, deny it was there. "Is it true that the inhabitants of Bergen County are going to the enemy as fast as ours are?" she asked, to change the subject.

He took the bait. "Going daily to the enemy in great numbers, Madam," he said. "Some carting for them, some going into their service, and others waiting on them for protection. The Tories are insolent and numerous—evils I might prevent could I be but reinforced," he added gloomily.

"I do not want that lead in my house," she said to Johannes, when Scott had gone. "Can you do something to have it removed?"

"I will speak to John Haring about it," he said. But he said it in a hopeless tone. The needs of the Continental army came before their wants.

"I believe I shall start writing it down," she said to him, as they prepared for bed.

CHAPTER 17

▼

CIVIL WAR

The things that were happening all around her that November of 1776 were so terrible that she was certain no one in the future would believe them, unless they were recorded as they happened.

The violent sacking of the house in Hackensack of their friend the minister Dirck Romeyn gave her the impetus. With Johannes, she drove to Hackensack to see the house.

It was a shocking sight. Even the very doors and windows had been smashed. Like a wrecked ship, the plundered, once-so-comfortable abode wallowed forlorn in the elements, without role or utility.

Joining them in the front yard, strewn with Romeyn household possessions and clothing, her friend Elizabeth Christie and her husband William, both dazed, supplied the details. "The British and Hessian troops and even their officers joined in," Elizabeth said.

"Not the officers!"

"Yes. And van Buskirk and his troops and their sluts."

"Disgusting!" said Margaret. "Van Buskirk was our friend not so long ago."

"And most disgusting, even the *dominie's* own servants and slaves joined in, cheering and laughing," William said.

Johannes felt his mind stagger. "His own slaves and servants?"

"They stole everything they could move," William Christie went on in a life-less voice. "Pewter, china, rugs, blankets, feather mattresses, bolsters, pillows, sheets, clothing. Then they stripped the barns of hay and grain. They made off with four hogs, all his milk cows, and a horse."

"A fifth hog, the poor thing squealing piteously, they killed and slaughtered on the cherry table in the *groote kamer*," Elizabeth said. "And divided the bloody parts among themselves and roasted them on the spit then and there. And ate them."

"They smashed what they couldn't move," said William, in that alarming dull and toneless voice. "The great tulipwood *kas*, the cherry table after they butchered the hog on it."

"I am afraid their rampage will give the signal for many more who recently called themselves Patriots to attack their neighbors and friends and relations," Johannes said.

The next morning she wrapped herself in her cloak, hitched a horse to a wagon, and drove down the lane and over the plank road to Casparus Mabie's store at the Slote, which in her girlhood had been her grandfather's store. She had lived in the house next to it from the time she was ten until she went to the city at sixteen. Eliza, she wondered, where are you, friend forever?

She purchased a dozen sheets of paper, two quills, dried ink powder, and a black-lead pencil. She had learned to prepare quills while at school, but not to the satisfaction of her employer Elbert Haring when, for four years before her marriage, she did the accounts at his bakery on Bleecker Street. Nor did her penmanship meet his standards. He had sent her to a punctilious English tutor in the city who perfected both her Italianate hand and her quill techniques.

The quills were long and hard, with good round barrels. With her penknife, she scraped off the scurf on the back of the barrel. Carefully, she cut the end half through and then turned the quill over to the belly side and cut it all the way through about a quarter to a half of an inch to make a fork. Then she put the blade of the penknife in the notch and forced the slit to the length she liked. She sharpened it to a fine point, and finally placed the inside of the nib on the nail of her thumb and cut the nib into the shape she liked. "There," she said. She mixed the ink powder with a little water, folded and cut the paper, and began to write. "It is my diary and I shall write in it every day," she told her household, "and I would appreciate some peace and quiet while I do it." Though she knew that was a wish in vain.

She wrote down all the details of the Romeyn attack, then recorded how they shot Albert Zabriskie dead in cold blood. And how Abraham van Buskirk, once claiming to be a Patriot, was now a commissioned officer, a lieutenant colonel, in the New Jersey Volunteers, a Loyalist outfit bloodthirsty for Patriots. And how the British commander Sir William Howe issued a proclamation offering amnesty to all rebels who renounced the war, and how many took him up on it.

John Haring fed her news. "With the main British army now pursuing Washington west of the Hackensack toward Pennsylvania, Bergen and Orange counties are left to the mercies of van Buskirk's Greencoats and the local Tories," he said. "We estimate that nearly 3,000 lukewarm Patriots and neutrals have joined them on the basis of General Sir William Howe's proclamation, with its added promises of protection for their lives and property. It is hard to believe, but Tories new and old try to bribe even soldiers in the Continental army to come over to their side."

"It's not so hard to believe," said Johannes. "They have the irresistible carrot of Patriot real estate confiscated by British officials to lure them with."

"And more news," said Haring. "The Loyalists are again marauding through the Ramapos and beyond, threatening to surround our army encamped near Suffern's Tavern."

Johannes was right in his prediction that the Tories who had ruined Romeyn's house would be emboldened by their success. Sure that the rebellion was on the verge of failure and there would be no price to pay for their savagery, these former Patriots now fell upon the houses of Romeyn's elders William Christie and Garret Lydecker, stripping them, and burning 4,000 fence rails on Lydecker's farm. Elizabeth Christie ran out into the yard in her nightclothes, screaming imprecations at them. But they were too busy pillaging to care.

With shaking hand, she recorded the names of those whose farms suffered the same shocking fate. Her tears fell on the pages as she wrote, making blots of the ink: Jacob Wortendyke, Thomas Blanch, Thomas Campbell, Johannes Terhune, David S. Demarest, Albert Terhune, Abraham Brouwer, John Mauritius Goetschius, Abraham de Voe, her cousin Theunis Blauvelt (not the traitor Theunis D. Blauvelt but another cousin of the same name), John Demarest, Wiert Banta. Looting and pillaging became such a matter of routine that the British and Hessian troops even absentmindedly plundered Tory homes. Wherever it happened, crowds gathered to watch, some solemn and angry, some cheering and jubilant, depending on their politics.

"I fear for *our* house," she said, shivering.

"I think it is far enough off the main road through Tappan that no harm will come to it," Johannes said, trying to soothe her.

"The house is only two miles from the center of Tappan," she said.

"I believe we are safe," he said grimly.

"I fear for it, nevertheless. And I fear worse things, too."

He frowned. Stories circulated of indecent treatment and actual ravishment, even by British officers, even of young girls. In a family of their acquaintance, a girl of thirteen was forced by a British soldier into a bed chamber, where he moved a heavy chest in front of the door, threw her on the bed, and despite her screams raped her while her frantic family tried in vain to break down the door. When he was done, he dragged her off to camp for two of his fellow soldiers to rape. In this case, the authorities hanged all three for their crime.

But this was not always the case. A gang of British soldiers raped married women, pregnant women, even one old woman of near seventy. "But," Margaret pointed out, "such is the nature of those indignities that the women who suffer them are often unwilling to have them made known, and so the rapists go free."

"Never venture far without the rapier," he said. He meant the little old-fashioned sword that had been in his family since anyone could remember. "It is old, but it is sharp, and it is manageable even by a woman. My grandmother cut off a wolf's ears with it."

*   *   *   *

Once word came that "Mr." Washington was on the other side of the Delaware with his barefoot, starving men contemplating his rude winter quarters, General Sir William Howe retired to New York to wait out the winter. "What is the point of making myself uncomfortable chasing the rebels into Pennsylvania? Winter will destroy them easily enough," he said, according to the spies in his midst.

Howe preferred to be warm and gay in New York, where he had taken a mistress, Mrs. Elizabeth Loring. To acknowledge her favors, he had appointed her husband to the lucrative post of commissary of prisons. Betsey Loring and Sir William were a familiar sight at the gaming tables, where in one night, it was reported in the papers, she lost 300 guineas, nearly a year's wages for her husband.

Ballads promptly circulated about them: "Sir William he, snug as a flea,/Lay all this time a-snoring,/Nor dreamed of harm as he lay warm/In bed with Mrs. Loring." And then there was the inevitable quatrain rhyming Loring and whoring. And another, urging the commander to rise and fight: "Awake, arouse, Sir Billy,/There's forage in the plain./Ah, leave your little Filly,/And open the campaign./Heed not a woman's prattle,/Which tickles in the ear,/But give the word for battle,/And grasp the warlike spear."

Sir William's admirers could not comprehend his behavior. "Why does he not go in pursuit of the deluded, misguided, bamboozled Whigs, the demagogue-beshackled, Congress-becrafted independents and cannonade them into nullities and nonentities? Give the word for battle! Grasp the warlike spear!"

Margaret was outraged by Howe's behavior. "Such blatant immorality," she stormed. "We must win the war and turn the decadent English out!"

She cursed, she prayed that he be shamed for his immoral conduct, as "A Tar" had called for him to be shamed for offering turncoats the confiscated properties of Patriots in return for their oath of allegiance. ("Oh, fie, Sir William, fie for shame!" one Patriot wrote to the *New York Journal* of John Holt. "Such proclamations become a general at the head of a victorious army, not the chief of a mongrel banditti composed of the sweepings of the jails of Britain, Ireland, Germany, and America. Fie, Sir William! Blush for your proclamation.")

Blush for Joshua Loring's strumpet, she wrote in her diary, furious.

*   *   *   *

One cold evening in early December of 1776, John Haring, now president pro tem of the New York Provincial Convention, Brigadier General John Morin Scott, and Colonel William Malcolm, who commanded the company of New York State troops encamped at Tappan, dropped in at Margaret and Johannes's house, stamping their feet free of snow and blowing on their fingers. They moved almost as one to the blazing hearth to warm themselves.

"What is the enemy up to this week?" asked Johannes, pouring them glasses of Madeira.

"They recruit ceaselessly around the neighborhood," Haring reported. "In this week alone, they enlisted thirty men without much trouble. Men once on our side," he added angrily.

"How to stop them," Scott muttered, packing tobacco into his pipe. "I have begged the Convention for two more regiments and a field piece or two. Worse, my brigade is scheduled to disband in a week, and I have begged as well for a bounty to persuade the men to stay on for a month. If it is not forthcoming, you cannot imagine of what infinitely serious consequence it will be for you here," he added. "Without proper support, all the country south of the Highlands, including Tappan, must submit to the enemy."

She shivered and drew her cloak around her. The men had brought the cold into the house with them, but it was not the cold air that chilled her. "And what did the Convention reply?" she asked nervously.

"It ordered me to move with my brigade to Haverstraw," Scott said. "Which I will do tomorrow. I am ordered to post my men in such a manner as to cover the stores on this side of the river and to prevent the advances of the enemy into the passes of the Highlands. Those are my orders. But the men will be gone in a week if I cannot promise them a cash bounty for staying."

"Cash is perilously scarce," said John Haring glumly.

"As bad as it is for us Patriots," Johannes said, "I have heard that some prudent Tories in the area have thought it wise to ship their effects to New York, less the Patriots turn on them in retaliation."

"They have already begun to do so," said Colonel Malcolm.

"Yes. I had intelligence this afternoon that the Bergen County militia undertook a raid of their own just yesterday, near New Bridge," said John Haring. "They caused a terrible uproar as they ran over the Tory ground and scattered the gangs. They captured one Parcels, said to be an arch Tory, and a stout negro fellow, the slave of Samuel Peek, known as a spy, and threw them into jail."

"That is cheering news for a change," Johannes said. "Samuel Peek is a bad man."

She had felt relatively safe with Colonel Malcolm and his troops camped on the ridge between her farm and the village of Tappan. "I am dismayed to think that you will be leaving us undefended," she ventured.

"I do not think my force sufficient to protect Tappan, alas," he said. "I have applied to move elsewhere."

"But how shall we manage without you?" she asked, shocked. "What shall we do?"

"I do not know, Madam," he said. "All I know is that I am not sufficient for your protection."

"What *shall* we do?" she asked, when the men had taken their leave.

"What *can* we do?" Johannes replied.

"You alarm me," she said. "You worry me. We cannot be helpless. I shall write to Colonel Malcolm this very night."

She took out her paper and quill pen and ink and sat for an hour by the light of the copper candelabra and sconces, writing. He sat up with her, reading a book, sipping his Madeira, staring into the flames of the fireplace when his concentration flagged, wrestling with the question, *what can we do?*

When she had finished she read it to him. "Our friends are so distressed here," she read, "that I hope you will think it your indispensable duty to remain and support them. As you know, the southernmost part of this county is ravaged by the enemy, plundering the friends of the country of their property, and disarming them. If some speedy relief is not afforded us in Tappan, I feel the most of the people will submit to the enemy, and if this takes place, it will greatly aid the enemy in crossing the mountains to attack us. Can you not stay to prevent that disaster?"

"You have said it as it is," he said. "Let us hope he listens."

In the morning, she gave the note to her cousin, Lt. Col. John David Blauvelt, under Malcolm's command, to deliver to him by hand.

In his tent on the high ground west of the village, east of the farmhouse where he had spent so many pleasant evenings, Malcolm read the note. He sighed. "I feel sympathy for the woman, but what can I do?" he said. "I am helpless."

Blauvelt stirred, uneasily.

Malcolm sighed again, heavily. "Well, there is this," he said. "A small thing. Tell your cousin that I have just heard this morning that General Heath, encamped at Haverstraw and Nyack, is at this moment moving toward Hackensack with 600 troops to settle the hash of the Tories. He intends to conclude the business that I began with the raid two days ago on New Bridge. Perhaps it will soothe her nerves to know he is on the way."

"It is good news," said Blauvelt. "She will be glad. We all will be."

"But tell her also," Malcolm added, "that I have received my orders to quit the area, and I shall do so at once."

"This will seriously discountenance the inhabitants," Blauvelt said.

"I cannot help that," said Malcolm. And to the dismay of the Patriots in Tappan, he broke camp that morning and marched away.

In a day, General Heath arrived and made camp on the same ridge, just west of the village. He marched on Hackensack the next morning, and it was soon learned that he had seized a large number of Hackensack Tories and a good deal of stolen firewood and foodstuffs on its way in boats to New York City to supply the British army.

"He arrested fifty Tories and seized fifty or sixty muskets," John Haring reported that evening. "His men confiscated a sloop loaded with hay and household goods bound for New York and fifty barrels of flour and rum and other stores from Tory homes, including a thousand pounds of cheese. A loaded brig and a loaded schooner made away, but the brig ran aground and the schooner overturned in the water, its goods lost."

It was the Patriots' turn to laugh and cheer, but only fleetingly, for they knew the tide would soon flow in the opposite direction again, and it did. Within days, small parties of the enemy made excursions into Tappan and once more plundered and disarmed the friends of the country, as the beleaguered Orangetown militia took after them in pursuit.

Now she wrote to General Heath, encamped on the same Ridge where Malcolm had been: "We beg you to consider how hard it is for our men to be gone from us, leaving the women and children to suffer," she wrote. "We must have assistance. If you can see fit to send a body of men to augment our numbers nothing will be wanting to drive the enemy out of our neighborhood."

General Heath sighed. "Women," he said. "They have no idea of the demands of war. But fortunately this time help is on the way." He had no time to write a reply to her. Instead, he sent an aide to Tappan to tell her of it.

The aide galloped up to her house that afternoon. "General Heath has asked me to inform you that General Washington has ordered a large body of the troops under the command of Brigadier General George Clinton to march immediately through the counties of Orange and Bergen to protect the well affected and to distress the enemy and harass the disaffected."

"Thank you, thank you," she said, nearly in tears.

"Madam," he said, bowing. He was gone as quickly as he had come.

Clinton's troops came as promised, but they did not stay. With much fifing and piping and drumming and clattering of wagons and neighing of horses, they marched through the village and on to other parts and were seen no more.

She was disgusted. "It is past time we moved what we can," she said. "We are too much a target." Her sweet-gum *kas* was too heavy to move, too full of linens and bedclothes and gowns and petticoats, and the cherry table was in use every hour of the day, but she had the rest of her good furniture and her precious gewgaws loaded into a wagon for transport to safety with the minister Samuel Verbryck in Clarkstown. They brought old tables and chairs and chests down from the garret to replace the good things, her mother-in-law Aeltie's old-fashioned things. Ruefully, she recalled the hurt feelings in the family when she had spurned those very objects, so long ago, in that simpler time, mid-century, when she had been a mere heedless bride. An eon ago. A world away.

She sat with Johannes before the fire. "Although General Heath's attack on New Bridge was successful," she said, "still it makes me uneasy to think that just an hour's march away from Tappan at Hackensack and New Bridge six companies of Regulars and three of Tories dally restlessly in winter quarters."

"Plus a regiment made up of 200 British and Hessian troops and 400 armed Tories," said Johannes.

"They can come at any time, marauding Tappan way," she said nervously. "And Dolly Zabriskie reports even larger numbers. She claims there are 2,000 troops at New Bridge."

"I wonder if Dolly and her husband are leaning to the King and exaggerate to alarm our side," he said.

"Who can you trust, if not a friend like Dolly?" she said.

"I trust no one," he said, "except you."

"Now you've made me doubt Dolly," she said.

*   *   *   *

Although General Washington, the guardian protector of the country, as he was called, was gone from New Jersey over the Delaware into Pennsylvania, she was consoled that much of the Continental army was encamped not far to the north. Three thousand five hundred American troops had moved from Peekskill to Smith's Clove on the Ramapo River, Stony Point, Haverstraw, Nyack, and to Tappan, where they made camp on the low hill just to the west of the village, the same ridge where Heath and Malcolm before him had camped. To the north, Forts Clinton and Montgomery were garrisoned.

And in all of these places, while the men busied themselves building log huts for the winter, Margaret and all the women of the area, whatever their politics, knitted socks and mittens for them and fashioned warm hats out of felt and went about the neighborhood collecting used coats and blankets and shoes for the men. They saved rags for bandages and to make paper, turned in lead window weights for bullets. Margaret hitched a horse to the wagon and drove with her daughters Aeltie and Elizabeth around the countryside collecting clothing. Sam rode shotgun beside them. Elizabeth had custody of the rapier.

On one such excursion, not far from Tappan, along the road east of the meadows at the bottom of the Bergen Woods in English Neighborhood, she learned that van Buskirk's hated Greencoats had quartered themselves among unwilling farm families. Their presence was untenable and their position vulnerable. "They are sitting ducks," she said to Johannes, when she got home. "Our side should undertake a duck hunt."

"We must inform John Haring. He can get word to General Clinton," he said.

This happened, and in the dark of the moon on the 19th of December, General George Clinton, encamped in the Ramapo Highlands, ordered his troops, 600 strong, to march some twenty-eight miles through a bitter cold night the whole length of Ulster and Orange counties to English Neighborhood, where they took twenty-three Greencoats prisoner, some muskets, a wagon, and eight horses.

Despite this little success, though, a troubled General Washington reported to the Continental Congress, now fled from Philadelphia to Baltimore, that the game was nearly up for the colonies. "Ten days more will put an end to our army," he wrote. "The troops are tired, cold, barefoot, ragged, some nearly naked, hungry, and worried. They are of a single mind to find their way back to their wretched homes, if they still exist, once their enlistments expire, which they are to do on the last day of the year 1776. Can you not find the wherewithal to encourage them to stay, our cause is lost."

Samuel Demarest, through a friendly spy in British headquarters, reported to the Tappan congregation that General Sir William Howe was of the same mind as his opponent "Mr." Washington. "General Howe firmly believes that it is just a matter of time until victory is his. He is certain that his proud army has only to wait for the Delaware to freeze over to march on Philadelphia and celebrate the New Year among the welcoming hordes of Loyalists in that gay city while the rebels fall apart and slink away home."

The people shivered and looked uneasily at each other.

"Yet, there is good news, for his brother, Admiral Howe, is not so confident of this," Demarest went on. "If my spy informs me correctly, Lord Richard was heard to say that almost all the people of sense and spirit are in the rebellion, and he said it in a very gloomy voice."

"Amen!" The people cheered and whistled and stamped their feet. "Amen!" "Amen!"

*   *   *   *

One person of sense and spirit saw that the present situation—the present discouraged winter—might cost the whole continent if the mood did not change. As he plodded across New Jersey with the retreating Continental army after the fall of Fort Lee, Thomas Paine began to compose in his mind a new pamphlet, writing down his thoughts every evening by candlelight in his tent. Fast and furiously, he wrote, and exactly one month to the day after the fall of Fort Lee, *The American Crisis* flew from the printer's shop into every American encampment and into every village and town in every colony in the land.

Margaret read it hungrily. "It is manna in these black days for my despairing spirit," she said to Johannes. "Listen to this!" She read it aloud to him:

"I call not upon a few, but upon all; not on this state or that state, but on every state. Up and help us! Lay your shoulder to the wheel! Let it be told to the world that in the depth of winter when no thing but hope and virtue could survive, the city and the country, alarmed at one common danger, came forth to meet and to repulse the evil."

She read and reread it. "I cannot read it without weeping," she said. "Listen to this: 'Say not that thousands are gone, turn out your tens of thousands! Throw not the burden of the day upon Providence, but show your faith by your works, that God may bless you.'

"And this: 'The heart that feels not now is dead. The blood of his children will curse his cowardice who shrinks back at a time when a little might have saved the whole and made them free.'

"And this: 'Had not the cowardly and disaffected inhabitants spread false alarms through the country, Jersey had never been ravaged. But once more we are again collected and collecting. Our new army is recruiting fast, and we shall be able to open the next campaign with 60,000 men, well armed and clothed. By perseverance and fortitude, we have the prospect of a glorious issue. By cowardice, a ravaged country, a depopulated city, slavery without hope. Look on this picture and weep over it! And if there yet remains one wretch who believes it not, let him suffer it unlamented.'"

She broke down, and he put his arms around her and held her and let her weep on his chest at Paine's description of him who "never appeared to full advantage but in difficulties and in action," of him whose mind was of a "natural firmness, a cabinet of fortitude," of him whom "God hath blessed with perfect health and given a mind that can even flourish upon care," of him whose qualities would lead his country out of despotism into freedom. *Help him, help him win,* she prayed.

"God will help him win," he said, as if he had read her thoughts.

"I have to believe it," she said. "I cannot give up hope."

∗   ∗   ∗   ∗

And one whose mind could flourish even in despair saw in that bleak and hopeless winter a chance to redeem himself after the calamities of the war so far: the losses in Brooklyn, the disorderly retreat from Manhattan, the ignominious lost battle in Westchester, the fall of Fort Washington and Fort Lee, the flight through New Jersey to the west bank of the Delaware.

On Christmas night, sure in his belief that nothing obliged him to retire from his enemy, rather conceiving it his duty to make head against them any chance he got, he rallied his officers and his troops and in a bitter sleet storm personally led them back across the swiftly flowing and ice-choked Delaware. His secret password for the expedition was "Victory or Death," for he knew that defeat would mean the end of the war, the end of the cause of liberty, the end of him.

At dawn, they fell upon Trenton, where 1,400 Hessians, certain there would be no attempt on them in the teeth of the ferocious nor'easter that raged around them, slumbered in their barracks, and in equally ferocious close-combat street fighting that morning they captured or killed a thousand of them and their officers. Once again, the weather was a friend to America. "Or Providence," people declared, when they learned of the victory—and of the precious booty: hundreds of muskets, bayonets, and swords, enough to equip several American brigades, six German cannon, three wagons full of ammunition. Patriots rejoiced in every colony, for now it seemed as if the tide had turned again, for good this time, and the cause of liberty was once again within their grasp.

Rejoicing was general, except in Bergen and Orange counties. There in the fraught territory between the rivers in the "neutral ground"—where feelings were anything but neutral—the success at Trenton and a week later another at Princeton seemed only to heighten the animosity of the Loyalists for the idea of independence from Great Britain. It made them all the more determined not to be independent.

"The church wars have sunk their fangs deep into Tory hearts and pumped them full of poison for which the victories at Trenton and Princeton are no antidote," said John Haring gloomily.

"In fact, just the opposite," Johannes said. "The specter of defeat excites them to swear to greater violence to come. And in this they see advantage in the army's enlistment terms expiring at the end of the year and the men running for home."

"Although I am unacquainted with military affairs," Margaret ventured, "militia terms are expiring, too, on December 31. What then are we to do for our protection?" They were at the parsonage visiting Haring and his wife Mary, who had not even been born in the days when Margaret kept Mary's father's books on Bleecker Street, and who was now nursing her second child. It made Margaret feel old. She was fifty-one.

"General Clinton is said to be on his way here," said Haring. "Maybe he will provide an answer. He will be stopping at the parsonage. Come back and ask him yourself."

"I shall," she said.

He arrived that week, on his way back to the Highlands. With his Colonels Pawling and Allison, he stopped for food and drink and local intelligence at the Tappan parsonage. Margaret took the opportunity to bring up the burning question of the defense of Tappan. "Although I am of course nothing of an authority on military matters," she began, "is it not possible for you to exhort the troops not to basely desert their bleeding country in its hour of need, not to suffer our cruel enemy to plunder and distress our friends. Exhort them to stay and serve another term?" She was begging, she knew, but she was not too proud to beg for such a cause.

He was surprised at her outspokenness. He bowed to her. "I shall exhort them, indeed, Madam, but you must know that I have no leverage with them."

"No leverage?"

"None. I am quite helpless," he said, to her dismay. "They know as well as do I that the enemy have so good intelligence of our every motion that only by routing them entirely would I have a probability of success. And my men are not sufficient for that task."

"Can you at least beg General Heath for a few field pieces to do the routing?" asked Johannes.

"Believe me, I have begged," Clinton said shortly. "Heath cannot spare them."

"But the enemy are imprisoning, plundering, and killing us," she said, as calmly as she could. "The day after the success at Trenton, 700 British and Tory forces marched north from Hackensack and raided Paramus and Hopperstown, captured seven Whig farmers, and threw them into an unheated prison in Hackensack."

"I am afraid it will only get worse in the time to come," he said. "But I have spoken truth, Madam. I cannot help you."

It was more than shocking to hear that their own army could not help them, but Colonel Pawling confirmed it. "You, Madam, you and your friends and relations and neighbors and strangers all through the counties of Bergen and Orange lie greatly exposed to both internal and external enemies. And as you know, your internal enemies have free recourse to New York City."

"By which you mean free recourse to the headquarters for all British activity in the colonies," Johannes said.

"Yes."

"You mean free recourse to British bribes to turn their coats if they haven't already," Margaret snapped. "And free recourse to British ears eager for intelligence and glad to pay for it."

"True. Matters are come to such a height," Colonel Allison added glumly, "that they who are friends of the American cause must for their own safety be cautious how they speak in public."

John Haring, sitting quietly by the fireside, stirred uneasily. He might have acknowledged this, but he was by nature a taciturn man. And, thought by some in the know to be one of George Washington's secret spies, he had more than most to watch out for among the inconstant, fickle, smiling summer Patriots in his neighborhood, and thus more to lose for his country than most.

✳   ✳   ✳   ✳

As the men had predicted, it got worse. And Margaret recorded it, writing by daylight at the cherry table in the *groote kamer* and again in the evening by candlelight, how the people of the neutral ground lived exposed and unprotected between the British army and the Continental army, ransacked by both.

Her cousins in the militia came daily to give her information: "Van Buskirk's Loyalists by the hundreds scout and pillage where they will," Johannes Blauvelt reported. "Worse, they act as protection for Tories and 'neutrals' who swear allegiance to the King in return for the opportunity of conveying their produce and their firewood to New York for sale to the enemy."

"The ground lies open to British and Hessian spies and recruiting agents who with cash and promises entice woodcutters and ironworkers in the Highlands to swarm to the British," Harmanus Blauvelt reported. "Slaves disappear in the night, promised their freedom if they go over to the King's side."

This was not news. Margaret and Johannes's two healthy slaves were among them. The two old sickly ones stayed, and the slow-moving Bett and her three children, they stayed.

It all incensed her, rendered her half witless with rage and frustration. "I feel demented!" she cried "But what is there to do?"

"Write another letter," said Johannes.

"Are you mocking me?"

"No!"

"Then I shall!" Grimly, she took up her pen and wrote to *him*, to beg *him* to stop it. "It is setting the people against the cause," she wrote. "The enemy forages at will, takes what they want of our animals, empties our barns and hay barracks, strips our orchards, loots our kitchen gardens."

And it wasn't only the enemy who plundered them. As *Dominie* Verbryck put it, "That which the palmerworm hath left hath the locust eaten; and that which the locust hath left hath the cankerworm eaten; and that which the cankerworm hath left hath the caterpillar eaten." British worms, Hessian worms, Tory worms, Patriot worms. They were everywhere.

He sighed when he read the letter. From Tappan. From that Dutch writing woman, no doubt, he thought. He was a little smitten by her, he must admit.

That comely intelligent face. That shapely form. In his mind, he conjured up a meeting with her, at a pleasant cotillion somewhere, where he could dance her up and down the hall, as he did with the wives of his officers, get to know her. But that would never be, foolish man, he thought. She is a proper Dutch house *frau*, not given to dancing, especially with men not her husband. Still, he would reply.

He took up his pen. "Though I know you are right that it will set the people against the cause if my Army forages on them, the Army must eat. Their horses must eat," he replied. But then that seemed to him too cold an answer. As if to give her some consolation, he concluded in a warmer way, "Madam, the Lord must help you. I cannot."

She kept his reply pressed into her Psalm book along with the first: Was it possible, she wondered, that he remembered her from that day so long ago? But of course he did not, she told herself furiously. How presumptuous of her even to think it!

And then she remembered that she was to learn poetry. "What is an ode, Johannes?" she asked him that night.

"An ode? An ode? What a question out of the blue!"

"Do you know the answer?"

"Of course," he said. "An ode is a poem written in praise of a distinguished personage, but also in praise of a lover, of wine, of friendship, of the simple life, of a great public figure, of any number of praiseworthy subjects."

"Ah," she said.

"Shall I read you one of Horace's odes?" he asked her.

"I would like that," she said.

"You're a curiosity to me, even after all these years," he said, going to get the book from his desk. "Asking such a thing without a warning. I didn't know you thought about poetry. You make me smile, my dear."

He opened his Horace. "He wrote this to Maecenas, his patron," he said. He read very slowly, as he had to translate from the Latin:

> Maecenas, born of monarch ancestors,
> The shield at once and glory of my life!
> There are who joy them in the Olympic strife
> And love the dust they gather in the course;

> The goal by hot wheels shunned, the famous prize,
> Exalt them to the gods that rule mankind;

This joys, if rabbles fickle as the wind
Through triple grade of honours bid him rise.

To me the artist's meed, the ivy wreath
Is very heaven: me the sweet cool of woods,
Where Satyrs frolic with the Nymphs, secludes
From rabble rout, so but Euterpe's breath

Fail not the flute, nor Polyhymnia fly
Averse from stringing new the Lesbian lyre.
O, write my name among that minstrel choir,
And my proud head shall strike upon the sky!

"He starts out by writing about his patron and ends by writing about himself," she said.

He laughed. "Horace is like that," he said. "Shall you now write odes?"

"No," she blushed. "I am sure my talents do not lie in that direction."

     *   *   *   *

From Tappan in January, New York Rangers Captain Robert Johnston was ordered to reconnoiter toward Hackensack to learn the British positions and to determine when they would leave the area for their winter quarters. But no sooner was this trusted Patriot just out of town than he and his troops were overcome by the temptation to strip the farms in Harrington, steal 400 pounds of copper hoops from the cooper, a pipe of wine, eleven wagonloads of leather, ten hogsheads of rum, gin, and brandy, furniture, clothing, linen, and bedding—and from both Tory and Patriot stores, tanneries, workshops, and houses.

The inhabitants were enraged, John Haring in particular. He had trusted and admired the man. "Johnston's conduct," he stormed, "is injurious to the rights of America and will make the inhabitants backward in going ascouting, for they are enemies to plundering. His conduct has much displeased the inhabitants of this place. I shall inform General Clinton. He should be court martialed and hanged."

"It is more than injurious to our rights," Margaret said sadly. "It is how war demeans even the finest of men and renders them brutal and immoral. I considered Captain Johnston to be a very fine and honorable man."

*   *   *   *

When, before Twelfth Night, the British army decamped from Hackensack to spend the winter more comfortably in New York City, Tories in the neutral ground shivered in their boots, for now that they had lost their protectors George Clinton's scouting parties were avid to round them up. Clinton's men gladly apprehended them and threw them into prison where they languished until guards could be spared to take them to the civil authorities in Morristown for trial. Clinton himself threatened them with hanging. "The option is mine," he said coldly, "and you can be sure I shall exercise it if I deem it to be an effective deterrent."

The worst of them, like Samuel and Jacobus Peek, thought it prudent to follow the Regulars into the city to avoid the vengeance of the Patriot neighbors they had plundered just a fortnight before. But before they could pack their possessions and make their getaway, John Haring had reported their actions to General Clinton, who happened to be passing through Tappan. "The two are with the enemy and have been very active in plundering our friends," Haring assured him.

Margaret confirmed this. "Samuel and Jacobus Peek were officers in the militia but when danger drew nigh they refused to march when ordered," she said. "They are both rank Tories. And though needless to say, I have no military expertise, I am of the opinion that they should be seized and incarcerated."

Clinton stared at her, again taken aback at such forwardness on the part of a woman, but this woman spoke her mind whenever she chose, apparently. Her husband must have no control of her at all, he thought.

He did not respond to her, but she noted in her diary that he ordered the two seized at Paramus and turned over to the civil authorities with the indication that his Brigade Major John Haring would produce testimony against them.

Even though they risked apprehension, many of the inhabitants of the area openly traded with the enemy, the condition of payment being their swearing allegiance to the King. Margaret began to record their names, but there were too many to keep up with: Casparus Westervelt, Cornelius Banta, Derick Banta, Derick Brinkerhoff, John Paulison, Lawrence van Horn, Martin Roelefson, Stephen Terhune, John Goetschius, Jacob Bogert, Henry Bogert, and dozens more.

"Some of them believe in their oath," she said to Johannes. "They believe it is the proper and legal thing required of them to be loyal to the King. But others are simply in it for the money and have no concern for either King or Country."

"Some who trade with the enemy are of our own family," he said sadly.

"No one can be trusted," she said. "Not even family and friends. Those thought to be Patriots go over to the Tory side as soon as they judge it the auspicious thing to do. I trust only you," she said. "And that is a terrible thing to say."

"Still," he said, "one has to be grateful for the Patriots who do not turn their coats when the moment calls for it."

"I am making lists of them, too," she said. Blauvelts, Harings, and Bogerts by the scores, Eckersons, Demarests, Huylers, Christies, Leydeckers, Brouwers, Zabriskies, and on and on. But it was not lost on her that all the same family names could be put on a list of Tories. A veritable civil war was going on.

*   *   *   *

During the day the Tories lay in wait in the woods, rose to break into Patriot houses at night, rouse Patriots from their sleep, haul them off to jail in New York City, burn down their houses and barns, strip their farms, steal their livestock, drive them into hiding if they managed to escape. No Patriot of an age to bear arms, sixteen to sixty, was safe in his home at night now. While the Tories carried out their nocturnal crimes, Patriot men banded together and slept in the woods for safety.

In March four Americans were carried off to prison in New York. In April, a Tory raid on Closter took three prisoners and seven wagonloads of rum, sugar, coffee, and chocolate. A week later 200 Tories captured a captain and three militiamen, twelve guns, six horses, a wagon, and trunks of goods. They took all to New York and paraded the captain through the streets, labeled as "the great rebel."

The next week a raiding party of twenty-five armed men seized the rich merchant and Tory hunter John Fell in his house in Hackensack and carried him off to the Provost's prison near City Hall. In May, 300 Tories attacked the picket at Paramus and drove the men into the woods, while a detachment captured a captain, a lieutenant, and three enlistees and conveyed them to the feared and fearsome Sugar House prison on Liberty Street. All is chaos and ruin, she wrote. It is verily as if hell has come to earth.

Her favorite cousin, Major Johannes Joseph Blauvelt, age 62, was seized at home by a band of Tories that included, much to her disgust, three of their Blauvelt relatives. On the other hand, her husband's relative Tory Peter T. Haring was apprehended by a party of American troops near Tenafly and taken to prison in Morristown. Two sons of Samuel Verbryck were captured and sent to the Sugar House. She sharpened the nib of her quill and made more lists. Carried off to prison in New York by their own neighbors, former friends, and even relations were Blauvelts, Christies, Brinkerhoffs, Harings, Coopers, Blanches, Tallmans, Wortendykes, Westervelts, Ver Valens, Ferdons, Heyers, Zabriskies, van Bussons, Lawrences, Bantas. It was endless.

*   *   *   *

With Willemptie and Willemptie's daughter Cathlyntie Mabie (some day to become Margaret's daughter-in-law, if all went according to Margaret's plans), Margaret went to New York to take food and clothing to her nephew Jacobus Blauvelt and her husband's nephew Abraham G. Haring and his cousin Cornelius Haring, all three young men held prisoners in the Reformed Dutch Church on William Street. What they found there made them nearly pass out with horror.

"Where are your clothes?" she asked, looking around her in disbelief at the scene. "What have they done to you?" The women pressed their handkerchiefs to their noses to stifle the stench.

The men, lying on the floor in filthy linen shirts, were so weak they could barely talk above a whisper. They pulled themselves to a sitting position, and together they managed to tell their tale. "We were relieved upon arrival of all our possessions and all the clothes on our bodies but our shirts. We were thrust in here with the hundreds of others you see all around us, without a blanket among us to cover our nakedness," said Cornelius. He spoke in a hoarse, halting croak. Around them was a sea of moaning, groaning humanity more dead than alive.

"Or straw to lie upon, or a fire to warm the air of the place," said Abraham in a labored voice. "The cold and damp have gone to our lungs and cause us to cough and wheeze so hard we think to die with the pain of drawing breath."

"I have heard it said it was better to die in battle than to be taken prisoner by the cruel British," Willemptie said in wonderment. "Now I believe it."

"Yes, how easy it is now to believe the brutality of the British, not so long ago our allies and 'cousins,'" said Margaret scornfully. "Your only thoughts were for your country, your families, your lives, your liberty, and this is what you get for it."

She opened her basket of food and poured cider for them. They drank greedily and sank their mouths into apples and sweet cake while their co-captives eyed them hungrily and jealously. The food gave them strength. She could hear it returning in their stronger voices.

"They starve us. We starve pitifully to death daily," said Jacobus hoarsely, "for the amounts the commissary allows, half a pound of bread and four ounces of pork per day, has in fact to serve for three days."

"Commissioner Loring pocketing the difference," said Margaret.

"The bread and pork we are given are spoiled and not fit to eat by humans."

"And the nasty, brackish water they give us is undrinkable, though we must drink it or die of thirst."

"The prisoners all grow sick not only in their lungs, but of the dysentery and fevers that kill some of us every day from having to lie in our own and each other's filth and breathe each other's poisonous breaths so crowded are we on top of one another."

And indeed there was hardly room for the ladies to turn around in the stinking den.

"It is disgraceful," said Margaret. "And I shall make complaint. What do your guards have to say about the conditions?"

"They say," said Cornelius, "'This is the punishment you deserve for your rebellion, you insolent curs. Indeed, you are treated too well. You have not received half you deserve. You deserve to be hanged. But if you will enlist into his Majesty's service, you shall have victuals and clothes enough.'"

"And what of the bodies of the dead?" Willemptie asked fearfully.

"The guards drag them out of the prison by a leg or an arm," said Abraham. "They pile them up in the dooryard, let them lie there till enough are collected to make a cart load. Then they drive the cart out to the ditches dug by the dead men's own countrymen when defending the city against the enemy in the summer of '76 and tip the corpses into the ditches and cover them with a little earth."

The women, stricken with the horror of it, traveled in silence back to Tappan, as if the inhumanity of their own kind had rendered them mute. If men treat each other so, what hope is there for the human race? Margaret wondered.

       ✳   ✳   ✳   ✳

On July 11, 1777, almost one year to the day when the *Phoenix* and the *Rose* appeared in the Tappan Zee, the authorities arrested forty-eight Bergen County Tories. Among them were three of Margaret's Haring in-laws. Three days later,

Major Samuel Hayes and a company of Americans crossed the Hackensack on flatboats and arrested fourteen more Tories at Secaucus, English Neighborhood, and New Barbadoes Neck. All were brought to trial, and about half, having taken the Patriot oath to save their necks, were acquitted, including, much to Margaret and Johannes's alarm, Johannes's two violently Tory uncles, Cornelius A. and Cornelius C. Haring. "Those two are better locked up," said Johannes.

Margaret's nephew Jacobus Blauvelt, age twenty-eight, along with one of Verbryck's sons, were soon exchanged for Peter T. Haring from Harrington, but poor Jacobus died in the defiled sanctuary before the exchange could take place, and the minister's son returned to his family so thin and sick and weak it was thought he could not live for long.

"Reprisals and counter reprisals give rise to the unending war within the war," she wrote. "Spies are everywhere and double agents aplenty. No one can trust anyone. British recruiters actively persuade enlistees, and prisoners on both sides pretend loyalty to whatever side they calculate it is to their advantage to claim. And few understand what is at stake. All is chaos and ruin. The land mourns. I mourn. We all mourn."

CHAPTER 18

▼

MASSACRE

She was hanging laundry on the line. All around her the children, black and white together, a dozen in all, were playing in the yard among the chickens and the ducks, swinging on the barn doors, balancing themselves on the split-rail fence, chasing each other hither and thither, wrestling and rolling about in the grass, ceaselessly in motion. Their constant activity exhausted her. She longed for peace and quiet, some privacy, but it was impossible with so many under foot. The household's laundry had to be washed and hung to dry. The meals had to be prepared, the floors swept, an endless, thankless task in itself with twenty and more living in the house. There was no rest in sight.

A horseman galloped down the lane. She looked up, startled. "Mother! Mother!" Isaac cried, as he galloped past the house, his blue linen hunting shirt flying behind him, waving to her with his hat.

"Our liberty! Mother! I am going for it!" he shouted, and he disappeared into the trees, heading for the river where he did shore duty.

Her eyes filled with tears. *Dear God,* she thought. *Trenton and Princeton.*

"I believe the successes at Trenton and Princeton have given the men their heart again," she said to Johannes that evening. "Now that spring is here." The militias, which had dissolved away after the evacuation of Fort Lee in November of '76, were regrouping in the spring of '77. "They are dreaming of their natural rights and ancient privileges again."

"Yes," he said, "they are determined to win their liberty. And this time minus the faithless who have since pledged their allegiance to the King."

"And minus the lukewarms," she said scornfully, "insisting they are neutral."

This was a sore point between them, because to her dismay, their son Abraham, the twin, the frail one, could not be persuaded to take the Patriot side. He had declared himself to have no fixed convictions on either side. "I am neutral in the fight," he said.

"How can a child of mine be neutral?" she harangued him. But he hung back.

"He's only sixteen," said Johannes.

"Why do you defend him? Sixteen is old enough to fight for his country," she said. "One can, indeed must, bear arms at sixteen. It is the law."

"He's young for his age. He will, when he's ready."

"We will have to pay to outfit a substitute for him," she fussed.

"That is understood. I am arranging it with your cousin."

"You shouldn't have spoken to my cousin without my knowing it," she snapped.

"I'm sorry," he said. "He inquired of me."

"He's bookish, like you," she said, meaning their son.

He laughed. His bookishness was always her fall-back accusation. "As if being bookish leads to neutrality? I'm hardly neutral. Besides," he added, "I need one son at least to help me in the fields. I am not used to sowing and mowing, seeding and reaping. It is a great deal of bother and fatigue to me."

She looked at him. He looked tired, and shabby, too, she noticed with a start. His hair needed cutting. His clothes were worn, his frock coat missing its buttons. He was fifty-seven and unaccustomed to farm work, that was certain. "We are both getting old for all the work of it all," she said.

Their other sons, Isaac, twenty-five and married, and John, twenty-two, were among the faithful. She walked with them of an evening to the hill behind Casparus Mabie's house where now a sentry kept watch day and night over the terrain. John explained how they had divided themselves into groups of four. "We have arranged that one man will serve as guard for a week while the other three tend to their fields. We plan to rotate duty over a month until all have served a week and all have taken care of their plowing and planting. We will help with yours," he added.

"The plowing and planting are so much harder now, with our slaves run off to the enemy," she fretted. "Your father will be glad to have your strong back. It is a strange sight to see him leave his books and toil in the fields, the poor man pushing a plow for the first time in his life."

From the sentry post, they walked to the field where the men drilled. "The Captain says we must drill until we can fire our muskets in unison," John said. "And scare off or better yet kill Buskirk's Greencoats when they come in the night."

"I hate to think of my sons killing anyone," she said.

"It is kill or be killed," Isaac said flatly.

"I know it," she said. "It is a terrible thing nevertheless."

"There are things more terrible than killing your enemy," he said.

"I fear we are becoming callous," she said. "War is hardening out hearts to moral things."

"It would be immoral not to war," said Isaac. "I want my liberty, and I will kill for it."

It was the duty of the Orangetown militia not only to protect the inhabitants from marauders on land, but also to guard the shores of the Hudson River to prevent the enemy from landing to plunder, burn, and destroy. John guarded the countryside. Isaac was in the shore guard. "Four British men-of-war already lie in the Tappan Zee," he said, "and it is only April. Last summer they didn't come until July."

"I suppose they are tacking about well out of musket range, like last year," she said.

"Yes. Our fire cannot reach them."

"I shall go to see them tomorrow," she said.

But the next day as she was getting ready to drive over to the river for an afternoon sighting of the squadron, Isaac galloped up to her door in a great sweat. "Last night the men-of-war launched two small boats and attempted to land at Nyack," he reported breathlessly. "We killed three of them and wounded more and drove the survivors rowing back to their ships."

"Come in," she said. "Come in and eat."

"I have not time," he said. "I must be back to my company."

"There is a *hutspot* of capon stewing," she said. It was one of the dishes Marytie had taught her to make, long ago. She could still remember Marytie chopping the bird into pieces, cooking it in water, adding clumps of toasted white bread, cinnamon, ginger, saffron, sugar, marrow, pitted dates, slices of lemon. She still did it the same way. But now, with so many mouths to feed, she had to triple the recipe. The house was filled with its fragrance.

"Oh, Mother," he said. "Capon *hutspot* I cannot resist. And I am hungry as always." He tied his horse to the hitching post in front of the house and followed her in. Bett was scrubbing the floor. Mrs. Scott was churning butter. Helena

Westervelt cut out blue linen for a rifle shirt such as the militia wore. It was their uniform, the field dress of almost the entire army as well, and much admired for its ability to strike terror in the enemy, who believed that everyone who wore it was a first-class marksman. Rachel was spinning. Aeltie, big with child again, carded. Children raced in from the yard after them, sensing food to be served.

She ladled the capon and dates into a bowl for him, cut a hunk of bread off the loaf, poured him a tankard of cider, sat across the table from him. He ate hungrily. He was a tall, rangy, good-looking man, with a crop of curly dark hair and those green eyes of his father's. She loved to dwell on his face, her first-born son. The stew was gone before she knew it.

She fixed him another bowl and cut more bread. "Did you kill any of them?"

"I hope so," he said. "It was too dark to tell who killed and who didn't. If I didn't kill any of them, I hope I wounded them. And I pray they die of their wounds."

She frowned.

"Don't frown," he said. "That is how it is."

"I can't help it," she said.

He finished eating. "That was good, Mother, but I must away," he said. "Good day, ladies." He bowed to them and rushed out the door to gallop away.

She stood in the doorway until he disappeared from sight down the lane, back to the shore guard. "Thou shalt not kill," she said to the women. "But how can we save our liberty if we don't kill those who would take it from us?"

"We can't," they said.

"We are becoming hardhearted," she said.

"That is the price of war," said Rachel.

She looked into the pot to calculate how many servings were left.

*   *   *   *

Other companies, led by other of her male cousins, nephews, in-laws, neighbors, scouted through the backcountry, while still others scouted in the county of Bergen. The men in the company that guarded Tappan assembled after sundown on the low ridge on the western edge of the village, then took to the woods to hide through the night, sleeping on their arms in shifts, while sentries patrolled, rotating sleep with picket duty until the dawn broke.

When his week on guard duty was over, John came home to help his father and brother in the fields, and they gathered to hear his news around the table in the *groote kamer*. "We are under orders to hold ourselves ready to march at a minute's warning, whenever an alarm is sounded," he said. "And the alarm sounds all too often."

"What do you do when it sounds?"

"Whenever the enemy appears, the guard that first discovers them gives the alarm by firing his gun, which is repeated by the next guard, and so continued, by which means the intelligence travels many miles in a few minutes, and all that are at home or in the fields must march to assist in driving off the brutes. Our colonel has written to General Washington to tell him how it is with us," he added.

"Has he replied?" she asked.

"Not yet. But we expect he will."

She smiled a little. "I expect he will."

"We join the first company we meet," he went on. "So we are all under different officers at different alarms. Some of our excursions last for eight and sometimes ten days, before we get home again. We are obliged to take our arms and equipment with us to our daily labor, to be ready to pursue the enemy at a moment's notice. It is difficult, especially for the married men. Their families much miss them when they are gone for so long."

"It is a trouble for the women and children to be alone without their men folk," Margaret agreed.

As they expected, the Great Man wrote back an encouraging note, which Colonel Blauvelt proudly read aloud to his friends and family. They were gathered under the grape arbor at Margaret's house to exchange news and gossip. Margaret successfully contrived to obtain this missive from her cousin on grounds of safekeeping. She took it directly into the house, read it to herself by the light of a candle and held it to her breast for a moment, before tucking it into her Psalm book along with the two notes he had written to her.

"With the militias better organized, things are looking up," Johannes was saying, as she returned.

"Yes," Thomas Blanch said. "There seems hope for a calm summer. The British are making no further attempts on the shore after losing three dead to our men and numerous wounded."

"The Tories resent General Howe's inaction. They call him Lord Dally, are impatient for him to move out and destroy us once and for all," said Samuel Demarest.

"Why does he procrastinate in New York? It is a puzzle."

"For reasons known to himself," Johannes said.

"In England, he is a Whig," Margaret said. No one took it as a *non sequitur*.

"Perhaps to give us time, I wonder?" Thomas Blanch said.

"Perhaps," said Demarest. "There is something strange about it."

"Although I am little acquainted with military matters," Margaret ventured, "the militia may be better organized this year, as you say, but do you not think it unfair that our militia have to defend Patriot farms for twenty-five miles around—and feed and arm themselves to boot?"

"It is most unfair," said Samuel Demarest, "for the Tories who maraud upon the people are fed and armed and moreover paid for their crimes by their masters."

"It is unfair," Johannes said, "but at least the unfairness of it stokes the anger not only of the militias toward the British, but of all inhabitants of our bent desiring to see the enemy ousted from our land."

"Amen," said Thomas Blanch, hoisting his tankard.

$$*\qquad*\qquad*\qquad*$$

The summer was not to be calm, though, for news came in July that the great Fort Ticonderoga, which since the exploits of Ethan Allen and the Green Mountain Boys and the hero Benedict Arnold had been in American hands, was abandoned to the British without a fight.

Despair settled in again. All seemed lost once more. "It is heartbreaking," she moaned. "We move ahead a step, and then they mow us down again." They sat around the table in the *speelhuis*, drinking Madeira, picking at nuts and apples.

"Yes," Johannes said glumly. "All General Howe has to do now is to order the fleet up the Hudson to capture the forts in the Highlands, cut the iron chain across the river at West Point, and link up with General John Burgoyne's army on its way down the Champlain Valley. Thus will New England be severed from the continent and the war won. It looks dark."

A worried John Haring agreed. "The complexion of things to the north and the preparations seen to be lately made by General Howe leave little room for doubt that he intends to form a juncture with Burgoyne," he said. "General Washington has moved his troops into the Ramapo Mountains, where he can cut Burgoyne off from Howe, but how effective he can be against such superior force is doubtful."

"How many men has Burgoyne?" she asked.

"Eight thousand."

"It seems hopeless," she said.

But their concerns were not fulfilled. Howe (perhaps thinking that the militia in the Champlain Valley would melt away at the sight of Burgoyne's advance, or perhaps, as people very often murmured, he was secretly sympathetic to the cause of the Americans) inexplicably sailed in mid-August south to Philadelphia instead of linking up with Burgoyne.

Washington was jubilant. "Now is the time for our most strenuous exertions," he crowed to his generals, champing to be after his enemy. "One bold stroke will free the land from rapine and devastation, and female innocence from brutal lust and violence. The eyes of all America and Europe are upon us. If I can win a decisive battle, France will come in on our side, and we will finish off the British! I shall advance at once on Philadelphia with all the force I can muster."

But his generals, more cautious, persuaded him against it. "Pursue Howe, but not to take Philadelphia, for that would be impossible," Greene and Knox argued. "Your Army is too feeble and ineffectual. Pursue Howe only to harass him while staying far enough in his rear to preserve such troops as you have." He listened to them and at last reluctantly agreed with them that his army, such as it was, was more important than Philadelphia. The Hudson River corridor was more important.

"But why didn't Howe see that?" Margaret wondered.

"Maybe he did," said Johannes.

"I believe it was Providence that directed him to cruise south rather than north," she said firmly. "I'm sure of it."

"Perhaps," he said. "Remember what the papers said after the Battle of Brooklyn, when he brought off his troops, surrounded on every side by their enemies, and secured their retreat across a river of which the enemy was in full possession. It was said to be a feat unparalleled in military history. Or a miracle."

"I remember very well what they said. They said that heaven had interposed on behalf of America that day by permitting such numbers to escape with glory from such a superior force."

"Let us hope and pray that heaven will interpose again," he said.

"I do, with all my heart, hope and pray it," she said. But in fact her heart was pessimistic. And in early September, when the Governor of New Jersey advised Congress that the British forces in New York under Sir Henry Clinton were about to invade New Jersey with 2,000 of his best troops, with another 6,000 said to be on their way from various quarters, she was sure the end was at hand.

"The Orange and Bergen county militia captains have begged the generals in the Continental army for help against the onslaught," John Haring said to the people gathered in the Tappan church to hear the bad news. "As we make no doubt they must be sensible, three or four hundred militia cannot stop the progress of such an enemy. If they have any regard for the sons of liberty, they must send us relief as quick as possible. We cannot maintain our ground much longer."

But relief came not. The generals politely regretted.

Margaret's thoughts turned to a matter that she had been brooding about for months, the 3,000 pounds of ammunition the army had stored in her cellar. "I don't like it being in our house," she said. "When will they come for it?"

He shook his head. "I don't know."

"And who will come for it? Us or them? And if them, what else will they take when they come? I beg you, I beseech you," she said, "to insist that they come and remove it."

"I wouldn't know whom to ask," he said.

"You promised to ask John Haring. Ask him. He will know."

"I think it is safe where it is," he said. "I think we are safe. We are enough off the beaten track."

*   *   *   *

But they came. That month, that dulcet September, three British regiments, the Grenadiers, and van Buskirk's New Jersey Volunteers marched north from Elizabethtown. At the same time, six companies and three regiments of the enemy landed at Fort Lee and marched south. And 300 troops disembarked at the Slote and headed down the plank road toward Tappan, the three forces converging on the village from and in all three directions until it was overflowing with soldiers and horses and wagons and tents and guns and ammunition and more soldiers.

The troops and the women who followed them were hungry. They took every thing they wanted from every place they found it. Willemptie watched, outraged, as a soldier grabbed a squawking chicken from her yard, wrung its neck, plucked its feathers, gutted it with his knife, threw the guts in the yard, and walked into her house without so much as a by your leave to cook it on her hearth. He sat on a chair watching it roast as he picked lice out of his hair, crunching them on the arm of the chair with his long dirty fingernails.

For nine days and nights that month Sir Henry Clinton's troops exchanged fire with the Dutch farmers and the militiamen of Orange and Bergen and Passaic counties, killing and maiming them for the pleasure of it, stealing all the cattle they could, burning their houses, plundering and looting at will. Van Buskirk's Greencoats were the cruelest of them all. "Van Buskirk," Margaret said in disgust. "To think that he was at the beginning a Patriot, one of us."

And on one of those lovely September evenings, when the western sky was still rosy with the setting sun, and a huge golden harvest moon lay for a moment balanced on the blue hills of the Nyack Range to the east, and the swallows dived in and out of the barn after the last insects of the evening, and the twittering blue jays and cardinals and mockingbirds were settling down in their nests, the bandits came at last to Margaret's house. Hearing them marauding toward them through the stubbled cornfields with wagons to carry their booty away, Johannes took the loaded musket from its place near the chimney and hustled all the women and children in the house to the barn. Then he disappeared.

With greedy cries they fell upon the house. She watched through a chink in the barn's siding as whooping and shouting they knocked the glass out of her windows with their musket butts and smashed in the doors to plunder, stealing every movable thing in the house, throwing their booty, all her precious treasures, into the wagons. She watched in a kind of imperturbable, dispassionate, stoic silence as laughing and cursing they rushed out of the back of the house to throw a feather mattress into the well and stuff one of her best petticoats into the privy. Another feather mattress they split with their bayonets and laughed at the feathers floating on the breeze that stirred the evening air. And she listened as inside the house they hacked her beloved furniture to pieces with axes. That will be my sweet-gum *kas*, she thought dully. That will be the cherry table.

Then they discovered the cellar and its guilty burden, the 3,000 pounds of the Continental army's ammunition, and their joy was complete. "This will bring a fine price in New York," she heard one of them gloat. They loaded the barrels into the wagons and started rattling off to the next farm, when through the chink in the barn wall she saw a straggler with a rifle heading toward the barn. To burn? To rape? To kill? To steal a horse?

A shot rang out, and the figure dropped to the ground in her kitchen garden. The marauders rolled on through the cornfields, did not miss him.

He was a young lad. They carried him into the wrecked, ruined house and laid him on a slashed mattress on the floor. There was a huge bloody hole in his shirt—it wasn't even the green shirt worn by van Buskirk's bandits, but just an ordinary linen work shirt, so he wasn't officially one of the bandits but a hanger on, or maybe not even that, maybe just an innocent passer by. She tried to stanch the blood with a towel, but it kept coming, flooded warm and bright over her hand.

By the light of the full moon, she recognized him from the neighborhood and he her. His wound would not let him speak, but mutely he implored her with his eyes to help him. She knew his family, had not known they were of the Tory persuasion. And perhaps they were not. They were not Dutch, and not churchgoers, so how could she know what they were or what they believed?

Though he was incapable of speech, his eyes begged for mercy. She reached for a cup and lifted his head and gave him a sip from a bucket of water that amidst the chaos of the room was inscrutably full and clean. Scripture came to her. "If you knew who it is that is saying to you 'Give me a drink,' you would have asked him and he would give you living water," she murmured. He seemed to understand that she was talking of eternal things, and that was, strangely to his unchurched soul, a comfort, by the look in his eyes. But if he swallowed the living water she offered him, and how could she know that? he could not swallow the actual water. It dribbled back out of his mouth, and he died, his eyes still fixed on her face.

"Now what?" she cried. "Now what do we do?"

"Close his eyes and cover him," said Johannes wearily. "We can't do anything until morning."

She lowered his head to the floor and closed his eyes, and her daughter Aeltie knelt beside her to straighten out his limbs. Her cousin brought a blanket from the wrecked *kas* to cover his form. The twins, Abraham and Elizabeth, tried to clear the house of debris, pushed and lugged the ruined furniture and household wreckage out the back door into the night. The slave woman Bett hustled her children and Rachel's and Aeltie's off to their beds. Mrs. Westervelt and Mrs. Scott gathered their own children and scuttled into the corners allocated to them. Rachel and Aeltie sought their ruined beds, and wearily Johannes placed his musket back on the wall and lay down in his clothes on their old *betse*, deprived of its soft feather mattress and bolsters and pillows and sheets.

She lay down on the floor on a pallet, next to the corpse. That was the Dutch custom, to stay with the body until it could be buried, stay with it all night so the rats wouldn't feed on it. At least she would have that to comfort his mother with in the morning, small comfort though it would be.

In the dark, she wept, for the boy, for themselves, for the wreck of her house, for the wreck of her country. But most of all for him, a mere boy, dead in front of her eyes. Yet she could not be angry with her husband for killing him.

He was their neighbor, true, and he was only a lad. But that was not apparent in the dark. In the dark, he was the enemy, heading for their barn with a loaded rifle in his hand.

As it sailed over the house, the moon flooded the room with light, and she lay awake for many hours as it moved across the room, cursing war and what it did to Christian men and gentle boys, made beasts or martyrs of them.

Not far away Johannes lay awake, too, fearful of their own sons, perhaps this very night in the way of Tory muskets.

They heard each other groan and sigh and toss all night.

*   *   *   *

"What a contemptible ruination they have made of our house," she said in the morning, after the boy's parents had come and taken away his body.

The whole household joined in pushing and pulling the wreckage out into a fallow field, where Johannes set it on fire. "There is almost nothing left," he said, awed.

"We will have to start over," she said.

He gazed at the place where he had shot the boy. "Did I sin in killing him?"

"We are at war."

"Yes."

"It's kill or be killed," she said shortly.

"Yes," he said. "But he was only a lad."

"You don't know what was in his mind," she said. "He carried a rifle. And it was loaded."

"Right."

*   *   *   *

That afternoon, John Haring cantered up on his strawberry roan. "I bring grim news," he said. "A raiding party led by General William Tryon visited the home of Colonel Hay at Haverstraw last night."

"Oh no," she moaned. "A party was here last night, too, as you can see."

"Yes, I see," he said. "A dreadful mess. But your house is standing. Not Hay's. They burned it and his barn and stables to the ground. They stole or wrecked all his fine furniture, took away his slaves and all of his livestock, and caused his wife and children to flee with only the clothes on their backs."

"His wife is a daughter of Judge William Smith, Sr., and a sister of William Smith, Jr., the Tory Chief Justice of New York," Johannes said, awed.

"Her social position did her no good amid the horrors of war," Margaret said.

"What good will anything do for any of us?" Mrs. Scott cried bitterly.

"Is the end near?" Margaret asked. "They say Burgoyne will capture the Hudson Valley, Howe will capture the capital, and under Sir Henry Clinton the British and Hessians in New York will cross the Hudson and occupy New Jersey."

"I cannot say. There were many raiding parties last night, a concerted effort to undermine us," said Haring. "But at least the Continental regiments camped in Westchester crossed the Hudson last night and gave chase. And at least Sir Henry, having collected as many cattle and sheep, hogs, and horses as he could handle, has returned to New York."

"To distribute his illegal booty among his Army," Johannes said.

"Yes," John Haring said, "according to my intelligence, he regards the booty as 'affording a seasonable refreshment without costing the Army or the government a shilling.'"

"The people's cattle and sheep and hogs and horses," Margaret fumed. "He is no better than a common thief."

In a week, a confident Sir Henry ordered his Major General John Vaughn to foray back up the Hudson to take the Highland forts for sure this time and to give an assist to Burgoyne. Vaughn easily took Fort Montgomery and Fort Clinton, and then he marched his men up to Kingston and burned it to the ground.

John Haring brought the news.

"All is lost," she moaned. "Now the end is at hand. It is over."

"No, it is not over," Haring said. "I have also come to tell you the good news, for the Lord had other plans for the British. I have come to tell you that the very day after they burned Kingston, we routed the British at Saratoga."

"What!"

"How?"

"With the help of thousands of angry New England militia. Determined not to be split off from the Continent or from their chance at independence from British slavery, they joined the regulars under Horatio Gates and Benedict Arnold and saved the day."

When the news reached Tappan, there was cheering in the streets and lanes and in the church and tavern. Samuel Verbryck ventured out of hiding in Clarkstown to preach a rousing sermon in the Tappan parsonage and declare the Battle of Saratoga to be the War's turning point.

"How did they do it?" people wondered.

"They used methods the British do not understand," John Haring said. "Methods learned from Indians, hit and run tactics, nighttime harassment, thin skirmish lines, unconventional formations from behind trees and even up in trees."

"Daniel Morgan's sharpshooters with rifles, knives, hatchets, and tomahawks forced the thought-to-be invincible Burgoyne to surrender! We are saved!"

"It is confirmation as strong as Holy Writ of God's will for his American colonies," Verbryck declared.

"In disgrace, Sir Henry Clinton and the British have abandoned the Highland forts to the Americans and sailed down to Philadelphia," John Haring reported.

*   *   *   *

"We can breathe again," sighed Johannes, "with Howe and Clinton in Philadelphia, the Continental army at Valley Forge, and Burgoyne a terror no more."

But in the early winter, just before Christmas, Margaret's nephew Isaac, the son of her brother Theunis and the spit and image of his grandfather, her father, fell out of an apple tree at age eleven and died of a broken neck. "Terror takes many shapes," Margaret said.

It was a tragedy almost unbearable, and an irony almost unbearable. "He was the apple of our eye," his mother wept, "and he died of an apple tree."

All grieved for him, a precious boy, handsome, quick, athletic, healthy, and sweet natured. "All the hope and promise of a free nation was ours to dream for him," said his father.

His parents' anguish was beyond measure. "Life is too cruel," his mother sobbed. Half mad with grief, she wished to die herself for lack of him. They had to restrain her, keep her in doors, assign someone to be with her every minute of the day and night.

"What is the loss of our mere property in comparison?" Margaret said to her household. She mourned not her smashed spinning wheels, and her sweet-gum *kas* chopped to pieces, and her gowns and petticoats and linens and bed coverings gone, she cared not for the vanished faience and pewter and redware, or that her house was cold and dark with her sconces and candelabra filched away, and rags stuffed in the shattered windows to keep the winter winds out. It was only her family that mattered.

She went to the boy's mother, her sister-in-law Jannetje Turneur, and lay beside her on her *betse*, stroking her, whispering comfort to her, lulling her to sleep, willing her to live. But the poor woman was inconsolable. "He is in a better place," Margaret whispered.

"No," Jannetje cried. "No, he is not in a better place. There is no better place. There is no heaven, if that's what you mean."

"We must believe there is," said Margaret. "The Bible says so, a place where sheep may safely graze."

"No! This is the place where sheep once safely grazed. There is no other!"

And then came another terror even closer to home. Her son John came to tell them of it. "Colonel Blauvelt has ordered me and Cornelius de Baun to reconnoiter within the British lines at Paulus Hook," he said. "We are to determine the extent of the trading between New Jersey and New York."

"You will be in great danger," she said, quivering.

"Yes, but it is common knowledge that the enemy in New York is being supplied from Orange and Bergen counties. The inhabitants have such egress and regress to the interior parts of the country to purchase provisions that they do not even bother to acquire passes. They simply load their goods into wagons and periaugers and drive or sail to the ferry. Colonel Blauvelt wants the exact supply routes through the country that he is in charge of to be uncovered and the traders arrested."

In a day or so, under orders from Colonel Blauvelt, John and Cornelius de Baun, spying a Loyalist with a full wagon and two negroes heading to the Sneden's Landing ferry to New York, apprehended him and his wagon and possessions and took him, loudly protesting his innocence, to militia headquarters. John Haring, with loaded musket, rode in the wagon beside the negro, who drove. The other negro sat in the back, beside the prisoner, tied to him with rope. Cornelius de Baun, musket at the ready, with John's horse on a rein, cantered alongside. All were on their guard, for in similar circumstances just months before, the prisoner had tried to escape, and his captors had shot him dead. That he was in fact innocent then made a great deal of trouble for the captors.

Now this prisoner, in an attempt to escape, tried to seize John's musket, whereupon Cornelius de Baun galloped up behind him and shot him dead.

As in the earlier case, a large reward was subscribed by van Buskirk to anyone who could bring in the two militiamen, and very soon Cornelius de Baun was captured by his Tory cousin Jacob de Baun and thrown into the Provost's prison, condemned to hang. Within a day, John Haring was also captured, and also by one of *his* cousins, and thrown into the same scurvy place, also sentenced to hang.

Margaret, beside herself, immediately obtained permission from her cousin Colonel Blauvelt to provision the men. Mrs. de Baun did likewise. But when the two mothers got to the prison with their baskets of food and sundries, they learned to their horror that their sons were handcuffed in the dungeon and could not be visited.

Margaret reported this to Colonel Blauvelt, who promptly went to Elisha Boudinot, the American commissary of prisoners, in Hackensack: "I have appointed their mothers to provide for them," he said, "but the women tell me that the men are in the dungeon, in leg irons and handcuffs and chained to the floor, allowed only one *hutsput* a day and a pint of water. This you may depend upon, Sir, is the truth. They will surely die unless you intervene."

"I shall intervene immediately," said Boudinot. But his attempts to exchange the men were denied.

"But they are regularly enlisted men, acting under orders, and should be treated as prisoners of war, not as common criminals," Blauvelt protested. "I offered that I myself be sent to the prison under a flag of truce to see what I could do, but the enemy rejected my offer."

"Nothing short of retaliation will teach Britons to act like men of humanity," Elisha Boudinot spat out. "Capture a Loyalist officer and throw him into jail, with irons on his hands and feet, chain him to the floor, and give him bread and water only. Until further notice," he added. "I shall inform General Washington of the case."

When he learned of the matter, and that the two prisoners were Dutchmen from Tappan (a town that had come to occupy a certain place in his imagination, though he had never yet been to it), General Washington himself wrote to Sir Henry Clinton to complain: "Two soldiers in the service of these states are suffering a confinement of peculiar severity, without a sufficient cause for so injurious a discrimination. I am persuaded," he wrote, "that I need only call your attention to the situation of these men to induce you to order them relief, and to have them placed precisely on the same footing with other prisoners of war."

After ten days, for some reason of his own, perhaps because he did not want to be accused of holding prisoners of war in chains, Sir Henry ordered the two men exchanged, an act for which he was abused by Tories for his sentimentality and by Patriots for the cruel and illegal treatment he had condoned for ten days.

"I wonder," Margaret mused, "did he free them because he is one of those Whiggish Englishmen who silently sympathize with men who insist on their ancient rights and privileges?"

"I think that is wishful thinking on your part," said Johannes. "I hear nothing good of Sir Henry."

There was great rejoicing in Tappan, when the two prisoners appeared, emaciated and covered with lice. While her son cleaned and groomed himself and laid his weary body down to rest, Margaret resorted to the smokehouse for the last of the last year's hams and put on a small, in fact, a rather meager, spread under the locust trees to celebrate his return. "I am reminded of happier days," she said to Johannes, "when family and friends gathered every Sunday in the good weather to picnic under the trees around the church."

"Now the church is a filthy hospital full of sick and dying men, vermin, lice, and disease, and warring armies consume the bounty of our fields," said Johannes.

"When will it end? How will it end?"

"I thought it had ended at Trenton," he said. "How wrong I was."

*　　　*　　　*　　　*

John had described to her the desolation of the countryside as he had seen it on the way up from prison and the Paulus Hook ferry, and after he was rested and well enough to return to his company, she decided to see for herself the devastation of that part of their Eden. She had an errand in Hackensack that would take her through that country: to find a few able-bodied day laborers to help Johannes in the fields, for it was planting time, soon to be cider-making time, and slaughtering time again. "It is a strange twist of fate that I have had to give up my books and farm my own farm at age fifty-seven," he said. "I can use a few strong men in the days ahead. But be careful. And take the rapier."

She hitched an ancient dray that had been overlooked by the raiders to a farm wagon, buckled the rapier on its leather belt around her waist, and with her cousin Rachel drove from Tappan to Closter to Hackensack. Sam rode beside them with a loaded musket. Within an hour, they were passing dozens of wrecked farmhouses, barns, outbuildings, burnt churches and courthouses, farmers staring mutely at fields reduced to stubble, women huddled over the smoldering hearths of wrecked houses trying to cook a meal for listless, hopeless families sitting about in shock.

"The ruination," said Margaret in awe. It was almost impossible to take it in.

"How ugly war is," Rachel shuddered.

"This is worse than ugly. This is hell come to earth," Margaret said, gazing around at the desolate landscape. "War has made a black, smoking hell of our beautiful green paradise."

"Yes," said Rachel. "It was our fair land, and then the armies came."

"But, we war for the best of reasons."

"Yes, to save the glorious plant of liberty, as they call it."

"And therefore we will win in the end. We must," said Margaret fiercely. "England cannot win, because the dream of freedom cannot be suppressed forever. No loving God would allow it."

It did not escape them that an elderly slave, too old and tired to even dream of freedom any longer, rode alongside them to protect them with his musket. "The dream of freedom belongs to the slaves, too," said Rachel.

Margaret sighed. "Slavery has become too troublesome to bother with, and perhaps it always has been," she said.

"And that is why," Rachel muttered, "between you and me, Sister, I wish they had all run away a long time ago."

"Yes. Run back to Africa. I wish it too."

"It was the African chiefs who sold them," said Rachel. "I don't think they want to go back there."

*   *   *   *

This all happened in the summer of 1778—the raid on her house, the cruel death of her nephew, the capture of her son. It was the summer when General Howe and his army suddenly abandoned Philadelphia for New York City, and when General Washington ordered a regiment of the Continental army back to Tappan, and others to the Highlands, while he took up a position across the Hudson in White Plains, where it was safer.

It was no secret that his main goal was to preserve his army, even if it meant that he could not support the militias, who especially in the neutral ground were on their own. He regretted the necessity. He regretted their constant engagement year in and year out, all on their own with no support from him. He regretted, but there was no help for it. They *were* on their own. He gave orders for the Tappan regiment to patrol to the south to prevent supplies from going to New York City, and the men brought back 300 cattle and eighty sheep for the use of the army.

"The people's cattle and sheep," Margaret said bitterly. "The poor hungry people's cattle and sheep."

With a regiment of Continentals guarding the area, *Dominie* Romeyn felt safe to come down from New Paltz to minister to his flocks. On the way, he stopped at Tappan to see John Haring and his wife Mary, living in the parsonage. Margaret and Johannes called on him as soon as they heard of his arrival.

"Of flocks I have just learned I now have two," he sighed. "My congregation in Hackensack has split in two, and so has my congregation in Schraalenburgh. One is Patriot and one Tory."

"And so, each church has two ministers?" Margaret said.

"Two ministers, two consistories, and two congregations under two roofs," he said. "And all related. That is the madness of it, cousins, brothers, and friends and neighbors pitted against each other."

"And both sides think they own the truth," John Haring said.

"Yes, and both point to the same Scriptures to prove it."

"And God disapproves of both," Romeyn said, "for their implacable and uncivil and unchristian lack of love for each other."

"It is all so unnecessary," Haring said. "But both sides will go on to the finish, for both sides are convinced of their correctness."

"I am hardly an expert, but they say that the Tories are patriots of their own sort," said his wife. "Loyal to their King." She had uncles among them and uncles she had once loved.

✳   ✳   ✳   ✳

As the fields were harvested that summer, men slept with their muskets at hand, expecting the British to raid once the crops were gathered into barns and hay barracks. And sure enough, on September 22, 1778, thousands, some said 16,000 British troops under Lord Cornwallis landed at Paulus Hook and marched north toward Liberty Pole and New Bridge, Schraalenburgh, Teaneck, the English Neighborhood, and Tappan. Meanwhile news came that Sir Henry Clinton was being conveyed north up the Hudson in a barge. "This is no mere foraging expedition," Johannes said to the friends gathered around the table in the *speelhuis.*

"No," said John Haring. "I am worried. It seems to be a new attempt to cut New England off from the continent so that the British can command the Hudson Valley."

"In Tappan," said Margaret, "I have counted no more than 200 of the Continental army left to stop the British advance."

Thomas Blanch looked at her sharply.

"The rest have withdrawn to safety over the Saddle River to Paramus," said Johannes. "There is only the militia to defend us."

"But how to defend Liberty Pole against seventeen British field pieces?" she demanded. "And New Bridge against daily reinforcements from New York? And Newark and Secaucus and New Barbadoes Neck from the flotillas that ferry in supplies?"

"My dear madam, where do you get your facts?" Thomas Blanch asked.

"I make it my daily business to survey the movements of the army camped in my neighborhood, and of suspected Tories too," she said. "And I listen. I keep my ear to the ground. And I am not alone."

"You spy?"

"We all spy," she said flatly. "Spinning and carding are not enough in these times. We gather information for our own good. And for yours."

"You are very outspoken," he murmured.

"I shall write to General Washington," John Haring said, "to report the distress the late movements of the enemy into the neutral ground have occasioned."

"Tell him that numbers of families are left destitute of not only every comfort and convenience but every necessity of life," she said. "Beg him to see fit to send a regiment to defend us."

"I shall do my best."

But again, the General wrote back a note of sorrow and encouragement. There was nothing he could do to help. Margaret also contrived to obtain this disappointing note from her cousin—for safekeeping, she promised—to add to the growing collection preserved in her Psalm book.

✳   ✳   ✳   ✳

The militiamen were brave and indefatigable, but they could not prevent the damages, even though they rode about urging the people to move their cattle, grain, and forage into swamps and woods, where the British could not easily find them. Nor could they prevent the damage to Patriots' houses and barns. Or to their persons. While in the area, *Dominie* Romeyn never slept in the same house two nights in a row, for there was a price on his head.

At this time, Johannes's cousin John A. Haring, a militiaman, received a severe cut with a saber on his head and was taken prisoner to the French Church in New York, where he would remain along with 400 others for three months under conditions described by General Washington when he learned of them as shocking to humanity.

Johannes went to see for himself and returned shaken. "The men are so crowded they cannot all lie down at the same time, but have to take turns," he reported. "They have received not a stick of wood from the provost marshal to build a fire or cook their pork. They have burned all the pews in the sanctuary for fuel for their cooking fires, and now that the pews are gone they eat their pork raw."

*   *   *   *

As women of her sentiments were doing all over New York and New Jersey, Margaret and her cousin Rachel, and her daughters Aeltie and Elizabeth, along with Willemptie and Cathlyntie Mabie, and Helena Westervelt and their other women friends, and even Mrs. Scott, for she was rallying, took it upon themselves to spy on the British. "We are able to make many observations on British movements and positions and numbers," they told John Haring. "But what should we do with the information? How shall we proceed?"

"Relay your information to Major Alexander Clough," Haring advised them. "He is General Washington's chief of intelligence and chief spy, stationed at Hackensack, below New Bridge. He is under the command of Colonel George Baylor, the son of an old friend and neighbor of General Washington in Virginia. Baylor leads a regiment of American light horse, Lady Washington's Guards."

"Where exactly will we find Major Clough?" Margaret asked.

"He has set up his headquarters in Abraham Vanderbeek's house near Paramus," Haring said.

Six of them went, Willemptie and Cathlyntie clad in their finest. The others, Margaret, Rachel, Aeltie, Elizabeth, Mrs. Westervelt, and Mrs. Scott, had lost their best gowns in the raid on the house, and since then had had to wear old petticoats and work gowns found stored away in the garret, or bought in second-hand stores. "There's a war on," said Margaret briskly. "We can't help what we look like."

They easily found the house of Abraham Vanderbeek, and an aide led them into the presence of. Major Clough. He was at his field desk, which was set up in the *groote kamer*. "What can I do for you, ladies?" he asked pleasantly enough.

Margaret was spokeswoman. She explained to him how they operated, what sort of information they could gather, what they could report to him on British movements in their own neighborhoods.

They were taken aback at his indifference. He actually stifled a yawn as she spoke, and at the end he smiled at them in a way they did not like, meaning he found their earnest Dutch manner and Jersey Dutch accents a little quaint, their offer a little comic. "All is under control," he drawled. "I advise you to go home to your families, ladies, and think no more of military matters."

They backed out of his presence. "I am completely mortified," said Margaret, back in the wagon. "What a rude man."

But soon after their interview with him, they were disturbed to learn from their friends and relations in the militia that Major Clough appeared to be condoning Tory traffic with New York.

"Perhaps that explains his indifference to us," Margaret said. "Is he is a traitor to His Excellency, a double agent?"

"Is Baylor as well, then?" Rachel wondered.

"I wonder," said Margaret.

They also learned that Major Clough had found not only their manner and accents quaint, he had found their dress quaint also and indeed had had a good laugh at their expense. In fact, he was quoted in the papers as recommending that, come winter, the Dutch women of Bergen County turn their many petticoats into warm waistcoats for the troops. "I have only to observe that having for above a century worn the breeches in the family, it is only reasonable that when winter comes again the men should make booty of their petticoats," he said.

Margaret was not amused. A number of her own treasured petticoats had vanished in that fearful raid upon her house. "And how would a Virginian know anything of Dutch women in Bergen County?" she said witheringly. He was in contempt of her court.

"If we think he is trafficking with Tories, we should inform General Washington," said Willemptie. "It is our duty."

"You are right. We should do that," said Margaret. "We will get our revenge on him by informing General Washington himself of the rumors that he may be a spy." She composed a careful letter to him.

He suspected at once who the writer was. It was that woman, that writing Dutch woman of Tappan. He recognized her name, he recognized the name of the place from which the letter came. He even recognized her careful Italianate hand. That same Dutch woman, that woman whose appearance had transfixed him for a moment that day so long ago. Was he on his way to Boston that time? Yes, Bunker Hill.

"She is right to spy, of course," he said to his aide. "I depend on spies. And women are as good at it as men. But she is wrong in her conclusions, for Clough is one of my spies."

He replied to tell her so, addressing his letter to the officer commanding the militia at Hackensack, with a copy to her: "Major Clough, commanding at Hackensack, is under the necessity of sometimes allowing persons to carry small matters into New York, and to bring a few goods out, that he may the better obtain intelligence. The persons employed in that way are sometimes stopped by the militia, under suspicion that they are carrying on a contraband trade. I have ordered Major Clough to acquaint the militia officers not to detain or molest any person showing a pass from him." In short, His Excellency had ordered Clough to send local people into the city to spy on the British positions. All *was* under control. Margaret was again mortified.

But then, on her copy of this letter, he thanked her for her concerns and suggested she relay any further intelligence to his good friend, Colonel George Baylor. Her spirits leaped. She could be of use to him after all! Before she put the letter away in her Psalm book, she pressed it to her cheek for a long moment.

*   *   *   *

But in fact, all was not under control. On the last Sunday evening in September 1778, under orders from General Washington in White Plains, Colonel Baylor and Major Clough, guided by Colonel Abraham Blauvelt, moved the regulars and the light horse guard from Paramus toward Tappan, to be safe from four advancing British regiments and fifty dragoons under the infamous General Charles No-Flint Grey. Grey was so called because he had destroyed an encampment of General Anthony Wayne's troops without firing a shot, by ordering his men to remove the flints from their muskets and gut the men with their bayonets, vicious three-sided blades that rendered wounds in flesh that could not be sewn up.

After that night, Colonel Blauvelt was not to be the same again. He relived the horror of it to the end of his life, waked in terror dreaming of it, sweating, his heart pounding. In broad daylight, he started at loud noises or sudden movements, was ever fearfully looking over his shoulder. He was not alone.

General Grey, never one to pass up a fight, ordered his regiments to pursue Baylor and Clough. A group of local Tories, who knew the roads and, better yet, the Tory barns where the Americans would settle for the night in presumed safety, guided Grey and his troops quietly through the dark forest.

Colonel Baylor, with twelve officers and 140 dragoons, all innocent of any danger, settled down for the night, some in the barns and outbuildings on the farm of one Cornelius Abraham Haring, uncle of Johannes, and some on the surrounding farms. Baylor posted a guard on the bridge over the Hackensack. Even though the British forces were only ten miles away, he felt himself and his men safe with the guard to alert them in case Grey should somehow discover them. He did not suspect that his host, Cornelius A. Haring, was a notorious Tory, or that Haring's close friend and neighbor Abraham Mabie was suspected by the locals of being an active spy for the British.

"What happened?" moaned Clough the next day. He was badly wounded and near death in the Tappan church. He and Colonel Baylor had tried to conceal themselves in the jambless Dutch fireplace of the house, but they were discovered and savagely bayoneted.

"It may never be known for sure, but it is believed one Abraham Mabie, a Tory, alerted the British to your positions," John Haring replied.

"At two in the morning," Baylor whispered in a labored voice, "I heard someone cry 'No quarter to rebels,' and they burst upon us and killed men outright with their bayonets. I do not know the numbers. But the screams and shrieks of the attacked must have waked the dead."

Thomas Talley, one of Baylor's Light Horse, badly wounded also, reported that even troops who begged to surrender were mercilessly gutted. "From a loft in the barn," he said, shivering in his shirt on the cot next to Clough's, "blood flowed through cracks in the floor to the ground below. I asked for quarter, and it was granted. But instead they pulled off my breeches and took my money and silver buckles, and ordered me into the barn. Here they struck me with bayonets about the breast and back until I became nearly insensible. They held a candle to my face to discover whether I was dead or alive, and left me for dead."

George Wyllis, badly wounded, reported the same, in a whisper: "The Captain said they must kill us all, and struck me a dozen times with the bayonet in my breast and back and stripped me and left me for dead, with two more who lay near me."

Margaret's cousin, Harmanus Blauvelt, reported that he had found himself surrounded. "I offered to surrender," he moaned, "but instead of giving me quarter, they fired upon me and wounded me in the thigh and then stabbed me in the arm with a bayonet and left me for dead. I am in very great pain from my wounds, and I fear their festering in this filthy hospital where we lie helpless."

The same scenes were enacted in other houses and barns in the neighborhood where the men slept, houses and barns owned by Demarests, Harings, Blauvelts, and Bogerts. The defenseless Americans begged and cried for mercy, but they were shown none. The next day, John Haring determined that of 116 troops of the regiment, eleven were bayoneted to death on the spot, seventeen were wounded and expected to die, eight severely wounded were taken prisoner, and thirty-one not injured were taken prisoner. Forty-nine lucky ones escaped into the woods.

In the morning, militiamen, weeping, buried the dead, including Major Clough.

General Grey's chief of intelligence, one Captain John André, soon to be Major, duly recorded the details of the night's evil work in his diary. And the British engineer Archibald Robertson sketched in his notebooks a view of the village from an eminence behind Casparus Mabie's house. No one could have told from the charming sketch what savagery had taken place there the night before. And no one could have known in 1778, but all recollected, when the infamous day came two years later, that Tappan, the Dutch church, and the noted house of Casparus Mabie on Main Street were to become well known to that same John André.

Sir Henry Clinton, mentor to Captain John André, returned to New York after the massacre highly satisfied. "It is a clever innovation, very clever, of Grey's to order his men to remove the flints from their muskets, so that they must to rely on their bayonets," he was overheard by a spy to say to his aide.

CHAPTER 19

▼

NADIR

The people were shocked and sickened for days and weeks after the terrible massacre. A great melancholy fell upon them. Grief overtook them. They could not sleep, could not speak, could not weep, or wept without stopping, felt their hearts would break, felt nothing, vomited, wrung their hands, shook their heads in disbelief, walked aimlessly about their despoiled land, could not walk but stayed indoors and stared at walls, too stunned for words with the brutality of it. How could it be that this terror had come upon them in the still of a soft and innocent September night? An old man hanged himself. A bereft woman filled the pocket tied around her waist with rocks and drowned herself in the Hudson River.

And to make it worse, to their disgust and distress, 6,000 British troops lingered on the ridge to the west of the village for a week, No-Flint Grey and Lord Cornwallis quartering themselves and their aides in the houses around the Green, without asking or thanking, or paying. The army took all it wanted of produce, cattle, and goods from the bereaved and helpless inhabitants, and all it wanted of food and drink from wherever and whomever they pleased.

The stench of their presence rendered the very outdoors noxious. "Six thousand shittings a day," Margaret calculated grimly. Their once lovely little Eden was befouled by the privies built out over the once pristine Hackensack River, the stinking necessaries thrown up at the encampment, the pits and ditches dug for shitting, the excrement covered with dirt once a day.

She recalled the words of Moses: "You shall have a place outside the camp and you shall go out to it; and you shall have a stick with your weapons; and when you sit down outside, you shall dig a hole with it, and turn back and cover up your excrement. Because the Lord your God walks in the midst of your camp, to save you and to give up your enemies before you, therefore your camp must be holy, that he may not see anything indecent among you, and turn away from you."

"When the wind blows from the east, the stench overcomes me," she moaned. "I am losing all hope."

"Do not be overcome," he said. "If you give up hope, then I will, and I do not want to."

"You are right. I must get hold of myself," she said. "I will not be overcome, not by my enemy. I will bury my grief. I will do something useful."

Petitions were unknown before the War. But now that she had learned of them and their effectiveness, she decided to organize one of her own, to Governor George Clinton. She sharpened her nib and wrote. "The enemy are now extending their ravages into this state and have made their appearance at Tappan with a large body commanded by Cornwallis in person. And after butchering in a most inhuman manner a number of Light Horse, they turned their cruelties to women and old men, whom they treated with every kind of brutality their perfidiousness could invent. The militia, knowing the small number of its whole force, has every reason to expect we must, unless immediately relieved, fall a sacrifice to the enemy. We have every reason to believe that no aid will be afforded from the Continental army. We throw ourselves on your mercy."

In her wagon with her cousin Rachel and Willemptie and Cathlyntie Mabie, and with the rapier in its leather sheath buckled around her waist, she went all over the neighborhood and up into Blauveltville to the north of Tappan and on to Clarkstown beyond that, getting more than a hundred people to sign the letter.

But Governor Clinton showed no mercy, sent no relief, afforded no aid. "I cannot help you, Madam," he wrote. "I am afraid you are on your own."

Then at last, when all the fields and orchards and vines were stripped and all the barns and hay barracks bare, Cornwallis's army struck its tents and departed for New Bridge. Following it went hordes of locals, fleeing with them. "Fleeing the dream of independence!" Margaret scorned. "Fleeing to slavery to British masters!" Among them, and it came as no surprise, was another of her Blauvelt cousins, a long-time British guide and spy.

Along the way, these traitors stole their neighbors' cattle and loaded what grain was left after the forage of the King's army into the King's wagons. Lukewarms and vague neutrals, they were now throwing in their lot with the British, who were sure to be victorious in the long run, or so they thought the massacre of Baylor and his troops had proved.

"But they don't know what I know," Margaret said grimly.

"And what is that?" Johannes asked.

"They don't know that the American general Lord Stirling has just called their brutal campaign into New Jersey the last effort of the expiring tyranny of Great Britain." She had read it in Hugh Gaine's *New York Gazette, and Weekly Mercury*—the Whig version he published out of Newark, not the Tory version he published in New York.

"I would like to believe it is the last effort the British would, or could, mount," Johannes said. "I would like to have faith that Providence will see to our rights and privileges."

"Let us have faith. And let our faith make us whole. We cannot lose hope."

"In fact," he said, "perhaps it is cause to rejoice that the lukewarms and neutrals have left the neighborhood, for who knows how lukewarm and neutral they really were?"

"Yes," she said. "Who knows what they were really thinking and doing? It is whispered everywhere that Abraham Mabie, who called himself a neutral, was spying for the British and would have had the time and opportunity to tip off Cornwallis and Grey to our positions on the night of the massacre."

"If so, he deserves to hang," said Johannes. "And I would run up the rope myself."

    *   *   *   *

With George Washington and the Continental army now encamped far to the south on the Raritan, only the exhausted local militia and a regiment of Continentals at Paramus protected the inhabitants of Tappan from the terrors of war. And with the departure of the British army, the murderous gangs from the Highlands returned again to wage war of their own kind on the people, plundering, abducting, killing, raping, burning.

Major Nathaniel Strong was shot dead in the middle of the night in his own house. "They came to our house, about twelve o'clock at night, he was in bed, and they broke and entered the outer door, broke a panel out of the door of the inner room," his poor distraught widow, her teeth chattering, told Margaret.

"They fired at him through a window, but he escaped. They called upon him to deliver up his arms and he should have quarter, but on setting down his gun, they shot through the broken panel twice, and he expired without speaking a word. They stole two bridles and a saddle and left."

"Oh, it is sheer havoc and terror," Margaret said, shivering. "Every night I and my household go to bed fearing a new break in, more plundering, maybe this time rape and murder."

"They come when they want to, and everything is theirs for the taking," Mrs. Strong said, shivering too, drawing her cloak around her. "Horses, saddles, watches, rifles, slaves, plate, cash, women's bodies."

"The militia pursues them into the Ramapo Mountains, and if they can, they retake the negroes and the horses and goods not already sold in the city," said Margaret.

"But Bergen County Tories allow gang members wanting to go to New York to sell their loot to hide out in their cellars during the daylight hours," Johannes said.

"Or in caves in their woods dug large enough to fit eight of the fiends at a time," Mrs. Strong said. "I know where some of them are."

"They as resourceful as can be," said Johannes. "They cross the Hackensack on log rafts and then on foot overland to the Hudson where they brazenly board ferries to New York with their plunder."

If they were captured, they were tried and hanged. Of two of them hanged at Hackensack that fall, the court said, "They were famous all over the country for robbery, house-breaking, pocket-picking, and horse-stealing, *all recommending qualifications in a Loyalist.*" Bergen and Orange county men were among those mountain gangs: William Stagg, Wiert Banta, David Rutan, Jacob Acker. And Tories all around them, Margaret knew, everyone knew, harbored them in their cellars in the day time: Jacobus Peek, Theunis Helm, Benjamin Demarest, John C. Haring, Isaac Mabie, too many to count.

*   *   *   *

Claudius Smith, the infamous leader of the gangs, was captured, tried, and hanged.

In revenge, the gangs went to the house of one John Clark. "It is about twelve o'clock," their leader shouted, "and by one o'clock, Clark, you shall be a dead man."

Afterward, his widow ran to Margaret's house. "They toyed with him for a while," she reported, weeping, "then took him out to the barn, and shot him through the breast. Then they drank a quantity of his rum, and after they had robbed a passerby of his cash, they went back to the mountains."

"Before they went, they handed me this paper and told me to make it known to one and all. But I do not know how to read," she added shamefacedly, drawing the paper from her pocket. She handed it to Johannes.

He took it to the candlelight. "A Warning to All Rebels," he read. "You are hereby forbid at your peril to hang no more friends to government as you did Claudius Smith. We are determined to hang six of you for one, for the blood of the innocent cries aloud for vengeance. There is companies of us, Indians as well as white men, and particularly numbers from New York that is resolved to be revenged on you for your cruelty and murders. We are loyal to our King. This is the first and we are determined to pursue it until the whole of you is massacred."

"I marvel at their reasoning," Margaret said. "*They* are the friends to government. *They* are the innocent. *They* are the loyal ones."

"It was Jacob Acker who enabled them. He has been engaged in assisting the enemy," John Haring said, when he learned of the case.

"Jacob Acker. And we counted him one of us!"

"I have learned he has given them all the information he was capable of to enable them to steal, plunder, and destroy property of those that were true to their country's independence and informed them where they might have an opportunity with safety to plunder and steal."

"You can trust no one," she said.

"And where is the Continental army while these atrocities are visited on the inhabitants of Orange and Bergen counties?" Johannes asked.

"They have a more important thing to do," said Haring. "To preserve themselves for greater battles yet to come, when the French finally decide to do what they have promised to do, come in on our side. I'm afraid it is left to an exhausted militia to defend their families and friends as best they can."

"At least the legislatures are making laws to deal with Tories," Johannes said. A commission for detecting and defeating their conspiracies had been established, Loyalists were deprived of the right to vote or hold office, they could be banished from the state of New York with little ado, and a commission was established to seize and confiscate Tory property, land, houses, slaves, livestock, and all personal effects. At once, fifty-nine New York Tories were convicted of treason and hanged. In all 1,500 estates were seized, hundreds of Tories banished. In New Jersey seventy-six estates were confiscated, the estates of Tory Ackermans, Blauvelts (Theunis and David), Hendricks, Bogerts, Vischers, Demarests, Harings (Peter T., John C., and Abraham), Leydeckers, Lents, Myers, Outwaters, Peeks, Smiths, van Buskirks (Abraham, Andrew, Cornelius, David, John Jacob, John, and Peter), van Horns, van Houtens, Zabriskies, and more.

✳   ✳   ✳   ✳

With the new laws in place, the winter was quiet, and Margaret was pleased that her son John took the opportunity to court Cathlyntie Mabie. They were married in the parsonage by *Dominie* Verbryck (the church still being used as a hospital for the sick and wounded) and acquired a simple house for themselves on the edge of the village Green. In back of their little house, John planted fruit trees and fashioned dome-shaped beehives out of straw for his bride. She was going into the honey business.

"I feel uneasy about their location," Margaret said to Johannes. "It is too exposed."

"Keep your own counsel," he advised. "Don't alarm them in their bliss."

"Yes," she said. "Besides, our own house was not too exposed, and look what happened to it." Still, in the spring of '79 when the raiders returned, she shivered for the couple's safety in that vulnerable spot on the edge of the Tappan Green. From Little Ferry on the Hackensack up though Teaneck, Paramus, English Neighborhood, Harringtown, and Tappan, and down through Closter and Hoboken, they raided and looted.

And one day, her fears were realized. They came without warning and cut down Cathlyntie Mabie's new little orchard and knocked over her beehives and stole the honey. They carried off her timber fences for their campfires. They torched the old stone barn and left the smoking ruins, laughing. Cathlyntie was as frightened and frantic as the bees that swarmed helplessly in her denuded orchard.

"The militia chased them," her cousin Abraham Blauvelt reported. "Nine of them put a party of about thirty men to flight, forcing them to drop their plunder and abandon one of their officers dead on the field. And Wiert Banta, so infamous for his complicated villainies, was shot through the knee requiring amputation. He will not be kidnapping and plundering the loyal subjects of the state of New Jersey again."

"Wiert Banta's father," Margaret said, "is uncle to the lieutenant in command of the militia, John Huyler."

"And so it goes."

That same Abraham Blauvelt called on Margaret to bring her some bad news, but before he could break it to her, she engaged him in her latest project: making a list of all the Patriot Blauvelts. Together, they could name more than fifty. "We must be the most numerous of all the Patriot families," she said with satisfaction.

After she had blotted the list and put it away for safekeeping, he told her what he had come to tell her: "Our friend Captain Jonathan Hopper of the Bergen County militia has had his throat cut by Tory raiders bent on stealing his horses."

She uttered a low moan. "Another senseless loss."

"He has been a good friend to both of us all our lives." They mourned together another senseless loss.

The fury of the Tory raids that spring caused Margaret to pen another letter to General Washington. "Those of our poor county and the county of Bergen are too weak and worn down with service and suffering to form an adequate defense. We beg Your Excellency for the help of the Army."

It was that persistent woman of Tappan again. He recognized her name, of course, her good penmanship. He was even sure now that she was the one he had seen in a crowd one day, on Broadway, near Hull's Tavern. But how could he be sure of such a thing? How could he put together a face in a crowd and this Dutch writing woman of Tappan? It was a mystery. But he well remembered that woman, whoever she was, who had willed him with her fierce eyes not to disappoint her, not to disappoint the country. As if he had a choice! He would not disappoint her or the country if his life depended on it, and it did, even though he could not help her or any of her sisters in their current plight.

"Madam," he wrote back, "The Army at Paramus and Kings Ferry is too remote to help you. They would be wasted in your troubled territory. I regret that I cannot distress the posts in order to cover your neighborhood."

She was crushed. She read it over and over again. "How shall we survive the chaos?" she cried aloud. "How shall we survive?" At last she put it away, with the others.

Bergen and Orange counties were now so troubled that its delegates to the Continental Congress feared to come home; in fact, most of them had no homes to return to. All lay in ruins.

✳   ✳   ✳   ✳

"I am going mad," Margaret said, in May. "I must get away from the bedlam of this household. I cannot think!"

"Where could you possibly go?"

"I shall go to Closter to visit Margrietie Brinckerhoff," she said. "She has no children in her house. It will be quiet and peaceful there. I shall stay a week and come home much refreshed."

"Go," he said reluctantly, "but be careful, my love. Take the rapier. And take Sam."

Two days later, on a beautiful Sabbath morning, as Margrietie Brinckerhoff and her household and her guest Margaret Blauvelt were preparing to go to church, a party of van Buskirk's men made their way up the Hudson to the Closter Dock and sneaked along the wooded Closter Dock Road until they reached the village, which the Tory papers had described as "abounding with many violent rebels and persecutors of loyal subjects where it was publicly posted that no quarter shall be given to the enemy."

The women watched in horror as the men seized Margrietie's husband Samuel Demarest and hog tied him, set the house, barn, wagon house, corncrib, and hay barrack on fire, wounded their son Hendrick, and killed their son Cornelius right before the women's eyes. The marauders carted Samuel and four neighbors off to New York to prison, and Margaret and Margrietie and the wives and daughters of the other abducted men, sobbing and keening, took up shovels and dug a grave with their own hands and buried Cornelius in it. Hendrick was alive only because his mother had thrown herself on his body when he fell of his wound.

The same morning, in nearby Schraalenburg, the militia encountered another party of Tories and took back ninety head of stolen cattle and a body of runaway slaves. In turn, the Tories burned three Patriot farmhouses to the west of Closter, all genteelly furnished, and four massive Dutch barns. John Haring wrote to George Washington to inform him: "Mr. Douwe Tallman, who was stabbed by the Tories on Sunday morning, died of his wounds on Tuesday," he wrote. "He wanted by a few weeks of being ninety years." It was said that the old man was bayoneted because he would not tell where he had buried his money and plate.

"Can it get any worse?" Margaret cried.

*   *   *   *

It got worse. In the middle of May when the orchards bloomed and apple blossoms and lilacs perfumed the air and baby birds twittered in their nests, they came again, Sir Henry Clinton's troops, a thousand strong from three directions. They moved through Closter, they crossed the Hudson from the former Fort Washington to the former Fort Lee, and van Buskirk's men moved up from Paulus Hook. In three prongs, they marched on Liberty Pole and Little Ferry, Hackensack, and New Bridge and Paramus. All along the way, they plundered farms and houses and terrorized the inhabitants.

Margaret read aloud to her household a note from a friend in New Bridge whose house had escaped the brutalities: "Their incursion was marked with desolation and unprovoked cruel murders. Not a house belonging to a Patriot escaped, excepting our own, praise God. Two negro women who were endeavoring to drive off some cattle belonging to their masters were murdered. The raiders breathed fire and sword and desolation, and those whom an ungovernable and rapacious soldiery have already plundered, they have utterly destroyed."

They learned from the papers that the same troops set fire to and destroyed a Presbyterian church and burnt every dwelling house and barn in its vicinity, including the house of the minister of that church, the Rev. Mr. James Caldwell, who was away from home. A soldier went up to this house, where in the front room Mrs. Caldwell, surrounded by her eight small helpless children, was nursing her infant. He put his gun to the window and calmly shot the lady through the lungs.

Then, with the children screaming in fear in the dooryard, he ordered a hole dug and her body thrown into it. And then he ordered the house to be set on fire and everything in it.

"This melancholy affair has had the effect of raising the resentment of the whole country to the highest pitch," John Haring stormed. "The people are ready to swear an everlasting enmity to the very name of a Briton. So far is this cruelty and devastation from terrifying them to submission, it rouses the most timid to feats of desperate heroism."

"The British are digging their own grave," Margaret said. "They will fail. They are too evil for God to allow them to succeed."

In the morning of the following day, as quickly as they had come they disappeared back to Hobuck Ferry and over the river to New York, and their women with them, pots and pans tied around their waists, pushing carts loaded with laundry and babies too.

But they returned. That summer, British men-of-war again occupied the Tappan Zee, as they did every summer. A raiding party landed at the Slote, where the spar *kill* emptied into the Hudson, and burned several barns to the ground. And as they did every summer the militia patrolled the shores by day and slept uneasily in houses and barns on the banks of the river by night.

Now spies behind the enemy lines reported that the British planned to obliterate the blockhouse at Stony Point, the southern gateway to the Highlands, surrounding it with a thousand men, as they had Fort Montgomery. But the

Americans under General Anthony Wayne destroyed the blockhouse first, and then marched into the Highlands from whose peaks they were able to look down upon four companies of the British 17th Regiment, who along with Loyalist troops and a detachment of Royal Artillery, occupied the ruins for six weeks. The Americans watched from above as the British cleared the woods, felling a thousand trees to build abatis to hide behind, the sharp branches pointed outward in every direction at their mortal enemy.

From the heights, they watched and waited, until General Washington ordered Wayne to attack. When the order came, on the night of July 15, 1779, as No-Flint Gray had done, Wayne ordered his men to remove the flints from their muskets.

His light infantry, elite troops drilled in the use of the bayonet, first killing every dog they could find along the route they would take, marched 1,350 strong in deepest quiet to the position. Then, on arrival at their destination, shouting imprecations, the troops charged up the hill to the blockhouse in the dead of night, overrunning it in thirty minutes.

After the event, it was reported that, on orders from His Excellency to be humane, the Americans at Stony Point under Mad Anthony Wayne displayed a quality of mercy and generosity unique in the war, if not in history. They did not use their bayonets. They took 500 prisoners and let the rest escape.

Wayne's men occupied the ruins, and Patriots up and down the Hudson Valley cheered and toasted Mad Anthony, the hero of the day.

A month later, the Americans brought off another glorious exploit when, with 600 men, Major Harry "Light-Horse" Lee, with bayonets drawn, captured the entire British garrison of 250 men at Paulus Hook, a peninsula that with the tide at flow became an island even as the men attacked. "They plunged through swamps deep in muck," John Haring reported to the Tappan people. "They waded through creeks and canals, and splashed across the moat, pushed through the abatis, stormed the parapet, and took the works. They pulled down the British flag and captured all the officers and men in the blockhouse. The Americans killed or wounded fifty and took 158 prisoners. The British were taken by such surprise that they did not get off even one round of artillery."

The people cheered and whistled, when they heard, and stamped their feet and clapped. "We are winning! We are winning!" they shouted.

"Not yet, but I believe winning is possible," said Haring cautiously. "But it will not be smooth sailing. The Loyalists are fierce and cruel. As Lee's men returned to their camp at Liberty Pole, van Buskirk's Greencoats attacked. Lee's troops returned the fire, then fled to safety at New Bridge, taking their prisoners with them."

Major Lee described his ordeal to General Washington, and it was soon made known far and wide. Margaret read the account of it in the papers to her household: "Major Lee, oppressed by every possible misfortune, at the head of troops worn down by a rapid march of thirty miles, through mountains, swamps and deep morasses, executed the impossible. Without the least refreshment during the whole march, ammunition destroyed, encumbered with prisoners, and a retreat of fourteen miles to make good, on a route admissible of interception at several points by a march of two, three or four miles, one body moving in his rear and another well advanced on his right, a retreat impossible to his left. Under all these distressing circumstances, he testified to his commander in chief that his sole dependence was in the persevering gallantry of the officers and the obstinate courage of the troops."

The women moaned and wept. "It is so hard for the men. It is so hard for us. How can we bear it much longer?"

"Don't weep and fret," said Margaret. "We should cheer for his feat, taking a British fort within earshot of British headquarters in Manhattan."

And indeed, his feat raised Patriot morale and was ballyhooed as one of those turning points of the war.

"Turning point," said Margaret disgustedly. "This war never seems to turn for good to its prayed-for end. We are on a seesaw. The ups and downs make me feel dizzy and ill."

"Well," said John Haring, "at least these two successes on the part of the Americans have discouraged Sir Henry Clinton from any further action this summer. He has consoled himself by ordering the court martial of the commander of the fort at Paulus Hook responsible for the debacle."

Still, the summer was a disaster for the inhabitants of the area, for now the Continental army moved in again, General Wayne camping to the north at Haverstraw, General Woodford to the northwest at Kakiat, Lord Stirling to the south at Paramus and New Bridge. And it was hungry. It had to be fed. Its horses had to be fed.

The people were helpless to resist as together the various regiments proceeded to forage all the way south to Paulus Hook, requisitioning a hundred wagons and collecting more than a hundred head of fat cattle and as much grain as they needed. They stripped the inhabitants of their corn, milk, ducks, chickens, sheep, pigs, took anything they wanted, entitled to it. The people were in despair, hungry themselves. Margaret noticed that they were getting thinner. It struck her, too, that her teeming household looked not only thin but also worn and shabby, the women's clothes wearing out, the children bursting out of their shifts and shirts. When will it end? she wrote in her diary. How are we to get through another winter?

And then the winter set in, the coldest, bitterest winter in recorded history, colder even than 1741, that winter when Margaret was a girl, the winter before the slave conspiracy trials. Snow fell endlessly, in storm after fierce storm, until the surface of the earth was buried six feet under it. The shallow Hackensack River froze solid. The Hudson River froze from shore to shore. The ice in the upper bay of New York harbor was eleven feet deep, so solid that battalions and their artillery could march back and forth over it. Water froze in wells; the people had to melt snow over fire for drinking water. The British cut down the trees in the city streets for fuel and hacked ships apart to burn. Sentries froze to death in their sentry boxes. Margaret mourned her best woolen petticoats, stuffed into the privy by the Greencoats. She had acquired replacements, though not nearly so good or so warm as the ones she remembered.

And yet even the winter was not the worst. The worst came in March of 1780 with news from spies that a raid on Hackensack was imminent. Lt. Colonel Richard Varick, two justices of the peace, two freeholders, the sheriff, an adjutant, and four militia captains wrote a hurried appeal to General Washington: "We, the subscribers, magistrates, sheriff and officers of militia residing at Hackensack and vicinity make application to you for a detachment or party from your command to assist in protecting us and our neighbors, the well-affected inhabitants to the American cause, against the incursions and depredations of small parties of the enemy and their vile abettors. We are credibly informed that the enemy will make an attack and incursion on the inhabitants of Hackensack within five days. The well-affected inhabitants, though willing to risk their persons in defense of their property, are too few in number for the purpose of repelling the enemy or keeping up continual guards and scouts for their security."

John Haring delivered it to Headquarters.

"Unfortunately, the appeal is too late," said General Greene. "Last night 300 British Regulars crossed the Hudson and landed at Weehawken. They marched to Hackensack, burned the courthouse and the houses of two Patriots to the ground, broke the doors and windows of every house they passed, took everything of value that they wanted. *Dominie* Romeyn saved his life by secreting himself behind the chimney of the house where he was staying and lying quietly on the ceiling beams until it was over."

The commander in chief stood at a window, staring bleakly into the dooryard of the farmhouse he had commandeered. "Few understand what a predicament we are in," he said, without turning from the window. "Congress especially does not understand it. Our resources are stretched to the limit. Our spirits are low. The people are weary to death of it all."

"We are indeed weary to death of it all," said Margaret, when Haring stopped by her house that night. "How much more can we bear?"

"They took prisoner fifty or sixty men," Haring said. "I regret to tell you, Margaret, that among them was your cousin, Captain Abraham A. Haring."

"He is cousin to all of us," Johannes said.

"And a good friend," said Haring.

"His wife, Margrietie Blauvelt, is also our cousin," said Margaret. "She is soon expecting a child, their first."

Two weeks after the Captain's capture, his wife gave birth to a son, and a week after the birth, on a Sunday in April, Margaret went to New York City to look for the Captain in the Sugar House Prison, for his wife was despondent.

"He is not here. He has been transferred to a prison ship," said his orderly, a Sergeant James Riker, also an inmate. "He has been taken to the *Scorpion.*"

Margaret gasped. "That means he is a dead man, or soon to be," she said. The *Scorpion* was an aging, dismasted man-of-war in Wallabout Bay, off the Brooklyn shore. If the prisons on Manhattan Island were loathsome hellholes, the dozens of gruesome floating jails in the bays and bights around Brooklyn were even worse. On the *Jersey*, the most notorious of them all, the 1,200 men on board were half-starved, beaten, and chained in their own excrement. On the impossibly crowded, vermin-infested decks, the prisoners were exposed to the elements and given rotten food to eat. (One survivor reported dining on the head of a sheep with the horns and wool still thereon.) All were exposed to lice, rampant camp fever, dysentery, yellow fever, and small pox.

"They die like flies in the ships," said Riker. "Whereupon their bodies are piled up on the shore until a large enough number make up a cart load. Then the carts are driven out to shallow ditches, where the corpses are tumbled in together and covered with a little dirt."

Or, if this was too much trouble, she learned, the corpses were simply tossed overboard or buried on the shore, where the tides and the surf soon washed the rotting, bloated forms to the surface. Survivors, if they were so fortunate, were no more than skeletons upon their release.

"Don't they know that this cruel and inhumane treatment makes Americans hate the British with such fury that their hatred assures an eventual American victory?" Margaret said on her return home.

She could not bring herself to tell the Captain's anxious wife the truth about her husband, but said rather that he was as well and cheerful as could be expected under the circumstances and was hoping to be exchanged for a British prisoner before too long. The poor woman, soon to be widowed, brightened with relief. "Thank you, dear Margaret, for this good news," she said. "You are so kind."

*   *   *   *

On her way out of the city that day, Margaret passed a group of women, followers of the British army, poor souls who were forced to tag along with their husbands, receiving food and protection in return for cooking, sewing, washing clothes, nursing the wounded, foraging for supplies, while caring for their own children to boot. Or in some cases it was not their husbands they followed, for some of them were indigents who had no husband or anyone to care for them, and so they attached themselves to the army as it moved, hoping for crumbs in return for their services. The authorities disapproved, but what could they do? The women and children were helpless.

One of these sorry homeless women looked at her curiously as she passed. "Margaret?" she called out. "Is it you?"

Margaret stopped and stared at the woman. She was black with dirt, and her clothing hung about her in filthy rags. Pots and pans dangled from her waist, and her unkempt hair straggled out of a too-small bonnet. "Could it be Eliza?" she asked.

"The same," said Eliza, through clenched lips. Her teeth were no more.

She had returned from wherever she had gone, but not on the arm of a handsome officer, and certainly not in brocade and silk.

They stared at each other. Margaret was conscious of her own neat and clean appearance. She wore a "new" dress, a cast-off found in a second-hand shop, a red printed shalloon, chosen this day because she thought its bright color would cheer the prisoners, and a neat white bonnet. "Dear Eliza," she said finally. "What happened to you?"

Eliza's eyes filled at first with anger and then sadness. "I have not been lucky," she said. "Men have not treated me well."

"Starting with your father," Margaret murmured, remembering that violent and possessive German.

"Is he alive? Is my mother alive?" Eliza asked. "No, they couldn't be, could they?"

"Neither one," said Margaret. "They died years ago, in Tappan."

"I would like to go there," Eliza said wistfully. "I would like to live in Tappan again. But I have no means to provide for myself, except this." She gestured toward the baggage wagons in the distance, where the camp-following women were required to keep themselves, out of sight of the officers, who found them an embarrassment and a nuisance. "I am too old and broken to work."

Margaret thought of their school days together forty years before, in the '30s, in a time when their little world was innocent and peaceful and they had thought it would always be so. They had had high hopes for themselves. She felt old and broken, too. "Who would have thought it would come to this?" she said.

"You seem to have done well enough for yourself."

"You have no idea. I cannot describe to you the misery that has descended upon Tappan since you last saw it," she said. "But if you will, you are welcome to come home with me. We will make room for you. Leave the pots and pans here for someone else."

"I can't pay you," said Eliza.

"You can help me in the house. We are so many these days. There is no end to the work. All the strong slaves have run away."

"I am not strong," Eliza said.

"You are strong enough for all practical purposes," Margaret said.

When they got to Tappan, Bett took one look at her and rushed to the corner of the *keuken* where they bathed, filled the wooden tub with hot water, and helped Eliza out of her filthy clothes, which Margaret gathered and threw on the rubbish heap. Bett doused Eliza's head with strong-smelling rosin and wrapped her hair in a towel to smother the lice. Naked, Eliza lowered her body, aged and misshapen, into the water and washed herself. The water was soon filthy. Bett emptied the tub and filled it again.

When she was clean, Margaret gave her a linen shift to wear and a cotton gown, with a checkered petticoat and a clean apron and set before her a bowl of cornmeal mush and milk. "You said when I left for England that you wished we would always be friends, Little One," Eliza said. "You are more than a friend. You are a saint."

"I am no saint," Margaret said ruefully. "I expect you to be a great help to me in the house, even if all you can do is keep a dozen children out from under my feet."

CHAPTER 20

▼

TREASON

But Eliza was right. She was no help at all to Margaret. No more the feisty woman who had set out for London to seek her fortune, she seemed to be lost in a daze, sat all day on a bench on the *stoep* gazing to the blue hills to the east, broken in body and spirit. Margaret wondered if she was losing her mind.

"What are you thinking of?" she asked her softly, sitting beside her on the bench.

"I am thinking of the cruelty of man to man," Eliza said after a long pause. "I am thinking of this cruel war."

"Yes, cruel is the word for it. You see what they've done to my house," Margaret said. "And to all the houses and barns of our friends and relations. We are forced to live not much better than the animals. No glass in the windows, no good furniture, everything gone or ruined."

"It's better than a baggage wagon," said Eliza. "Cruel enemy. Cruel war."

Johannes cantered up the lane from the village, dismounting just in time to hear this. "Cruel war indeed," he said. "And it seems that of British cruelty there is no end. There has been a dreadful raid on Hopperstown. I have met your cousin in the village, Margaret. He was at Hopperstown with the militia. He is following me with the details."

Soon down the lane in his blue rifle frock galloped her cousin Colonel Abraham Blauvelt. They sat under the grape arbor on as fine a morning as there ever was and heard the story. "At sunrise this very morning, Cornet George Spencer of the Queen's Rangers and twelve of his men galloped through Hopperstown to the headquarters of Major Thomas Byles of the 3rd Pennsylvania Regiment. It was a sturdy stone house," he reported breathlessly.

"The servants of Major Byles and a few of the officers under his command slept in a wooden house nearby. At the sound of the galloping horsemen, the servants woke frightened from their sleep and began to fire from the windows of the house on the British. Spencer ordered six or eight of his men to dismount and fire into the windows of the stone house at random, where his spies had informed him Byles and some of his officers slept, while the rest of his men, screaming imprecations, broke down the door of the wooden house. The terrorized servants within came out with their hands up.

"When the officers in the stone house did not surrender, Spencer ordered his men to break down the door. This proved impossible, so Spencer ordered his men to bring fire from the now-emptied wooden house and set the cedar-shingled roof of the stone house on fire, forcing Major Byles and his officers to abandon the building, which was soon engulfed in flames, with the distraught officers in their nightclothes gazing at it from the yard. Spencer offered Major Byles and his officers good usage if they would surrender.

"He also advised them that 500 infantry composed of Hessians and Green-coats and a hundred cavalry were on the way. Judging that it was in vain to attempt a further defense against so large a force and judging it impossible to escape, Major Byles reluctantly surrendered, assuming the promise of good usage to him and his men. Major Byles failed, however, to present the hilt of his sword in front when surrendering, as was customary, the cornet said later. So he gave his men the order to shoot. They shot him through the breast. He is expected to die of his wounds."

"I am aghast," said Johannes. "He offered him good usage."

"What were our other losses?" she asked.

"Besides Major Byles, the Americans lost in killed, wounded, and captured were two captains, four lieutenants, and about forty rank and file. Three militia-men were wounded (the militia having immediately turned out at the sound of the guns). I was fortunate. They fired at me, but missed. The British lost thirty in killed, wounded, and captured, for indeed the Hessian infantry and van Buskirk's cavalry did arrive as promised to swell the ranks of Spencer's dozen Rangers. And of course the survivors made it their business to loot and burn the houses and barns of the terrorized inhabitants of the village. Then they withdrew to the Hudson.

"We harried them all the way to Fort Lee, causing them to abandon much of their loot along the sides of the road and to allow their prisoners to escape. At the Fort, our men, screaming curses and imprecations, pursued the fleeing troops down the Palisades to the river where we took back four wagons and sixteen horses, while the British in panic leaped onto their waiting vessels."

"Why did the British choose Hopperstown? It is such an innocuous place," Margaret wondered.

"Because," he said, "they suspected that the Continental army stores its ammunition in Hopperstown cellars." When Margaret heard this, she relived the memories of the night when they had come to her house and wrecked it and made off with the casks of ammunition hidden in her cellar, the night the boy had died before her eyes. She was overcome with sadness and buried her face in her hands to hide her tears.

"This is not all," Abraham continued. "Soon others came and looted and plundered and then burned to the ground the house and barn of Major John Goetschius."

"No!" she moaned. Goetschius was a favorite of hers among his generation, the son of a fiercely patriotic *dominie* in the Reformed church, just a few years older than her own eldest son.

"He is considered by some in a position to judge to be the most active and spirited officer on the continent, bar none," said Johannes. "At least his life was spared."

"Yes," said Abraham. "He was fortunate to be away from home at the time."

"And then?"

"And then, the terrorists continued on their merry way to Hendrick Kuyper's house, destroyed the dwelling house, two barns, a cow shed, a brewery, took away a negro man, two negro women, and three negro children, destroyed Kuyper's fences and made off with a good periauger, wagons, sleighs, a riding chair, horses, cattle, sheep, Bibles, linen, silver, furniture, and money."

There was no end to it. In June, Abraham and another cousin, James Blauvelt, came to tell of more savagery. "This day, the British and their loyalist friends burned the house and barn of Jacob Ferdon, the house of David Banta, the house of David S. Demarest, the house and barn of David B. Demarest, the house and barns of Derrick Banta, John Banta's farmhouse and outbuildings, and robbed and plundered Abraham Vanderbeek and family of all they possessed. Then in one final act of evil, they burned the whole town of Schraalenburgh and left it a heap of rubbish, with a party of runaway negroes abetting the destruction."

*   *   *   *

She stood up in the church that Sunday. "To defend the people of Bergen and Orange counties are some mere seventy-five militiamen," she declared, "while the British, 200 strong, are operating out of a said-to-be impregnable blockhouse at Bull's Ferry, marauding, plundering, burning houses and barns at will. And their men-of-war cruise the river looking for suitable landing spots to do more of the same. *What are we to do?*"

"Attack the blockhouse," men shouted.

John Haring stood. "That blockhouse is garrisoned by wretched banditti and horse thieves. It is where they store the booty of the Tory raiders. I shall bring up the matter with General Wayne," he said.

"Attack it," shouted the people. "Urge him to attack it."

Thus it came about that General Anthony Wayne sought and received General Washington's approval to attack the Bull's Ferry blockhouse, and this he undertook to do with two brigades and a regiment of dragoons, joined by the local militia under the valiant Major Goetschius.

Margaret's son Isaac was among them. "A thousand troops in all, we crept through the woods during the whole of a night," he reported, when it was over. "We seized the landings on the Hudson beneath the Palisades with all the British boats at their moorings, and in the morning we had the blockhouse surrounded. But we could not take it. It was impregnable indeed. Fearing reinforcements from the British encamped on the east shore of the Hudson, we burned the British boats at anchor and retreated, driving the local cattle lowing and bleating before us, with British soldiers and local Tories harrying us all the way to New Bridge."

Major John André, Sir Henry Clinton's aide and chief intelligence officer, now penned a mock-heroic ballad about the aborted raid and published it in Rivington's *Gazette*. Deriding "Mad" Anthony Wayne, the hero of the Battle of Stony Point, as a rustic "warrior drover" herding bleating cattle through the countryside, the ballad mocked not only him but the "many heroes brave and bold from New Bridge and Tappan" who retreated with him.

"He was Captain John André the night of the massacre," Johannes recalled.

Margaret, furious that her brave and bold friends and relations, so loyal to the cause, were treated with such derision, wrote again to General Washington to bring their plight to his attention: "The well-affected inhabitants are perfectly worn down with a long series of incessant watchings and fatigues," she pleaded.

"The inhabitants of this county, already plundered, diffused and worn out, and who for their spirit of perseverance deserve a better fate, must unless speedily saved, soon fall a sacrifice to enemy violence." This time, it was a cry for help that did not go unheard.

He sighed. It was that persistent Dutch woman of Tappan again. He conjured up her face, her comely face, on which he had read all the complicated feelings he well knew not just she but all the people on his side had for him: their trust, their loyalty, their approval, their love, and more, their fervent belief in their liberties that he had sworn to defend, their determination that he should not disappoint them. He would not, if he had to die doing it.

But he hadn't the time to respond to her every missive. She must have nothing better to do than write letters, he thought to himself. "To this request, in lieu of writing, I shall act, and the message will be loud and clear," he said to his aide Joseph Reed. "The people of that place have suffered enough. I shall order Generals Wayne and Erskine to find a site on the Hudson River between Closter and Sneden's Landing for a blockhouse to match the Bull's Ferry blockhouse, one with equally impregnable stone walls two feet thick."

"Sir!" said Reed.

"It will serve as living quarters for the officers of a garrison of about seventy-five Continentals that will encamp around it for the purpose of watching the movements of the enemy's forces and spying on British headquarters in the city. In the case of an attack," he went on, "the building is to be designed large enough for all seventy-five men to crowd in with the officers."

"Sir!"

"Below the blockhouse, a separate Water Guard will harass British shipping on the Hudson, with two cannon on the brink of the hill trained on the river."

"Yes, Sir!"

On horseback, galloping from place to place, the two generals considered three possible sites for the blockhouse. They settled on Sneden's Landing.

When they learned of the possibility of such a fortress in their midst, the people marveled. It was the wonder of the neighborhoods. "In four years, it is the first sign from the Continental army that we matter," said Johannes.

"Indeed, the first sign that we exist, except to forage upon, as it passes to and fro," she said.

Even greater was the wonder when, on August 8, 1780, His Excellency himself and the main body of his army decided to encamp at Tappan, to stay for fifteen days, it was rumored. Margaret's first thought was of her appearance, and her first impulse to find a looking glass to see what she looked like after living for four years under the utmost strain and duress. Her glass (that pride and joy she had acquired in happier days) had disappeared in the raid on her house.

"Mrs. Hart is said to have a looking glass," said Helena Westervelt. Mrs. Hart was a Tory woman living in the neighborhood, and thought to be a spy for the British. Margaret swallowed her pride and drove her wagon over to the woman's house.

Mrs. Hart would have liked to slam the door on her visitor, for Margaret Blauvelt's activities on behalf of the rebels was well known, but she bit her pride: the rebels, after all, were camped just over the brow of the hill. She brought the looking glass from her house and handed it to Margaret.

Margaret stared at herself in disbelief. "Good grief," she murmured. Her face was thin and gaunt, her forehead plowed with furrows. Her blond hair had gone white. This she had known, because she could see it when she brushed it. But it had grown long and lank, too, since the loss of her scissors in the raid, too long to pile up on her head, as she used to. It hung about her face in stringy locks. It was her face, though, that was the shock. Not only thin and gaunt, her skin had cracked into a mass of tiny fine lines, as if the mirror had cracked and crazed and reflected itself upon her. But it had not. The glass was as good as new. Even more alarming, her very expression was altered and almost unrecognizable. She appeared tense and worn and worried, when she had once looked … expectant. Expectant that a pleasant life lay before her, that the war would be brief, that the war would be won, that the war would make them free.

She was like Eliza, old. "I'm an old woman," she said wonderingly. She was fifty-five.

"Your hair needs cutting," said the Tory woman, studying her.

"I have no scissors," Margaret said.

"Nor have I."

They looked at each other. "Come back tomorrow," said Mrs. Hart.

The next day, Margaret returned with her hairbrush. And Mrs. Hart produced a pair of shears that looked capable of cutting through tanned hide.

Well away from the house, behind the barn, where the hair would be found by the birds and mice for their nests, Mrs. Hart brushed Margaret's hair and cut it carefully with her mighty shears. "I used to wear it up, held with a tortoise-shell comb," said Margaret. "I lost it in a raid on my house. It belonged to my husband's great-grandmother. I wore it piled up on the top of my head, with the comb in it."

(*Her stately head*, the Tory woman thought, *her slender figure*, though she would not go so far as to compliment her, or tell her that it was said all about that she had once been as striking a woman as there was to be seen in the counties of Orange and Bergen.) "I have such a comb," she said. "It might be the same comb."

"Did you acquire it illicitly?" Margaret asked.

"My husband acquired it in a raid on a house," she said.

"What have we come to, plundering each other?" said Margaret. "What will the Lord make us pay for it?"

"You can have the comb," said Mrs. Hart curtly. "It may well be yours, for all I know."

When she was finished cutting, they walked back to the house. The woman went in and soon came out with the comb. One of the teeth was broken. "But it is my comb," Margaret said. "My own comb. I am glad to have it back. Thank you." She pulled her hair back from her face and secured it on top of her head with the comb.

"The back needs a ribbon," said the Tory woman. She produced one from the pocket around her waist and with it tied Margaret's hair in a neat queue at the nape of her neck.

"You have your teeth," she said wistfully. "And they are white." Hers were black, those she still possessed.

"I never smoked a pipe," Margaret said. It was family wisdom, passed down from Grietje Cosyns and Marytie her daughter-in-law, and her daughter-in-law Aeltie, that pipe smoking disfigured a woman, caused her teeth to blacken and fall out.

"I never did either," said the Tory woman. "They turned black anyway."

Margaret wanted to pay her for the ribbon and offered her a sixpence. But the Tory woman would not take it. One never knew, she reasoned to herself, when one might need a friend in the rebel camp. Especially these days.

*　　　*　　　*　　　*

In Tappan, His Excellency made his headquarters in Grietje Cosyns' house, built in 1700 by her third husband, Daniel De Clarke.

Soon after settling in, on a bright August's day, he mounted his tall white charger Nelson and galloped over to inspect the site for the blockhouse. A hugely excited retinue of townspeople followed on horseback, on foot, in carts, and in wagons. Margaret and as many of her household as could fit in the wagon were among them, including Margaret's daughter-in-law Cathlyntie Mabie, pregnant with her first child. Even Eliza had bestirred herself to see him.

"It is too thrilling for words to be in his presence," Rachel whispered.

"I can hardly bear it," Margaret said. "My heart is beating fit to burst."

Hearts everywhere were suffused with love and admiration for him, overcome with gratitude. Hearts felt as if they would fairly explode with the joy and pride of him. Eyes filled with tears at the sight of his majestic form and his elegant equipage, at the thought of the sacrifices he had made and would continue to make for their sorrowing selves, their beleaguered country. He had refused a salary from the Congress, worked for nothing in his fierce resolve to free them from their British masters. He had not had a single day of rest in two years. He had not seen his beloved Mount Vernon in four years.

He cantered ahead of the crowd, pleased with the level roads leading to the site, and with the eminences on the north and south sides of the road. "Perfect for gun batteries," he said, pointing with his sword. He was pleased, too, with the rising ground overlooking the Hudson River to the east and the landscapes to the south, north, and west, suitable for cannon commanding all the country, as General Wayne had promised. "The site is acceptable in every detail," he said to Wayne, beside him. "Start digging the foundations at once."

And then he wheeled about on his great steed, glancing over the pursuing crowd, for he assumed she was there. And at once he saw her, standing up in her wagon, her eyes piercing him. Still the same, he thought, after all these years. A good-looking woman. Yet altered too, her face thinner than he remembered, aged by misfortune and worry and sorrow, her clothing unmodish and tattered, like all of theirs. It was a terrible thing, this war he had to fight.

He lifted his hat and inclined his head to her. Without taking her eyes off his face, she inclined her head to him in return and made an awkward sort of curtsey. Proud Dutch woman not used to bending her knee, he thought. But her eyes filled with tears, he saw, and her lips trembled.

She turned away from him to the woman at her side. Her body shivered and shook with emotion suddenly released, and she fell on the woman's neck. "When will it end?" she sobbed. "When will we be free? How long must we suffer?"

Many broke down with her, including Rachel, and bystanders said afterward that his eyes filled with tears, too, as he lifted his tricorn to all of them and galloped away on further inspections.

*   *   *   *

His army occupied the country for miles around that hot August. General Lafayette with his light infantry camped on the west bank of the Hackensack. Ten regiments from Massachusetts, New York, New Jersey, Pennsylvania, and Connecticut circled the village of Tappan on the east all the way to the Slote, under Generals Hand, Poor, McDougall, Howe, Greene, Lord Stirling, St. Clair, Parsons, and von Steuben.

And one day, on his bay mare, dapper blue-coated Benedict Arnold, Washington's trusted general, the hero of Fort Schuyler and the Battle of Saratoga, and the late commandant of the city of Philadelphia, passed through the village on his way to take command of West Point. The people poured out to hail him for his spectacular defeat of Burgoyne at Saratoga, the victory that had made France sit up and listen—and decide that it would be in its best interests for it to throw its support to the Americans, although it had not yet made good on that promise. All knew he was one of Washington's bravest and favorite and most trusted generals, "judicious, of great activity, enterprise and perseverance," His Excellency had written to the Continental Congress in a fruitless attempt to get that body to honor Arnold.

For the acclaim was not unreserved. All knew also that, in the spring just passed, the Congress had court-martialed Benedict Arnold, and George Washington had had to reprimand him for "reprehensible, imprudent and improper behavior" having to do with certain business dealings undertaken to ease his financial problems. No one knew, though, until the summer gave way to autumn, how embittered this fierce, impetuous, and temperamental favorite was over his insulting treatment by the Congress and the humiliating public reprimand by his commander in chief.

*   *   *   *

While the blockhouse was under construction, His Excellency ordered the Bergen County militia to patrol the shores of the Hudson. Margaret's cousin Abraham Blauvelt told of how the Great Man himself galloped up to them at the site of the construction and commanded them to be diligent and watchful and promised he would send a company of his regular troops to reinforce them, which promise he kept. Her cousin Harman Blauvelt of the Tappan militia and her son-in-law Cornelius Blauvelt soon drilled on the Tappan Green under the direction of Baron von Steuben himself.

There was constant commotion, but at least not the stench of the British. His Excellency was particular about his troops' sanitary arrangements. But there was plundering again. His men were hungry too. "You will make the forage as extensive as possible in the articles of hay and grain," he ordered, "as well as in cattle, hogs, and sheep fit for slaughter, and horses fit for the use of the Army."

John Haring waited upon him in the familiar house of his great-grandmother, where he worked at his field desk in the *groote kamer*. "The people are being brought to a starving condition by the Army's robbing them of their cattle, sheep, hogs, and fowl, and almost all of their corn, potatoes, and other vegetables," he said.

"Such are the necessities of an Army." His voice was grim.

Haring pressed on. "The Continentals in a violent manner abuse the well-affected, run about with clubs and bayonets upon pikes as bad as our enemies ever have done and steal their household property."

Washington flushed in anger and ordered his officers to punish the offenders and restore the looted goods. Comestibles were one thing. Household goods an entirely unmilitary other. One soldier was hanged on the spot for his robbing rascality. Another villain was ordered shot to death. Two soldiers received a hundred lashes for robbing a widow. Four more soldiers were hanged for robbery, and at last the desired effect was achieved. The people breathed a little easier.

Two weeks later, as suddenly as he had come, the Great Chief departed Tappan, with the army. By the time they left, not only Cathlyntie Mabie's bees and honey were gone, gone too, and everyone else's as well, were her cows, her sheep and hogs, chickens and ducks, her stores of corn and grain, her fields of fragrant buckwheat. Even her new pewter spoons were gone. She had melted them down for musket balls for her soldier husband. Their first child was due in a month.

The army moved down into Bergen County, where His Excellency made his headquarters in the fine Dey mansion, and where, it was rumored, he was laying his plans to attack Manhattan Island. General Nathaniel Greene stayed behind in Tappan to supervise the final phases of the blockhouse construction.

All of Tappan and the neighboring villages were astir with excitement at the rumors of the attack on New York, especially when the Minister of France, incognito, paid a surprise visit to view the works, on his way to Rhode Island to inspect the French army encamped there and the French fleet biding its time off Newport.

Margaret rejoiced. "It is a sign," she said, "another proof that the French are finally serious, are finally coming to help us win the war!"

He was elated, too. "Finally," he said to his aide Joseph Reed. "The flighty, fickle French seem to have finally decided to join us, to unite their forces with ours in an attack on New York City that will send the enemy packing back to Britain."

This did not happen. On the 18th of September, General Washington left his army on the Hackensack and went to Hartford for a conference with the Count de Rochambeau, commander general of the French army, and Admiral de Grasse in command of the French navy, both dillydallying at Newport. Between the two Frenchmen, the idea was to determine what action to take against the British forays into the South, and what actions to *pretend* to be interested in taking, to appease George Washington's ambitions.

It was later said to be one of those many turning points of the war that Washington left Hartford on the 23rd, as planned, to confer with Benedict Arnold at Colonel Beverly Robinson's lonely mansion on the east bank of the Hudson, where Arnold had made his headquarters. Indeed, it was widely agreed to have been a Providential happening that he arrived there within one half-hour of the news of the arrest of Sir Henry Clinton's chief intelligence officer, Major John André, with the plans to West Point concealed in his boots between his stockings and his flesh. Plans in the handwriting of Benedict Arnold.

Arnold immediately understood what he had to do. Within that fateful half-hour, he ordered a horse to be saddled, and he galloped to the river, where six oarsmen rowed his barge down to the Tappan Zee. Here the waiting British man-of-war *Vulture*, which had brought André thither from New York a few nights previously to meet with his accomplice, weighed anchor and promptly conveyed the traitor to New York and the disappointed arms of Sir Henry, who had been prepared to pay Arnold 20,000 pounds for the plans to the Point.

The affable, handsome, and accomplished young Major André, who was captured at Tarrytown some forty-eight hours before Arnold (or George Washington) learned of it, was taken first to North Castle, the nearest military post, and then to Lower Salem, while a letter detailing his capture was inexplicably transmitted to the traitor Arnold, permitting him to escape. The next day André was taken to the Robinson House, now deserted by Arnold, where he passed the day, under heavy guard. No one was sure what to do with him.

The third day he was escorted under strong guard to West Point and from there by barge to King's Ferry at Stony Point, and then overland to Tappan, which they reached on the afternoon of September 28. That same day, the day André arrived at Tappan, Cathlyntie Mabie, in her little house on the north side of the Green, delivered into the hands of her mother her first-born child. She named him John Haring after his father, his father's father, and his grandfathers back to the beginning in America.

From West Point, a shaken George Washington conveyed the news to General George Clinton. "I have been witness to a scene of treason as shocking as it was unexpected," he said. "Benedict Arnold, my trusted friend, has made a dastardly plot to sacrifice the key to the Continent, in return for the sum of 20,000 pounds sterling."

Clinton was horrified. "What shall you do?"

"I shall set out for Tappan again and the trial," he said. "What else can I do?"

*   *   *   *

He arrived in Tappan, still in shock and dismay, a little later on the same day as André, to the great excitement of the inhabitants. Of course, Margaret deserted her post at Cathlyntie's bedside and ran across the Green and down the lane and over the spar *kill* to catch a glimpse of him. As she ran, she recalled how she had deserted those little boy cousins of hers in the old days, back in the '40s, when she had hurried to see the conspiracy trials.

As he had in August, he repaired to Grietje Cosyns' house and ordered the court martial of the charming little spy. "Let André and his accomplice, Joshua Hett Smith of Haverstraw, be kept in separate houses in camp and kept perfectly secure," he ordered. "Let them be guarded by strong and trusty guards, trebly officered that a party may be constantly in the room with them. They must be so guarded as to preclude a possibility of their escaping, which they will certainly attempt to do."

André's prison was the house of Cathlyntie Mabie's girlhood, the five-bay center-hall dwelling, two rooms deep, both upstairs and down, that her father had built a year or two before she was born and that was now owned by her brother, whose family had had to vacate it for the use of the Army.

General Nathanael Greene was quartered in the front room on the south, André in the front room on the north. André's bedchamber was the rear room off the front room on the west. Nathanael Greene's bedchamber was upstairs, in the room where Cathlyntie had slept with her sisters. Smith was held in the Tappan church. George Washington's cook, Samuel Fraunce, sent meals to both prisoners at the General's behest.

"André is a man of infinite artfulness who will leave no means unattempted to make his escape and avoid the ignominious death that awaits him," Colonel Scammell informed the guards. "Watch him with every precaution. Never let him out of your sight for a moment."

The next day, September 29, in the Tappan Reformed Church, a court of inquiry made up of Major Generals Nathanael Greene, William Alexander, the Marquis de Lafayette, Baron von Steuben, Arthur St. Clair, and Robert Howe, and Brigadier Generals James Clinton, John Glover, Edward Hand, Jedediah Huntington, Henry Knox, Samuel Parsons, John Paterson, and John Stark found the prisoner guilty as a spy from the enemy, and declared that, agreeable to the law and usage of nations, he ought to suffer death.

General Washington was informed of the verdict and asked for his opinion of the sentence. "Gentlemen," he said in a low voice, betraying no emotion, "we have all been outlawed as traitors, so either he hangs or we do." He ordered him to be executed on the gallows on October 1, at 5 p.m.

Spies sped to British headquarters in New York with the news that André, Sir Henry Clinton's surrogate son and great favorite, would hang unless exchanged for Arnold, for General Washington had let it be known indirectly that only Arnold delivered to him alive could spare André's life.

Both Sir Henry and the traitor Arnold himself wrote letters to His Excellency pleading for André's release, and the execution was delayed for a day to hear a delegation from Sir Henry argue for his exchange, for which there were precedents. But in this case only Arnold would suffice. "But if I start handing over my paid turncoats," Sir Henry Clinton reasoned, "the supply will rapidly decline. Besides, Arnold is more valuable to us in our service than dead. I will not put him forth in exchange."

Major André also wrote to George Washington, who read the letter and then gave it to Greene to read to the generals: "I pray you to exert sympathy towards a fellow soldier and adopt the mode of his death to the feelings of a man of honor. Let me hope, Sir, if aught in my character impresses you with esteem towards me, I shall experience the operation of these feelings in your breast by being informed I am not to die on a gibbet but rather shot as a gentleman and an officer."

"What shall you reply?" General Wayne inquired.

"I shall not dignify it with a reply," he said coldly. "He shall hang, as I have said. Tomorrow at noon."

André's servant arrived on the eve of the trial with the prisoner's regimentals, for the spy had made the serious breach of military procedure of being discovered behind enemy lines out of uniform, disguised in the dress of a country person.

At noon on October 2, armed guards marched him from his quarters in the Mabie house to the gallows on the hill. He wore a handsome scarlet coat, trimmed with green, and buff under-clothes, vest, and breeches. His hair was tied with a black leather ribbon in back, under a hat trimmed with gold brocade.

The crowds were immense. Hundreds, maybe thousands, poured into Tappantown from every direction to see the spy hanged. Not one to enjoy the spectacle of a man swinging from a gibbet—she had had in 1741 enough hangings to last a lifetime—from this hanging Margaret could not stay away. With her cousin Rachel, she stood among the crowd and the 500 American troops milling in the street in front of the house. They followed the procession up the hill to the site where he would be put to death.

The route was lined on both sides of the road leading to the gallows on the hill by guards, 300 in all, it was said. Generals on horseback led the procession, followed by a horse-drawn Army baggage wagon containing the black-painted coffin, and then by officers on foot, surrounding André in their midst, while he walked companionably arm in arm with his two guards, one on the right and the other on the left. "As if he were going to a picnic," Rachel murmured.

At the summit of the hill, when he saw the gibbet, André blanched and fell back a step. Until that moment, he had believed death would be by firing squad. It was not so ordained. For him, a gentleman and an officer, to be hanged like a common criminal was to suffer an irremediable public humiliation, and one the public would never forget, he knew.

He was instructed to climb upon the baggage wagon and then to step into his own coffin, at which the crowd, visibly shocked, drew its collective breath sharply. He took off his hat and placed it in the coffin and then paced the coffin from head to toe, as if measuring it, or taking its measure. The officers wanted to get it over with. He was offered an opportunity to speak his last words. "All I request of you is that you bear witness that I meet my fate like a brave man," he said in a soft, clear voice. Again, the crowd took in its breath.

The hangman was a frightful-looking creature with a two-weeks' growth of hair on his face, which as Margaret inspected him more closely appeared to be covered with soot and grease to disguise him from those who knew him or from those who might see him again some day. As if not wishing to be touched by the blackened ghoul, the elegant prisoner roughly removed the noose from the loathsome hangman's hand and placed it over his own head, with the knot directly under his right ear, and drew it snugly to his neck. "Tie his arms behind his back, just above the elbow," ordered the officer in charge. This was done.

"Giddyap!" the hangman cried harshly, flicking his whip. The horse stepped smartly forward, pulling the wagon from under the gallows, and the prisoner swung in a mighty arc, back and forth.

He remained hanging for twenty minutes, and Margaret had never heard a greater silence than that which surrounded the sight of the dead figure so smartly clad in his red and green uniform.

They cut the body down and removed its outer clothing, laid it in the black coffin in its buff undergarments. She lingered with Rachel until the crowd had dispersed, then went to look at the corpse in his coffin. They were shocked at how his handsome face had swollen and blackened so horribly that it was unrecognizable. "It is an eye for an eye, a life for a life, I know," she said, "but he didn't take anyone's eye, let alone life. Why did he have to die, only doing his job for his King and country, after all?" She felt overcome with melancholy, and then anger that the real traitor, Benedict Arnold, had gone free.

From the grove of trees at the edge of the hill, she could look down the road leading to the bridge over the spar *kill* to Grietje Cosyns' house. The shutters on the west side of the house were closed. The commander in chief had not attended the execution, must have ordered the windows facing the gallows hill to be shuttered. "So that he did not have to hear the crowd, see the gallows?" Rachel wondered.

"Or so that he did not have to be reminded of another hanging, of Nathan Hale, hanged in the service of his country by the enemy he had spied upon at his Commander's behest?" said Margaret.

"I have heard it said many times," said Rachel, "that he is a man of tender heart, for all his warrior head."

"Nathan Hale died for George Washington, as John André died for Sir Henry Clinton," Margaret said shortly. "So it is, by the strange logic of war."

He would remain in Tappan for another five days, but she did not see him again. He kept to himself in his Headquarters, writing, it was said. She would not see him again until May of 1783, when he returned to Tappan to work out the terms of the British surrender with Sir Guy Carleton.

CHAPTER 21

▼

VICTORY

From the time of the discovery that the trusted Arnold had gone to the enemy, a whole year elapsed before the French finally decided to act. In the summer of 1781, the French fleet under Admiral de Grasse was tacking about off the Virginia capes, the people learned, just waiting for the American commander, encamped for safety in the Ramapo Mountains, to join the battle. "As if *he* has not waited long enough for the French to join the battle," Margaret said fiercely.

The moment word came in September of 1781 that the time was ready, he broke camp in the Highlands and ordered the Continental army, along with the French army, encamped at White Plains, to the Chesapeake and thence to Yorktown. Moving rapidly, he first took care, though, with documents he arranged to be intercepted, to deceive Sir Henry Clinton into believing that New York or Staten Island was the target of the two advancing armies.

While New York frantically prepared itself for its defense, part of the French army passed through Tappan in a whirlwind of motion and commotion, the birds of the air no match that sweet July morning for fifes and drums and marching feet, creaking wagons, neighing horses. Ragged children capered after them down the lanes, but their exhausted elders, ragged too, lacking the energy even to wave, stood silently on the sidelines to watch the army pass.

A month later, at Yorktown, on October 17, 1781, six and a half years after the Battle of Lexington, Lord Cornwallis, trapped on the peninsula between the forces of Washington and Rochambeau on land and the French fleet at sea, had no recourse but to surrender his whole army, 7,241 men. His bands played the mournful tune "The World Turned Upside Down" during the surrender proceedings, while long lines of sullen, scowling Redcoats marched to an appointed field to lay down their arms. A year later, in November, 1782, John Jay and John Adams and Benjamin Franklin signed a preliminary peace treaty with the English recognizing the United States of America as an independent nation.

*   *   *   *

It took another six months to arrange the end of the end. On May 6, 1783, General George Washington and Sir Guy Carleton themselves came to Tappan, again to Grietje's house, to arrange the evacuation of New York, to discuss a general exchange of prisoners, of which the American army held 6,700. (And for whose keep the Americans now had the effrontery to demand compensation!) And to compensate both sides' property rights: the restitution of Englishmen's confiscated estates and the property they would abandon when they left, and the return to their owners of Americans' slaves and other movables.

Margaret went, of course, along with everyone else to the Hudson River to see Sir Guy and company rowed in barges upon the shore in front of the sandstone Onderdonk house.

Just as they arrived at the spot, *he* galloped up on his magnificent white charger, tall, commanding, *majestic,* she would put it, accompanied by his Life Guard in their smart blue and white uniforms. Disembarked from his barge, Sir Guy soberly waded toward him through little rippling waves.

A great and palpable eagerness in the people to see the hero, the godlike man, the genius of freedom, caused them to crowd forward almost as one. "Strange is the impulse felt by almost every breast to see the face of this great good man," Johannes murmured.

He had other things on his mind than to glance about the crowd for a familiar female face. But she was free to dwell on his and on his every movement, and she did.

As if he felt her eyes on him, he turned, wheeling about on his horse. There she was, in the shade of a locust tree. She had that urgent, expectant look again, as if she were willing him, waiting for him to do ... *something important.* She was in her mid-fifties, he reckoned, but she was a handsome woman still, though thin and worn now, and her clothing quite in tatters. The war had aged her, the long turbulent years of revolution and, for her in the neutral ground, the savage civil war that ran alongside it. Well, they had all aged. Revolution had taken its toll on him too.

Now it was over. He had done what she wanted, *something important.*

He lifted his hat to her. Without taking her eyes off him, she bobbed her head and did that curious rendition of a curtsey, a social air obviously foreign to her, an English thing for a proud Dutch lady to do. She did it for *him.*

He felt strangely fortified by her devotion, her fierce and inexplicable almost mother-love for him. Inexplicable because she was not his mother. Yet in some way, she was his mother, he understood. She and those women like her who had sacrificed and endured so much for the cause were the mothers of their country, as he was being called its father for all that he had endured and sacrificed. His eyes moistened. It had been a terrible thing, that war.

He turned away to greet a dyspeptic Sir Guy Carleton, waiting for him on the sandy beach.

*   *   *   *

The two commanders, after the landing ceremonies and the shaking of hands all around, rode together to Tappan in a chariot brought down from Newburgh, drawn by two matched pairs, accompanied by Major Fish and a command of 300 Light Infantry.

Margaret, in the excited gaggle of spectators, among them the Lieutenant Governor of New York and Chief Justice William Smith, walked the three miles to the little hamlet of Tappan behind the triumphant troops.

When the two commanders and their aides reached Grietje's house, they were saluted with drums beating and fifes piping and flags flying, and they spent an hour in congratulations and conversation in the dooryard. They then went into the house for the negotiations, which lasted for three hours. Meanwhile, the crowds waited in the shade of the locust trees to see what expressions would be on their faces when they came out to the sumptuous dinner arranged in a tent on the lawn by Black Sam, Mr. Samuel Fraunce, proprietor of the tavern on Broad Street that bore his name.

They stopped their talks at four, and Washington offered his guests wine and bitters. Their faces seemed all conviviality and harmony when they emerged, but that, it turned out, was the wine and bitters, for word soon spread through servants who had been in the room with them that in fact the negotiations had been terse and acerbic.

"As to the slaves," Carleton had announced, with a frisson of glee, when this matter was on the table, "the British have already embarked thousands of them to other parts, having long ago promised them their freedom in return for their loyalty to the King. Including one female slave escaped from Mount Vernon," he couldn't help but add.

General Washington fumed at this lost opportunity to restore the slaves to their owners. He brought his boot down heavily upon the wide oak planks of the floor to indicate his displeasure.

But maybe it is just as well, he thought, gazing beyond Carleton's head out the window at the tent where their repast would take place. Always in the back of his mind was the knotty problem of the slaves, the nation's, and his and Martha's. The war had been about freedom. Surely, the slaves deserved theirs. He had long had an inclination to free his, but he was not at liberty to free Martha's, and he was reluctant to break up their families by freeing his and parceling out hers to new owners. Their freedom or their family: it befitted a Solomon to decide. Perhaps the solution was to decree that they all be freed. All of them in all the colonies. But then, he was merely a retiring commander in chief, not a king.

The elegant repast of Black Sam was served to thirty men of both armies, and it lasted for two hours, and the more Madeira they consumed, the more all seemed jolliness and good fellowship.

"As if all the years of killing and maiming and robbing and burning and plundering and rape were no more than a nightmare, now forgotten upon waking," Margaret said bitterly, walking home with her whole household in the early dusk. "They have made a ruin of our land, and now they smile and drink together and toast each other. It is sickening."

But, of course, the next day, she joined the crowds that followed the commander in chief and his aides and officers down the Oak Tree Road to Sneden's Landing, where the dignitaries went on board Sir Guy's frigate the *Perseverance* for another elegant dinner. This affair was preceded by a seventeen-gun salute, the first official British recognition of the little upstart nation that, against all odds and probabilities, had defeated the mighty British Empire.

General Washington was much gratified by Sir Guy's toast to him. "When the illustrious part that you have played in this long and laborious contest becomes a matter of history," Sir Guy said, raising his glass, "fame will gather your brightest laurels from the banks of the Delaware rather than those of the Chesapeake."

"In other words," said his aide Joseph Reed afterward, "the war was won at Trenton and Princeton in 1776."

"Yes," he said. "And what mad pride impelled them to pursue it for five more years?"

"And what blind ambition?"

"Yes," he said. "What blind ambition."

He was conveyed back to Tappan for the night, past ruined farms and broken, silent people, standing along the road, some of them weeping.

"And what ideas but that of freedom on the one hand and power on the other has caused both, mighty empire and upstart nation, in their mutual savagery, to render a once Edenic land a state of devastation?"

✳   ✳   ✳   ✳

This is exactly what Margaret was thinking too, as she followed his carriage back to Tappan.

The melancholy vestiges of war, as her cousin John Bogert had called them in a letter to her, were everywhere apparent: Fine sturdy houses now but weed-filled cellar holes, blind men, crippled boys, worthless money. The once-fruitful, fertile land was now one vast common covered promiscuously by weeds, briars, and grasses, and in some places not a creature left to cut down the overgrown meadows. In the neutral ground, even the highways were lost, and known only by the ruins of the stone walls that had bordered them.

"What cruel changes does the destructive hand of war make wherever it approaches!" this cousin wrote to her from New Brunswick, where he was teaching and hoping to resume his study for the ministry. "The land mourns. The joyful husbandman is no more seen pursuing his daily labors, and those poor inhabitants of this place who remain on the land have no longer that plenty stored that formerly made them the happiest of men. Their hard-earned property, the provision they had made to render their old age comfortable has been wrested from them. Once prosperous families, having lost husbands, fathers, brothers, by tears and entreaties have managed to retain at most one last cow for their subsistence. These, dear cousin, are the circumstances of our country today. What hearts of steel must the authors of the war have, how void of rational reflection their minds! Is there not some curse, some hidden thunder in the heavens, to blast those wretches who sought their greatness by our country's ruin?"

John Haring called on her the next day. She read the letter to him. He sighed. "He speaks truth," he said. "The authorities in New Jersey have conducted a survey to appraise the country's ruin. It is soon to be published. They found in just five counties 2,000 instances of destruction by the British and several hundreds by the American soldiers."

"If they had only listened to us in 1775," said Johannes, "there would be no broken people, ruined houses, courthouses, churches, schools, wharves, ships, cattle, crops, slaves, household goods all either ruined or pillaged away."

"The once-fair land mourns indeed," she said. "And the once-prosperous people mourn the once-fair land."

"At least we are free," said John Haring.

"We are free," she said, "but we have paid a high price for it, and we shouldn't have had to pay any price. It was ours to begin with."

*   *   *   *

She had more to mourn than the land, although that was bad enough. During the seven terrible years of war, she had lost: Her father, Isaac, in September 1776. Her mother, Elizabeth van Houten, not long after. Also in 1776 an infant daughter of her nephew Abraham's, he an ensign in the Orangetown militia.

Almost every year had brought a new blow, or two.

Her darling nephew Isaac, dead from climbing an apple tree, 1777. His brother, her nephew Jacobus, the same year, dead a British prisoner-of-war. She had visited him and given him apples and cake and cider to drink.

Her merry little grandson Johannes, dead at three years in 1778.

Her cousin Abraham A. Haring, captain in the Orangetown militia, taken away by the British in 1780 and never heard from again. Presumed to have died on the British prison ship where he was last reported seen.

Her nephew Isaac's child Jacobus, died at age one in 1781

Her grandson Gerrit, died at age one in 1782.

And after the war, it continued:

Their *dominie* for thirty-four years, Samuel Verbryck, died in 1784.

Her brother Theunis died of cancer in 1785.

Worse, her son John, Cathlyntie's husband, died in June 1787, leaving his widow and two sons, ages five and two. Her only comfort was that he and Cathlyntie Mabie had together joined the Tappan Reformed Church on April 12, 1787, just two months before he was carried off by a summer ague.

Then, another blow too hard, Aeltie, her first born, followed John to the grave at age forty in 1789.

Finally, Cathlyntie, a daughter to her in all ways but one, sickened and died in 1796, at age thirty-eight.

But at least, before she died, Margaret, always thinking, had had the presence of mind to call Cathlyntie's first-born son, Johannes, to his mother's bedside and have her speak to him of Geertje Bogert, an only child and only seven at the time.

It seemed preposterous to the feeble and ailing Cathlyntie to try to interest Johannes, a harum-scarum sixteen, in a neighborhood seven-year-old female child as a future wife, but Margaret insisted. "It is a good thing," she said, fiercely.

In the four years that were left to Margaret after Cathlyntie drew her last, she never lost an opportunity to drill into the mind of Johannes (he was her grandson, after all; she had the right to drill) that it was in his best interest to marry Geertje Bogert, the only child of Sarah Onderdonk and Cornelius Bogert. "She will have all those long green fields to herself when they are gone," she said, "and that idyllic house site on a knoll facing south overlooking the dancing spar *kill* below and the blue hills of the Nyack range in the distance. You can always improve the house, it needs improving," she added. "But no one will ever improve on that site."

$$* \qquad * \qquad * \qquad *$$

It came to pass, just as Margaret had desired, although she did not live to see it. Her grandson Johannes Haring and Geertje Bogert married, and it was a marriage of true love, like Grietje Cosyns' to Jan Pietersen Haring, and Marytje's to Cosyn, Aeltie's to Jan, Margaret's to Johannes, Cathlyntie's to John. The family was fortunate in that way. The men were the salt of the earth, good providers and good lovers, and they chose good women, brainy and beautiful and passionate women—women full of high ideals.

When she was about twelve, Geertje got the idea, when he looked her way in church, what he was thinking of. But then, he had long green fields, too, in his future, from his dead father's father. Why shouldn't they look at each other and think of those fields?

When it was time, he came, on horseback up the lane her father's father's father made and married her her sixteenth April, when the apple orchard bloomed pink and white and the willows greened along the creek and the redbud flushed the blue hills.

They walked together that first besotted summer, when work was done, to the clean, clear cedar-shaded Hackensack. The cool water was just deep enough to cover their nakedness when she stood on tiptoe on the red sun-flecked bottom to make love to him. The pale sand was fine as flour where he laid her down to dry, her young belly already curving to the setting sun with child.

Eden. For a while.

The poor thing was dead at thirty-eight, the same age as the mother-in-law she had never known, leaving him with eight blond *kinder* to bring up, four sons and four daughters, and her own bereft parents to care for in their old age.

And then, in 1798, her beloved Johannes passed away after a long illness. "I set my cap for you," she whispered to him as he died, "and you did not disappoint me, *mijn lieveling.*"

Almost worse than any death to her, her son Abraham joined the *conferentie* church after the war and married a daughter of it, he and his lost to her as if to a common grave.

Of her five children, then, only her eldest son Isaac and her daughter Elizabeth, the twin of Abraham, were left to bury her, when it was her time. She prayed they would live so long.

*   *   *   *

When news came in December of the last year of the century of the great man's death, on December 14, 1799, Margaret's mourning was as deep for him as for any of her blood relations, including her husband, her daughter, her son, and her lamented child gone to the other side of the church.

She followed the mourning of the nation in the papers, starting with the eulogy of Light-Horse Harry Lee delivered on the day after Christmas. "First in war, first in peace and first in the hearts of his countrymen. Pious, just, humane, temperate and sincere, uniform, dignified and commanding. Correct throughout, vice shuddered in his presence and virtue always felt his fostering hand." She consumed the words with her eyes and committed them to her memory.

Such was the man for whom the nation mourned, the Indispensable Man, the generous deliverer of his country's right.

He had not disappointed! He had delivered them from slavery!

She recalled the story of the old soldier who long after the War was over had met him in the White House. And who in an outpouring of love and gratitude had spoken out: "I thank God that I have an opportunity of seeing my old Commander once more. I have seen him in adversity, and now seeing him in glory, I can go home and die contented."

It was her wish, too, to die contented, and she would die contented, she fancied, if, to be close to him in death as it had not been possible in life, she could die in the same year as he had died.

And strangely enough, this eccentric wish was answered. Three hundred and sixty-five days after the Indispensable Man breathed his last, she expired, on December 13, 1800.

Even stranger, but for its being a Leap Year, she would have died on the first anniversary of his death.

She was seventy-five.

*   *   *   *

After burying her, Elizabeth found, in her mother's Psalm book, a scrap of paper, along with several letters in a hand she did not recognize at first.

"It's called *Ode*, this scrap of paper," Elizabeth said. "But it ends with an Amen. More a prayer than a poem, wouldn't you say?"

"Let me see it," said her daughter, Margaret Eckerson.

Her mother handed it to her, and the girl read:

> *To you, Great Chief, in your dark tomb*
> *All honor and glory be due.*
> *You fought and won our liberty.*
> *You set your people free.*
> *Hail, Matchless First of Men,*
> *All honor and glory to you.*
> *Amen.*

"Dear Mother, always thinking," Elizabeth sighed, "even though, in my opinion, it is not much of an ode."

She took the scrap from her daughter and put it back in the Psalm book. "These little letters appear to have been from him," she added. "General Washington. Odd of him to be writing to her, wasn't it?"

"Perhaps not so odd," said Margaret thoughtfully.

"She was right, though," Elizabeth said. "He did indeed set us free."

"Yes, he did," said Margaret. "And now, I have been thinking, Mother," she added crisply. "We are free. It is time to set the slaves free. It is way past time. Do you agree?"

Elizabeth gazed at her daughter. "Eleven years old and thinking already," she murmured. "I named you well, little Margaret. And you are right, yes. It is way past time."

978-0-595-47316-8
0-595-47316-4

Printed in the United States
121971LV00001B/201/P